Typographic Design:
Form and Communication

Fifth Edition

Saint Barbara. Polychromed
walnut sculpture, fifteenth-
century German or French.
The Virginia Museum of Fine Arts.

Typographic Design:
Form and Communication

Fifth Edition

Rob Carter

Ben Day

Philip Meggs

JOHN WILEY & SONS, INC.

This book is printed on acid-free paper.

Published by John Wiley & Sons, Inc., Hoboken, New Jersey
Published simultaneously in Canada

For general information on our other products and services
or for technical support, please contact our Customer Care
Department within the United States at (800) 762-2974, outside
the United States at (317) 572-3993 or fax (317) 572-4002.

Wiley also publishes its books in a variety of electronic formats.
Some content that appears in print may not be available in
electronic books.

Library of Congress Cataloging-in-Publication Data:

Carter, Rob.
   Typographic design : form and communication / Rob Carter,
Ben Day, Philip Meggs. -- 5th ed.
      p. cm.
   Includes bibliographical references and index.
   ISBN 978-0-470-64821-6 (pbk.: acid-free paper);
   ISBN 978-1-118-12966-1 (ebk)
   1. Graphic design (Typography)
   I. Meggs, Philip B. II. Day, Ben. III. Title.
   Z246.C217 2011
   686.2'24--dc22
                                                    2011017540
Printed in the United States of America
10 9 8 7 6 5 4 3 2 1

In memory of our friend, colleague, and teacher Ben Day (1942–2011)

"The whole duty of typography,
  as with calligraphy,
  is to communicate to the imagination,
  without loss by the way,
  the thought or image
  intended to be communicated
  by the Author."

Thomas James Cobden-Sanderson

Contents

Typography has undergone continuous change over the past six decades. It is the authors' intention to provide a concise yet comprehensive overview of the fundamental information necessary for effective typographic-design practice. A knowledge of form and communication encompasses a range of subjects, including our typographic heritage, letterform anatomy, visual organization, and the interface between form and meaning.

In addition to these fundamentals, this volume presents other topics critical to informed design practice. Recent research provides the designer with an expanded awareness of legibility factors, enabling increased communicative clarity. Technological complexity requires comprehension of earlier and current typesetting processes, for both affect the language of typography. Theoretical and structural problem-solving approaches, evolved by design educators, reveal underlying concepts. Case studies in applied problem solving demonstrate a knowledge of typographic form and communication. A chapter devoted to typographic design process reveals traditional as well as nontraditional methods and practice. An understanding of typographic classification and form subtlety is gained from the study of type specimens.

Through the twelve chapters of this book, the authors share a compilation of information and examples with practitioners and students. It yields both insights and inspiration, bringing order to the complex and diversified subject of typographic design.

Typography is an intensely visual form of communication. Because this visible language communicates thoughts and information through human sight, its history is presented here in chronological visual form on four timelines. This evolution is shown in the context of world events, architectural development, and art history.

The first timeline predates typography. It begins with the invention of writing over five thousand years ago and ends with the invention of movable type in Europe during the middle of the fifteenth century. The second timeline covers the long era of the handpress and handset metal types. This period, from Gutenberg's invention of movable type to the end of the eighteenth century, lasted about three hundred and fifty years. In the third timeline, the Industrial Revolution and nineteenth century are revealed as an era of technological innovation and an outpouring of new typographic forms. The fourth timeline begins with the year 1900 and covers the twentieth century, when type was shaped by the aesthetic concerns of modernism, the need for functional communication, and technological progress. In the late twentieth century, the digital revolution in typography occurred, followed by the dawning of a new century and millennium.

From the origins of writing to Gutenberg's invention of movable type: 3150 B.C.–A.D.1450

Note: Picture credits and further descriptive information for timeline illustrations start on page 348.

1.
c. 3150 B.C.: The earliest written documents are impressed clay tablets from Sumer. The signs represent clay tokens, which were used for record keeping before the invention of writing.

2.
c. 3000 B.C.: Cuneiform, a very early writing system, consisting of wedge-shaped marks on clay tablets, was invented by the Sumerians.

2500 B.C.: Egyptians begin to make papyrus, a new writing material derived from the stems of the papyrus plant.

3.
c. 2600 B.C.: Completion of the pyramids at Giza, Egypt.

4.
c. 2400 B.C.: False-door stele inscribed with hieroglyphic writing, from Old Kingdom Egypt.

5.
c. 2100 B.C.: Cuneiform tablet listing expenditures of grain and animals.

6.
c. 1800–1400 B.C.: Stonehenge, a megalithic monument of thirty-foot-tall stones set into circular patterns.

7.
c. 1570–1349 B.C.: Polychromed wood sculpture from New Kingdom Egypt, with hieroglyphic inscriptions.

8.
c. 1450 B.C.: Detail, *The Book of the Dead* of Tuthmosis III, hieroglyphic writing on papyrus.

c. 3150 B.C.

1.

2.

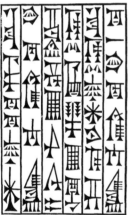

3.

4.

7.

5.

8.

6.

9.

c. 1500 B.C.: The twenty-two characters of the Phoenician alphabet.

c. 800 B.C.: Homer writes the *Iliad* and *Odyssey*.

540 B.C.: The first public library is established in Athens, Greece.

10.

389 B.C.: Inscription in the Phoenician alphabet on a fragment of a marble bowl.

11.

Fourth century B.C.: Greek manuscript writing.

12.

448–432 B.C.: The Parthenon, temple of the goddess Athena, on the Acropolis in Athens, Greece.

13.

414–413 B.C.: Fragment of a Greek record of sale, carved on stone.

c. 160 B.C.: Parchment, a new writing material made from animal skins, is developed in the Greek state of Pergamum.

44 B.C.: Julius Caesar is murdered.

14.

c. 50 B.C.–A.D. 500: Roman square capitals *(capitalis quadrata)* were carefully written with a flat pen.

c. A.D. 33: Crucifixion of Christ.

15.

c. 79: Brush writing from a wall at Pompeii, preserved by the volcanic eruption of Vesuvius.

105: Ts'ai Lun invents paper in China.

16.

150: The Roman codex, with folded pages, begins to be used alongside the rolled scroll.

16.

c. 100–600: Roman rustic writing *(capitalis rustica)* conserved space by using more condensed letters written with a flat pen held in an almost vertical position.

c. 1500 B.C.

9.

11.

13.

12.

10.

MARTISQ·DOLO

14.

15.

CONNERTANTPRIA
SINMANIBUSUESTRI
VLTROASIAMMACNO

16.

17.
118–25: The Pantheon, Rome.
18.
Undated: The fluid gestural quality, harmonious proportions, and beautiful forms of Roman writing are effectively translated into the permanent stone carving of monumental capitals *(capitalis monumentalis)*.

19.
312–315: Arch of Constantine, Rome. Carved into marble, monumental Roman capitals survived the thousand-year Dark Ages.

325: Emperor Constantine adopts Christianity as the state religion of the Roman Empire.

c. 400–1400: During the thousand-year medieval era, knowledge and learning are kept alive in the Christian monastery, where manuscript books are lettered in the scriptoria.

452: Attila the Hun invades and ravages northern Italy.

476: Emperor Romulus Augustulus, last ruler of the western Roman Empire, is deposed by the Ostrogoths.
20.
533–49: Church of Sant' Apollinare in Classe, Ravenna.
21.
Third–sixth centuries: Uncials are rounded, freely drawn majuscule letters, first used by the Greeks as early as the third century B.C.

22.
Third–ninth centuries: Half-uncials, a lettering style of the Christian Church, introduces pronounced ascenders and descenders.
23.
Sixth–ninth centuries: Insular majuscules, a formal style with exaggerated serifs, was developed by Irish monks from the half-uncials.

A.D. 118

17.

19.

18.

20.

musadquequamuisconsci
mitatisnostraetrepidatio
murtamenfideiaxestuincit
21.

mortuautfcm
22.

magnum quod erit
23.

4

732: The Battle of Tours ends the Muslim advance into Europe.

800: Charlemagne is crowned emperor of the Holy Roman Empire by Pope Leo III.

24.
c. 800: Portrait of Christ from *The Book of Kells,* a Celtic manuscript.

868: The earliest extant printed manuscript, the *Diamond Sutra,* is printed in China.

25.
Tenth century: High Cross at Kells, Meath County, Ireland.

26.
c. Eleventh century: Round tower on the Rock of Cashel, Tipperary County, Ireland, a lookout and refuge against Viking invaders.

27.
Eighth–twelfth centuries: Caroline minuscules became the standard throughout Europe after Charlemagne issued his reform decree of 796, calling for a uniform writing style.

1034: Pi Sheng invents movable type in China.

1096–1099: The First Crusade.

28.
1163–1250: Construction of Notre Dame Cathedral, Paris.

29.
Eleventh–twelfth centuries: Early Gothic lettering, a transitional style between Caroline minuscules and Textura, has an increased vertical emphasis.

30.
Twelfth century: Bronze and copper crucifix from northern Italy.

1215: The Magna Carta grants constitutional liberties in England.

31.
Thirteenth–fifteenth centuries: Gothic Textura Quadrata, or Textura, the late Gothic style with rigorous verticality and compressed forms.

1347–1351: First wave of the Black Death, a plague that decimates the European population.

32.
Thirteenth century: Byzantine School, *Madonna and Child on a Curved Throne.*

A.D. 732

24.

25.

26.

31.

27.

early gothic

29.

30.

28.

32.

33.
Thirteenth–fifteenth centuries: Rotunda, a more rounded Gothic letter, flourished in southern Europe.

34.
Fourteenth century: Lippo Memmi, *Saint John the Baptist.*

35.
1420–36: Filippo Brunelleschi, dome of Florence Cathedral.

36.
Fifteenth century: First page of a block-book, *Apocalypse.* Woodblock printing probably appeared in Europe before 1400.

37.
1440–45: Fra Filippo Lippi, *Madonna and Child.*

1431: Jeanne d'Arc is burned at the stake.

c. 1450: Johann Gutenberg invents movable type in Mainz, Germany.

38.
c. 1450–55: Page from Gutenberg's 42-line Bible, the first European typographic book.

39.
Woodblock print of the hand-printing press, with compositors setting type from a typecase in the background.

40.
The cathedral in the medieval city of Mainz, Germany.

c. 1200

34.

37.

35.

Rotunda

33.

36.

38.

39.

40.

Typography from Gutenberg to the nineteenth century: A.D. 1450–1800

The humanist philosophy that flowered during the Renaissance embraced the study of classical literature, a belief in human dignity and worth, a spirit of individualism, and a shift from religious to secular concerns.

1450–1500: Books printed in the first half-century of typographic printing are called Incunabula.

41.
1465: Sweynheym and Pannartz, the first type designed in Italy. It had some Roman features.

42.
1467: Sweynheym and Pannartz, the first Roman-style type, influenced by Roman inscriptional capitals and manuscripts written in Caroline minuscules.

43.
1470: Nicolas Jenson, early Venetian roman typeface.

44.
1475: William Caxton, typography from the first book printed in the English language.

45.
c. 1485: Filippino Lippi, *Portrait of a Youth*.

46.
1486: Erhard Ratdolt, the earliest known specimen sheet of printing types.

1492: Christopher Columbus lands in America.

47.
c. 1494: Scholar and printer Aldus Manutius established the Aldine Press in Venice to publish works by the great Greek and Roman thinkers.

48.
1495: Francesco Griffo (punch cutter for Aldus Manutius), roman type first used in *De aetna* by Pietro Bembo.

1450

bat ille ihesus: q quom pmū auses uocareͭ moises figurā psentiens iussit eū ihesum uocari: ut dux militie delectus esset aduersus amalech qui oppugnabant filios israhel: et aduersariū debellaret p nois figuram: et populū m

41.

esse sensum semitas queritur. tanq illi ad cogitandum rheda & quadrigis opus eēt. Democritus quasi in puteo quodam sic alto ut fundus sit nullus: ueritatem iacere demersam nimirum stulte

42.

ab omnipotenti deo missus deus uerbum quasi lucis isi cunctis annūciat. Non hinc aut aliunde: sed undiq; cun ad deum uerum: græcos simul et barbaros omnem sexū

43.

In the tyme of p troublous world/ and of the hons beyng and reyȝnyng as well in the rop englond and fraunce as m all other places vn

44.

47.

46.

45.

lud admirari, quod uulgus solet: magnu esse scilicet tantas flammas, tam immen sos ignes post hominum memoriam sem

48.

49.
1501: Francesco Griffo, the first italic typeface, based on chancery script handwriting.

50.
Home of Albrecht Dürer, Nuremberg, Germany.

51.
Woodblock initial by Geoffroy Tory, who returned to France from study in Italy in 1505, inspired by roman letterforms and Renaissance design ideals.

52.
1523: Lodovico Arrighi, an Italian writing master, introduces his formal chancery italic type.

53.
1517: Martin Luther posts his ninety-five theses on the door of Wittenberg Palace Church, launching the Reformation.

54.
1525: Albrecht Dürer, construction of the letter *B*.

54.
1529: Geoffroy Tory, construction of the letter *B*.

55.
1519–47: Pierre Nepveu, Chateau of Chambord, France.

56.
c. 1480–1561: Claude Garamond, outstanding designer of Old Style typefaces during the French Renaissance.

1501

50.

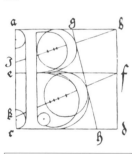

53.

55.

51.

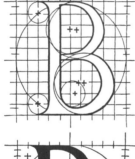

54.

56.

49.

52.

8

57.

c. 1540: Titian, *Portrait of Cardinal Pietro Bembo.*

1543: Copernicus publishes his theory of the heliocentric solar system.

58.

1544: Simone de Colines, title page with woodcut border.

59.

1546: Jacques Kerver, typography, illustration, and decorative initials, which were combined into a rare elegance during the French Renaissance.

60.

After 1577: El Greco, *Saint Martin and the Beggar.*

1582: Pope Gregory XIII initiates the Gregorian Calendar, which is still in use.

1584: Sir Walter Raleigh discovers and annexes Virginia.

61.

1595: Johann Theodor de Bry, illustrative initial *E.*

1603: Shakespeare writes *Hamlet.*

62.

1607: Carlo Maderna, façade of St. Peter's, the Vatican.

1609: Regular weekly newspapers appear in Strasbourg, Germany.

63.

1621: Jean Jannon, typefaces upon which twentieth-century Garamonds are based.

64.

1628: The Vatican Press, specimen of roman capitals.

c. 1540

58.

FRANCISCVS

64.

59.

61.

62.

60.

57.

La crainte de l'Eternel eſt le chef de ſcience: mais les fols meſpriſent ſapiéce &

63.

65.
1632–43: The Taj Mahal, India.
66.
c. 1630: Sir Anthony van Dyck, portrait of *Henri II de Lorraine.*

1639: The first printing press in the British Colonies is established in Massachusetts.

1657: First fountain pen is manufactured, in Paris.
67.
c. 1664: Jan Vermeer, *Woman Holding a Balance.*

1666: The great fire of London.

1667: Milton publishes *Paradise Lost.*

68.
c. 1670: Christoffel van Dyck, Dutch Old Style type.

1686: Sir Isaac Newton sets forth his law of gravity.
69.
1675–1710: Sir Christopher Wren, St. Paul's Cathedral, London.

During the eighteenth century, type design went through a gradual transition from Old Style to Modern Style fonts designed late in the century.

1700: The emergence of the Rococo Style.
70.
1702: Philippe Grandjean (punch cutter), Romain du Roi, the first transitional face.

71.
1709: Matthaus Poppelmann, Zwinger Palace, Dresden.

1709: England adopts the first modern copyright law.
72.
1720: William Caslon, Caslon Old Style types, which from this date were used throughout the British Empire.

1632

65.

66.

Ad me profectam effe aiebant. D. quid Quæfo, igitur commorabare, ubi id
68.

69.

sa doctrine et de ses lois. Après, il nous fait voir tous les hommes renfermés en un seul homme, et sa femme même tirée de lui ; la concorde des mariages et la
70.

67.

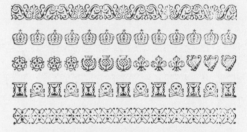

72.

ABCDEFGHIKLMN
OPQRSTUVWXYZJ
Quoufque tandem abutere, Catilina, patientia noftra ? qu
Quoufque tandem abutere, Catilina, patientia noftra? quam-

This new Foundery was begun in the Year 1720, and finifh'd 1763; and will (with God's leave) be carried on, improved, and inlarged, by WILLIAM CASLON and Son, Letter-Founders in LONDON.

71.

73.
1722: Castletown, near Dublin, Ireland.

1738: First spinning machines are patented in England.

74.
1744: Benjamin Franklin, title page using Caslon type.

75.
1750: François Boucher, *The Love Letter*.

76.
1750s: John Baskerville creates extraordinary transitional typefaces.

77.
1765: Thomas Cottrell introduces display types two inches tall (shown actual size).

78.
1768: Pierre Simon Fournier le Jeune, ornamented types.

79.
1773: Johann David Steingruber, letter *A* from *Architectonishes Alphabet*.

80.
1774: John Holt, broadside of the American revolutionary era, using Caslon type.

1775: James Watt constructs the first efficient steam engine.

1776: American Declaration of Independence is signed.

81.
1784: François Ambroise Didot, the first true Modern Style typeface.

1789: The fall of the Bastille launches the French Revolution.

82.
1791: Giambattista Bodoni, Modern Style typefaces of geometric construction, with hairline serifs.

1791: American Bill of Rights guarantees freedoms of religion, speech, and the press.

1793: French King Louis XVI and Marie Antoinette are sent to the guillotine.

1796: Aloys Senefelder invents lithography.

1799: Nicolas-Louis Robert invents the papermaking machine.

1722

73.

75.

76.

M. T. CICERO's
CATO MAJOR,
OR HIS
DISCOURSE
OF
OLD-AGE:

With Explanatory NOTES.

PHILADELPHIA:
Printed and Sold by B. FRANKLIN,
MDCCXLIV.

74.

LA
DIVINA
COMMEDIA
DI
DANTE ALIGHIERI
CON
ILLUSTRAZIONI

TOMO I.

PISA
DALLA TIPOGRAFIA
DELLA SOCIETÀ LETTERARIA
MDCCCIV.

HISTOIRE
DE
LOUIS DE BOURBON,
SECOND DU NOM,
PRINCE
DE CONDÉ,
PREMIER PRINCE DU SANG,
Surnommé *LE GRAND.*

LIVRE PREMIER.
1621-1643.

LOUIS DE BOURBON, second du nom, naquit à Paris 1621. le 7 Septembre 1621 ; il fut titré *Duc d'Enguien,* nom heureux qui rappelloit la mémoire du vain-

82.

80.

To the PUBLICK.

78.

C

77.

79.

lumes in-4° sur papier-vélin de la fabrique de messieurs Matthieu Johannot pere et fils, d'Annonai, premiers fabricants de cette sorte de papiers en

81.

The nineteenth century and the Industrial Revolution: A.D. 1800–1899

The Industrial Revolution had a dramatic impact upon typography and the graphic arts. New technology radically altered printing, and designers responded with an outpouring of new forms and images.

83.
c. 1803: Robert Thorne designs the first Fat Face.

1804: Napoleon Bonaparte crowned Emperor of France.

1808: Beethoven composes his Fifth Symphony.
84.
1812: Jacques-Louis David, *Napoleon in His Study* (detail).

1814: Friedrich Koenig invents the steam-powered printing press.

85.
1815: Vincent Figgins shows the first Egyptian (slab-serif) typefaces.
86.
1815: Vincent Figgins shows the earliest shaded type.

87.
1816: William Caslon IV introduces the first sans serif type.
88.
1818: Page from *Manuale Tipographico,* which presented the lifework of Giambattista Bodoni.
89.
1821: Robert Thorne, Tuscan styles with splayed serifs.

1800

84.

83.

85.
ABCDEFGHIJK

86.
ABCDEFGHIKM

87.
LETTERFOUNDER

89.
Manchester

❖ PARANGONE ❖

Quousque tandem abutêre, Catilina, patientiâ nostrâ? quamdiu etiam furor iste tuus nos eludet? quem ad finem sese effrenata jactabit audacia? nihilne te nocturnum præsidium Palatii, nihil urbis vigiliæ, nihil timor populi, nihil concursus bonorum omnium, nihil hic munitissimus habendi se-

MARCUS TULL. CICERO
ORATOR ATQUE PHILOSOPHUS.

CHERASCO

88.

90.

1822: Thomas Jefferson, Rotunda of the University of Virginia in the neoclassical style based on Greek and Roman architecture.

1822: Joseph Niepce produces the first photographic printing plate.

91.

c. 1826: Bower, Bacon and Bower, early reversed type entitled White.

1826: Joseph Niepce takes the first photograph from nature.

92.

1827: Darius Wells invents the mechanical router, making the manufacture of large display wood types possible.

93.

1833: Vincent Figgins introduces outline types.

94.

1836: Davy and Berry, poster printed with wood type.

1830s–80s: Wood-type posters and broadsides flourished in America and Europe.

95.

1836: Vincent Figgins, perspective type.

96.

1837: Handbill set in Fat Face.

1837: Victoria crowned queen of England.

1822

STOCKS

THEATRE-ROYAL, NORWICH.

FOR THE BENEFIT OF

R. Battley, FRUITERER.

On THURSDAY, 12th May, 1836,
Will be performed the POPULAR PLAY, of The

CASTLE SPECTRE.

Earl Osmond....Mr. MADDOCKS
Reginald....Mr. HAMERTON   Kenric....Mr. G. SMITH
Earl Percy....Mr. NICHOLS   Saib......Mr. HARRISON
Father Philip..Mr. GRAY   Muley....Mr. BRYAN
Motley......Mr. GILL   Hassan....Mr. NANTZ.

Angely....Mrs. G. SMITH
Alice......Mrs. WATKINSON | Evelina....Miss HONEY.

END OF THE PLAY,

A COMIC SONG
BY MR. MARTIN.

To conclude with the NAUTICAL DRAMA, of The

PILOT, OR, A
STORM AT SEA!

The Pilot, Mr. MADDOCKS
Barnstable, Mr. G. SMITH—Captain Boroughcliffe, (a regular Yankee), Mr. GILL
Long Tom Coffin, Mr. NANTZ
Captain of the Alacrity, Mr. HAMERTON—Colonel Howard Mr. GRAY
Lieutenant Griffith, Mr. TAYLOR—Serjeant Drill, Mr. NICHOLS.
Sailors, Soldiers, &c.
Kate Plowden, Mrs. PLUMER—Cecilia, Miss HONEY
Irish Woman, Mrs. WATKINSON.

DAVY & BERRY, PRINTERS, ALBION OFFICE.

94.

HOUSEHOLD FURNITURE, PLATE, CHINA-WARE, JEWELS, WATCHES

93.

DARIUS WELLS.

92.

90.

95.

Working Men, Attention!!

Globe Office
Saturday, November
20, 1837

It is your imperious duty to drop your *Hammers and Sledges* ! one and all, to your post repair, *THIS AFTERNOON*, at *FIVE* o'clock P. M. and attend the

GREAT MEETING

called by the papers of this morning, to be held at the CITY HALL, then and there to co-operate with such as have the GREAT GOOD OF ALL THEIR *FELLOW CITIZENS* at Heart. Your liberty! yea, your *LABOUR!!* is the subject of the call: who that values the services of HEROES of the *Revolution* whose blood achieved our Independence as a Nation, will for a moment doubt he owes a few hours this afternoon to his wife and children?

HANCOCK.

96.

91.

97.

c. 1840–52: Sir Charles Barry and A. W. N. Pugin, Houses of Parliament, inspiration for the Gothic Revival.

98.

c. 1841: Wood and Sharwoods, ornamental type.

During the 1840s, ornamented type becomes increasingly important.

99.

1845: Robert Besley, the first Clarendon style.

1848: The California gold rush begins.

1851: Joseph Paxton designs the Crystal Palace.

100.

1853: Handbill combining Egyptian, outline, and decorative types.

101.

1854: Broadside using elongated Fat Face fonts.

1854: The United States makes its first treaty with Japan.

102.

1859: William H. Page and Company, Ornamented Clarendons.

1856: Sir Henry Bessemer develops process for converting iron to steel.

1859: Charles Darwin publishes *Origin of Species by Means of Natural Selection*.

c. 1840

97.

100.

98.

101.

102.

audacia tua? nihilne te noc
dium palatii, nihil urbis vigi

99.

103.

1860: *Charleston Mercury,* broadsheet announcing the dissolution of the Union.

1861–65: American Civil War.

1863: Abraham Lincoln signs the Emancipation Proclamation.

104.

c. 1865: Honoré Daumier: *The Third-Class Carriage.*

1866: The first successful transatlantic cable is laid.

1867: Alfred Nobel invents dynamite.

1867: Christopher Sholes constructs the first practical typewriter.

105.

1868: Currier and Ives, *American Homestead Winter.*

106.

c. 1875: J. Ottmann, chromolithographic card for Mrs. Winslow's Soothing Syrup.

1876: Alexander Graham Bell invents the telephone.

1877: Thomas Edison invents the phonograph.

1879: Thomas Edison invents the electric lightbulb.

107.

1883: The Brooklyn Bridge is opened to traffic.

1883: William Jenney designs the first skyscraper, a ten-story metal frame building in Chicago.

108.

c. 1885: Maverick & Wissinger, engraved business card.

109.

c. 1880s: Lettering printed by chromolithography.

110.

1886: Ottmar Mergenthaler invents the Linotype, the first keyboard typesetting machine.

1861

105.

107.

106.

109.

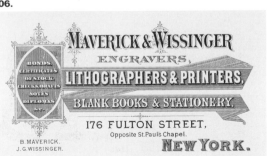

108.

110.

103.

104.

15

111.
1887: Advertisement for Estey Organs.

1887: Tolbert Lanston invents the monotype.

112.
1889: Alexandre Gustave Eiffel, the Eiffel Tower.

113.
c. 1890s: Coca-Cola syrup jug.

114.
1892: Paul Gauguin, *By the Sea.*

115.
William Morris' typeface designs: 1890, Golden; 1892, Troy; 1893, Chaucer.

116.
1891–98: William Morris' Kelmscott Press launches a revival of printing and typography.

117.
1892: William Morris, page from *News from Nowhere.*

1887

111.

112.

113.

114.

This is the Golden type.
This is the Troy type.
This is the Chaucer type.
115.

116.

Afloat again CHAPTER XXIV. UP THE THAMES. THE SECOND DAY.

THEY were not slow to take my hint; & indeed, as to the mere time of day, it was best for us to be off, as it was past seven o'clock, & the day promised to be very hot. So we got up and went down to our boat; Ellen thoughtful and abstracted; the old man very kind and courteous, as if to make up for his crabbedness of opinion. Clara was cheerful & natural, but a little subdued, I thought; and she at least was not sorry to be gone, and often looked shyly and timidly at Ellen and her strange wild beauty. So we got into the boat, Dick saying as he took his place, "Well, it is a fine day!" and the old man answering "What! you like that, do you?" once more; and presently Dick was sending the bows swiftly through the slow weed-checked stream. I turned round as we got into mid-stream, and waving my hand to our hosts, saw Ellen leaning on the old man's shoulder, and caressing his healthy apple-red cheek, and quite a keen pang smote me as I thought how I should never see the beautiful girl again. Presently I insisted on taking the sculls, and I rowed a good deal that day; which no doubt accounts for the fact that we got very late
230

117.

118.

1893: Henri van de Velde, title page for *Van Nu en Straks*.

1895: The Lumièire brothers give the first motion-picture presentation.

119.

1897: Edmond Deman, title page in the curvilinear Art Nouveau style.

120.

1890s–1940s: Inspired by Kelmscott, Americans Frederick Goudy and Bruce Rogers bring renewed excellence to book and typeface design.

121.

1897: Will Bradley, title page in his "Chap Book" style, reviving Caslon type and colonial woodcut techniques.

1898: Zeppelin invents his airship.

122.

1899: Josef Hoffmann, catalogue cover for a Vienna Secession exhibition.

123.

1898–1902: Hector Guimard, entrance to Paris Metro Station.

1893

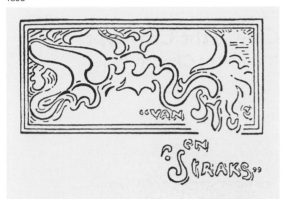

118.

119.

122.

120.

121. **123.**

Typography in the twentieth century: 1900–2000.

The twentieth century was a period of incredible ferment and change. Unprecedented advances in science and technology, and revolutionary developments in art and design have left their marks on typography.

124.
1900: Peter Behrens, dedication page from *Feste des Lebens und der Künst*.

1903: The Wright brothers succeed in the first powered flight.

1905: Einstein proposes his theory of relativity.

125.
1909: Filippo Marinetti founds Futurism, experimentation with typographic form and syntax.

126.
c. 1910: German sans-serif "block style."

127.
1913: Wassily Kandinsky, *Improvisation 31 (Sea Battle)*.

1914–18: World War I.

c. 1915: Kasimir Malevich, Suprematist painting shown at the *0.10* group exhibition launching Suprematism.

128.
c. 1916: Bert Thomas, British war bonds poster.

1917–22: The Dada movement protests the war and conventional art.

129.
1917: John Heartfield, Dadaist advertisement.

130.
1917: Vilmos Huszar, De Stijl magazine cover.

1918: Czar Nicholas II and his family are executed.

131.
1919: Raoul Hausmann, Dada poem.

1900

124.

126.

125.

127.

129.

128.

130.

131.

1920

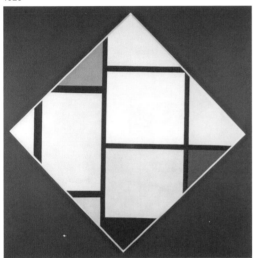

132.

133.

DIE KUNSTISMEN

HERAUSGEGEBEN VON EL LISSITZKY UND HANS ARP

LES ISMES DE L'ART

PUBLIÉS PAR EL LISSITZKY ET HANS ARP

THE ISMS OF ART

PUBLISHED BY EL LISSITZKY AND HANS ARP

EUGEN RENTSCH VERLAG
ERLENBACH-ZÜRICH, MÜNCHEN UND LEIPZIG

135.

139.

bauhaus

136.

137.

KABELS

ZELFINDUCTIE
N.K.F
NEDERLANDSCHE KABELFABRIEK
DELFT

140.

138.

1929: The New York Stock Market collapses, and the Great Depression begins.

141.

1930: Paul Renner, prospectus for Futura.

142.

1930: Chrysler Building, an example of Art Deco decorative geometric style.

143.

1931: Max Bill, exhibition poster.

144.

c. 1932: Alexey Brodovitch, exhibition poster.

1933: Adolf Hitler becomes chancellor of Germany.

145.

1936: Walker Evans, photograph of sharecropper family.

1939: Germany invades Poland; World War II begins.

146.

1942: Jean Carlu, advertisement.

147.

1944: Max Bill, exhibition poster.

1945: Atomic bombs destroy Hiroshima and Nagasaki; World War II ends.

148.

1948: Paul Rand, title page.

1929

141.

147.

143.

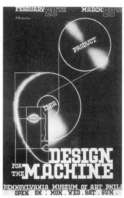

144.

148.

145.

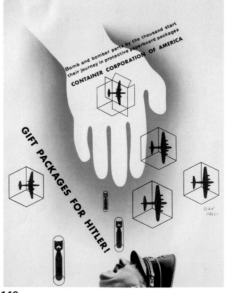

146.

142.

149.
1948: Willem de Kooning, *Painting.*
150.
1950: Ladislav Sutnar, book cover for *Catalog Design Progress.*

1950: North Korea invades South Korea.

151.
1950–55: Le Corbusier, Notre Dame de Haut.

1952: School segregation is declared unconstitutional by the Supreme Court of the United States.

152.
1952: Henri Matisse, *Woman with Amphora and Pomegranates.*
153.
1955: Josef Müller-Brockmann, concert poster.
154.
1956: Saul Bass, advertisement for Container Corporation of America.

155.
1956: Willem Sandberg, book cover for *experimenta typografica.*

1957: Russia launches Sputnik I, the first Earth satellite.

156.
1959: Saul Bass, film title.
157.
1959: Frank Lloyd Wright, the Guggenheim Museum, New York.
158.
1958: Carlo L. Vivarelli, magazine cover.

1948

149.

152.

157.

150.

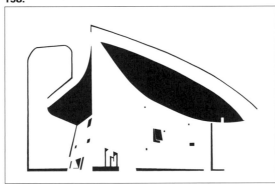

158.

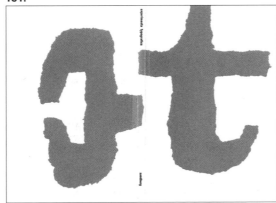

151.

155.

153.

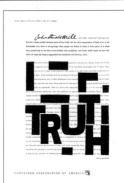

154.

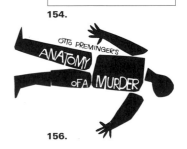

156.

21

159.
1959: Henry Wolf, magazine cover for *Harper's Bazaar.*
160.
c. 1959: Gerald Holton, "peace symbol."

161.
1959: Otto Storch, figurative typography.
162.
1960: Karl Gerstner, advertisement.
163.
c. 1960: Herb Lubalin, advertisement.

164.
c. 1961: George Lois, pharmaceutical advertisement.
165.
1962: Eero Saarinen, Dulles International Airport.

166.
1963: President John F. Kennedy is assassinated.
166.
1965: Seymour Chwast and Milton Glaser, poster.

167.
1965: The U.S. Marines land in force in Vietnam.
167.
1966: George Lois, magazine cover for *Esquire.*

1959

159.

160.

DIVINE TO EAT, EASY TO MAKE, AND BEAUTIFUL TO LOOK ON: ELEGANT PARFAITS. THERE ARE TWO TYPES: THE FRENCH, WHICH IS A CREAMY, DELICATE, COOL (BUT NOT ICY) MIXTURE WITH A BASE OF SUGAR, EGGS, CREAM, FRUIT AND/OR FLAVORINGS; AND THE AMERICAN, MADE WITH COMMERCIAL ICE CREAMS OR SHERBETS OR BOTH WITH A SURPRISE INGREDIENT, SUCH AS FRUITS, CORDIALS, COGNAC, NUTS, SAUCES (SEE McCALL'S FINE SAUCE RECIPES ON PAGE 00). WITH AMERICAN PARFAITS, YOUR IMAGINATION CAN HAVE FREE REIN. WITH THE FRENCH, HOWEVER, YOU MUST FOLLOW RECIPE DIRECTIONS TO THE LETTER. PARFAIT MEANS, OF COURSE, PERFECT, AND WE CAN IMAGINE FEW MORE PERFECT DESSERTS, ESPECIALLY IF YOU WANT TO SHOW OFF, FOR THESE ARE TRULY SHOWOFF RECIPES! FROM THE COOK'S STANDPOINT, THERE IS A REAL ADVANTAGE IN SERVING FROZEN DESSERTS. FOR THE OBVIOUS REASON, THEY MUST BE MADE WELL AHEAD AND REFRIGERATED. THUS, THE BIG DESSERT PROBLEM IS OUT OF THE WAY WHEN IT'S TIME TO PREPARE THE MAIN PART OF THE MEAL. AT FAR RIGHT, YOU SEE AN AMERICAN PARFAIT, VANILLA ICE CREAM LAYERED WITH PISTACHIO AND TOPPED WITH WALNUTS AND WHIPPED CREAM. THE STRAWBERRY AND APRICOT PARFAITS ARE BOTH CLASSIC FRENCH. FOR THE RECIPES, TURN TO PAGE 00, WHERE YOU WILL FIND THE FRENCH AS WELL AS GOOD VARIATIONS OF THE QUICK AND POPULAR AMERICAN PARFAITS. THEN, PLAN A PARTY.

161.

163.

164.

165.

"Oh my God –we hit a little girl."

The true story of M Company. From Fort Dix to Vietnam.

167.

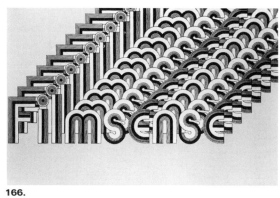

162.

166.

168.

c. 1968: Seymour Chwast and Milton Glaser, poster.

169.

1968: R. Buckminster Fuller, American Pavilion, Montreal World's Fair.

170.

c. 1967: Symbol for the environmental movement.

171.

1969: First Moon walk by Commander Neil Armstrong.

172.

1972: Wolfgang Weingart, typographic interpretation of a poem.

173.

1974: Herb Lubalin, newspaper cover for *U&lc.*

174.

1974: Cook and Shanosky, standard symbol signs.

1975: The Vietnam War ends.

175.

1976: American Revolution bicentennial, symbol design by Bruce Blackburn.

1968

168.

169.

170.

171.

172.

173.

174.

175.

176.
1977: Pompidou National Center of Arts and Culture, Paris.

177.
1977: Bill Bonnell, RyderTypes trademark.

178.
1978: Willi Kunz, poster design.

179.
1979: Richard Greenberg, film titles.

1979: Soviet troops invade Afghanistan.

1980s: Digital typography and computer technology impact typographic design, leading to electronic page design by the end of the decade.

180.
1981: Bitstream founded; first independent digital type foundry.

180.
1982: Pat Gorman and Frank Olinsky, Manhattan Design, MTV logo.

181.
1983: Michael Graves, Portland, Oregon, city hall.

182.
1984: Warren Lehrer, page from *French Fries.*

1984: Apple Macintosh computer, first laser printer, and PageMaker page layout software are introduced.

183.
1985: Zuzana Licko, Emperor, early bitmapped typeface designs.

1986: Fontographer software makes possible high-resolution font design on desktop computers.

1988: Tiananmen Square massacre.

1977

176.

177.

179.

181.

182.

Fredrich **Cantor**

strange VICISSITUDES

June 17
July 8
78

FOTO
492 Broome Street
New York, NY 10013

178.

Emperor 8
Emperor 10
Emperor 15
Emperor 19

183.

184.
1990: David Carson, page from *Beach Culture*.

185.
1991: Ted Mader + Associates, book jacket.

Experimental digital typefaces:

186.
1990: Barry Deck, Template Gothic (Emigre).

187.
c. 1991: Jonathan Barnbrook, Exocet Heavy (Emigre).

188.
1993: Jonathan Hoefler, HTF Fetish No. 338.

1990: Reunification of Germany.

189.
1991: Erik Spiekermann, Meta (FontShop).

1991: Persian Gulf War.

1991: Fall of Communism in Russia; apartheid ends in South Africa.

190.
1992: Robert Slimbach and Carol Twombley, Myriad, Adobe's first Multiple Master typeface.

191.
1992: Ron Kellum, Topix logo.

192.
1993: James Victore, poster.

193.
1994: Netscape founded, early Web browser.

1990

184.

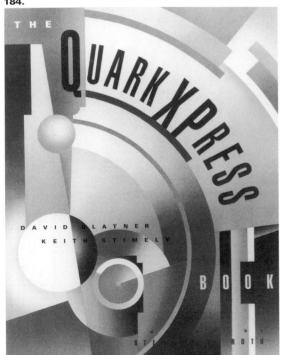

185.

186.
ABCDEFGHIJK

187.
ABCDEFGMOL

188.
EXCESSIVE?

189.
MetaMeta**Meta**Meta

190.

191.   **193.**

192.

194.
1994: Matthew Carter, Walker typeface with "snap-on" serifs.

195.
1995: Landor Associates, Xerox /The Document Company logo.

196.
1996: Stefan Sagmeister, poster.

197.
1997: Frank Gehry, Guggenheim Museum, Bilbao, Spain.

198.
1997: Paula Scher and Keith Daigle, book jacket.

1997: Dolly the sheep, first adult animal clone.

Digital versions of classical typefaces:

199.
1989: Robert Slimback, Adobe Garamond.

200.
1994–95: Janice Fishman, Holly Goldsmith, Jim Parkinson, and Sumner Stone, ITC Bodoni.

201.
c. 1996: Zuzana Licko, Mrs. Eaves roman.

202.
1998: Neville Brody, conference poster.

1994

194.

197.

202.

198.

195.

Adobe Garamond

199.

ITC Bodoni Roman

200.

Mrs Eaves Roman

201.

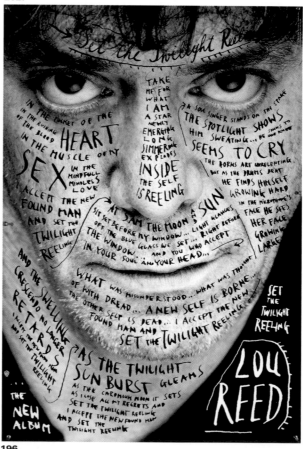

196.

A new century and millennium begin: 2000

203.
2000: Wolfgang Weingart, book cover.

2001: Al-Qaeda Terrorists attack the World Trade Center towers and Pentagon.

204.
2001: Jennifer Sterling, calendar page (detail).

205.
2001: Jim Sherraden, book cover for *Hatch Show Print*.

206.
2002: Emil Ruder, new edition of *Typographie.*

207.
2002: Irma Boom, telephone card.

2003: The United States invades Iraq.

208.
2003: Philippe Apeloig, poster.

2004: A powerful earthquake in Southeast Asia causes a tsunami, killing tens of thousands of people in nearly a dozen countries.

2000

203.

204.

206.

207.

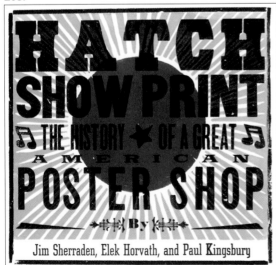

205.

208.

209.
2003: Max Kisman, typeface poster.

2003: *Design Observer* is founded. This Web site is devoted to a broad range of design topics focused on graphic design, communication arts, print, typography, and criticism.

210.
2004: Jianping He, Page from Hesign International, GmbH, Web site.

211.
2004: Brian MacKay-Lyons, Bryan Anderson, and participants of Ghost Lab 6, Kingsburg, Nova Scotia.

212.
2005: Lawrence Weiner, typographic installation.

213.
2005: Mevis & Van Deursen, book cover.

2005: Death of Pope John Paul II marks end of an era for the Roman Catholic Church and of modern history.

214.
2005: Jean-Benoît Lévy, Swiss Einstein stamp.

2003

209.

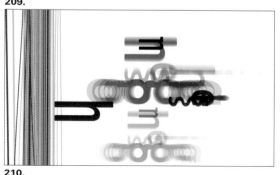

210.

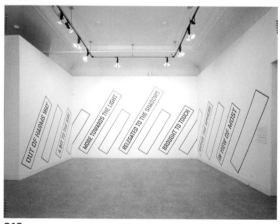

211.

213.

214.

212.

215.

2005: Martin Venezky, spread from his book, *It is Beautiful... Then Gone.*

216.

2005: Joost Grootens, book design for the *Metropolitan World Atlas* (see Chapter 9).

2006: North Korea tests its first nuclear weapon.

2007: *Harry Potter and the Deathly Hallows* is released, selling over 11 million copies in the first 24 hours and becoming the fastest-selling book in history.

217.

2007: Helmut Schmid, new edition of *Typography Today.*

218.

2007: Experimental Jetset, poster for the documentary film, *Helvetica,* by Gary Hustwit.

219.

2007: Lanny Sommese, poster for the Central Pennsylvania Festival of the Arts.

220.

2008: Ed Fella, promotional flyers.

2005

215.

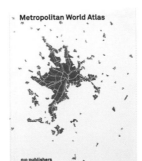

Metropolitan World Atlas

o10 publishers

216.

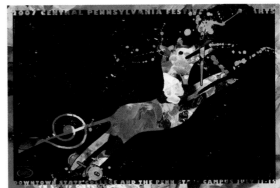

219.

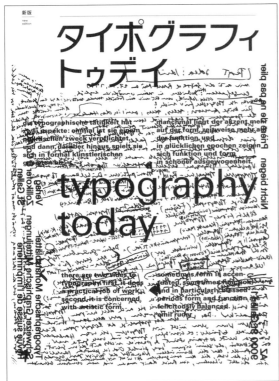

217.

218.

220.

29

221.
2009: Harmen Liemburg, poster for *Ultralight,* a travelling exhibition.

222.
2010: Mirko Ilić Corp., typographic illustration for the *New York Times.*

223.
2010: *The Sound of Red Earth* by Stephen Vitiello. Sound installations for the 20th Kaldor Public Art Project, Sydney Park Brickworks, Sydney, Australia. Photo by Paul Green, courtesy of Kaldor Public Art Projects.

224.
2010: Skolos and Wedell, poster for and AIGA Boston event honoring Matthew Carter.

225.
2010: Doug and Mike Starns, sculptural *T* for the *New York Times Magazine.* © 2011 Doug + Mike Starns.

2009

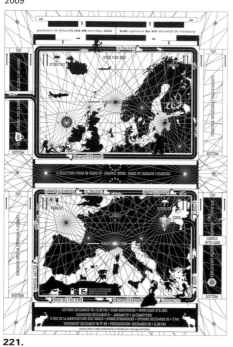

221.

222.

224.

223.

225.

Typographic design is a complex area of human activity, requiring a broad background for informed practice. This chapter explores the basic language of typography. Letterforms, the fundamental components of all typographic communications, are carefully examined. Nomenclature, measurement, and the nature of typographic font and family are presented.

The alphabet is a series of elemental visual signs in a fixed sequence, representing spoken sounds. Each letter signifies only one thing: its elementary sound or name. The twenty-six characters of our alphabet can be combined into thousands of words, creating a visual record of the spoken language. This is the magic of writing and typography, which have been called "thoughts-made-visible" and "frozen sounds."

1.
Strokes written with the reed
pen (top), and brush (middle),
and carved with a chisel
(bottom).

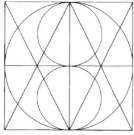

2.

3.
Capital and lowercase
letterform construction.

The four timelines in chapter one graphically present the evolution of letterforms and typographic design from the beginning of writing to the present. Our contemporary typographic forms have been forged by this historical evolution. Typography evolved from handwriting, which is created by making a series of marks by hand; therefore, the fundamental element constructing a letterform is the linear stroke. Each letter of our alphabet developed as a simple mark whose visual characteristics clearly separated it from all the others.

The marking properties of brush, reed pen, and stone engraver's chisel influenced the early form of the alphabet (Fig. **1**). The reed pen, used in ancient Rome and the medieval monastery, was held at an angle, called a cant, to the page. This produced a pattern of thick and thin strokes. Since the time of the ancient Greeks, capital letterforms have consisted of simple geometric forms based on the square, circle, and triangle. The basic shape of each capital letter can be extracted from the structure in Figure **2,** which is composed of a bisected square, a circle, a triangle, an inverted triangle, and two smaller circles.

The resulting vocabulary of forms, however, lacks several important attributes: optically adjusted proportions, expressive design properties, and maximum legibility and readability. The transition from rudimentary mark to letterforms with graphic clarity and precision is a matter of design.

Because early capital letters were cut into stone, these letters developed with a minimum number of curved lines, for curved strokes were difficult to cut (Fig. **3**). Lowercase letters evolved as reed-pen writing. Curved strokes could be written quickly and were used to reduce the number of strokes needed to write many characters.

The parts of letterforms
Over the centuries, a nomenclature has evolved that identifies the various components of individual letterforms. By learning this vocabulary, designers and typographers can develop a greater understanding and sensitivity to the visual harmony and complexity of the alphabet.

The following list (Fig. **4**) identifies the major components of letterform construction. In medieval times, horizontal guidelines were drawn to contain and align each line of lettering. Today, letterforms and their parts are drawn on imaginary guidelines to bring uniformity to typography.

Baseline: An imaginary line upon which the base of each capital rests.

Beard line: An imaginary line that runs along the bottoms of descenders.

Capline: An imaginary line that runs along the tops of the capital letters.

Meanline: An imaginary line that establishes the height of the body of lowercase letters.

x-height: The distance from the baseline to the meanline. Typically, this is the height of lowercase letters and is most easily measured on the lowercase *x*.

All characters align *optically* on the baseline. The body height of lowercase characters align optically at the x-height, and the tops of capitals align optically along the capline. To achieve precise alignments, the typeface designer makes optical adjustments.

Apex: The peak of the triangle of an uppercase *A*.

Arm: A projecting horizontal stroke that is unattached on one or both ends, as in the letters *T* and *E*.

Ascender: A stroke on a lowercase letter that rises above the meanline.

Bowl: A curved stroke enclosing the counterform of a letter. An exception is the bottom form of the lowercase roman *g,* which is called a loop.

Counter: The negative space that is fully or partially enclosed by a letterform.

Crossbar: The horizontal stroke connecting two sides of the letterform (as in *e, A,* and *H*) or bisecting the main stroke (as in *f* and *t*).

Capline

Meanline

x-height

Baseline

Beard line

Descender: A stroke on a lowercase letterform that falls below the baseline.

Ear: A small stroke that projects from the upper right side of the bowl of the lowercase roman *g*.

Eye: The enclosed part of the lowercase *e*.

Fillet: The contoured edge that connects the serif and stem in bracketed serifs. (Bracketed serifs are connected to the main stroke by this curved edge; unbracketed serifs connect to the main stroke with an abrupt angle without this contoured transition.)

Hairline: The thinnest stroke within a typeface that has strokes of varying weights.

Leg: The lower diagonal stroke on the letter *k*.

Link: The stroke that connects the bowl and the loop of a lowercase roman *g*.

Loop: See *Bowl*.

Serifs: Short strokes that extend from and at an angle to the upper and lower ends of the major strokes of a letterform.

Shoulder: A curved stroke projecting from a stem.

Spine: The central curved stroke of the letter *S*.

Spur: A projection – smaller than a serif – that reinforces the point at the end of a curved stroke, as in the letter *G*.

Stem: A major vertical or diagonal stroke in the letterform.

Stroke: Any of the linear elements within a letterform; originally, any mark or dash made by the movement of a pen or brush in writing.

Tail: A diagonal stroke or loop at the end of a letter, as in *R* or *j*.

Terminal: The end of any stroke that does not terminate with a serif.

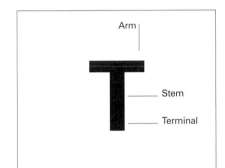

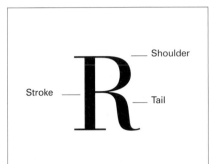

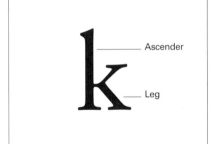

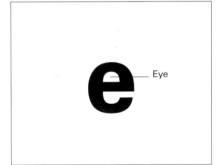

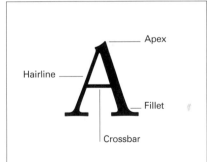

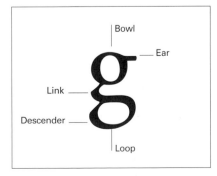

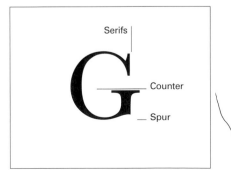

4.

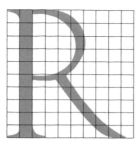
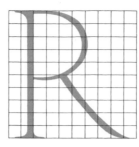
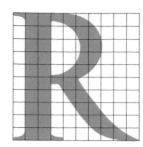

5.

1499 Old Style

1757 Baskerville

1793 Bodoni

1816 First sans serif

c. 1928 Ultra Bodoni

1957 Univers 55

6.

Proportions of the letterform

The proportions of the individual letterform are an important consideration in typography. Four major variables control letterform proportion and have considerable impact upon the visual appearance of a typeface: the ratio of letterform height to stroke width; the variation between the thickest and thinnest strokes of the letterform; the width of the letters; and the relationship of the x-height to the height of capitals, ascenders, and descenders.

The stroke-to-height ratio. The roman letterform, above, has the stroke-width-to-capital-height proportion found on Roman inscriptions (Fig. **5**). Superimposition on a grid demonstrates that the height of the letter is ten times the stroke width. In the adjacent rectangles, the center letter is reduced to one-half the normal stroke width, and the letter on the right has its stroke width expanded to twice the normal width. In both cases, pronounced change in the weight and appearance of the letterform occurs.

Contrast in stroke weight. A change in the contrast between thick and thin strokes can alter the optical qualities of letterforms. The series of *O*s in Figure **6,** shown with the date of each specimen, demonstrates how the development of technology and printing has enabled typeface designers to make thinner strokes.

In the Old Style typography of the Renaissance, designers attempted to capture some of the visual properties of pen writing. Since the writing pens of the period had a flat edge, they created thick and thin strokes. *Stress* is the term to define this

thickening of the strokes, which is particularly pronounced on curves. Note how the placement of weight within the Old Style *O* creates a diagonal axis. As time has passed, type designers have been less influenced by writing.

By the late 1700s, the impact of writing declined, and this axis became completely vertical in many typefaces of that period. In many of the earliest sans-serif typefaces, stress disappeared completely. Some of these typefaces have a monoline stroke that is completely even in weight.

Expanded and condensed styles. The design qualities of a typographic font change dramatically when the widths of the letterforms are expanded or condensed. The word *proportion,* set in two sans-serif typefaces, demonstrates extreme expansion and condensation (Fig. **7**). In the top example, set in Aurora Condensed, the stroke-to-height ratio is one to nine. In the bottom example, set in Information, the stroke-to-height ratio is one to two. Although both words are exactly the same height, the condensed typeface takes up far less area on the page.

X-height and proportion. The proportional relationship between the x-height and capital, ascender, and descender heights influences the optical qualities of typography in a significant way. The same characters are set in seventy-two-point type using three typefaces with widely varying x-heights (Fig. **8**). This example demonstrates how these proportional relationships change the appearance of type. The impact of x-height upon legibility will be discussed in Chapter Four.

8.
On the same-size body (72 point), the x-height variation between three typefaces – Garamond 3, Bodoni, and Univers – is shown. The proportion of the x-height to the point size significantly affects the appearance of type.

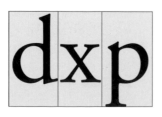
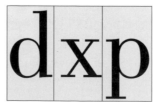
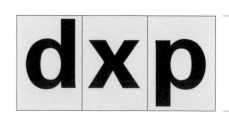

72 points

PROPORTION PROPORTION PROPORTION

A font is a set of characters of the same size and style containing all the letters, numbers, and marks needed for typesetting. A typographic font exhibits structural unity when all the characters relate to one another visually. The weights of thick and thin strokes must be consistent, and the optical alignment of letterforms must appear even. The distribution of lights and darks within each character and in the spaces between characters must be carefully controlled to achieve an evenness of tone within the font.

In some display faces, the font might include only the twenty-six capital letters. In a complete font for complex typesetting, such as for textbooks, it is possible to have nearly two hundred characters. The font for Adobe Garamond (Fig. **9**) includes the following types of characters.

Capitals: The set of large letters that is used in the initial position.

Lowercase: The smaller set of letters, so named because in metal typesetting these were stored in the lower part of a type case.

Small caps: A complete set of capital letters that are the same height as the x-height of the lowercase letters. These are often used for abbreviations, cross references, and emphasis.

Lining figures: Numbers that are the same height as the capital letters and sit on the baseline.

Old Style figures: A set of numbers that are compatible with lowercase letters; *1, 2,* and *O* align with the x-height; *6* and *8* have ascenders; and *3, 4, 5, 7,* and *9* have descenders.

Superior and inferior figures: Small numbers, usually slightly smaller than the x-height, used for footnotes and fractions. Superior figures hang from the capline, and inferior figures sit on the baseline.

Fractions: Common mathematical expressions made up of a superior figure, an inferior figure, and a slash mark. These are set as a single type character.

Ligatures: Two or more characters linked together as one unit, such as *ff.* The ampersand is a ligature originating as a letter combination for the French word *et* ("and") in medieval manuscripts.

Digraphs: A ligature composed of two vowels which are used to represent a dipthong (a mono-syllabic speech sound composed of two vowels).

Mathematical signs: Characters used to notate basic mathematical processes.

Punctuation: A system of standard signs used in written and printed matter to structure and separate units and to clarify meaning.

Accented characters: Characters with accents for foreign language typesetting or for indicating pronunciation.

Dingbats: Assorted signs, symbols, reference marks, and ornaments designed for use with a type font.

Monetary symbols: Logograms used to signify monetary systems (U.S. dollar and cent marks, British pound mark, and so on).

7.

abcdefghijklmnopqrstuvwxyz
ABCDEFGHIJKLMNOPQRSTUVWXYZ
ABCDEFGHIJKLMNOPQRSTUVWXYZ
1234567890& 1234567890& 1234567890&
¼½¾ ⅛⅜⅝⅞ ⅓⅔‰ 1234567890/1234567890-

 fffiflffiffl ÆŒßRpæœ√π=±+÷∞°-‒—
ÂÅÁÇÍÎÏØÓÒÔÚ(.,;:'"!?^"''"'""^˘˜‹›«»`
áéíóú åäëïöüàèìòùâêîôûøÁÉÍÓÚÅÄËÏÖÜ
™©®@#s¢¢ᴆ₡£¥%^*
{}[]|¡¢§¶•†‡

9.

15.

Optical relationships within a font

Mechanical and mathematical letterform construction can result in serious spatial problems, because diverse forms within an alphabet appear optically incorrect. These letterform combinations show the optical adjustment necessary to achieve visual harmony within a font.

AEVO

10.

Pointed and curved letters (Fig. 10) have little weight at the top and/or bottom guidelines; this can make them appear too short. To make them appear the same height as letters that terminate squarely with the guidelines, the apexes of pointed letters extend beyond the baseline and capline. Curved letterforms are drawn slightly above and below these lines to prevent them from appearing too small.

HBESKX38

11.

In two-storied capitals and figures (Fig. 11), the top half appears too large if the form is divided in the mathematical center. To balance these letters optically, the center is slightly above the mathematical center, and the top halves are drawn slightly narrower than the bottom half.

Horizontal strokes (Fig. 12) are drawn slightly thinner than vertical strokes in both curved and straight letterforms. Otherwise, the horizontals would appear too thick.

Tight junctions where strokes meet (Fig. 13) are often opened slightly to prevent the appearance of thickening at the joint.

Letters combining diagonal and vertical strokes (Fig. 14) must be designed to achieve a balance between the top and bottom counterforms.

ETO

12.

M

13.

NK

14.

Strokes can be tapered slightly to open up the spaces, and adjustments in the amount of stroke overlap can achieve a harmony of parts. Letters whose vertical strokes determine their height (Fig. 15) are drawn slightly taller than letters whose height is determined by a horizontal stroke. Optically, they will appear to be the same height.

MBNB

16.

The stroke weight of compact letterforms (Fig. 16), such as those with closed counterforms, are drawn slightly smaller than the stroke weight of letterforms having open counterforms. This optically balances the weight.

OHQ

17.

Curved strokes are usually thicker at their midsection than the vertical strokes, to achieve an even appearance (Fig. 17).

These adjustments are very subtle and are often imperceptible to the reader. However, their overall effect is a more ordered and harmonious visual appearance.

Unity of design in the type font

Tremendous diversity of form exists in the typographic font. Twenty-six capitals, twenty-six lowercase letters, ten numerals, punctuation, and other graphic elements must be integrated into a system that can be successfully combined into innumerable words.

Letterform combinations from the Times Roman Bold font (Fig. 18) demonstrate visual similarities that bring wholeness to typography. Letterforms share similar parts. A repetition of curves, verticals, horizontals, and serifs are combined to bring variety and unity to typographic designs using this typeface. All well-designed fonts of type display this principle of repetition with the variety that is found in Times Roman Bold.

Curved capitals share a common round stroke.

DCGOQ

The diagonal strokes of the *A* are repeated in *V W M*.

Lowercase letters have common serifs.

AVWM jiru

F E B demonstrates that the more similar letters are, the more common parts they share.

Repetition of the same stroke in *m n h u* creates unity.

FEB mnhut

Likewise, the letters *b d p q* share parts.

bdpq SCGH

Capital serifs recur in similar characters.

BRKPR atfr

ZLE MYX

Subtle optical adjustments can be seen. For example, the bottom strokes of the capital *Z* and *L* have longer serifs than the bottom stroke of the *E*. This change in detail compensates for the larger counterform on the right side of the first two letters.

bq bhlk ceo

18.

An infinite variety of type styles is available today. Digital typography, with its simple and economical introduction of new typefaces, has made the entire array of typefaces developed over the centuries available for contemporary use. Numerous efforts have been made to classify typefaces, with most falling into the following major categories. Some classification systems add a decorative, stylized, or novelty category for the wide range of fanciful type styles that defy categorization. A selection of decorative typefaces appear on pages 332 and 333.

Old Style

Old Style type began with designs of the punchcutter Francesco Griffo, who worked for the famous Venetian scholar-printer Aldus Manutius during the 1490s. Griffo's designs evolved from earlier Italian type designs. His Old Style capitals were influenced by carved Roman capitals; lowercase letters were inspired by fifteenth-century humanistic writing styles, based on the earlier Carolingian minuscules. Old Style letterforms have the weight stress of rounded forms at an angle, as in handwriting. The serifs are bracketed (that is, unified with the stroke by a tapered, curved line). Also, the top serifs on the lowercase letters are at an angle.

Italic

Italic letterforms slant to the right. Today, we use them primarily for emphasis and differentiation. When the first italic appeared in the earliest "pocket book," printed by Aldus Manutius in 1501, it was used as an independent typestyle. The first italic characters were close-set and condensed; therefore, Manutius was able to get more words on each line. Some italic styles are based on handwriting with connected strokes and are called scripts.

Transitional

During the 1700s, typestyles gradually evolved from Old Style to Modern. Typefaces from the middle of the eighteenth century, including those by John Baskerville, are called Transitional. The contrast between thick and thin strokes is greater than in Old Style faces. Lowercase serifs are more horizontal, and the stress within the rounded forms shifts to a less diagonal axis. Transitional characters are usually wider than Old Style characters.

Modern

Late in the 1700s, typefaces termed Modern evolved from Transitional styles. These typefaces have extreme contrasts between thick and thin strokes. Thin strokes are reduced to hairlines. The weight stress of rounded characters is vertical. Serifs are horizontal hairlines that join the stems at a right angle without bracketing. The uppercase width is regularized; wide letters such as *M* and *W* are condensed and other letters, including *P* and *T*, are expanded. Modern-style typefaces have a strong geometric quality projected by rigorous horizontal, vertical, and circular forms.

Egyptian

In 1815, the English typefounder Vincent Figgins introduced slab-serif typestyles under the name Antique. At the time, there was a mania for ancient Egyptian artifacts, and other typefounders adopted the name Egyptian for their slab-serif designs. These typestyles have heavy square or rectangular serifs that are usually unbracketed. The stress of curved strokes is often minimal. In some slab-serif typefaces, all strokes are the same weight.

Sans Serif

The first sans serif typestyle appeared in an 1816 specimen book of the English typefounder William Caslon IV. The most obvious characteristic of these styles is, as the name implies, the absence of serifs. In many sans serif typefaces, strokes are uniform, with little or no contrast between thick and thin strokes. Stress is almost always vertical. Many sans serif typefaces are geometric in their construction; others combine both organic and geometric qualities.

The development of photo and digital technology has stimulated the design and production of countless new typefaces whose visual characteristics defy standard classification. The visual traits of these "hybrid" forms may fall into more than one of the historical classifications presented on the preceding two pages. The following is a classification system derived from the visual features common to letters throughout the typeface kingdom. It may be used for comparative purposes to pinpoint the most dominant traits of specific typefaces. Type designers use these variations to create a family of typefaces. The type family is discussed on pages 45–48.

Serifs:

Serifs provide some of the most identifiable features of typefaces, and in some cases they reveal clues about their historical evolution. The serifs shown are those that appear most frequently in typefaces.

Weight:

This is a feature defined by the ratio between the relative width of the strokes of letterforms and their height. On the average, a letter of normal weight possesses a stroke width of approximately 15% of its height, whereas bold is 20% and light is 10%.

Width:

Width is an expression of the ratio between the black vertical strokes of the letterforms and the intervals of white between them. When white intervals appear larger, letters appear wider. A letter whose width is approximately 80% of its height is considered normal. A condensed letter is 60%, and an expanded letter is 100% of its height.

Posture:

Roman letters that slant to the right but are structurally the same as upright roman letters are referred to as oblique. Italic letters, which are based on handwriting, are structurally different from roman letters of the same type family. Italic letters with connecting strokes are called scripts. The angle of posture varies from typeface to typeface; however, a slant of approximately 12% is considered to be normal.

Thick/thin contrast:

This visual feature refers to the relationship between the thinnest parts of the strokes in letters and the thickest parts. The varying ratios between these parts produce a wide range of visual textures in text type.

A high contrast A medium contrast A low contrast A no contrast

x-height:

This proportional characteristic can vary immensely in different typefaces of the same size. Typically, x-heights are considered to be "tall" when they are at least two-thirds the height of capital letters. They are "short" when they measure one-half the height of capital letters.

d extra tall d tall d medium d short d extra short

Ascenders/descenders

Ascenders and descenders may appear longer in some typefaces and shorter in others, depending on the relative size of the x-height. Descenders are generally slightly longer than ascenders among letters of the same typeface.

dp extra long dp long dp medium dp short dp extra short

Stress:

The stress of letters, which is a prominent visual axis resulting from the relationships between thick and thin strokes, may be left-angled, vertical, or right-angled in appearance.

O left-angled O vertical O right-angled

Typographic measurement

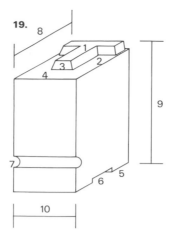

19.

1. Face (printing surface)
2. Counter
3. Beard
4. Shoulder
5. Feet
6. Groove
7. Nick

8. Point size (body size)
9. Type-high (.918″ height)
10. Set width

Our measurement system for typography was originally developed for the handset metal type invented by Johann Gutenberg around 1450. The rectangular metal block of type (Fig. **19**) has a raised letterform on top, which was inked to print the image.

Metal type measurement

The small sizes of text type necessitated the development of a measuring system with extremely fine increments. There were no standards for typographic measurements until the French type designer and founder Pierre Simon Fournier le Jeune introduced his point system of measurement in 1737. The contemporary American measurement system, which was adopted during the 1870s, has two basic units: the point and the pica (Fig. **20**). There are approximately 72 points in an inch (each point is 0.138 inches) and 12 points in a pica. There are about six picas in an inch.

Metal type exists in three dimensions, and an understanding of typographic measurement begins with this early technology. The depth of the type (Fig. **19,** caption 8) is measured in points and is called the point size or body size. All metal type must be the exact same height (Fig. **19,** caption 9), which is called type-high (.918 inch). This uniform height enabled all types to print a uniform impression upon the paper. The width of a piece of type is called the set width (Fig. **19,** caption 10) and varies with the design of each individual letter. The letters *M* and *W* have the widest set width; *i* and *l* have the narrowest. The length of a line of type is the sum of the set width of all the characters and spaces in the line. It is measured in picas.

Before the development of the point and pica system, various sizes of type were identified by names, such as *brevier, long primer,* and *pica;* these became 8-point, 10-point, and 12-point type. The chart in Figure **21,** reproduced from a nineteenth-century printers' magazine, shows the major point sizes of type with their old names.

0   1   2 Inches

0 1 2 3 4 5 6 Picas	6 Picas = 1 Inch
0 12 72 Points	12 Points = 1 Pica
	72 Points = 1 Inch

20.

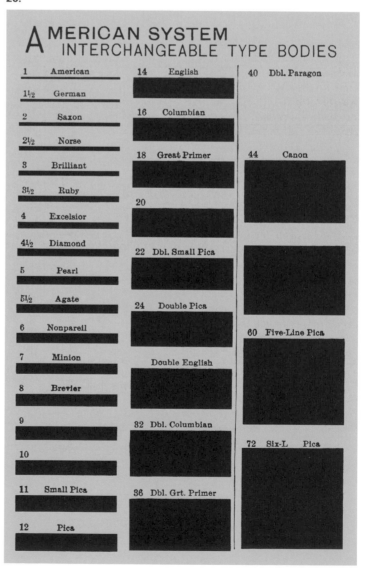

21.

Reproduced actual size from *The Inland Printer,* April 1885.

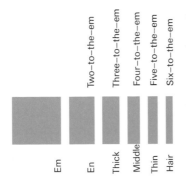

Two-to-the-em
Three-to-the-em
Four-to-the-em
Five-to-the-em
Six-to-the-em

Em   En   Thick   Middle   Thin   Hair

This line has word spacing with em quads.

This line has word spacing with en quads.

This line has word spacing with thick quads.

This line has word spacing with middle quads.

This line has word spacing with thin quads.

This line has word spacing with hair quads.

Type that is 12 point and under is called text type and is primarily used for body copy. Sizes above 12 point are called display type, and they are used for titles, headlines, signage, and the like.

Traditional metal type had a range of text and display sizes in increments from 5 point to 72 point (Fig. **22**). The measurement of point size is a measurement of the metal block of type including space above and below the letters; therefore, one cannot measure the point size from printed letters themselves. This is sometimes confusing. Refer to the labels for x-height, cap height, and point size on Figure **22** and observe that the point size includes the cap height plus a spatial interval above and below the letters.

Spatial measurement

In addition to measuring type, the designer also measures and specifies the spatial intervals between typographic elements. These intervals are: interletter spacing (traditionally called letterspacing), which is the interval between letters; interword spacing, also called word-spacing, which is the interval between words; and interline spacing, which is the interval between two lines of type. Traditionally, interline space is called leading, because thin strips of lead are placed between lines of metal type to increase the spatial interval between them.

In traditional metal typography, interletter and interword spacing are achieved by inserting metal blocks called quads between the pieces of type. Because these are not as high as the type itself, they do not print. A quad that is a square of the point size is called an *em.* One that is one-half an *em* quad is called an *en.* In metal type, other smaller divisions of space are fractions of the em (Fig. **23**). These metal spacers are used for letter- and wordspacing, paragraph indentions, and centering or justifying lines of type.

5 Point
6 Point
7 Point
8 Point
9 Point
10 Point
11 Point
12 Point
14 Point
18 Point
24 Point
30 Point
36 Point
42 Point
48 Point
54 Point
60 Point
72 Point

Cap height   Body size

22.

43

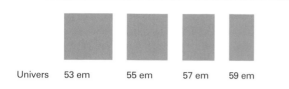

Univers 53 em 55 em 57 em 59 em

24.

This line is set with plus ten units of interletter spacing.
This line is set with normal, unaltered interletter spacing.
This line is set with minus five units of interletter spacing.
This line is set with minus ten units of interletter spacing.
This line is set with minus twenty units of interletter spacing.

26.

For design considerations, the em of a condensed type style can be narrower than a square, and the em of an expanded type size can be wider than a square. This is demonstrated by the em quads from four styles in the Univers family of typefaces (Fig. **24**).

While *em* and *en* are still used as typographic terms, spacing in digital typesetting and desktop publishing is controlled by a computer, using a unit system. The *unit* is a relative measurement determined by dividing the em (that is, the square of the type size) into equal vertical divisions. Different typesetting systems use different numbers of units; sixteen, thirty-two, and sixty-four are common. Some desktop publishing software even permits adjustments as small as twenty-thousandths of an em. The width of each character (Fig. **25**) is measured by its unit value. During typesetting, the character is generated, then the typesetting machine advances the number of units assigned to that character before generating the next character. The unit value includes space on each side of the letter for normal interletter spacing. Adding or subtracting units to expand or contract the space between letters is called *tracking.* Changing the tracking changes the tone of the typography (Fig. **26**). As will be discussed later, tracking influences the aesthetics and legibility of typesetting.

Some letter combinations, such as *TA,* have awkward spatial relationships. An adjustment in the interletter space to make the interval more consistent with other letter combinations is called *kerning.* In metal type, kerning was achieved by sawing notches in the types. Contemporary typesetting software can contain automatic kerning pairs, and the designer can manually change the kerning between characters when these awkward combinations appear.

| 13 Units | 10 Units | 9 Units | 5 Units | 10 Units | 11 Units |

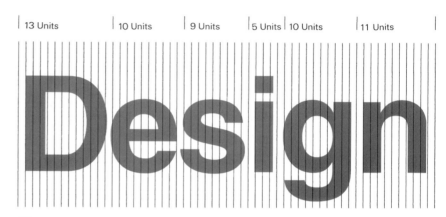

25.
The unit value of each letter in
the word *Design* is shown.

In this setting, minus one unit
is used for tighter interletter
spacing.

In this setting, minus two
units is used. The letters touch.

A type family consists of a group of related type-faces, unified by a set of similar design characteristics. Each face in the family is an individual one that has been created by changing visual aspects of the parent font. Early type families consisted of three fonts: the regular roman face, a bolder version, and an italic. The roman, bold, and italic fonts of the Baskerville family (Fig. **27**) demonstrate that a change in stroke weight produces the bold version, and a change in stroke angle creates the italic. The bold font expands typographic possibilities by bringing impact to titles, headings, and display settings. Today, italics are primarily used for emphasis as a variation of roman. In addition to weight and angle changes, additional members of a type family are created by changing proportions or by design elaboration.

Weight changes. By simply changing the stroke width relative to the height of the letters, a whole series of alphabets, ranging from extremely light to very bold, can be produced. In England, a classification standard has been developed that contains eight weights: extralight, light, semilight, medium, semibold, bold, extrabold, and ultrabold. Most type families do not, however, consist of eight weights. Four weights – light, regular or book, medium, and bold – are often sufficient for most purposes. In the Avant Garde family (Fig. **28**), stroke weight is the only aspect that changes in these five fonts.

Proportion. Changing the proportions of a type style by making letterforms wider (expanded) or narrower (condensed), as discussed earlier, is another method for adding typefaces to a type family. Terms used to express changes in proportion include: ultraexpanded, extraexpanded, expanded, regular, condensed, extracondensed, and ultracondensed.

Sometimes confusion results because there is no standardized terminology for discussing the variations in type families. For example, the regular face is sometimes called *normal, roman,* or *book.* Light weights are named *lightline, slim,* and *hairline. Black, elephant, massive, heavy,* and *thick* have been used to designate bold weights. Names given to condensed variations include *narrow, contracted, elongated,* and *compressed.* Expanded faces have been called *extended, wide,* and *stretched.*

27.

Baskerville

Baskerville

Baskerville

AVANT GARDE

AVANT GARDE

AVANT GARDE

AVANT GARDE

AVANT GARDE

28.

Futura Italic
Baskerville Italic
Bodoni Italic

29.

Angle. In our discussion about the basic classification of typefaces, italics were presented as a major independent category. They were first introduced four hundred years ago as a new style. Now italics serve as a member of type families, and they are used for contrast or emphasis. Italic fonts that retain curvilinear strokes inspired by handwriting are called cursives or scripts. In geometric typefaces constructed with drafting instruments, the italic fonts created by slanting the stroke angle are called obliques. Baskerville Italic (Fig. **29**) is a cursive, demonstrating a handwriting influence; Futura Italic is an oblique face; and Bodoni Italic has both cursive and oblique qualities. Although the Bodoni family was constructed with the aid of drafting instruments, details in the italic font (for example, some of the lower serifs) evidence a definite cursive quality.

Elaboration. In design an elaboration is an added complexity, fullness of detail, or ornamentation. Design elaboration can be used to add new typefaces to a type family. These might include outline fonts, three-dimensional effects, and the application of ornaments to letterforms. Some of the variations of Helvetica (Fig. **30**) that are available from the German firm of Dr. Boger Photosatz GmbH include outlines, inlines, perspectives, rounded terminals, and even a chipped antique effect.

While many elaborations are gaudy and interfere with the integrity and legibility of the letterforms, others can be used successfully.

Goudy Handtooled (Fig. **31**) is based on Goudy Bold. A white linear element is placed on each major stroke. Dimensionality is suggested, and the face alludes to incised inscriptional lettering.

Decorative and novelty type styles should be used with great care by the graphic designer. At best, these can express a feeling appropriate to the content and can allow for unique design solutions. Unfortunately, the use of design elaboration is often a mere straining for effect.

The Cheltenham family
One of the most extensive type families is the Cheltenham series of typefaces (Fig. **32**). The first version, Cheltenham Old Style, was initially designed around the turn of the century by architect Bertram G. Goodhue in collaboration with Ingalls Kimball of the Cheltenham Press in New York City. When this typeface went into commercial production at the American Type Founders Company, designer Morris F. Benton supervised its development. Benton designed about eighteen additional typefaces for the Cheltenham family. Variations developed by other typefounders and manufacturers of typesetting equipment expanded this family to more than thirty styles. The design properties linking the Cheltenham family are short, stubby slab serifs with rounded brackets, tall ascenders and long descenders, and a moderate weight differential between thick and thin strokes.

Cheltenham
Cheltenham
Cheltenham
Cheltenham
Cheltenham
Cheltenham
Cheltenham
Cheltenham
Cheltenham
Cheltenham
Cheltenham
Cheltenham
Cheltenham
Cheltenham
Cheltenham
Cheltenham
Cheltenham
Cheltenham
Cheltenham
Cheltenham
Cheltenham

32.

Goudy Handtooled

31.

30.
Elaborations of
Helvetica Medium.

					39 Univers
	45 Univers	46 *Univers*	47 Univers	48 *Univers*	49 Univers
53 Univers	55 Univers	56 *Univers*	57 Univers	58 *Univers*	59 Univers
63 Univers	65 Univers	66 *Univers*	67 Univers	68 *Univers*	
73 Univers	75 Univers	76 *Univers*			
83 Univers					

33.

The Univers family

A full range of typographic expression and visual contrast becomes possible when all the major characteristics – weight, proportion, and angle – are orchestrated into a unified family. An exceptional example is the Univers family (Fig. **33**). This family of twenty-one type styles was designed by Adrian Frutiger. Instead of the usual terminology, Frutiger used numerals to designate the typefaces. Univers 55 is the "parent" face; its stroke weight and proportions are the norm from which all the other designs were developed. The black-and-white relationships and proportions of Univers 55 are ideal for text settings. Careful study of Figure **33** reveals that the first digit in each font's number indicates the stroke weight, three being the lightest and eight the heaviest. The second digit indicates expansion and contraction of the spaces within and between the letters, which results in

expanded and condensed styles. Roman fonts are designated with an odd number, and oblique fonts are designated with an even number.

In the design of Univers, Frutiger sparked a trend in type design toward a larger x-height. The lowercase letters are larger relative to ascenders, descenders, and capitals. The size and weight of capitals are closer to the size and weight of lowercase letters, creating increased harmony on the page of text. Because the twenty-one members of the Univers family share the same x-height, capital height, and ascender and descender length and are produced as a system, they can be intermixed and used together without limitation. This gives extraordinary design flexibility to the designer (Fig. **34**).

34.
Typographic interpretation of
The Bells by Edgar Allan Poe
using the Univers family.
(Designer: Philip Meggs)

Hear the

sledges with the **Bells**

SILVER **Bbeellss- -**

What a world of **merriment** their *melody* foretells!

*H*ow they *tinkle,*

tinkle,

tinkle, in the icy air of night!

While the stars that

o v e r s p r i n k l e

All the heavens seem to t w i n k l e

With a *crystalline* delight:

Keeping *time, time,* **time,**

In a sort of **R**unic rhyme,

To the **tin**tin*nab*u**la**tion that so *musically* wells

From the *bells,* bells, Bells,

Bells,

BELLS, **Bbeellss- -**

From the *jingling* and the *tingling* of the bells.

3 Syntax and Communication

Like the anatomy of typography, typographic syntax and communication have a language that must be learned to understand typographic design. Syntax is the connecting of typographic signs to form words and sentences on the page. The elements of design – letter, word, line, column, and margin – are made into a cohesive whole through the use of typographic space, visual hierarchy, ABA form, and grid systems.

Typographic syntax

In grammar, syntax is the manner in which words are combined to form phrases or sentences. We define typographic syntax as the process of arranging elements into a cohesive whole. The study of typographic syntax begins with its basic unit, the letter, and progresses to word, line, column, and margin.

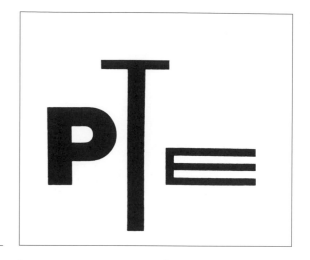

1.

2.

1.
This composition demonstrates contrasting visual characteristics of three letterforms. (Designer: Robert Boyle)

2.
Through precise letterform drawing and carefully considered form-to-counterform interaction, two dissimilar letters form a cohesive sign. (Designer: Gail Collins)

3.
Two letterforms are each broken into two geometric shapes of varying size and density, and the four resulting forms are combined into a delicate, asymmetrically balanced symbol. (Designer: Frank Armstrong)

The letter

Our initial discussion of typographic syntax addresses the intrinsic character of the individual letter. This well-drawn form, exhibiting subtlety and precision, is the unit that distinguishes one family of type from another. It exists in various weights, sizes, and shapes (Fig. **1**).

Although the letter typically functions as part of a word, individual letters are frequently combined into new configurations. As shown in Figures **2** and **3,** combinations of letters *A* and *g* and *P* and *Q* are unified to create a stable gestalt. In the illustrated examples, there is an expressiveness and boldness to the individual letters. The syntax displayed here is an example of letter combinations acting as signs, extracted from a larger system of signs.

A typographic sign is visually dynamic because of its interaction with the surrounding white space or void – the white of the paper. This form-to-void relationship is inherent in the totality of typographic expression. The repetition of the letter *T* in Figure **4** is balanced and complemented by its white space. In the title page for Hans Arp's book *On My Way,* the visual interplay between the three letterforms animates the page (Fig. **5**). This equilibrium and spatial interaction and the manner in which it is achieved will be discussed further in our study of typographic space.

Contemplating this ability of space to define form, Amos Chang observed, ". . . it is the existence of intangible elements, the negative, in architectonic forms which makes them come alive, become human, naturally harmonize with one another, and enable us to experience them with human sensibility."

4.
It is the figure/ground reversal in the repetition of the letter *T* that creates a balanced and expressive poster. (Designer: Willi Kunz)

5.
A dynamic composition is formed by the precise spatial location of the letterforms *a, r,* and *p,* which also spell the author's name. (Designer: Paul Rand)

4.

3.

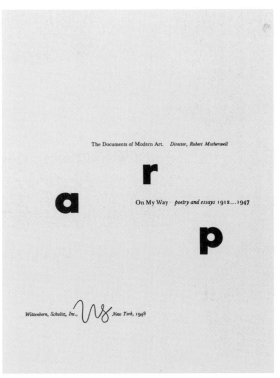

5.

6.

A star, a glass, and a word contribute to form a sign for *joy*. The word's meaning is expressed visually and poetically. (Designer: Frank Armstrong)

7.

Word-to-word interaction exhibits rhythmic recurrences of form and counterform. Individual letterforms are paired, and their corresponding interior counters are related here. (Designer: John Rodgers)

8.

This dissection of the word *Camerata* displays the letterform combinations and the relationships between consonants and their connecting vowels. Contrast and repetition create lateral movement within a word, and the overall arrangement relates to the word's meaning. (Designer: Sergio de Jesus)

6.

8.

C   a   a

C a   **m** r

Camerata

am

m e

e

7.

ce   oo

ll   d

cellar door

9.

The word

By definition, a word has the potential to express an idea (Fig. **6**), object, or event. Word signs are independent of the things they represent, yet by design they can be made to signify and reveal their meaning.

Form and counterform relationships, found within individual letterforms, also exist within individual words. Speaking on the structural consideration of form and counterform and the designing of typefaces, Adrian Frutiger stated: "The material of typography is the black, and it is the designer's task with the help of this black to capture space, to create harmonious whites inside the letters as well as between them."

By observing this principle and by combining form and counterform into word units, the designer discovers subtle typographic connections and rhythms (Fig. **7**). The word unit is a constellation of individual letterforms, suggesting a union and forming a cohesive whole. Optically adjusted spaces and consistent counterform relationships assure the overall clarity of this union.

Discussing interletter spacing, the painter and graphic artist Ben Shahn tells about his training as an apprentice who lettered on lithographic stones in 1913. The shop foreman explained, "Imagine you have in your hand a glass that will hold only so much water. Now you must provide space between your letters – whatever their slants and curves may be – to hold just that much water, no more or less." The universal principle for spacing letters is this: the typographer, calligrapher, or designer attempts

to make the interletter space between each pair of letters appear equal to the space between every other pair of letters. Because these counterform spaces have such different configurations, this spacing must be achieved through optical balance rather than through measurement.

Figure **8** shows a dissection of the word *Camerata,* displaying various interletter relationships, including both geometric and organic features. In this example, the word's internal pattern is created by the visual properties of the individual letterforms and their various juxtapositions. This arrangement displays the nature of the internal pattern. *Camerata* is an Italian word meaning "a room full of people"; this meaning supplies yet another interpretation of the overall pattern.

A concern for form and counterform is evident in the equilibrium that is established among the letterforms comprising the word *Camerata.* It is extremely important to see the interior rhythms of a single word. In the example shown, the letters *C, m, r,* and *t* function as elements of contrast, while the three *a*s and the *e* act as the unifying elements. A similar use of contrast and repetition is demonstrated by the progression of letterforms within the corporate logotype for Olivetti (Fig. **9**).

Obviously, not all words offer the potential for such a rich typographic internal pattern. The complex and lively forms reproduced here clearly show the variety and fullness of form that exists in some deceptively simple word units.

9.

In the Olivetti logo, the x-height establishes continuity, and the five ascending vertical forms create a horizontal rhythm. The repetition of rounded forms (*o and e*) and the "echo effect" of a rounded form followed by vertical strokes create a lively unity; the angled strokes of the letter *v* introduce an element of contrast. (Designer: Walter Ballmer)

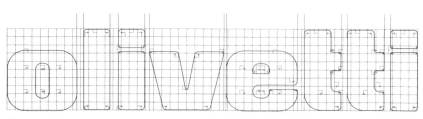

9.

Of all the achievements of the human mind, the birth of the alphabet is the most momentous.

13.

10.

Symmetrical placement produces a quiet, balanced configuration.

11.

Asymmetrical placement achieves a dynamic division of space on the page. (Designer: Ivy Li)

The line

Words are joined to form verbal sentences and typographic lines. The configuration and placement of lines of type are significant structural concerns. In its most basic form, a line of type consists of a single point size and a single weight extended horizontally over a specific line width.

Lines of type can be arranged symmetrically (Fig. **10**), or asymmetrically (Fig. **11**). The viewer/reader must sense a clearly established relationship between individual lines of type and the surrounding space (Fig. **12**).

The smallest change in point size, weight, or line length controls the overall emphasis given to a line of type. The designer or typographer must determine when the overall effect is balanced and fully integrated. All design considerations – typeface selection, alignments, and spacing – should display connections that are apparent and distinct (Fig. **13**). Jan Tschichold states, "The relationship of the sizes must in any case be clearly visible, its effect must be lively, and it must always follow the sense of the text exactly."

The length of a group of lines of type can be equal (justified), unequal (flush left/ragged right, ragged left/flush right), or centered. The examples in this section illustrate various typographic alignments. Typographic form becomes lively and harmonious through these alignments, which enhance individual lines of type and activate the surrounding space (Figs. **14** and **15**).

The placement of punctuation marks is of special significance to these alignments. In Figure **16** punctuation marks extend into the margin. Slight adjustments and subtle refinements heighten the degree of unity.

Typographic rules are used in conjunction with type and separate one line of type from another or one group of typographic lines from another as in Figure **12**, or in footnotes. Rules are found in a variety of forms (Fig. **17**) and numerous sizes and weights. (The use of visual punctuation, including typographic rules, is detailed in *Visual Hierarchy*.)

Earlier, we discussed kerning and the optical spacing of letterforms. Control of these factors makes possible a judicious use of letterspacing in a line of type. The orientation of lines raises a multiplicity of other spacing concerns; for example, interword spacing, interline spacing, and line-to-page relationships, as well as the establishment of columns and margins.

12.

Type and rules combine to bring a sense of unity to the page. Note the recurrence of similar space intervals and the attention given to individual line breaks (the rhythmic pattern of line endings). (Designer: Cheryl Van Arnam)

13.

This multiple-line composition contains varying line weights, yet expresses wholeness through the careful placement of all elements. It displays the diversity possible in the spacing of lines of type. (Designer: Wolfgang Weingart)

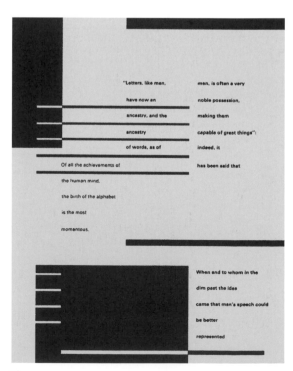

12.

"Bauhaus Masters"
Marcel Breuer
Paul Klee
Herbert Bayer

"Bauhaus Masters"
Marcel Breuer
Paul Klee
Herbert Bayer
16.

14.
Complex and subtle relationships in interline spacing are
achieved here by varying
type size, weight, and spatial
interval, which separate
the statements for the reader.
The overall effect is rhythmic
and expressive. (Designer:
Frank Armstrong)
15.
In this conversation, the
placement of lines and
intervals reflects the dialogue.
(Designer: Warren Lehrer)
16.
In the top setting the lines
are flush left, but the edge
appears uneven because of
the punctuation. In the bottom
version, "hanging" the
punctuation into the margin
is an adjustment resulting
in an optically aligned edge.
17.
Hierarchical clarity can be
established by using this
standard collection of
typographic rules to separate,
emphasize, and bring order
to parts of information.

14.

15.

Straight-line rule

Bar rule

Bracket rule

Swelled rule

Oxford rule

Leader

17.

18.

Four columns of type are arranged horizontally, allowing ample breathing space for the photographic images at the bottom of the spread. The depth of the columns make possible a clear integration of typographic and pictorial form. (Designer: John Malinoski)

19.

Eight columns of type create a vertical movement. Their uneven heights serve to balance the space and create a lively rhythm. The use of photographs and color breaks the overall grayness of the text. (Designer: John Malinoski)

Video stills: *Flight Song*, 1996–2001 (left) and *Floor Show*, 1999–2001.

sound in his work, and he does not spare us the abrasive scraping of that chair across the floor. It becomes the fingernails of life across the cosmos of a blackboard.

In the world of print, children were seen and not heard but, on the internet, children are heard and not seen. Richard Carlyon, *A Saying of Sorts*

This question is everywhere in Carlyon's work: Who are we immutably? Who is technology turning us into?

The phrase 'I wouldn't have believed it if I hadn't seen it' really should be 'if I hadn't believed it with all my heart, I wouldn't have seen it.' Richard Carlyon, *A Saying of Sorts*

In the center monitor of the extraordinary three-part *Pacer's Song*, the artist appears formally dressed in a black suit and informally undressed in bare feet, a recurring motif that often seems to symbolize, or embody, the fragile human body and its flawed beauty. He slaps (those sounds again) up and down another one of his bare-bones interiors, this time a hall. He sits in a chair, gets up again, paces, drags the chair through an open door. Then from a different angle: he drags the chair down the hall, drags it back, sits again, paces, drags the chair off-screen, pushes/slides the chair down the hall,

drags the chair down some steps with it awkwardly thumping behind him. He finally stops and, apparently having given up on the chair, simply walks up and down the stairs. Though we never see his face, the uncertainty and anxiety of this pacer are palpable. Meanwhile, the videos on the left and the right contain images from movies jaggedly edited in Carlyon's favorite style. They repeat motions at irregular intervals, sometimes creating what look like little skips, and sometimes creating longer motions: a woman or a man running up stairs, doors opening and closing to we know not what, together with the image of a key and the phrase, "took me just half an hour to find it" — all hypnotically repeated and filled with dread, sometimes faintly (who is behind that door?) and sometimes startlingly (men falling violently downstairs). The pacer in the center video has plenty to be pacing about. We don't know what's going to happen when we get to the top of that staircase, or who is behind that door, or when we're going to tumble down that staircase to our own death.

Anyone can name anything. Richard Carlyon, *A Saying of Sorts*

I'm not sure that Carlyon names, but I certainly think he renames; and I think he is passionately involved in the task of allowing the viewer the fearful pleasure of naming or renaming.

Video stills: *Nomad's Crossing* (left) and *Their Then Now*, both 1999–2000.

An error: failure to adjust from a preconception to an actuality. Richard Carlyon, *A Saying of Sorts*

I believe Carlyon's work is saturated in this idea. In *Difficulty and Desire*, he sits in shadow, in front of a window, a still fan resting in the window, the sign of some building behind him. He intones, almost inaudibly, "She was a visitor," over and over again, moving his head slowly from left to right. (This line comes from composer Robert Ashley's opera, *That Morning Thing*.) Then the image changes: the fan is now running, and you can clearly see that the sign behind him says UNIFORMS. There's also another sound, like a beast lowing. Then someone else seems to be saying, "She was a visitor." Carlyon reappears, eerily lit; holding the mask of a black and bearded man to his face, which he then removes to reveal another mask, plastic and opaque, covering his own face. The piece is clearly about identity, about the transient or elusive or unknowable nature of identity. But it is also clearly about a perceptual shift from the preconception that we can know ourselves to the actuality that this is impossible, that identity is always flexible, that perhaps we should even consider another identity all together.

Making something real by rendering it is not the same as making it recognizable. Richard Carlyon, *A Saying of Sorts*

Carlyon was undoubtedly interested in what was real. But real did not mean recognizable. It meant repeating an image or an action until it became unrecognizable, until it became invested with new meaning — perhaps more authentic meaning. For all of his variety, experimentation, curiosity, and endless reinvention, he strikes me in a way as a very old-fashioned artist. Images in art have never meant to be read realistically; they are meant to be read mythically, symbolically, or metaphysically. Rotting fruit in seventeenth-century Dutch still-life painting is never rotting fruit; it is death. Images are meant to be explored and discovered. Richard Carlyon understood to the core of his artistic being that exploration and discovery are an essential part of the pleasure of art. I would venture to say that in *A Saying of Sorts* and *Pacer's Song*, among other video works, he conveys this understanding with real greatness. But I will let him have the last word in our conversation because he should. Talking with Dick always made me excited about the possibilities of being alive. These videos do, too. If he hadn't believed it with his whole heart, they remind us, then he wouldn't have seen it.

Hassidic Jews believe that every object in the world has divine sparks trapped within it. Mind you, this includes roofing nails and peanut butter. The ordinary is not ordinary. The obvious is not obvious. Richard Carlyon, *A Saying of Sorts*

Wesley Gibson is a writer living in San Francisco, California. He has written art reviews and catalogues and is the author of a memoir, *You Are Here*, and a novel, *Shelter*.

38

39

18.

19.

Column and margin

As an extension of the spatial qualities inherent in single letters, pages also possess form and counterform relationships due to the interaction of columns and their surrounding spaces. Functional clarity and visual beauty are established in the harmonious relationships of these spaces.

Three specific variables related to columns govern these relationships: the proportion of column height to width, texture (the tactile appearance of the type), and tone (the lightness and darkness of type). It is through the manipulation of these contrasting variables that pages are spatially activated, optically balanced, and hierarchically ordered. Additionally, the height and width of columns (and their adjoining space intervals) should be carefully examined to ensure adequate legibility (for further discussion, see Chapter 4).

When organizing text columns, either horizontal or vertical movements may be emphasized. One will often dominate, as shown in Figures **18** and **19**. Eye movement across the page (side to side and top to bottom) is controlled by column rhythms, typographic weights, and rules functioning as visual punctuation. By the manipulation of these elements, the designer groups information according to its role in a given layout and guides the eye methodically through the space of the page. Each of the vertical columns in Figure **20**, for example, separates specific categories of information to make them easier to find. The first column, with bold-weight type, contains general information and is dominant; the two right-hand columns, with lightweight type, contain secondary information and are subordinate.

20.

Columns and margins are carefully balanced through the use of contrasting type sizes and weights and of two rule weights. (Art Director: Bart Crosby; Designer: Carl Wohlt)

21.

In this annual report there are subtle spatial relationships. These include the form/counterform of the column to the margin; the placement of the heading and subheading, which extend into the margin for emphasis; and the column mass to rules, photograph, and caption. (Designer: Frank Armstrong)

22.

This magazine page exhibits the needed contrast between text and caption elements. The column width of the text is double the column width of the caption. (Art Director: Ben Day; Designer: Anne Stewart)

The one- and two-column arrangements shown in Figures **21** and **22** illustrate some of the possibilities for text-column placement. In the two-column arrangement, the column depths are equal. Vitality and contrast are achieved by the placement of the adjacent photograph, its caption, and the bar rule containing the title. In both examples, the caption-column width and the text-column width are of different lengths, providing sufficient contrast to indicate to the reader that the caption is not part of the text. Such contrasts in column size, shape, texture, and tone are used to distinguish between different kinds of information and to provide visually luminescent pages.

Figure **23** is another example of how columns contrast with one another. Differences in the columns are produced by changing the interline spacing and the size and weight of the text type. Relative to one another, the columns can be seen as open or closed, light or dark.

The difference in tonality, which is an important design consideration, hierarchically leads the eye from one element to the next, and finally into the white of the page (for further discussion, see *Visual Hierarchy*). The critically determined spatial intervals create an engaging visual rhythm.

The size of type may vary from column to column (Fig. **24**) or within a column (Fig. **25**). As indicated in the latter diagram, type that is larger or heavier in weight appears more dense and is therefore emphasized on the page. Changes in density provide a kind of contrast that makes it possible to balance various typographic elements and add rhythmic qualities to the page.

The scale and proportion of columns, intervals between columns, and margins and their relationships to one another must be carefully adjusted as determined by the kinds of information they support. In Figure **21,** generous, unequal margins frame a single column of quiet text type for a hospital's annual report, while in Figure **19,** narrow margins surround quickly read narrow columns for an efficient-looking publication about computers.

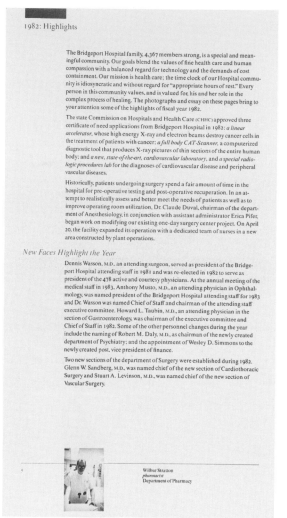

21.

23.

This experimental text composition reveals various combinations of typographic texture and tone.

24.

Variation in size, column to column.

25.

Variation in size within a column.

25.

24.

Margins not only frame parts within pages, they also contain supportive elements (marginalia) such as running heads, folios, and captions.

The elegant margins shown in Figure **26** have proportions identical to the page. The margin ratio is two margin units to three to four to six, as indicated. In other words, the bottom margin is twice as high as the top margin. Jan Tschichold has pointed out that this complex series of column-to-margin ratios, based on the golden section, is found in numerous medieval manuscripts. (For further discussion about margins, see Chapter Five, *The Typographic Grid.*)

Paragraph breaks within a column greatly influence the relationship between a column of text and its surrounding margins. A break may be introduced as an indention, as a space interval, or as a combination of both. Designers have also developed their own ways to indicate paragraphs (Fig. **27**). The overall page organization will determine the most suitable method.

When columns, margins, and their interrelationships are clear and appropriate to content, the result is a printed page of distinction. Every problem demands a fresh approach, yet an ordered unity that is responsive to the meaningful blend of form and counterform is always the goal.

independence in the student.

• "Accordingly, handicraft in the workshops was right from the start, not an end it itself, but laboratory experiment preparatory to industrial production. If the initial products of the Bauhaus looked like individual craft products, this was a necessary detour for the groping student whom we avoided to prod with a foregone conclusion.

• We salvaged the best of experimental education and added to it a carefully constructed program of information-based design that produced non-commercial products that worked. It was a different school with different people with different goals in a different time. Our aim was to produce designers who had the will, the ability, and the ethical base to change American production for the better.

• I was somewhat concerned that this might be a middle of the road

27.

Placement of a bullet (a typographic dot used for emphasis) upon intercolumn rules designates new paragraphs in this booklet design. (Designer: Jeff Barnes)

by Joseph Dyer

Haydn, Poulenc and the Princesses

22.

The whole duty of typography, as with calligraphy, is to communicate to the imagination, without loss by the way, the thought or image intended to be communicated by the author. And the whole duty of beautiful typography is not to substitute for the beauty or interest of the thing thought and intended to be conveyed by the symbol, a beauty or interest of its own, but,

The whole duty of typography, as with calligraphy, is to communicate to the imagination, without loss by the way, the thought or image intended to be communicated by the author. And the whole duty of beautiful typography is not to substitute for the beauty or interest of the thing thought and intended to be conveyed by the symbol, a beauty or interest of its own, but, on the one hand, to win access for that communication by the clearness and beauty of the

The whole duty of typography, as with calligraphy, is to communicate to the imagination, without loss by the way, the thought or image intended to be communicated by the author. And the

23.

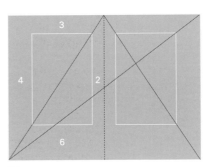

26.

Typographic space

28.

Spatial elements are balanced through the principle of visual compensation, achieving equilibrium and tension. Elements form relationships with other elements through carefully planned juxtapositions and alignments. Tension exists between the edge of the composition and adjacent elements. These basic forces affect typographic organization and help achieve dynamic, asymmetrical composition. (Designer: Jean Brueggenjohann)

"Speech proceeds in time and writing proceeds in space." Applying Karl Gerstner's statement to typographic design, typographic space is the rhythmic and dimensional field in which typographic communication exists. This field consists of positive form (the typographic elements) and void (the spatial ground) upon which the elements are arranged. Unity within the space is achieved by visual compensation; that is, the spatial balance and arrangement of typographic elements. Amos Chang, discussing the relationship between compensation and visual dynamics, wrote, "This process of growth from deficiency to compensation brings inherent movement to physical form . . . we may borrow an important rule of balance from the anatomy of a zoological being, man in particular . . . man's body is in a state of balance when his arms and legs are in a position to be moved effectively to compensate for position changes of the body."

Visual compensation is achieved by balancing elements against each other, adjusting their sizes, weights, spatial intervals, and other visual properties until unity and equilibrium are achieved (Figs. **28–30**). In Figure **31,** two contrasting letterform pairs are balanced. The letterform pair *fj* suggests contraction and consonance, while *gv* expresses expansion and dissonance. Consonance is a harmonious relationship between similar or corresponding elements, while dissonance is a discordant relationship between dissimilar elements. In Figure **32,** dissonant elements are combined with consonant form-to-void relationships, resulting in a state of visual balance and unity.

29.

Pictorial and typographic elements are placed in asymmetrical balance. Two pointed arches balance three rounded arches, and the ruled line moving into the margin corresponds to the letterspaced word *Messiah*.

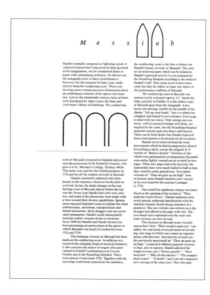

30.

This dynamic poster combines both large three-dimensional letterforms and a complex arrangement of two-dimensional elements. Spatial wholeness emerges from the arrangement: overlapping of elements is precise and expressive. Compensation is achieved through careful placement, with attention given to the surrounding void. (Designer: Frank Armstrong)

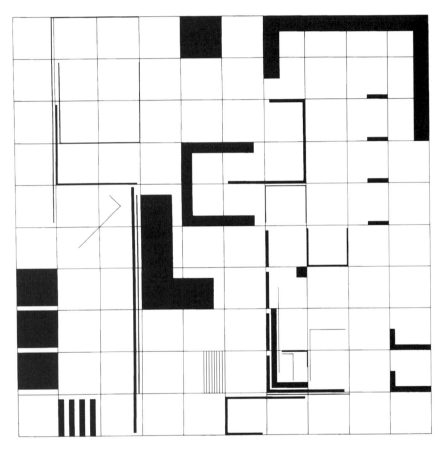

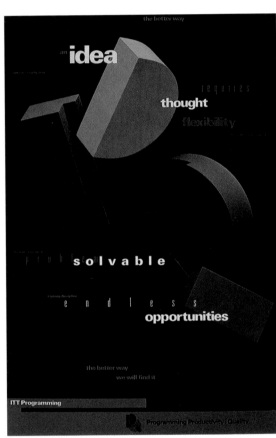

31.
(Designer: Lark Pfleegor)

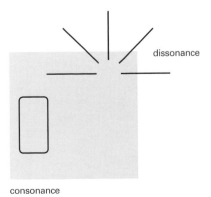

dissonance

consonance

32.

The contrast between geometric and gestural letterforms is dissonant. Unity is achieved by carefully planned shape correspondences and form-to-void relationships.

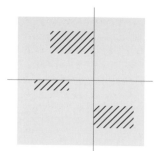

33.
Alignments create visual relationships between forms in space. (Designer: Jennifer Mugford Wieland)

34.
In this asymmetrically balanced composition, the edge of the type column aligns with the central axis of the circle. (Designer: Sergio de Jesus)

The structure of typographic space can be defined by alignments (Figs. **33–35**) and form-to-void relationships that establish a composition's underlying spatial order. This substructure is developed and enhanced through optical adjustment (Fig. **36**). Often inconspicuous, optical adjustment is the precise visual alignment of typographic elements in space based not on mathematical but perceptual alignment. The designer's understanding and use of optical adjustment is necessary for visual clarity.

Visual compensation and optical adjustment within the typographic space link printed elements and the spatial ground. This structural integration is not an end in itself; its order, simple or elaborate, acts as a stimulus, controlling the visual dynamics of the message transmission and response.

Nathan Knobler's observation in *The Visual Dialog* that "psychologists tell us that the need to understand, to find meaning in the world around us, is coupled with the need for stimulation and involvement" applies to design. To communicate with clarity and exactitude, the designer must be aware of the need to stimulate and involve the viewer. In typographic problem solving, the designer creates complex, highly interactive spatial environments (Fig. **37**) that establish coherence between the viewing experience and typographic form, between the verbal statement and written language.

Boston University
School of Visual Arts

Faculty Exhibition in New York

Sculpture Center
167 East 69th Street
New York

35.
Typographic elements are aligned with the horizontal and vertical edges of the geometric configuration.

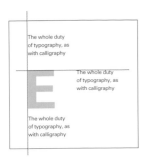

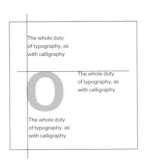

36.
Dotted lines indicate the use
of alignments to relate forms
to each other. Note the optical
adjustment in relating the
large *O* to the text type.

37.
In this exhibition catalog
cover, horizontal and vertical
alignment of elements bring
order to a dynamic, asym-
metrical design. Texture and
tone create a vibrant lumi-
nosity. (Designer: Wolfgang
Weingart)

Visual Hierarchy

38.
Type style, size, color, weight, and spacing are consistent, resulting in an even texture and tone. Visual hierarchy is almost nonexistent in this arrangement.

39.
A spatial interval equal to one line space separates the title from the other information, giving it prominence in the composition.

40.
Setting the title in bolder type further separates it from the overall tone and texture, increasing the hierarchical contrast.

A visual hierarchy is an arrangement of elements in a graduated series, from the most prominent to the least prominent, in an area of typographic space. When establishing a visual hierarchy, a designer carefully considers the relative importance of each element in the message, the nature of the reader, the environment in which the communication will be read, and the need to create a cohesive arrangement of forms within the typographic space.

The study of visual hierarchy is the study of the relationships of each part to the other parts and the whole. When elements have similar characteristics, they have equality in the visual hierarchy, but when they have contrasting characteristics, their differences enable them to take dominant and subordinate positions in the composition.

Contrast between elements within the space is achieved by carefully considering their visual properties. Important contrasts used to create hierarchical arrangements include size, weight, color, and spatial interval. The location of an element within the space plays an important role in establishing a visual hierarchy. The spatial relationships with other elements can also influence an element's relative importance in the arrangement.

Principles used to achieve visual hierarchy through careful contrast between the elements are demonstrated by the nine small diagrams on this page (Figs. **38–46**). The nine typographic designs on the opposite page (Figs. **38a–46a**) correspond to these diagrams.

38.

39.

40.

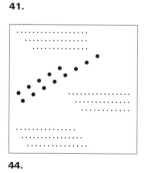

41.

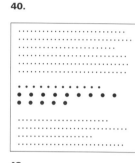

42.

43.

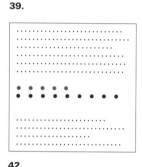

44.

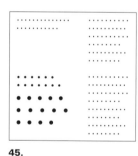

45.

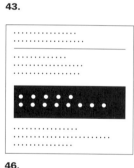

46.

41.
Changing the size and weight of the title makes it even more prominent in the visual hierarchy.

44.
The diagonal position of the title increases its prominence in the space. The smaller type elements align with the diagonals of the title's baseline and posture, unifying the composition.

42.
Color or value can create another level of contrast that can be controlled by the designer to create hierarchy.

45.
This composition demonstrates how extreme contrasts of type size and weight increase visual hierarchy and legibility from a distance.

43.
Two sizes and three weights of type are used to create subtlety and variety within the composition.

46.
Reversing the title from a black rectangle heightens contrast and increases the visual hierarchy. A ruled line separates the secondary type into two zones of information.

38a.

The Modern Literature

Society presents a lecture

by Raoul Ramirez,

Professor of Literature

Santaneo State University

Modern Hispanic Poetry

7:30 pm March 23

The Humanities Center Auditorium

Admission is free

38a.

39a.

The Modern Literature
Society presents a lecture
by Raoul Ramirez,
Professor of Literature
Santaneo State University

Modern Hispanic Poetry

7:30 pm March 23
The Humanities Center Auditorium
Admission is free

39a.

40a.

The Modern Literature
Society presents a lecture
by Raoul Ramirez,
Professor of Literature
Santaneo State University

Modern Hispanic Poetry

7:30 pm March 23
The Humanities Center Auditorium
Admission is free

40a.

41a.

The Modern Literature
Society presents a lecture
by Raoul Ramirez,
Professor of Literature
Santaneo State University

Modern
Hispanic Poetry

7:30 pm March 23
The Humanities Center Auditorium
Admission is free

41a.

42a.

The Modern Literature
Society presents a lecture
by Raoul Ramirez,
Professor of Literature
Santaneo State University

Modern
Hispanic Poetry

7:30 pm March 23
The Humanities Center Auditorium
Admission is free

42a.

43a.

The Modern Literature
Society presents a lecture
Santaneo State University
Professor of Literature

Raoul Ramirez
Modern Hispanic
Poetry

7:30 pm March 23
The Humanities Center Auditorium
Admission is free

43a.

44a.

The Modern
Literature
Society presents
a lecture

Modern
Hispanic Poetry

by Raoul Ramirez,
Professor of Literature
Santaneo State
University

7:30 pm March 23
The Humanities Center
Auditorium
Admission is free

44a.

45a.

Santaneo State
University
Professor of Literature

Raoul
Ramirez
Modern
Hispanic
Poetry

The Modern
Literature
Society
presents
a lecture

7:30 pm
March 23
The
Humanities
Center
Auditorium
Admission
is free

45a.

46a.

The Modern Literature
Society presents a lecture

by Raoul Ramirez,
Professor of Literature
Santaneo State University

Modern
Hispanic Poetry

7:30 pm March 23
The Humanities Center Auditorium
Admission is free

46a.

47.
The letters *f* and *j* are typographic counterparts because their forms correspond. Integration and equilibrium are achieved. (Designer: Lark Pfleegor)

When creating a visual hierarchy in typographic space, a designer balances the need for harmony, which unifies a design, with the need for contrast, which lends vitality and emphasis. As in music, elements can have a counterpart or a counterpoint relationship. Typographic counterparts are elements with similar qualities that bring harmony to their spatial relationship (Figs. **47** and **48**). Elements have a counterpoint relationship when they have contrasting characteristics, such as size, weight, color, tone, or texture. Counterpoint relationships bring opposition and dissonance to the design (Fig. **49**).

Typographic elements can have both counterpart and counterpoint relationships. In Figure **50,** extreme scale contrasts create a counterpoint relationship, while the modular letters, constructed from parallel horizontal and vertical elements, become typographic counterparts. Because the forms correspond, the *A*s (Fig. **51**) are counterparts, but their extreme scale contrast permits them to have a dissonant counterpoint relationship in the space. When organizing typographic elements into a visual hierarchy, it is useful to consider counterpart and counterpoint relationships.

48.
In this diagram, forms in the photograph and the letter *S* correspond. This counterpart relationship creates unity between these unlike elements. (Designer: Ivy Li)

49.
In these arrangements, the dominant elements (addition and multiplication signs) have a counterpoint relationship to the text blocks due to contrasts of scale and weight. Because the text blocks echo the structure of the addition and multiplication signs, and the elements have a balanced arrangement in the space, unity is achieved. (Designer: Lark Pfleegor)

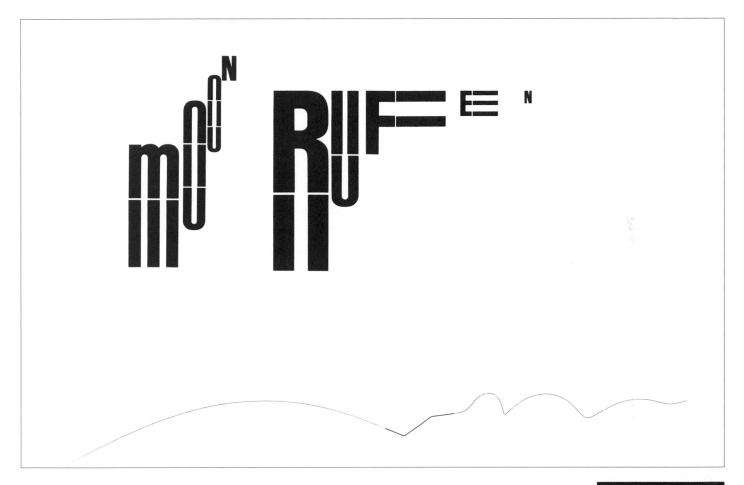

50.
A hierarchy of size gains unity and rhythm through the modular construction of letterforms. *Rufen* means "to call." (Designer: Wolfgang Weingart)

51.
The repetition of the letter *A* in two different point sizes creates a dynamic hierarchical structure. (Designer: Paul Rand)

53.

In these typographic exercises, rules and space intervals are used as visual punctuation. (Designers: Bryan Leister and Rebecca Lantz)

 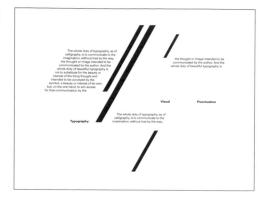

53.

52.
The word *sassafras* calls for a response, and the phrase *a flavoring agent* provides the reply. (Designer: Ivy Li)

Often, typographic elements in a visual hierarchy can be designated as questioning forms and answering forms (Fig. **52**). The typographic unit assigned the questioning role invites or calls for an answer. In a sense, the answering form has a counterpart relationship to the questioning form because it completes the communication. The most prominent visual element of a typographic hierarchy is frequently a questioning form. Consider the role of both typographic form and pictorial form: do individual components of a composition suggest a question or an answer? The questioning component expresses dissonance (unrelieved tension), while the answering component expresses consonance (relieved tension).

A typographic arrangement is partly governed by visual punctuation. As a writer uses standard punctuation marks to separate words and clarify meaning, a designer introduces visual punctuation (space intervals, rules, or pictorial elements) to separate, group, or emphasize words or lines. Visual punctuation (Figs. **53** and **54**) clarifies the reader/viewer's understanding of the content and structure of a typographic arrangement. Visual punctuation helps to clarify the meaning of the typographic message, while visual emphasis or accentuation is used to make one element more important. Emphasis is relative to the contrasting properties of elements; for example, in Figure **54** the word *collage* is dominant in the visual hierarchy due to its scale, weight, and position.

Visual accentuation is giving emphasis or stress to properties (round and straight, thick and thin, geometric and organic, etc.) of typographic and pictorial signs, usually through contrast with dissimilar elements. The bold and compelling mark combining the letter *A* and the scroll of a violin in Figure **55** is an example of visual accentuation through contrast. The geometric properties of the letter *A* are accentuated in opposition to the organic properties of the musical instrument. In this example, details in both the letter and pictorial form are accentuated or deleted, yet the legibility of the original letter and object has been retained. The letter *A* and the violin are incomplete, yet each retains its essence.

Typographic joinery is the visual linking and connecting of elements in a typographic composition through structural relationships and form repetition. The assembly of separate typographic elements to form a unified sign is seen in the logotype for the American Broadcasting Corporation (Fig. **56**). The pronounced geometry and emphasis given to the circular forms joins the forms through the use of the repetition. The shape of the circle is common to every part of this mark. The three letterforms and their circular container are blended to become one sign.

Some typographic designs are seen from different distances (far, middle, close). The viewer's perceptions are greatly influenced by shifts in the viewing experience. Attention to visual hierarchy and the perceptual environment is vital in graphic media (signage, posters, and exhibitions) where the viewing experience is in constant flux (Fig. **57**).

Typography's hierarchical order derives from the basic process of pattern-forming found in nature, in verbal and written language, the arts, and computer technology. This is aptly described by Gyorgy Doczi, speaking of his research on proportional harmonies in art and design. "The rhythms of writing are created by the same pattern-forming process of sharing that creates rhythms of dance, music, and speech. Movements shared make dance, patterns shared make music and speech."

The shared patterns of typography find expression through visual dynamics that enable it to function as both a message-carrier and a rhythmic, visual structure. The typographic message, with all its limitless thought and diversity of form, is shaped by this subtle and meaningful hierarchical language.

ABC abc abc abc

56.

A mark's unity is dramatically enhanced as typographic joinery becomes more refined. (ABC logo, Designer: Paul Rand)

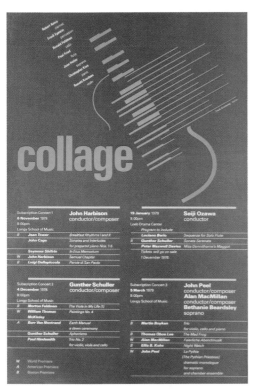

54.

54.

In this poster, a complex system of rules separates, connects, and emphasizes the names of composers, conductors, and information about numerous events. In the top area of the poster, ruled lines perform a different function: they combine to create a rhythmic visual sign for music. (Designer: Frank Armstrong)

55.

This symbol demonstrates visual accentuation. Striking visual contrast is achieved through the opposition of straight and curved edges and shapes. (Designer: Nick Schrenk)

55.

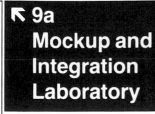

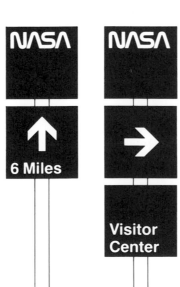

57.

In this signage for NASA, viewing context determines the visual hierarchy. For example, the size and position of the arrow in the interior directional signage are quite different from the size and position of the roadside signage. (Designer: Danne and Blackburn)

57.

ABA form

59.
Even though the functions of the small text block and the photograph are unrelated, these elements correspond to one another because of their similar sizes.

60.
Letters, when combined together as text, provide a treasury of textural contrasts. Corresponding textures reveal visual links between elements.

61.
When typographic elements possess contrasting tonal qualities, the eye perceives an implied three-dimensionality.

In typographic communication, visual relationships are established through an active dialogue between two fundamental design principles: repetition and contrast. Using these principles the typographic designer imbues messages with visual order and rhythmic variety.

Musical structure is also based upon repetition and contrast, and because it is linear in nature, a quality that is common also to typography, it provides an excellent model for understanding basic typographic structure. The primary structural pattern of music is the three-part form of statement-departure-return (ABA). The unifying components (the two *A*s) function as repetition, while the middle component (the *B*) functions as contrast. Arnold Schoenberg observed that "the principle function of form is to advance our understanding. It is the organization of a piece which helps the listener to keep the idea in mind, to follow its development, its growth, its elaboration, its fate." This quote also clarifies the mission of typographic form, where relationships between visible typographic elements are guided by the dynamics of ABA form.

The viewer of typographic communication perceives form relationships as being either in opposition or correspondence. This principle suggests that a fully integrated typographic composition depends upon the successful blending of elements of contrast and repetition. The viewer seeks a variety that stimulates both eye and mind, while structuring the communications experience. This is the dual basis of ABA form.

A   B   A   B

59.

A   B   A   B

60.

A   B   A   B

61.

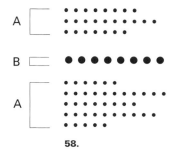

58.

ABA form in typography, as in music, is based upon a fundamental three-part structure where two *repeating* parts are in correspondence, and a third *contrasting* part stands in opposition (Fig. **58**). This fundamental structure, however, may be found in abundant variation. This is true because contrasting and repeating typographic elements within a composition are governed by the dynamic principles of proportion and rhythm. It is via these principles that ABA form grows in complexity and diversity. By definition, proportion in ABA form is the ratio determined by the quantity, size, weight, texture, tone, shape, color (or other syntactic quality) of similar and dissimilar typographic elements (A**A**BA**A**BA**A**). Rhythm is established in the intervals of space separating these elements (A**A** . B . A**A** . B . A**A**). The following examples illustrate this idea:

When typographic elements are similar in size to one another, an immediate correspondence between these elements is established (Fig. **59**). This correspondence is heightened because the tonality of the photograph and small text block is darker than the tone of the larger text block. In the middle diagram, the correspondence between the smaller text blocks is also magnified (Fig. **60**). A third variation is created by altering the tone of the elements: a bold typeface is introduced in the smaller text blocks, linking them together. Here, the factors of both scale and tone establish a distinct pattern of repetition and contrast (Fig. **61**). In an applied example – the design of a concert poster – the recurrence and contrast of typographic tone and texture are demonstrated (Fig. **62**).

62.

This poster is zoned into three spatial corridors: two columns of text, finely textured and light in tonal value, flank a dynamic arrangement of music-related visual signs, coarser in texture and darker in tone. (Designer: Ben Day)

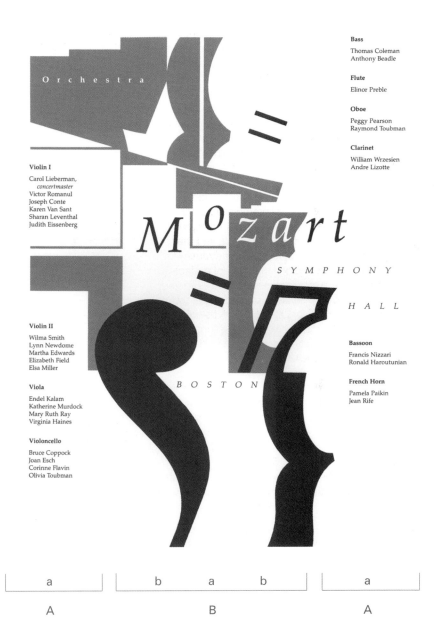

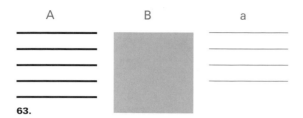

A   B   a

63.

Further variations in ABA form are discovered when elaborations (ABa, ABAb or AbAc) of corresponding elements occur to establish subtle contrasts (Fig. **63**), or when primary and secondary relationships occur in compositions simultaneously (Fig. **64**). The foregoing examples show the influence of proportion upon the relationships between typographic elements. The rhythmic patterns in each of these examples are identical, with equal or nearly equal intervals of space separating the elements. In a detail of the concert poster (Fig. **65**), a distinct rhythm composed of unequal spatial intervals between typographic elements can be observed. This rhythmic pattern may be viewed on two levels: the major group (A . B . A), and the minor group (**a** . bb . . **a** . b . . **a** . bb . . **a,** etc.). The intervals between these elements facilitate the functional grouping of the parts of the message: the "instruments" are separated from the "performers" by a "1X" interval of space, and each of these groupings is separated one from another by a "2X" interval of space. Other syntactic traits bind and isolate the parts: the "instruments" are bold in typographic weight, linking them together, while the "performers" are light in weight. At the same time, all these typographic elements share the same type size to distinguish them from the location of the event, which is presented in a larger, italic, all-capitals typeface.

64.

The relationships established by the three vertical columns of equal width (ABA) achieve visual dominance over the three horizontal bands (aba). The small column of text (c), which departs from the visual pattern of the main unit in position and type weight, provides an additional variation.

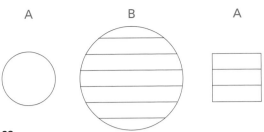

66.
Shape relates the first and middle forms; texture relates the middle and right forms; and size relates the left and right forms.

In this example, it is also possible to observe a phenomenon that appears at first as a contradiction in terms, but nonetheless is a condition in typographic design: perceiving typographic forms that are *simultaneously* in correspondence and opposition. This is a concept that is linked to a fundamental design notion: achieving unity within diversity (Fig. **66**). ABA form variations are capable of unifying diverse forms through visual correspondence while at the same time bringing variety to similar forms through opposition. The skilled designer manipulates typographic elements to achieve this essential balance.

ABA form is composed of both simple and complex patterns that give order and emphasis to the visual linking of typographic elements. These are not fixed systems but are a way of understanding the interrelationships of typographic form. About music Joseph Machlis stated, "The forms . . . are not fixed molds into which the composer pours his material. What gives a piece of music its aliveness is the fact that it adapts a general plan to its own requirements."

a   **Bass**

b   Thomas Coleman
b   Anthony Beadle

a   **Flute**

b   Elinor Preble

                          A

a   **Oboe**

b   Peggy Pearson
b   Raymond Toubman

a   **Clarinet**

S Y M P H O N Y

H A L L   B

a   **Bassoon**

b   Francis Nizzari
b   Ronald Haroutunian

                          A

a   **French Horn**

b   Oaneka Oaujub

65.

67.
This poster announcing a
production of the play
M. Butterfly by David Henry
Hwang clearly demonstrates
the three spatial zones
composing a basic and
rhythmic ABA form
relationship. (Designer:
David Colley)

partial production funding by a grant from the Illinois Arts Council
butterfly decal courtesy of Art Mart
graphic design: David Colley

Legibility

Typographic legibility is widely misunderstood and often neglected by designers. Yet it is a subject that requires careful study and constant evaluation. Legibility is achieved by controlling the qualities and attributes inherent in typography that make type readable. These attributes make it possible for a reader to comprehend typographic forms with the least amount of difficulty.

Typographers and designers have a definite responsibility to their readers to communicate as clearly and appropriately as possible. This responsibility is suggested by Henry David Thoreau in *Walden:* A written word is the choicest of relics. It is something at once more intimate with us and more universal than any other work of art."

aaaddd

1.
As the top stroke of the letter *a* rises to become the ascender of the *d*, intermediate forms are not easily deciphered by the reader.

As signs representing sounds in spoken language, letters are basic to legible typography. The primary purpose of a letterform is to convey a recognizable meaning to the mind. Therefore, letterforms must be designed with clarity, each being distinct within the alphabet. The contrast among individual characters makes it possible for the reader to decipher written information without confusion.

The most legible typefaces are those timeless examples characterized by three qualities upon which legibility is dependent: contrast, simplicity, and proportion. These typefaces exemplify beautiful and functional letterforms. A close look at typefaces such as Garamond, Baskerville, and Bodoni will reveal why their forms are as vital now as when they were first designed. (See the type specimens in Chapter Twelve.) The use of well-designed typefaces, however, is no guarantee that typography will be legible. Effective typography depends upon such factors as the communications context and the subtle adjustment of letterforms and their spatial relationships, each of which may have an effect upon how easily typography is read. Making type legible is a masterful achievement, requiring a process of intelligent decision making.

In the strictest sense, legible typography is a means of communicating information objectively. However, typographic designers sometimes bend the traditional criterion of legibility for expressive purposes. Designers, with their instinctive curiosity, have experimented with typography, playing with forms, imposing new meaning, and changing the standards of typographic communication. Innovative typography poses original questions, challenges edicts of the past, and redefines the concepts of legibility and functionality.

This chapter approaches legibility as an art of spatial synthesis. As an art, it is not absolute. Therefore, information derived from legibility research should be considered only a guideline. The knowledge designers have of legibility is based upon a legacy of typographic history and a keen awareness of the visible world. This knowledge will continually evolve, creating new standards for readability and functional typography.

Distinguishing characteristics of letters
The alphabet consists of twenty-six letters, each of which has evolved over the centuries to a unique place within this system of signs. This evolution has occurred gradually. It is no accident that the individual shapes of letterforms have developed out of a need to improve the communication process. As the alphabet has evolved, it has become a flexible system of signs in which all letters are distinct, yet all work together harmoniously as visible language.

In spite of the innumerable variations of size, proportion, weight, and elaboration in letterform design, the basic structure of each letterform must remain the same. For example, the capital *A* always consists of two oblique strokes joined at the top and connected by a horizontal stroke at their midsection. Sufficient contrast must exist between the letters in a font so that they can be easily distinguished (Fig. **1**).

2.
Four groupings show the structural relationships of all letters in the alphabet. The divisions are based upon the dominant strokes of each letter.

il

acegos

bdfhjmnpqrtu

kvwxyz

EFHILT
COQS
BDGJPRU
AKMNVWXYZ

3.
The upper halves of words
are read with ease, while the
lower halves are less legible.

Letters can be clustered into four groups, according to their contrasting properties. These are letterforms with strokes that are vertical, curved, a combination of vertical and curved, or oblique (Fig. **2**). From these groupings, one notices that letters are not only similar in many ways but that there are also some important differences. Obviously, letters with similar characteristics are more likely to be confused, while letters with distinct qualities provide contrast within a word. Letters within a word are most legible when they are taken, in equal number, from each group.

A closer look at the alphabet reveals additional characteristics distinguishing letters. The upper halves of letters provide more visual cues for letter recognition than the lower halves (Fig. **3**). Likewise, the right halves of letters are more recognizable than the left halves (Fig. **4**). Dominant letters within the alphabet that aid in word recognition are those that have either ascenders or descenders. Through tests, researchers have contributed valuable information about the comparative legibility of each letter in the alphabet. Findings vary only slightly. Lowercase letters can be rank ordered according to their distinctiveness as follows: *d k m g h b p w u l j t v z r o f n a x y e i q c s.* This varies, however, with different typefaces.

The most frequently used letters, such as the vowels *a e i o u,* are among the most illegible, and *c g s x* are easily missed in reading. Other letters that often cause confusion and are mistaken for one another are *f i j l t.* For example, the words *fail, tail,* and *jail* each begin with letters of similar shape and could easily be misread. The eye could possibly perceive *f* as *t,* or *t* as *j* (Fig. **5**). The designer should carefully study the words in display typography to identify such potential problems in legibility.

4.
More letters remain recognizable when only their right halves are exposed; however, there are exceptions (*b, p*).

fail
tail
jail

5.
Words have a tendency to be misread and confused with each other when composed of letters of similar shape.

6.

7.

DANCER
DANCER
DANCER

G
DANCER
DANCER
G

shape

SHAPE

8.
Word recognition is based on word structure, a combination of word shape (defined by the contours of the letters) and internal word pattern. The word set in lowercase letters is more distinct than the word set in all capitals, because its irregular word shape makes it more recognizable.

The perception of a letter is based upon the form/counterform relationship. Counterforms are as significant to legibility as the shapes of the letters themselves. This principle relates to all aspects of visual phenomena. A dancer manipulates space with the body, "making shape," defining, and redefining space (Fig. **6**). If the shape of a letter is changed, so is the way in which that letter is perceived. Letter shapes are cues that distinguish one letter in the alphabet from another (Fig. **7**).

Much controversy has surrounded the issue of the comparative legibility of serif and sans-serif typefaces. One argument claims that serif text type is more readable because the serifs reinforce the horizontal flow of each line. Serif typefaces also offer more character definition: for example, the serif on the bottom horizontal stroke of a capital *E* accentuates the difference between it and a capital *F.* However, the relative legibility between serif and sans-serif typefaces is negligible. Reader familiarity and the control of other legibility factors (to be discussed later) are far more significant than the selection of a serif or sans-serif typeface. (See the text-type specimens in Chapter Twelve to compare the legibility of serif and sans-serif type.)

The nature of words
While individual letters as discrete units, affecting all other spatial and aesthetic considerations, are the basis for a discussion of legibility, one reads and perceives words and groups of words and not just letters. In discussing typographic legibility, Frederic Goudy observed that "a letter may not be considered apart from its kinsmen; it is a mere abstract and arbitrary form far remote from the original picture or symbol out of which it grew, and has no particular significance until it is employed to form part of a word."

There are two important factors involved in the reading process: word shape and internal pattern. Words are identified by their distinctive word shapes, strings of letters that are instantaneously perceived, permitting the reader to grasp content easily (Fig. **8**). Counterforms create internal word patterns that provide cues for word recognition.

```
O R D W

R D W O

D W O R

R O W D

W O R D

O W R D
```
9.

When these internal spaces are altered sufficiently, the perceptual clarity of a word may also be altered. The weight of letters is vital to word recognition and influences an adequate internal pattern. The combination of word shape and internal pattern creates a word structure, an all-inclusive term describing the unique composition of each word (Fig. **9**).

Capital and lowercase letters

If text is set entirely in capital letters, it suffers a loss of legibility and the reader is placed at a significant disadvantage. Type set in this manner severely retards reading – more so than any other legibility factor. Figure **8** demonstrates that a word set in all capital letters is characterized by a straight horizontal alignment, creating an even word outline with letters of similar shape and size. A reader is not provided with the necessary visual cues that make words recognizable.

TEXT SET IN ALL CAPITAL LETTERS ALSO USES A SIGNIFICANTLY GREATER AMOUNT OF SPACE THAN TEXT SET IN LOWERCASE LETTERS OF THE SAME SIZE. AS MUCH AS 35 PERCENT MORE SPACE CAN BE CONSUMED WHEN USING ALL CAPITAL LETTERS.

On the other hand, text set in lowercase letters forms words that are distinct, based upon their irregular word shape and internal pattern. A variety of letter shapes, ascenders, and descenders provides rich contrasts that assure satisfactory perception. Once a specific word shape is perceived, it is stored in the reader's memory until the eye confronts it again while reading. A reader can become confused if a word takes on an appearance that differs from the originally learned word shape.

Interletter and interword spacing

The spacing of letterforms has a significant impact on legibility. Most readers are unaware of the typographic designer's attention to this detail. Minute spatial relationships are controlled to create not only readable but beautiful and harmonious typographic communication. It takes great skill to specify spaces between letters and words, determining proper spatial relationships. Letters must flow rhythmically and gracefully into words, and words into lines.

Typographic texture and tone are affected by the spacing of letters, words, and lines. When the texture and the spatial intervals between typographic elements are consistent, the result is an easily readable text. Texture is also affected by qualities unique to the design of specific typefaces. Sometimes designers arrange type for specific spatial effects, sensitively balancing norms of legibility with graphic impact. (See the text-type specimens in Chapter Twelve.)

Too much or too little space between letters and words destroys the normal texture intended by the typeface designer. As you read this sentence, notice that the narrow letter and wordspacing causes words to merge together visually. Likewise, the extremely wide letterspacing of this sentence is also disruptive for the reader.

There is often a danger of misfit letter combinations, which, in earlier typesetting systems such as Linotype, could not be easily corrected. (If the type size is small and evenly textured, this is a minor problem.) With phototypesetting and digital typesetting, these details can be corrected easily. The kerning of specific letter combinations can be programmed into the typesetting system. As type is set, appropriate letterspacing appears automatically (Fig. **10**).

9.
Letters can be grouped in myriad combinations. Words that are perceived as having meaning are those with which we have become familiar over time. They form a distinct and familiar shape.

Reading is disrupted by inappropriate wordspacing.

10.
Misfit letter combinations and irregular spacing can be a problem, particularly for display type. Optical adjustments should be made to achieve spatial consistency between elements.

SPACING
SPACING

EdwardoJohnston,oaocalligrapher, advocatedoaowordospaceoequaloto aolowercaseoo.

11.

AaronrBurns,ranrinfluential typographer,rsuggestedrwordrspacing equalrtorarlowercaserr.

Space between letters and words should be proportional to the width of letters. This proportion is often open to personal judgment (Fig. **11**). With experience and practice comes an understanding of the spacing that is suitable to a particular design project.

Type size, line length, and interline spacing
Critical to spatial harmony and legibility is an understanding of the triadic relationship of type size, line length, and interline spacing. When properly employed, these variables can improve the legibility of even poorly designed letterforms or enhance the legibility of those forms considered highly legible.

It is difficult to generalize about which sizes of type should be used, how long lines should be, or how much space should be inserted between lines. These decisions are based upon comparative judgments. The guidelines discussed in this section can never replace the type designer's sensitively trained eye for typographic detail. The normal reading distance for most printed matter is from twelve to fourteen inches, a fact to be kept in mind when making decisions about type size, since it affects the way in which a specific type size is perceived.

Text type that is too small or too large makes reading difficult. Small type reduces visibility by destroying counterforms, which affect word recognition, while large type can force a reader to perceive type in sections rather than as a whole. According to legibility research, the most legible sizes of text type at normal reading distances range from 9 to 12 point. This range results from the wide variation of x-height in different typefaces.

That is, when typefaces of the same point size are placed side by side, they may appear to be different sizes, because their x-heights vary radically. This is important to keep in mind when selecting typefaces and sizes.

An interesting comparison is the relationship between Univers 55 and Baskerville. Univers 55 has a very large x-height, with short ascenders and descenders. It appears much larger than Baskerville set in the same size, which has a smaller x-height and large ascenders and descenders. (See text column specimens in Chapter Twelve.)

Type sizes larger than 12 point may require more fixation pauses, making reading uncomfortable and inefficient. A fixation pause occurs when the eye stops on a line of type during reading, actually perceiving the meaning of groups of words. When there are fewer fixation pauses, there is greater reading efficiency and comprehension. When text type is smaller than 9 point, internal patterns can break down, destroying legibility. The reading audience is also a major consideration. For example, children learning to read need large type sizes in simple formats, as do adults with poor eyesight.

An appropriate line length is essential for achieving a pleasant reading rhythm, allowing a reader to relax and concentrate on the content of the words. Overly short or long lines will tire a reader. Excess energy is expended when reading long lines, and it is difficult to find the next line. A short column measure requires the eye to change lines too often, and there is an inadequate supply of horizontal perceptual cues. Compare the legibility of this paragraph with the legibility of Figures **12** and **13**.

An appropriate line length is essential for achieving a pleasant reading rhythm, allowing a reader to relax and concentrate on the content of the words. Overly short or long lines will tire a reader. Excess energy is expended when reading long lines, and it is difficult to find the next line. A short column measure requires the eye to change lines too often, and there is an inadequate supply of horizontal perceptual cues.

13.

An appropriate line length is essential for achieving a pleasant reading rhythm, allowing a reader to relax and concentrate on the content of the words. Overly short or long lines will tire a reader. Excess energy is expended when reading long lines, and it is difficult to find the next line. A short column measure requires the eye to change lines too often, and there is an inadequate supply of horizontal perceptual cues.

12.

Interline spacing intervals

Interline spacing intervals

14.

Certainly, every typographic problem has its own legibility requirements. The following data can serve as a point of departure in determining how to create legible typography. Line length is dependent upon both the size of type and the amount of space between lines. When working with the optimum sizes of 9-, 10-, 11-, and 12-point text type, a maximum of ten to twelve words (or sixty to seventy characters) per line would be acceptable. This would equal a line length of approximately 18 to 24 picas. An optimum line length for the average 10-point type is 19 picas.

The amount of interline spacing is dependent upon several factors. Generally, lines with no added space between them are read more slowly than lines with added space. Proper interline spacing carries the eye naturally from one line to the next. When there is inadequate space between lines, the eye takes in other lines as well. If lines are too widely spaced, a reader may have trouble locating the next line. As column measure increases, the interline spacing should also increase to maintain a proper ratio of column length to interline spacing.

Typefaces with larger x-heights need more interline spacing than those with smaller x-heights. Also, when working with display types, the frequency with which ascenders and descenders occur makes a difference. They can optically lessen the amount of white space between lines. Optical adjustments in display types should be made when spaces between lines appear inconsistent because of ascenders and descenders (Fig. **14**). Generally, the maximum line length for text type with a small x-height – used without interline spacing – is about sixty-five characters. When text type with a large x-height is used without interline spacing, legibility is diminished when line length exceeds about fifty-two characters.

Research has shown that for the optimum sizes of text type (9, 10, 11, and 12 point), one to four points of interline spacing can be effectively added between lines to increase legibility. Remember, this is not to say that type set outside these optimum specifications will be illegible, for critical judgment can ensure legible typography without inhibiting fresh approaches.

Weight

When considering the legibility of a typeface, the thickness (weight) of the strokes should be examined. A typeface that is too light or too heavy has diminished legibility. Light typefaces cannot be easily distinguished from their background, while a typeface that is too heavy has a tendency to lose its internal pattern of counterforms.

Typefaces of median weight are most legible.

Weight can be used advantageously to provide contrast and clarity between typographic page elements such as titles, headlines, and subheads. A heavier or lighter weight can emphasize one piece of information over another, thereby making information more comprehensible.

Extreme thick and thin strokes within letters of a particular typeface make reading more difficult, preventing smooth transitions from one word or group of words to the next. Thin strokes are less visible, creating confusion with letters of similar shape. When a typeface with extreme contrasts between thick and thin strokes is used in a text setting, a dazzle or sparkle effect is created. The reader begins to have difficulty distinguishing the words, and legibility decreases significantly.

In text type, weight change significantly affects legibility.

Character width

The shape and size of the page or column can influence the selection of character width. For example, a condensed typeface might be selected for a narrow page or column, achieving proportional harmony and an adequate number of characters and words to the line.

The width of letters is also an important legibility factor. Generally, condensed type is more difficult to read. A narrower letter changes the form/counterform relationship, causing letters to have an extreme vertical posture that can alter eye movement and reading patterns, diminishing legibility.

In text type, legibility is affected when condensed or expanded typefaces are used.

Italics and Obliques

Similar to other situations where typeforms deviate from a reader's expectations, italics impede reading. An extreme italic slant can slow the reading process and is disliked by many readers. However, italic type can be very effective when used as a means of providing emphasis.

15.

Black type on a white background and on a light gray background prove highly legible. Legibility suffers as the contrast between type and its background diminishes. The color temperature of the paper upon which type is printed and the choice of typeface also have a relative affect upon legibility.

16.

Legibility is greatly compromised when type and background are assigned complementary colors. Adjusting the value of either color improves contrast and thus legibility. In this example, the backgrounds of the complementary colors blue and orange are lightened, for improved legibility.

**Black type on
a white background**

**Black type on
a light gray background**

White type on
a light gray background

**White type on
a dark gray background**

**White type on
a light gray background**

15.

PMS Reflex Blue type on a
PMS 021 Orange background

PMS 021 Orange type
on a PMS Reflex blue background

PMS Reflex Blue type on a 50% tint
of PMS 021 Orange background

PMS 021 Orange type
on a dark blue background

16.

Legibility and color

Incorporating color into type significantly affects legibility, and the most important consideration when working with type and color is to achieve an appropriate contrast between type and its background. The degree of legibility sought depends entirely upon the intent of the designer and the nature of the content.

It has long been considered that black type on a white background is most legible. While this combination remains an excellent choice, other alternatives may offer equal if not improved legibility due to improved digital and printing technologies, and the fact that color is a relative phenomenon (Fig. **15**). When applied to type, color should be evaluated in relationship to the conditions in which it is read. In print, for example, one should consider the specific nature of the paper. If the paper is white, is it a warm or cool white? Is the surface of the paper rough or smooth? Is it coated or uncoated? What typeface is being considered, and in what size will it appear?

Generally, all legibility guidelines related to working with color and type in print apply also to type appearing on a computer screen. However, the use of color and type on a screen should also take into consideration the conditions of screen resolution and luminescence, as well as whether the type is static or in motion. Digital technologies have vastly changed the way in which designers use color and type, making it possible to easily assign color from palettes containing millions of colors. Also, the range of typographic applications continues to expand, with type asserting a role not only in printed and environmental communi-cations, but also in on-screen media such as the Internet.

Appropriate contrast between type and its background requires that designers carefully weigh the three basic color properties of hue, value, and saturation. By definition, *hue* and *tone* are simply more specific names for color. *Value* refers to the lightness or darkness of a color, and *saturation* – also called *chroma* or *intensity* – is the relative brightness of a color.

17.

The analogous hues yellow-green and blue are sufficiently different in value, resulting in an acceptable combination. A moderate adjustment of the yellow-green to a lighter value further improves legibility.

18.

Red and orange hues exist very close to each other on the color wheel, and when used for type and background do not offer sufficient contrast. A tint or shade of one of the colors, however, improves legibility.

19.

By scrutinizing the roles of value and hue contrast, the legibility of most typefaces can be improved. Typefaces that are visually challenging due to extreme proportions (heavy, light, wide, or thin) can be made more legible by assigning appropriate color combinations.

20.

The smaller and more delicate the type, the more contrast is needed to ensure adequate legibility.

All colors possess characteristics of hue, value, and saturation, and when combining color and type, balancing these properties is a critical legibility concern. For example, the highly saturated, complementary colors blue and orange offer maximum hue contrast, but when applied to type and background the effect is one of vibration that quickly tires the eye. These colors compete in brightness and vie for attention. If the type or background is lightened or darkened by selecting a tint or shade of the hue, legibility is improved (Fig. **16**).

But not all fully saturated hues are of the same value. Two highly saturated, analogous colors, for example, such as blue and green, provide sufficient contrast without a dizzying effect. (Analogous colors are those that appear in close proximity on a color wheel.) Because the green is actually lighter in value and brighter in saturation than the blue, there may be no need for further adjustment (Fig. **17**). However, if analogous colors are too close to each other on the color wheel, adjustments in contrast will be necessary (Fig. **18**).

Of all the contrasts of color, value affects legibility most significantly. Value contrasts effectively preserve the shapes and formal details of letters, thus making them more easily recognizable.

Typefaces possess unique shapes, proportions, and individual characteristics that should be taken into consideration when selecting color. A typeface with fine serifs, ultrathin strokes, small counters, or any number of other visual eccentricities may appear illegible if color is not carefully articulated. By turning value or intensity up or down in these situations, legibility can improve greatly (Fig. **19**).

The type size is also an important consideration in the planning of color. At smaller sizes, type requires backgrounds that are significantly different in hue and/or value (Fig. **20**).

Blue type on a green background

Blue type on a light green background

17.

Violet type on a blue background

Light Violet type on a blue background

18.

Univers 47, a condensed typeface

Univers 47, a condensed typeface

Bauer Bodoni Black, a typeface with extreme thick and thin strokes

Bauer Bodoni Black, a typeface with extreme thick and thin strokes

19.

7-point Minion Regular

10-point Minion Regular

20.

color   color

color   color

color   color

21.

If you find it necessary to present large amounts of text type in color, try increasing slightly the amount of space between lines. Even an additional point of space can make a significant difference, and a reader might be encouraged to continue rather than stop.

If you find it necessary to present

large amounts of text type in color,

try increasing slightly the amount

of space between lines. Even an

additional point of space can make

a significant difference, and a reader

might be encouraged to continue

rather than stop.

22.

The type size is also an important consideration in the planning of color. At smaller sizes, type requires backgrounds that are significantly different in hue and/or value (Fig. **20**).

Whether type is printed on paper or appears on-screen, an optical effect referred to as "typographic color" occurs. Not to be confused with the particular hue of a typographic element, this effect is the result of the visual qualities inherent in individual typefaces and the spacing of letters, words, and lines of type (Fig. **21**). Typographic color is an important tool, for it is an effective means by which hierarchical order and emphasis are achieved between different typographic elements. Also, if a large amount of text is set in an elaborate or unusual color setting, an increase in the space between lines can significantly improve legibility (Fig. **22**).

The reading process can be severely retarded when reading type on textured or photographic backgrounds, for they potentially interfere with the internal patterns of words and their distinctive word shapes. This problem is further exacerbated when such backgrounds and the type appearing on them are incompatible in color for reasons stated earlier in this discussion.

21.
Words set in various typefaces appear different in "color." As interletter spacing increases, the words also appear lighter in tone.

22.
The illusion of "lighter" or "darker" text is achieved with the introduction of additional interline spacing, and in some situations, legibility is improved.

Compare the legibility of
the justified and unjustified
columns.

Justified and unjustified typography

Traditionally, it was common practice to set type in a justified alignment. This was done for reasons of efficiency; in addition, it was more familiar and was considered to be more refined. In the 1920s, designers began to question this typographic convention and experiment with alternative text-setting styles. Unjustified and asymmetrical typography began to find widespread acceptance. Among experimental typographic designers was Herbert Bayer, who said, "I have long believed that our conventional way of writing and setting type could be improved for easier reading. In my first typographic works in the early twenties, I started to abandon the flush-left-and-right system for short lines of text and have introduced the flush-left system, leaving a ragged-right outline."

There are appropriate reasons for setting either justified or unjustified typography, but type set flush left and ragged right promotes greater legibility. If properly used, flush-left, ragged-right typography provides visual points of reference that guide the eye smoothly down the page from line to line. Because each line is either shorter or longer than the next, the eye is cued from one to another. In a justified setting, all lines are of equal length. Lacking are visual cues that promote easy reading.

With the use of unjustified typography, wordspacing is even, creating a smooth rhythm and a consistent texture. The indiscriminate placement of additional space between words in order to justify lines causes awkward gaps or "rivers" in paragraphs, which are disruptive to reading. Hyphenations at the end of lines should be used – but not overused – whenever possible to keep wordspacing consistent.

When setting ragged-right text, care should be taken not to rag the type too much. Uncontrolled line breaks of erratic rhythm can create awkward spaces that inhibit reading. In ragged-right type, care should be given to the selection of interline spacing, for it influences legibility and appearance. Spatial consistency and rhythmic line breaks result from careful typographical decisions.

The breaking of lines can be determined by the author's meaning rather than by appearance. This method, sometimes referred to as "thought-unit" typography, arranges lines into discrete parts related to the meaning of the text. Ragged-right lines may be of any length, with line breaks that are logical and focus on the intended message of the writer (Fig. **23**).

Paragraphs and indentions

An important goal for a designer is to distinguish typographically one thought from another, clarify content, and increase reader comprehension. Clear separation of paragraphs in a body of text is one way to accomplish this goal.

It is common practice in the design of books, magazines, and newspapers to indent each paragraph, usually with moderate indention of one to three ems. It is also typographic practice not to indent the first paragraph in an article, chapter, or advertisement so that the square corner of the first column can be maintained.

Paragraphs can also be separated by inserting additional space between them. This space should be proportional to the amount of interline spacing, which corresponds to the vertical measurement of the typographic grid. Paragraphs are often separated by one line space. This method should be avoided if the original copy is full of short, choppy paragraphs. Spaces between such paragraphs could be very disturbing, consuming too much space. Indentions and additional linespace are also used to establish order within complex tabular matter, such as financial charts and scientific data.

23.

Thought-unit typography from
the Washburn College Bible.
(Designer: Bradbury Thompson)

1:1 In the beginning
God created the heaven and the earth.

2 And the earth was without form, and void;
and darkness was upon the face of the deep.
And the Spirit of God
moved upon the face of the waters.

3 And God said,
Let there be light:
and there was light.

4 And God saw the light, that it was good:
and God divided the light from the darkness.

5 And God called the light Day,
and the darkness he called Night.
And the evening and the morning
were the first day.

6 And God said,
Let there be a firmament
in the midst of the waters,
and let it divide the waters from the waters.

7 And God made the firmament,
and divided the waters
which were under the firmament
from the waters
which were above the firmament:
and it was so.

8 And God called the firmament Heaven.
And the evening and the morning
were the second day.

9 And God said,
Let the waters under the heaven
be gathered together unto one place,
and let the dry land appear:
and it was so.

10 And God called the dry land Earth;
and the gathering together of the waters
called he Seas:
and God saw that it was good.

11 And God said,
Let the earth bring forth grass,
the herb yielding seed,
and the fruit tree yielding fruit after his kind,
whose seed is in itself, upon the earth:
and it was so.

12 And the earth brought forth grass,
and herb yielding seed after his kind,
and the tree yielding fruit,
whose seed was in itself, after his kind:
and God saw that it was good.

This is Garamond
This is Garamond
This is Garamond
24.

25.

New legibility issues emerged when the digital revolution occurred in typography and design. This includes concerns relating to software, discussed in this section, and problems related to on-screen display, covered in Chapter Eight. Electronic page design offers designers more possibilities for type manipulation than ever before, resulting in an obligation to know more about the cultural and formal evolution of typography than in times past. Without adequate knowledge of typographic legibility, it is easy for designers to blindly follow fads, succumb to common visual clichés provided by software, or thoughtlessly yield to the built-in defaults of a computer application. Legibility is a concern that should be continually addressed as technology changes. Because designers now work at a keyboard, they are directly responsible for composing legible type – a task once accomplished by sending specifications to a compositor at a typesetting firm.

As a result of desktop technology and type-design software, new typefaces and revivals of old typefaces are being released at an unprecedented rate. Some of these are well designed; others are not. Many typefaces from various digital foundries carry the same name, yet their design is far removed from the original (Fig. **24**). It is not enough to make typeface selections on the basis of name alone; designers should make visual comparisons before deciding which typefaces are most suitable for a task.

Tools available in desktop software enable type to be outlined, stretched, rotated, skewed, mirrored, placed on a curved baseline, and manipulated in innumerable other ways. Upon determining the objectives, requirements, and limitations of the typographic problem at hand, designers can creatively employ these tools while also addressing legibility needs. These tools are best used to express visual ideas, rather than to merely embellish a page. Though type set on a curved baseline loses legibility compared to type set on a horizontal baseline, it can still be addressed by carefully spacing the letters and choosing an appropriate typeface.

Gross distortion of the optical relationships within a font occurs when only one axis, such as its width or height, is changed, as shown in Figure **25**. Adobe introduced its multiple-master font technology around 1992 to address the need to alter letterforms by changing more than one axis while maintaining their design integrity. Multiple-master type is discussed in Chapter Seven.

Typographic experimentation on the computer allows designers to probe the relationships between type, space, and expression. Syntactic exploration reveals boundless potential to inform, amuse, and astonish. In recent years designers have extended their range of possibilities by approaching work as play and tools as toys. One example of the expressive potential of computer-manipulated type is seen in a page from a series of experiments created to document wanderings in canyons of the Utah desert (Fig. **26**).

24.
Three typefaces have the same name, but significantly different properties. The size, weight width, and shape of characters differ from one to the other.

25.
When letters are stretched horizontally or vertically on a computer to create condensed and expanded letterforms, their proportions change. The optical relationships of the original typeface design are destroyed.

26.
Experimental typography exploring computer manipulation of type. (Text: Ann Zwinger; Design: Rob Carter)

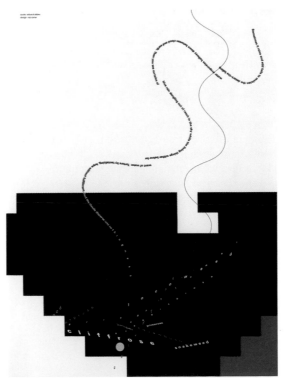

Typographic details

In typography, paying attention to detail is a fact of life. Every letter, word, and line of type is a subject of detail, and as such, it is the designer's responsibility to be alert and aware of these details. To those just learning the intricacies of typographic form and nuance, adherence to the following recommendations will be highly beneficial, and practicing them will eventually become second nature.

These recommendations apply primarily to normative typography, which supports the idea that "The whole duty of typography, as with calligraphy, is to communicate to the imagination, without loss by the way, the thought or image intended to be communicated by the author." Expressive forms of typography may intelligently ignore these recommendations all together.

	Recommended	Not recommended
When working with typography, begin with the same typeface and type size. Add additional typefaces, sizes and other variations such as type weight only as needed.	The whole duty of typography, as with calligraphy, **is to communicate to the imagination,** without loss by the way, the thought or image intended to be communicated by the author.	The whole duty of typography, as with calligraphy, is to communicate to the imagination, *without* **loss** by the way, the THOUGHT or image intended to be communicated by the author.
Contrast is one of the most important principles in typographic design. Any shift in typeface, type size, or type weight should be emphasized.	The whole duty of typography, as with calligraphy, **is to communicate to the imagination, without loss by the way, the thought or image intended to be communicated by the author.**	The whole duty of typography, as with calligraphy, is to communicate to the imagination, without loss by the way, the thought or image intended to be communicated by the author.
Interletter, interword, and interline spacing should be based on the spatial character of the typeface in use. This applies to both text and display settings.	The whole duty of typography, as with calligraphy, is to communicate to the imagination, without loss by the way, the thought or image intended to be communicated by the author.	The whole duty of typography, as with calligraphy, is to communicate to the imagination, without loss by the way, the thought or image intended to be communicated by the author.
Never place two word spaces after periods, commas, semicolons, question marks, and exclamation marks.	The whole duty of typography, as with calligraphy, is to communicate to the imagination, without loss by the way, the thought or image intended to be communicated by the author. And the whole duty of beautiful typography is not to substitute for the beauty or interest of the thing thought	The whole duty of typography, as with calligraphy, is to communicate to the imagination, without loss by the way, the thought or image intended to be communicated by the author. And the whole duty of beautiful typography is not to substitute for the beauty or interest of the thing thought
When setting flush-left, ragged-right or flush-right, ragged-left text, the effort to create pleasing, feathered rags will prevent text blocks from acquiring awkward shapes.	The whole duty of typography, as with calligraphy, is to communicate to the imagination, without loss by the way, the thought or image intended to be communicated by the author. And the whole duty of beautiful typography is not to substitute for the beauty or interest of the thing thought and	The whole duty of typography, as with calligraphy, is to communicate to the imagination, without loss by the way, the thought or image intended to be communicated by the author. And the whole duty of beautiful typography is not to substitute for the beauty or interest of the thing
Manually kern and letterspace display type settings. This is always an optical consideration, and the computer is no substitute for the trained eye.	**The whole duty**	**The whole duty**

	Recommended	Not recommended
Two forms of dashes are desirable: an en-dash with space before and after, and an em-dash with no space. Never use double dashes, and use an en-dash to connect numbers.	The whole duty of typography – as with calligraphy— is to communicate to the imagination, without loss by the way, 2011– 2020	The whole duty of typography--as with calligraphy--is to communicate to the imagination, without loss by the way, the thought or image 2011-2020
Do not use dashes where hyphens are required.	The whole duty of typography, as with calligraphy, is to communicate to the imagination, without loss by the way, the thought or image intended to be communicated by the author.	The whole duty of typography, as with calli-- graphy, is to communicate to the imagination, without loss by the way, the thought or image intended to be communicated by the author.
A common mistake is to substitute double prime marks for quotation marks and primes for apostrophes. Prime marks are used to indicate inches and feet.	The whole duty of typography, as with calligraphy, is to "communicate" to the imagination, without loss by the way, the thought or image intended to be communicated by the author.	The whole duty of typography, as with calligraphy, is to "communicate" to the imagination, without loss by the way, the thought or image intended to be communicated by the author.
To achieve optical alignment, it is desirable to "hang" punctuation at the edge of text blocks.	"The whole duty of typography, as with calligraphy, is to communicate to the imagination, without loss by the way, the thought or image intended to be communicated by the author."	"The whole duty of typography, as with calli- graphy, is to communicate to the imagination, without loss by the way, the thought or image intended to be communicated by the author."
Avoid typing three periods to make an ellipsis. Ellipses can be made by using available key commands and with the pull-down menu or type option + semicolon.	The whole duty of typography…as with calligraphy, is to communicate to the imagination, without loss by the way, the thought or image intended to be communicated by the author…	The whole duty of typography . . . as with calligraphy, is to communicate to the imagination, without loss by the way, the thought or image intended to be communicated by the author . . . .
It is not necessary to insert an additional word space between initial letters.	**T.M.**	**T. M.**

	Recommended	Not recommended

The first paragraph at the top of a page does not require indentation because it does not need to be distinguished from a paragraph above it.	The whole duty of typography, as with calligraphy, is to communicate to the imagination, without loss by the way, the thought or image intended to be communicated by the author.
	    And the whole duty of beautiful typography is not to substitute for the beauty or interest of the thing thought and intended to be conveyed.
		The whole duty of typography, as with calligraphy, is to communicate to the imagination, without loss by the way, the thought or image intended to be communicated by the author.
		    And the whole duty of beautiful typography is not to substitute for the beauty or interest

Avoid using three or more consecutive hyphenations at the ends of lines, as they create a distracting pattern in text.	The whole duty of typography, as with calligraphy, is to communicate to the imagination, without loss by the way, the thought or image intended to be communicated by the author.	The whole duty of typography, as with calligraphy, is to communicate to the imagination, without loss by the way, the extraordinary thought or image intended by the author.
Using bullets as the default method of distinguishing items within lists provides an acceptable solution, but other devices can integrate more effectively within text.	☐ The whole duty of typography, ☐ as with calligraphy, is to communicate ☐ to the imagination, without loss by the way, ☐ the thought or image ☐ intended to be communicated by the author.	• The whole duty of typography, • as with calligraphy, is to communicate • to the imagination, without loss by the way, • the thought or image • intended to be communicated by the author.
Using a baseline grid aids in aligning adjacent columns of text and in maintaining proportional harmony among individual text units.	The whole duty of typography, as with calligraphy, is to communicate to the imagination, without loss by the way, the thought or image intended to be communicated by the author.	The whole duty of typography, as with calligraphy, is to communicate to the imagination, without loss by the way, the thought or image intended to be communicated by the author.
When using contrasting type weights in the same size, reduce the size of heavier text to make it appear the same size as lighter text.	**The whole duty of typography,** as with calligraphy, is to communicate to the imagination, without loss by the way, the thought or image intended to be communicated by the author.	**The whole duty of typography,** as with calligraphy, is to communicate to the imagination, without loss by the way, the thought or image intended to be communicated by the author.
Be careful not to overlook using appropriate accents and symbols in text.	**sauté**	**saute**

A grid is a skeletal framework used by designers
to organize information within a spatial field.
It is a system characterized by the dualities of
freedom and constraint, simplicity and complexity.
It provides a strategy for composing text and other
visual information in two- and three-dimensional
space, including those of printed materials,
film, computer screens, built environments,
and typographic installations. Grid systems
aid designers in making information clear and
optimally accessible – highly desirable traits
in a world increasingly inundated by visual noise.
When used effectively, typographic grids provide
form and space with proportional harmony
and aesthetic beauty. The final result is clearer
and more accessible communication.

1.

In 1925, Jan Tschichold designed this cover for the journal *Typographische Mitteilungen*. His 24-page insert for this journal presented and advocated asymmetrical typography to its readers. This marked a movement toward a new language of typographic form and structure. (Designer: Jan Tschichold)

Background

The grid as we know it today is rooted in the earliest written forms, from columnar cuneiform tablets impressed by the Mesopotamians as early as 3000 B.C., to Hieroglyphic writing on papyrus (see Chapter 1, Figs. **5, 8**).

The mechanization of printing in Europe during the fifteenth century led to structural conventions and typographic principles that have survived for centuries. The architecture of moveable type and the mechanics of letterpress printing yielded rectilinear structures – text set into blocks framed by margins. Beginning with Gutenberg's 42-line Bible (Europe's first typographic book) other similarly structured books were created during the Renaissance in Germany, France, and Italy (see Chapter One, Figs. **38, 49,** and **59**).

The development of the modern grid cannot be attributed to a single individual or to an accidental discovery. It is the result of many pioneering efforts, including experiments by renegade designers associated with the movements of Futurism, Dadaism, Constructivism, and de Stijl, breakthroughs initiated at the Bauhaus, and the functionalist works and writings of Jan Tschichold (Fig. **1**). The grid finally emerged as a programmatic system of mathematical precision in Switzerland during the 1950s. Among others, designer Max Bill embraced absolute order in his work. During the last half of the 20th century, the typographic grid achieved universal acceptance as a visual organizational tool.

Now, grids are ubiquitous carriers of information, to the degree that we are not consciously aware of them on a daily basis. Yet the grid, artifice of time and space, is woven deeply into our subconscience. Grids serve as the underlying structure for modelling and archiving human thought, interactions, and events.

typographische mitteilungen

sonderheft

elementare typographie

zeitschrift des bildungsverbandes der deutschen buchdrucker leipzig ● oktoberheft 1925

natan altman
otto baumberger
herbert bayer
max burchartz
el lissitzky
ladislaus moholy-nagy
molnár f. farkas
johannes molzahn
kurt schwitters
mart stam
ivan tschichold

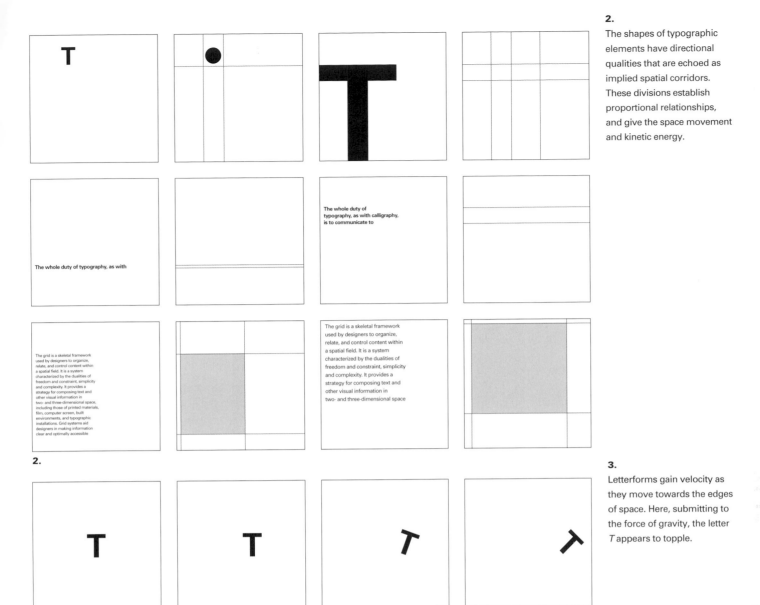

The shapes of typographic elements have directional qualities that are echoed as implied spatial corridors. These divisions establish proportional relationships, and give the space movement and kinetic energy.

The whole duty of typography, as with

The whole duty of typography, as with calligraphy, is to communicate to

The grid is a skeletal framework used by designers to organize, relate, and control content within a spatial field. It is a system characterized by the dualities of freedom and constraint, simplicity and complexity. It provides a strategy for composing text and other visual information in two- and three-dimensional space, including those of printed materials, film, computer screen, built environments, and typographic installations. Grid systems aid designers in making information clear and optimally accessible

The grid is a skeletal framework used by designers to organize, relate, and control content within a spatial field. It is a system characterized by the dualities of freedom and constraint, simplicity and complexity. It provides a strategy for composing text and other visual information in two- and three-dimensional space

2.

3.

Letterforms gain velocity as they move towards the edges of space. Here, submitting to the force of gravity, the letter *T* appears to topple.

3.

Structure and space
Space is the common denominator for all typographic communication. When typographic elements are introduced into space, they create subliminal divisions, and these divisions create spatial structure. As typographic elements shift syntactically in size, weight, and position, new structures emerge (Fig. **2**).

Another way of thinking about type and its relationship to space is to imagine a letterform as a point in space, the extension of a point as a line in space (line of text), and the extension of a line as a plane in space (text block). This analogy suggests that typographic elements are kinetic in nature, that they are in perpetual motion.

Consider the single letterform. When centered it appears motionless. When placed off center, it appears to move, gaining velocity as it approaches the outermost boundaries of the space. Rotate the letter and it appears to tumble. Lines of type are put into motion – from the direction of their origin (usually left to right) – at the moment they are read. They suggest horizontal movement, unless of course they are positioned vertically or at an angle in space. The kinetic possibilities of typographic elements are potentially endless (Fig. **3**).

Firmly grounded by gravity, we are oriented to the earth in terms of the horizontal and the vertical. We perceive the natural world according to these opposites, and we create the built environment in relationship to them. We are more comfortable with the horizontal – in this realm we feel safe. The vertical dimension is more challenging – we are afraid of both flying and of falling.

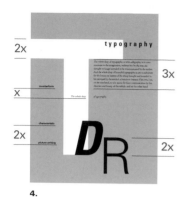

4.

4.
This exploratory composition exhibits modular relationships among elements. (Designer: Debra Thompson)
5.
Removing the square from a golden rectangle leaves another golden rectangle.

6.
The golden rectangle can be drawn by making a square, dividing it in half, and striking an arc from the half-point of one side of the square to the opposite corner of the square.

7.
Medieval manuscript (Psalterium) from the 12th century. Shown is a page of text with 3-line and 1-line initials proportioned according to the golden ratio.

Proportion

Divided space is perceived as a system of proportional relationships. To work effectively with the typographic grid is to understand that it also is a system of proportions. A grid ratio, which is a mathematical relationship between two or more grid measurements, governs the size and placement of typographic elements. The ratio X:2X (one unit to two units), for example, indicates the basic grid ratio. This stepped progression of X:2X establishes an underlying proportional system among the parts (Fig. **4**).

Designers most often rely upon an innate sense of proportion. But it is helpful also to consider models that have been handed down over centuries. The most familiar of these is the golden section, which is a law of proportionality found frequently in nature, the human body, and used throughout centuries in art, architecture, design, and music. First developed by Vitruvius, the golden section is basically a relationship or ratio between two numbers (or objects) wherein the ratio of the smaller number to the larger number is the same as the sum of both numbers. The algebraic expression of this relationship is a : b = b : (a+b). Stated numerically, the ratio is 1 : 1.618, and stated in percentages the ratio is 38% to 62% (Fig. **5**). The golden section, which can easily be constructed from the square (Fig. **6**), dominated as the proportional system for the design of medieval manuscripts (Fig. **7**).

The Fibonacci sequence is another important proportional model. Closely related to the golden section, this is a mathematical sequence wherein a number is the sum of the two preceding numbers – in other words, you add the two current numbers to get the third number. The progressive series of mathematical relationships found in the Fibonacci sequence can be observed throughout nature, from sea shells and pinecones to the arrangement of seeds on flowering plants (Fig. **8**).

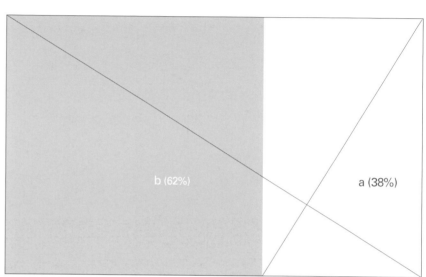

b (62%)   a (38%)

5.

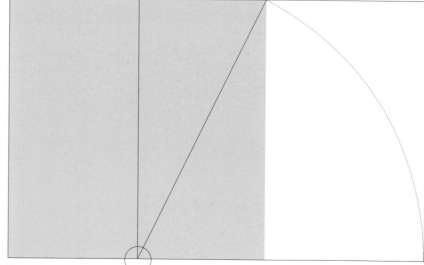

6.

0+1=	1
1+1=	2
1+2=	3
2+3=	5
3+5=	8
5+8=	13
8+13=	21
13+21=	34
21+34=	55
34+55=	89
etc.	

7.

The square

A natural division of the golden section is the basic square. This archetypal form has influenced the development of the modern grid perhaps more than any other system of proportion. Squares in combination lend an infinite variety of visual patterns. In Japan, for example, the tatami mat, a straw floor covering based on double square modules, is a system for creating asymmetrical spaces in traditional Japanese homes (Fig. **9**).

Paul Rand used squares as metaphorical building blocks, and as an organizational strategy for a book cover. It appears as contemporary today as it was when it was created in 1955 (Fig. **10**). A Web site for the Spanish type foundry Type-o-tones utilizes squares as the navigational system for the site (Fig **11**).

8.

The golden spiral winds through a series of conjoined golden rectangles. The spiral is linked to many forms in nature and is related to the Fibonacci sequence.

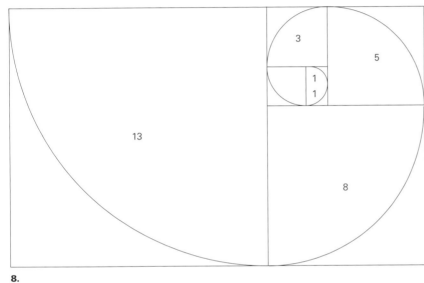

8.

10.

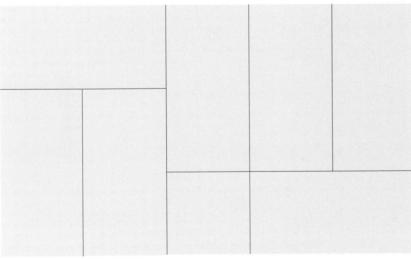

9.

11.

9.
An example of a tatami mat layout illustrates the flexibility and proportional beauty of this modular system.

10.
A book cover divided into a grid of eighty squares is used as an organizational system. Five squares forming the Swiss cross provides a window into Swiss architecture. (Designer: Paul Rand)

11.
Located within assigned squares, spinning letterforms and animated images entice users to navigate the website. (Designer: type-ø-tone)

A square subdivided into a 256-unit grid of smaller squares displays an enormous range of proportional possibilities (Fig. **12**). The language of the horizontal and the vertical was elevated to spiritual status by practitioners of the de Stijl movement. In his studied paintings, Piet Mondrian sought to reveal proportions of perfect harmony, proportions that could also be infused into the designs of everyday living (see Chapter One, Fig. **132**).

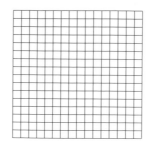

12.
Selectively removing lines from the grid to discover new spatial divisions is a process that trains the eye for proportional possibilities. The golden rectangle is revealed in examples below.

12.

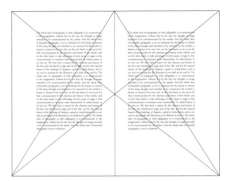

13.

In this classic example,
both text and page size share
golden mean proportions.

Single column grids

When text appears as a simple, linear narrative,
as in the traditional novel or exhibition panel,
it is often best to set it as a single block. There exist
many ways to orient single text blocks to pages
(or other spatial fields). These choices are most
often related to budget constraints, standard paper
sizes, and the function of typographic information.
Some designers still find it rewarding to revisit
the golden section from time to time (Fig. **13**).
But more often than not, alternative approaches
to proportions are developed. The designer's own
intuitive sense of proportion is nurtured through
observation and practice.

The problem is always to consider the text block
and the margins of the page as a proportional
system. Margins function to set the typographic
stage; they may be dynamically asymmetrical
or quietly symmetrical. Margins also accomodate
marginalia – separate typographic parts that
support the text. These include folios, running
heads, running feet, and notes. The negative space
of margins flows gently into the text, a mingling
of positive and negative space (For further
discussion, see *"Column and margin,"* pp. **57–59**).
The text block can be sized and adjusted within
the page to attain a variety of proportional
relationships (Fig. **14**).

14.

14.

The manner in which text
blocks are placed on the page
can greatly affect the overall
tone of the communication.
These sample layouts suggest
an abundance of possibilities.
Note the different ways
in which text blocks, images,
and marginalia are organized
to define the space.

Single column grids may appear quite unremarkable to the average reader, but in reality effective layouts are crafted with the utmost concern for minute detail. Choosing the right typeface for the content; adjusting letter, word, and line spacing for optimum legibility; and developing the proportions to set an appropriate tone are some of the issues that require the designer's attention (Figs. **15–17**).

15.

Cover and spread from a small book published in 1957 by the German publisher Insel-Verlag. The lively texture of Fraktur type contrasts with the quiet of generous margins.

16.

An exhibition catalog combines the photography of Leo Divendal and a childhood story by dancer and actor Christopher Milo. The text, set within narrow margins, reflects the expanse of the New Mexico landscape where the photographs and the story originate. (Designer: Rob Carter)

17.

Set within comfortable margins, the text of this intimate book is a thoughtful reflection on the selection of photographs for the book and an exhibition on the newly released photographs of Otto Frank. The book respectfully displays the photographs, which are positioned on the pages along with the text so as not to bring attention to themselves. (Designer: Victor Levie)

15.

The Road
to Raton

Story by Christopher Milo
Photography by Leo Divendal

Anne Frank   en familie

Foto's van Otto Frank

miles south from the mission, and is surrounded by a square with many shops that sell Mexican and Indian artifacts. The old La Fonda Hotel stands on the northwest corner of the square.

For the first time on the whole trip, Barbara started hollering at top of her lungs. She slept most of the way, but now needed to be changed. Aunt Bernice said, "Just a little longer there big girl, we'll soon be home." We wound higher and higher as we left Santa Fe. A thick forest brush and tall pine trees formed along the edge of both sides of the road. The snow was packed down into ridges made from the tires of the cars. At times the road was slippery and made the station wagon skid on what was nothing more than a one lane path. We, or a oncoming car, had to back up to let the other pass. This was scary because the station wagon was bigger and needed more room, so Uncle Jack had to hold on tight and make some clever moves around the other cars. Aunt Bernice said, "Just ahead of the next clump of pine trees, Sonny, the ranch is coming up!"

The Ranch

A very large house made of logs sat in a meadow off the road to the right. It was nestled neatly against a low wooded area, with a porch that circled all around it. The road continued past the log cabin, along a string of huts, then disappeared over the hill into the pine brush. On the other side of the road, in what Uncle Jack called the east meadow, stood a big barn, a silo, a smaller log cabin and a draw well with a bell on top. I counted ten sheep grazing in the meadow and two cows sat at the end near the tree line. The side of the hut with the huts, or coops, was at least a half acre of very dry dirt packed down from the cold and filled with hundreds and hundreds of chickens. Each coop had a fenced in yard covered with thin meshed wire that stretched from the top of the coops to the fences. There was one small slat door that opened into the coops, just off the main house. Once you were in the first yard, you had to go through another slat door to get into each coop yard. This kept the chickens from flying out, but also kept them separated so you'd know what chicken laid what eggs and when she laid them.

De fotokeuze
door Victor Levie

Anne Frank was voor mij altijd op de achtergrond. Zoals velen had ik genoeg aan de verhalen van mijn moeder en vader over de oorlog. Wie er wel of niet waren teruggekomen van de ouders, broers, ooms en tantes, neven en nichten, vrienden en vriendinnen. De portretfoto's op de kaptafel van mijn grootmoeder, waar ik met een schuin oog naar keek als ik bij haar op bezoek was.

De fotoalbums van de familie Frank veranderden dat. De beelden die Otto Frank, met een Leica en een goed oog, van zijn familie maakte, zijn intrigerend. Niet iedereen had in die tijd al een fototoestel en je kan zien dat het vastleggen een belangrijk moment is dat bijna nooit onopgemerkt voorbij gaat. Vast thema waren zijn twee dochters Anne en Margot; zij poseerden duidelijk voor de camera.

16.

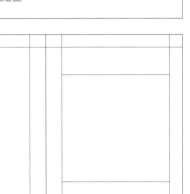

17.

18.

Horizontal lines running along the *x*-axis and vertical lines running along the *y*-axis are the elements composing a basic grid.

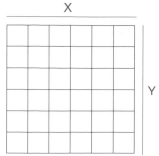

X

Y

19.

The multi-column grid is a structure with features specifically suited to the physical properties of typographic elements.

Multi-column grids

An elemental grid is based upon a "Cartesian" co-ordinate system of intersecting, perpendicular axes. It consists of rectangular modules defined by a network of horizontal and vertical lines (Fig. **18**).

Before any decision can be made about the construction of the typographic grid, the designer must first become thoroughly acquainted with the amount of text, its content, the audience for which it is intended, and the medium used for its delivery. A book, an exhibition, a Web site – each requires special consideration. Though the designer thoroughly grasps the material to be organized, grid structures often require adjustment throughout the design process.

Multi-column grids possess unique anatomical characteristics. These include margins that provide boundaries for typographic elements and define the "active" space of the page; text columns; gutters that separate text columns; and flow lines that create a dominant axis for the alignment of elements from page to page. The baseline grid represents the baselines of the primary text, which run from the top margin to the bottom margin. These horizontal divisions of space aid the designer in aligning text elements from column to column (Fig. **19**).

To structure type is to organize typographic forms into a unified whole, and to establish visual pathways between them. Two columns or many columns can be employed depending upon the complexity of the content. Multi-level information, as found in most typographic communication today, can be translated into clear and accessible typographic layouts (Fig. **20**).

The type area within a grid is composed of vertical columns. The width of text columns and the intervals between them should promote optimum legibility when required. The size of type should be measured on the column width to achieve the ideal number of characters per line.

**Typographic Design:
Form and Communication**

The whole duty of typography, as with calligraphy, is to communicate to the imagination, without loss by the way, the thought or image intended to be communicated by the author. And the whole duty of beautiful typography is not to substitute for the beauty or interest of the thing thought and intended to be conveyed by the symbol, a beauty or interest of its own, but, on the one hand, to win access for that communication by the clearness and beauty of the vehicle, and on the other hand, to take advantage of every pause or stage in that communication to interpose some characteristic & restful beauty in its own art. We thus have a reason for the clearness and beauty of the first and introductory page and of the title, and for the especial beauty of the headings of chapters, capital or initial letters, and so on, and an opening for the illustrator as we shall see by and by. The whole duty of typography, as with calligraphy, is to communicate to the imagination, without loss by the way, the thought or image intended to be communicated by the author. And the whole duty of beautiful typography is not to substitute for the beauty or interest in the thing thought and intended

| margins | text columns | column interval | flow line | baseline grid |

19.

When working with multi-column grids, it is essential to balance three interdependent variables. These are type size, line length, and interline spacing (leading). An adjustment to any one of these aspects will most likely require an adjustment to the others. Changing the size of type, for example, will most likely create a need to adjust the line length. Since the typographic space is divided horizontally into columns of varying widths, it is possible to control these variables while also creating a rhythmic visual field. (For further discussion, see *"Type size, line length, and interline spacing,"* pp. **80** and **81**.)

Rhythm is achieved by the repetition and contrast of columns and other visual elements. White space rhythmically separates elements and breathes energy into the typographic field.

In the normative sense, column intervals separating text columns are adjusted to enable the eye to flow logically from one column to the next without confusion about reading direction. However, exploring unconventional gutter intervals can lead to striking typographic rhythms and patterns.

20.
Sample multi-column grids ranging from two to eight columns. As the number of columns increases, so too does the number of organizational possibilities. Note how the use of white space both separates and connects elements to achieve a clear and logical informational hierarchy, and how columns are adjusted in length to achieve a pleasing "rag" along the bottom of the pages.

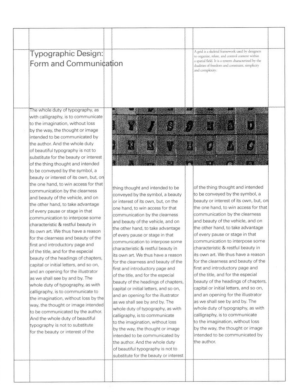

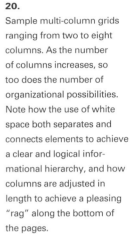

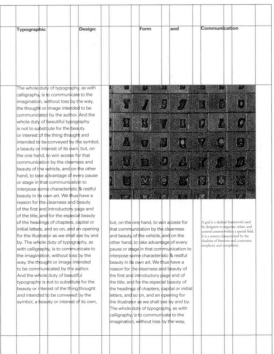

Grids may consist of primary and secondary divisions of space. For example, the grid used in this book consists of two columns as the dominant structure, with an optional structure of five columns (note the visible grid lines on this page). Concurrent grids not only provide added flexibility, they also enable the designer to layer typographic elements, achieving the illusion of three-dimensional space (Fig. **21** and **22**).

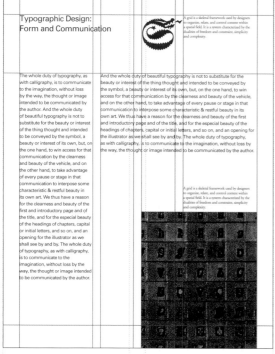

21.

22.

21.
Concurrent grids and multi-column grids with irregular column intervals can be used to accommodate information desiring special treatment. Specific parts of information can inhabit assigned columnar zones to preserve their autonomy. In the example shown, the far right column is reserved for the display of alphabetic characters.

22.
Multi-column grids can be applied to many different situations, as in this format consisting of three panels, each divided into three columns.

Experimentation with multi-column grids can yield visually surprising and functional results. Columns can be shifted horizontally and vertically, placed at opposing angles, or behave in ways extending typographic tradition. However, such effects should only be used when they contribute to the interpretation of the text (Figs. **23–26**).

23.

Strict adherence to a two-column grid proves an orderly environment for the presentation of text and paintings by artist and designer Bart van der Leck. (Designer: Wigger Bierma)

24.

The purity and serenity of climbing is reflected in this elegant and restrained design. The magazine layout consists of three columns that facilitate a balanced integration of text and spectacular photographs. (Editor/Creative Director: Christian Beckwith; Designer: Sam Serebin)

24.

23.

25.

In a book entitled *The Best Dutch Book Designs*, text columns shift laterally to achieve a woven texture. The columns are assigned texts in both Dutch and English. (Designer: Typography, Interiority, & Other Serious Matters)

26.

For the *One Hit Wonders* exhibit in the Rock and Roll Hall of Fame and Museum in Cleveland, Ohio, multiple columns featuring song titles, artist's names, and descriptive text arch dramatically along a curved wall to achieve both visual resonance and maximum interpretive clarity. (Project Directors: Bruce Burdick and Susan Burdick; Graphics Director: Stuart McKee, The Burdick Group)

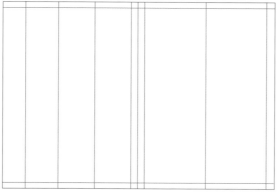

25.

26.

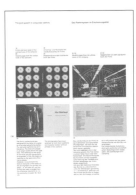
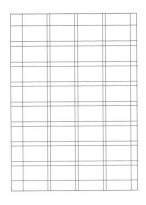

28.

28.
The cover, an interior page, and the grid of Josef Müller-Brockmann's classic book, *Grid Systems*. (Designer: Josef Müller-Brockmann)

27.
A 36-module grid extracted from 4,096 individual square units represents but one of an enormous range of grid constructions. In this example, the smaller vertical divisions function as a baseline grid. The complexity of this system offers a wide range of compositional choices. However, the goal remains to organize a collection of elements into a cohesive whole.

Modular grids

When is the adoption of a modular grid more desirable than the standard columnar grid? Though these two methods for organizing information are cousins, the modular grid offers opportunities to present more complex informa-tion with a high degree of accuracy and clarity.

Modules are formed by the intersections of horizontal and vertical lines. These units provide zones for the placement of different parts of information. The goal is to create a distinct hierarchy between units of information. This is achieved by understanding the different levels of information and representing them as contrasting elements.

At first, the modular grid appears mathematical, repetitive, and unimaginative. But it is important to think of the grid as a system for organizing information and not as a physical, inpenetrable fortress. Grids systems are flexible, and they evolve as the designer works to understand and represent information. Figure **27** displays a modular grid system consisting of thirty-six square modules. This example shows modules of equal size, but grid systems can be developed with modules consisting of any number of proportions. The beauty of the system is that modules can be combined into varied sizes and shapes to serve as zones for content elements.

As a general rule, the more complex the grid structure, the more flexible the organizational possibilities. The process of organizing material within a grid structure is a balancing act between variety and unity. Too much of either denies design of hierarchical clarity.

An excellent model for illustrating the modular grid is the work of Josef Müller-Brockmann, a major contributor to its wide acceptance (Fig. **28**). A leader in the development of the International Typographic Style during the 1950s and 1960s, Müller-Brockmann sought pure objectivity in typography and graphic expression.

His work, including posters that remain as fresh today as they were when first designed, attest to the power and visual impact of his work. This rational philosophy, which he shared with other pioneers of the movement, was assimilated throughout Europe and into the United States. In his 1981 book, *Grid Systems,* Müller-Brockmann states, "The use of the grid as an ordering system is the expression of a certain mental attitude inasmuch as it shows that the designer conceives his work in terms that are constructive and oriented to the future."

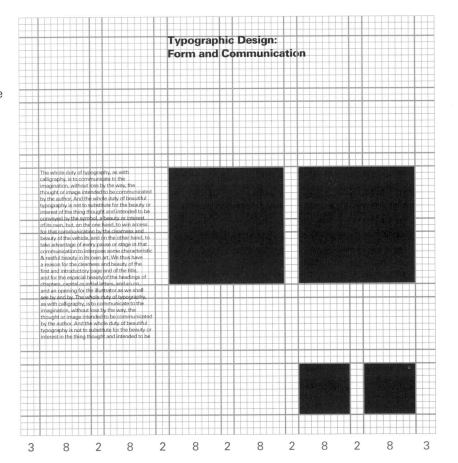

27.

Grids allow for the distribution of typographic elements into a clearly intelligible order. Within the internal structure created, headlines, text, captions, images, and other parts of the message are integrated. The areas occupied, which correspond to specific modules or groups of modules, are referred to as spatial zones. After identifying all the parts of a message, the designer assigns them to specific zones. The result is a logical hierarchy of parts, and information that is more accessible to readers (Fig. 29).

In the tradition of modern design, the spatial zones within a typographic grid are not violated. The designer works within the grid framework to objectively present information, while utilizing the principles of ABA form to establish relationships between the parts and to embue the composition with rhythmic and textural variety. But rules can be broken and risks are possible; skilled designers are capable of violating the grid to optimize clarity and maximize visual effect.

29.

Progressing from simple to complex, these grids systematically illustrate a diverse number of modular configurations.

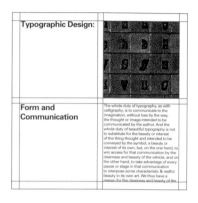

29.

30.

Spatial interaction and compositional balance are achieved when modules define void spaces that are integral to the geometry of the page.

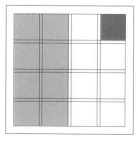 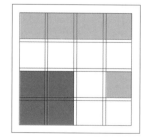 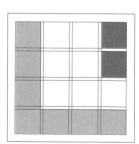

A successful grid is a performance, a concerto of typographical instruments working independently yet together. In the end, individual images and sounds work toward a common goal. What is perceived as the whole is greater than the virtuoso of any individual part (Fig. **30**).

The following examples reveal variations on the modular typographic grid used inventively across various media. In a highly complex information environment, it is necessary to provide audiences with articulate structures that also resonate visually. This is as true for books as for Web sites and other delivery venues (Figs. **32–36**).

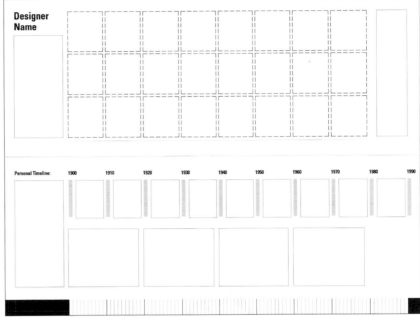

The book *American Graphic Design Timelines* features a highly flexible grid that makes it possible for readers to compare and contrast timelines of several design and related themes, including major events in world and U.S. history, cultural events, American graphic designers, companies, organizations, and publications (Fig. **31**).

Timelines in all sections are organized in a nine-column grid, with each column corresponding to a decade in the twentieth century.
As readers turn the pages, this time-oriented structure remains constant from section to section, making it possible for information to be studied in context.

Depending upon need, several pathways through the book may be taken by readers. It may be read traditionally as a linear narrative from section to section, or it may be used as a reference book where readers make specific connections by comparing the information found on the timelines. (Designer: Keith Jones)

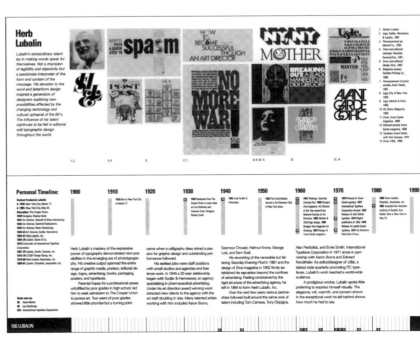

31.

32.
The MeBox is a customizable cardboard box storage system. The ends of each box have a grid of perforated disks that can be punched out as needed to make initials, numbers, symbols, and text. The boxes can be arranged in rows to create longer messages. (Designer: Graphic Thought Facility, London)

33.
Visual unity among the many components of the Grasslands outdoor exhibition is established through a modular system of squares. By combining the smallest square unit into larger groups of rectilinear units, images and type are presented in many different sizes for visually dynamic displays. (Exhibition designers: Michael Mercadante and David Whitemyer; graphic designer: Polly Baldwin)

34.
The Web site for Demographik – a design agency based in Florida that develops media solutions – is based on an animated system of square modules. While navigating the site, "tiles" appear to lift from the surface of the screen, casting shadows, and dynamically spinning into new locations where transformed spaces reveal information about the company. (Designer: Juan Benedit)

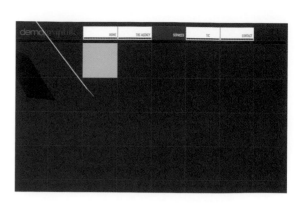

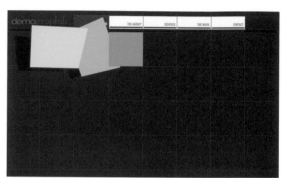

32.

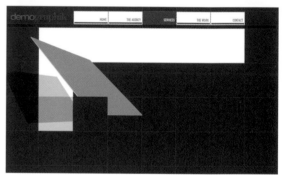

33.

34.

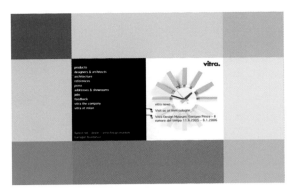

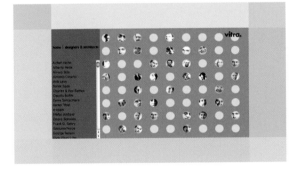

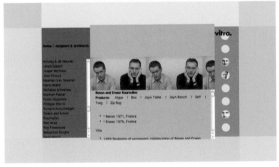

35.

36.

35.
Vitra, in collaboration with internationally renowned designers, is a manufacturer and developer of high-quality furniture. Visitors to the Vitra Web site are stimulated by an expansive and layered modular environment. Typography is integrated into modular units with refined simplicity, while vivid color, contrasting shapes, and visual repetition yield drama and sophistication. (Designer: Uli Weidner, Virtual Identity AG)

36.
IF/THEN is a book utilizing concurrent grid structures that provide visual variety while also preserving unity among pages. (Designer: Mevis & Van Deursen)

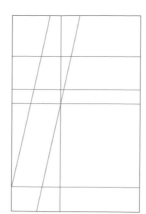

37.
The improvisational structure inherent in this poster is built upon dynamic relationships between horizontal, vertical, and diagonal axes. (Designer: David Colley)

Improvisational structures

Improvisational structures evolve in response to the specific elements of information as opposed to modular grids, which are predetermined organizational devices. A complete grasp of the visual material in question enables designers to understand the relationships between parts and to create visual hierarchies among them. In the metaphorical sense, typographic designers are information architects – they "build" typographic environments for clear and accessible information.

Typographical materials are the building blocks of improvisational structures. Once it is known which elements are dominant, subdominant, and subordinate, they are translated into typographic forms reflecting their hierarchical status. These forms, consisting of different sizes and shapes, are then introduced into the spatial field and intuitively arranged until a rational and aesthetic solution is found. For a poster announcing a lecture series, designer David Colley has organized the information into five distinct zones: title, speakers, venues, sponsor, and tertiary information. The improvised structure not only communicates clearly through legible typography and the effective organization of contrasting parts, it also provides a dynamic viewing experience based on the language of asymmetrical composition (Fig. **37**).

This flexible construction process involves inserting typographic forms in space to establish form and content relationships, substituting these forms with revised forms as necessary, and omitting forms that are inconsequential.

Working with improvisational structures calls for a firm understanding of asymmetrical composition, the dynamics of positive and negative space, and the essential role of visual contrast among typographic elements.

37.

Typographic messages pervade our culture to the degree that they are often taken for granted or not noticed at all. Typographic messages are most effective when they are distinguished from the competition. Messages that clearly communicate and are etched into the mind and memory are those characterized by absolute clarity in form and content. This chapter introduces typography as a language of potent visible signs, a language capable of educating, persuading, informing, and entertaining. When typographic signs are created with an informed eye and mind, they achieve both lucidity and aesthetic beauty.

1.

ping pong
   ping pong ping
   pong ping pong
     ping pong

1.

A multidimensional language

The typographic message is verbal, visual, and vocal. While typography is read and interpreted verbally, it may also be viewed and interpreted visually, heard and interpreted audibly. It is a dynamic communication medium. In this sense, early twentieth-century typography became a revolutionary form of communication, bringing new expressive power to the written word. Consider the concrete poem "ping pong" (Fig. **1**). The geometric structure of this poem is composed of a repetition of the words *ping* and *pong*. As these words are repeated, they signify the sound of a bouncing ping-pong ball, and the circular letters *p, o,* and *g* reflect the shape of the ball. The full impact of this poem is achieved when it is read aloud. By hearing the sounds and viewing the typographic forms, the typographic message is strengthened.

Significant departures from the use of conventional typographic forms occurred in Europe at the beginning of the twentieth century. During this activist period, experimentation in all the visual and performing arts was affected by potent social and philosophical changes, industrial and technological developments, and new attitudes about aesthetics and modern civilization. Typographic design was pulled into this artistic revolution as poets and visual artists realized that both meaning and form could be intensified in typographic communications.

The Futurist manifesto, written by the Italian poet Filippo Marinetti in 1909, profoundly influenced thinking in Europe and Russia. Futurism praised technology, violence, danger, movement, and speed. Futurist typography, known as "free typography," demonstrated these ideas in a highly expressive manner (Fig. **2**; and see Chapter One, Fig. **125**). The chill of a scream was expressed in bold type, and quick impressions were intensified through italics. Letters and words raced across the page in dynamic motion.

Among the movements affected by Futurism were Dadaism in France, Switzerland, and Germany; de Stijl in Holland; and Constructivism in Russia. Each of these historical movements has had a penetrating effect upon typography. Artists and

designers associated with these movements saw typography as a powerful means of conveying information relating to the realities of industrialized society (Figs. **3–5**; also see Chapter One, Figs. **129–35**). They disdained what typography had become: a decorative art form far removed from the realities of the time. The architect Otto Wagner further emphasized that "all modern forms must be in harmony with the new requirements of our time. Nothing that is not practical can be beautiful." Written in 1920, the second de Stijl manifesto clearly demonstrated the concern for a new, expressive typography (Fig. **6**). With dramatic changes taking place in the form and content of typography, the typographic message became a multifaceted and expressive form of communication. Typography needs to be read, seen, heard, felt, and experienced.

1.
"ping pong" (Poet: Eugen Gomringer)

4.
Title lettering for *De Stijl.*
(Designer: Theo van Doesburg)

2.
Les mots en liberté futuristes.
(Designer: Filippo Marinetti)

3.
Cover of the first issue of *Der Dada.* (Editor: Raoul Hausmann)

5.
Constructivist cover design for *Veshch, Gegenstand, Objet.* (Designer: El Lissitzky)

BERLIN 1922

OBJET

ВЕЩЬ

N=3

REVUE ● INTERNATIONALE ● DE L'ART ● MODERNE
МЕЖДУНАРОДНОЕ ● ОБОЗРЕНИЕ ● СОВРЕМЕННОГО ● ИСКУССТВА
INTERNATIONALE ● RUNDSCHAU ● DER KUNST ● DER GEGENWART

GEGENSTAND

THE WORD IS DEAD…
THE WORD IS IMPOTENT
asthmatic and sentimental poetry
the "me" and "it"
        which is still in common use
        everywhere…
is influenced by an individualism fearful of space
        the dregs of an exhausted era…

psychological analysis
and clumsy rhetoric
have KILLED THE MEANING OF THE WORD…

the word must be reconstructed
        to follow the SOUND as well as
        the IDEA
if in the old poetry
        by the dominance of relative and
        subjective feelings
the intrinsic meaning of the word is destroyed
we want by all possible means
        syntax
        prosody
        typography
        arithmetic
        orthography
to give new meaning to the word and new force
to expression

the duality between prose and poetry can no longer
be maintained
the duality between form and content can no longer
be maintained
Thus for the modern writer form will have a directly
spiritual meaning
it will not describe events
it will not *describe* at all
but ENSCRIBE
it will recreate in the word the common meaning of
events
a constructive unity of form and content…

Leiden, Holland, April 1920.

        Theo van Doesburg
        Piet Mondrian
        Anthony Kok

As a dynamic representation of verbal language, typography must communicate. This functional role is fulfilled when the receiver of a typographic message clearly and accurately understands what is in the mind of the transmitter. This objective, however, is not always accomplished. With a proliferation of typographic messages littering the environment, most are missed or ignored. The messages that are noted, possessing effective qualities relating to form and content, are appropriate to the needs of both message transmitter and message receiver.

The impact of an effective typographic message cannot be easily measured. Some may assume that since printed and broadcast messages are ephemeral, they have little impact upon their audience. This assumption is false. Because typographic ephemera are rhetorical, they often have a long-range effect upon a message receiver, influencing change within the context of social, political, and economic events. The symbol of solidarity expressed by Polish workers (Fig. **7**), the social statements made with graffiti in urban environments, and the typography on billboards aimed at passing motorists all operate as purposeful messages directed toward a predetermined audience within a specific context.

Effective typographic messages result from the combination of logic and intuitive judgment. Only the neophyte approaches this process in a strictly intuitive manner; a purely logical or mechanical procedure undermines human expression. Keeping these two extremes in balance requires the use of a functional verbal/visual vocabulary capable of addressing a broad spectrum of typographic communication.

6.
De Stijl manifesto of 1917.

10.

| to scrape | to crease | to peel | to melt | to splinter |

Verbal/visual equations

Language, in any of its many forms, is a self-contained system of interactive signs that communicate ideas. Just as elocution and diction enhance and clarify the meaning of our spoken words, typographic signs can be manipulated by a designer to achieve more lucid and expressive typographic communication.

Signs operate in two dimensions: syntactic and semantic. When the mind is concerned with the form of a sign, it is involved with typographic syntax. When it associates a particular meaning with a sign, it is operating in the semantic dimension.

All objects in the environment can potentially function as signs, representing any number of concepts: a smog-filled city signifying pollution, a beached whale representing extinction, and confetti implying celebration – each functions as a sign relating a specific concept.

Signs may exist at various levels of abstraction. A simple example will illustrate this point. Let us consider something as elemental as a red dot. It is a sign only if it carries a particular meaning. It can represent any number of things: balloon, ball, or Japanese flag. The red dot becomes a cherry, for example, as the mind is cued by forms more familiar to its experience (Fig. **8**).

The particular syntactic qualities associated with typographic signs determine a specific meaning. A series of repeated letters, for example, may signify motion or speed, while a small letter in a large void may signify isolation. These qualities, derived from the operating principles of visual hierarchy and ABA form, function as cues, permitting the mind to form concepts. Simple syntactic manipulations, such as the repetition of letters, or the weight change of certain letters, enable words visually to mimic verbal meaning (Fig. **9**). In another example, the letter *E* has been visually altered, relating it to the meaning of specific descriptive words (Fig. **10**).

8.
Signs exist at various levels of abstraction. A form is a sign, however, only when it carries a message. As the mind is cued by forms familiar to experience, information is conveyed.

9.
Syntactic manipulations are controlled by such factors as repetition, size change, position change, or weight change. These enable words to visually mimic verbal meaning.

10.
These elaborations of the letter *E* express a variety of concepts. (Designers: Carol Anthony, Linda Dronenburg, and Rebecca Sponga)

leav e

in ter val

di e t

ststutter

dro p

9.

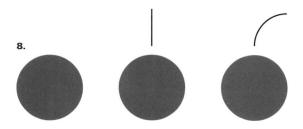

8.

11.

Typographic signs combine
to form a more complex
sign, suggesting a decorated
Christmas tree. (Designer:
Donna Funk)

In language, signs are joined together to create messages. Words as verbal signs, grouped together in a linear fashion, attain their value vis-à-vis other words through opposition and contrast. Words can also evoke meaning through mental association. These associative relations are semantically derived. Since typography is both visual and verbal, it operates in a linear fashion, with words following each other in a specific sequence, or in a nonlinear manner, with elements existing in many syntactic combinations. For example, in the visual poem "O Christmas Tree," the choice of the typeface, Futura Light, is very important. The capital letter *O* is a perfect circle, signifying ornaments; the linear strokes of other letterforms suggest the texture of evergreen needles (Fig. **11**). This typographic message is derived from the mental associations formed by contrasting typographic signs.

Two terms important to the understanding of signs are denotation and connotation. When considering the meaning of typographic signs, denotation refers to objective meaning, the factual world of collective awareness and experience. For example, a denotative interpretation of a yellow *O* would be: "This is a yellow letter *O*" or "This is a yellow circle." Connotative interpretations of the yellow *O* might be: "This is the sun, a slice of lemon, or a golden ring." Connotative observations are often conditioned, for they relate to overtones and are drawn from prior personal experience.

Typographic signs are both verbal and visual. The associations formed between the verbal and visual attributes are verbal/visual equivalencies, which are found in a variety of configurations. These reveal the associative nature of signs composing the typographic message and help us further understand its multifaceted attributes. Figures **12–24** illustrate the nature of some of these verbal/visual equations.

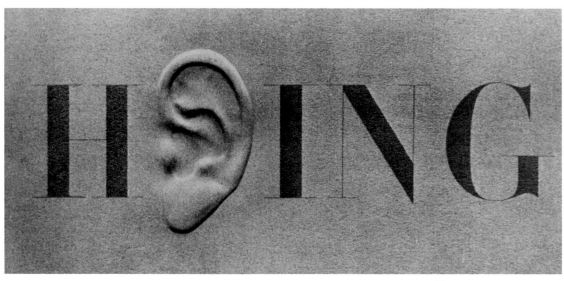

12.

Visual substitution: The visual
sign of an ear is substituted
for the letters *E, A,* and *R.*
(Designer: Lou Dorfsman)

14.

Simultaneity: The numeral *8* functions as the letter *g* in this logotype used for a group exhibition of paintings by the early-twentieth-century American art group The Eight.

Eight

15.

Visual transformation: A mother, father, and child are suggested through the visual transformation of the letters *l* and *i*. (Designer: Herb Lubalin)

Families

Taking Things Apart and Putting Things Together

what chemistry is what chemists do and what the results have been

sponsored by the American Chemical Society on the occasion of its 100th anniversary

Union Carbide 270 Park Ave. New York, N.Y. 10017

April 5-May 28,1976 9:30-4:30 weekdays Closed April 16,17 and Sundays Admission: free

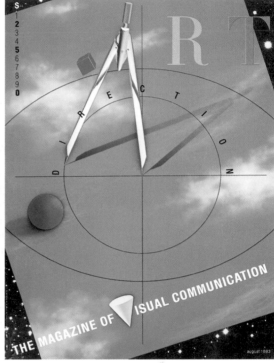

13.

Visual substitution: The visual sign of a compass is substituted for the letter *A* and an inverted cone is substituted for the letter *V*. (Designer: Harold Burch)

16.

Visual exaggeration: The irregular syntactic treatment of typographic signs exaggerates the process of taking things apart and putting things together. (Designer: Steff Geissbuhler)

the American premiere at the Depot in Urbana
of the play by Marcel Achard

translated by Sue Huseman Moretto
directed by Jose Moretto

October 31, November 1, 2, 3 1974
November 7, 8, 9, 10
at 8:00 pm, Friday and Saturday also at 10:30 pm

tickets at Record Service
704 South Sixth Champaign
and at the Depot 223 North Broadway
on nights of performance

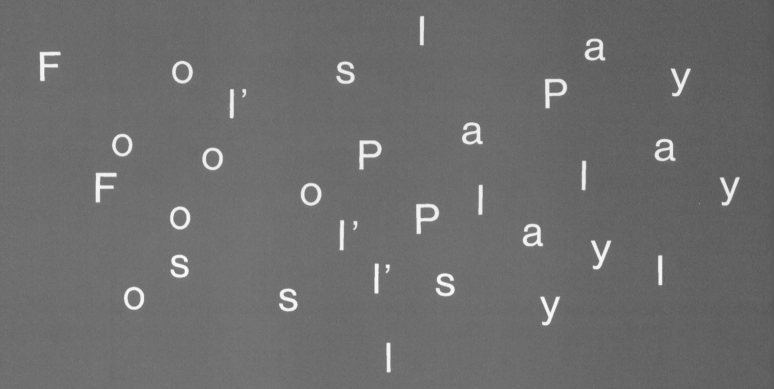

18.

Form combination: Visual and verbal signs are combined into a single typographic statement, creating trademarks that suggest the nature of various industries: an electrical contractor, a maker of plastic fibers for carpets and draperies, and a lithographic printer. (Designer: Don Weller)

18.

19.

Form combination: Verbal signs are combined with visual signs (cables). The resulting forms suggest the qualities of cable transmission. (Designers: Jerry L. Kuyper and Sheila de Bretteville)

20.

Parallel form: The Olivetti logotype and electronic calculator have similar visual characteristics that parallel each other. (Logotype design: Walter Ballmer)

21.

Verbal/visual correspondence: The syntactic qualities of this typographic sign correspond to the graffiti found in an urban environment. (Designer: Jeff Barnes)

22.

Verbal/visual correspondence: The visual characteristics of this typographic sign correspond to the form of a zipper. This is achieved by a repetition of letters and a horizontal shift within the word. (Designer: Richard Rumble)

19.

CBS

CABLE

20.

city

21.

17.

Visual exaggeration: The repetition and playful treatment of typographic forms effectively reinforces the content of the drama *Fool's Play,* for which this poster was designed. (Designer: David Colley)

ZIIIIIIIIIIIIPPPER

22.

23.

24.

23.
Verbal/visual correspondence:
The visual qualities of the
typefaces chosen for the
signs *Gandhi, Garbo, and Poe*
make direct reference to time
and culture. The message
is further strengthened by
the sounds associated with
the words. (Designer: David
Colley)

24.
Verbal/visual correspondence:
The visual repetition of this
word – unified by the shared
letters *u* and *n* – express the
concept of unity. (Designer:
Steff Geissbuhler)

Function and expression

Functionalism is a term used to describe the utilitarian and pragmatic qualities of designed objects. During the early twentieth century, functionalism was generally equated with designed objects of clarity, purpose, and unornamented simplicity. However, it has since evolved as a subjective notion that varies widely according to the needs of the audience and the objectives of the designer.

For example, if comfort in the design of a chair is defined as plushness and cushiness, an upholstered automatic recliner complete with footrest and vibrator might satisfy the criteria of a functional chair.

In contrast to the automatic recliner is the red/blue chair, a central artifact of the de Stijl movement, designed in 1918 by Gerrit Rietveld (Fig. **25**). Members of de Stijl sought a restrained expression and a new philosophy for living. With its hard, flat surfaces, the red/blue chair appears very uncomfortable; however, Rietveld's desire was for the chair to promote alert mental activity through rigid support. The seat and backrest planes are attached at only one edge, enabling the pliable wood to adjust to the user's weight. In this regard, the chair functions according to Rietveld's intentions. In an interior environment, Rietveld's red/blue chair has the presence and visual harmony of a piece of sculpture. The needs for a functional object (seating) and for aesthetic experience are fulfilled in this one object.

In typography, function is the purposeful communication of information to a specific audience. Although the range of possible typographic design solutions is infinite, the appropriateness of a solution always depends upon the purpose for which it was intended. Varying degrees of formal reduction or elaboration can be effective when solving specific typographic problems.

25.

25.
Red/blue chair, 1918.
(Designer: Gerrit Rietveld)

26.
The elemental shape and sequence of letters in the word *eye* visually suggest two eyes and a nose. Set in News Gothic, this typographic configuration serves as the masthead for *eye, The International Review of Graphic Design.* (Designer: Stephen Coates)

27.
Required to appear on all food packaging in the United States, the standardized *Nutrition Facts* label clearly provides consumers with important information about the nutritional value of foods. Typography responsibly assumes an objective, informational role. (Designer: Berkey Belser)

28.
The "A" stamp is the official priority stamp of the Swiss Post Office. A simple configuration of three interlocking shapes suggests an uppercase *A*. The trilogy of shapes represents the co-dependent parts of the mailing process: message, sender, and receiver. (Designer: Jean-Benoît Lévy)

29.
The vitality of *Rolling Stone* magazine is revealed in this monumental, three-dimensional letterform, a deconstructed element used in the traveling exhibition *The 30th Anniversary Covers Tour.* (Designer: J. Abbott Miller, James Hicks, Paul Carlos, and Scott Davendorf)

30.
This sequence of frames represents the animated "splash page" of a Web site designed to teach children how to read. The letter *O,* containing the remaining vowels, rolls onto the screen. As the letterforms transform in color, they roll off of the screen and disintegrate. (Designer: John Stratiou)

Formal reduction can be used to create optimum clarity and legibility, presenting complex information, such as news or scientific data, in a clear and straightforward manner. Orderly presentation guides the eye from one element to another, preserving reader interest and attention (Figs. **26** and **27**).

Another approach, expressionism, accomplishes its purpose through formal elaboration and ornamentation, creating visual impact. When appropriate, attention can be given to experimental, expressive, and ornamental possibilities. Ornament serves a variety of practical needs. Because it is semiotic, iconographic, and historical, it identifies the object with which it is associated. Expressive and ornamental typographic forms place objects in time, reveal their purpose, and clarify their structures (Figs. **28–30**). The formal elaboration of objects in architecture, industrial design, and the fine arts can significantly influence typographic possibilities. Figures **71** and **119** (Chapter One) and **31–33** possess strong ornamental qualities. Innovative typography can emerge when a designer fully understands communication needs and is able to assimilate a diversity of visual ideas.

On this subject, Ladislav Sutnar commented that "an eccentric visual scandal or visual shock of the outrageous and of the unexpected can catch the attention of the astonished eye . . . it may also delight the eye to see a fresh design concept or a message so orderly presented as to make comprehension fast and easy." A designer can avoid conventional solutions to typographic problems when innovation is appropriate. A single approach to typographical design, induced by stylistic convention and predetermined formulas, is a routine activity lacking the vitality of meaningful typographic invention. Sound principles and a trained vision should supersede dependency upon preconceived formulas. For typography to be truly functional, satisfying the needs of an audience, a designer must understand both the verbal and visual attributes of a typographic message.

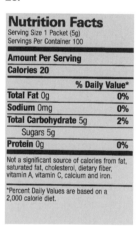

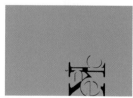

30.

26.

Nutrition Facts
Serving Size 1 Packet (5g)
Servings Per Container 100

Amount Per Serving

Calories 20

	% Daily Value*
Total Fat 0g	0%
Sodium 0mg	0%
Total Carbohydrate 5g	2%
Sugars 5g	
Protein 0g	0%

Not a significant source of calories from fat, saturated fat, cholesterol, dietary fiber, vitamin A, vitamin C, calcium and iron.

*Percent Daily Values are based on a 2,000 calorie diet.

27.

28.

Rolling Stone

Madonna
On Being a Star

"It's enough having
my breasts as an appendage.
When you jump up and
down, or dance, or run,
or whatever, they're there.
I can't imagine having
a third thing hanging off my body.
How dreadful."

29.

31.

A field of typographic forms, illustrations, and the colors orange and black charge this poster with expression. (Designer: Todd Timney)

31.

A field of typographic forms, illustrations, and the colors orange and black charge this poster with expression. (Designer: Todd Timney)

32.

This view book acquires its robust and expressive quality through vivid color, varying typographic textures, and structural complexity. (Design: Rob Carter)

33.

Expressive text type is achieved on a spread of the book *Elvis+Marilyn* by its configuration into the letter *R*. (Designer: Mirko Ilić)

The invention of typography has been called
the beginning of the Industrial Revolution. It is
the earliest mechanization of a handicraft: the
handlettering of books. Typographic design has
been closely bound to the evolution of technology,
for the capabilities and limitations of typesetting
systems have posed constraints upon the design
process. At the same time, typesetting has offered
creative challenges as designers have sought to
explore the limitations of the available systems
and to define their aesthetic and communicative
potential.

From hand composition to today's electronically
generated typography, it is important for designers
to comprehend the nature and capabilities of
typographic technologies, for this understanding
provides a basis for a thoughtful blending of design
and production.

1.
Composing stick.

Hand composition

The traditional method of setting foundry type by hand is similar to the method used by Gutenberg when he invented movable type in 1450. For centuries, hand composition was accomplished by assembling individual pieces of type into lines. A typographer would hold a composing stick (Fig. **1**) in one hand while the other hand placed type selected from a type case (Fig. **2**) into the stick. Type was set letter by letter, line by line, until the desired setting was achieved. When it was necessary to justify a line, additional spaces were created in the line by inserting metal spacing material between words. Letterspacing was achieved by inserting very thin pieces of copper or brass between letters until words appeared to be evenly spaced. When additional space between

lines was desired, strips of lead were inserted between the lines until the type column was the proper depth. By adding lead, the exact proportion and size of the column could be formed, assuring readability through consistent spacing.

Once type was set, it was "locked up" in a heavy rectangular steel frame called a *chase* (Fig. **3**). This was done on a table called a *stone.* The type was surrounded by wood or metal spacing material, called *furniture,* and the contents of the chase were made secure by tightening steel, wedgelike devices called *quoins.* After the type was secured in the chase, it was ready to be transferred to a press for printing, and after printing, the individual pieces of type were distributed back into the type case by hand.

2.
Type case.

Chase

Wood furniture

Type

Quoins

3.
A chase containing type "locked up" and ready for printing.

Hand composition was tedious and time consuming. When typesetting became automated as a result of the invention of Linotype and Monotype machines, hand composition was used only for setting small amounts of type or for display type. Currently, hand composition is obsolete as a practical means of setting type, but as an art form there has been a revival. Private presses produce limited-edition books and a variety of experimental materials by hand. Many of our typographic conventions and traditions have their origins in the rich heritage of handset metal type.

Linotype

One of the most profound developments in typesetting technology was the invention of the Linotype machine (Fig. **4**) by Ottmar Mergenthaler in 1886. This machine represented the first great step toward typographic automation. Its name was coined because it produced a single line of type to a predetermined length specified by the keyboard operator.

The operation of the Linotype was based on the principle of a circulating matrix. Each time a key was pressed, a single brass matrix (Fig. **5**) was released from an overhead magazine, divided into ninety vertical channels, each containing matrices for one character. The magazine was the character storage case for the machine. Once an entire line had been typed, the matrices moved into an automatic casting mechanism where the line of type was cast from molten lead. As each line was being cast, the operator typed the next line. After the casting process was complete, cast lines of type called slugs (Fig. **6**) were ejected from the mold, and the matrices were automatically returned to their appropriate slot in the magazine for reuse.

The advantages of machine composition as compared to hand composition were obvious. It was faster and more accurate; the problem of type distribution (returning characters to the type case) was eliminated, for the cast lines of type were simply melted, and the lead was reused. Justification of type was automatic, eliminating the tedious process of inserting spaces between letters and words. A standard Linotype could cast lines up to thirty picas in length.

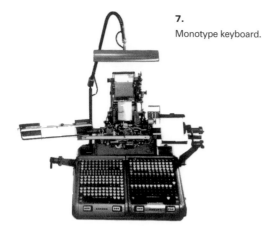

An important development for linecasting type was the Teletypesetter. This perforated tape-driven machine – an attachment to Linotype and Intertype – was introduced in 1928. Tape, which was punched by a machine similar to a standard typewriter, could be generated from a distant office and transmitted to the linecaster by wire, which made the machine invaluable to news services.

Monotype

Another significant achievement leading to fully automated typesetting was the Monotype machine, invented by Tolbert Lanston in 1887. This machine cast one character at a time rather than an entire line. it was composed of two parts: a keyboard and a typecaster (Fig. **7**). When an operator typed at a keyboard, a perforated paper tape was generated. This coded tape was used to drive the second part of the system – the typecaster. Compressed air, blown through the punched holes of this revolving spool of coded paper, determined which characters would be cast by the typecaster. Actual casting of type occurred when hot metal was forced into matrices from the matrix case (Fig. **8**). Once the cast characters had cooled, they were placed into a metal tray called a galley, where the lines were assembled. Monotype lines could reach a maximum length of about sixty picas.

Monotype became an efficient way to set type for several reasons. Corrections could be made by changing individual letters instead of complete lines. Therefore, complex typesetting, such as scientific data and tabular information, was easier. The Monotype matrix case held many more characters than a Linotype magazine, and the casting machine was relatively fast, casting one hundred fifty characters per minute. Since the system consisted of two separate machines, an operator could generate type away from the clatter of the casting machine. In fact, several operators could keyboard information for later setting.

8.
Monotype matrix case.

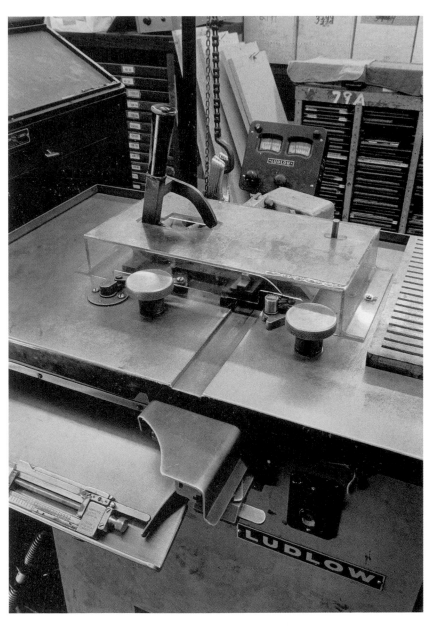

Ludlow

Ludlow, a semiautomatic linecaster, is another machine that found a place in the development of automated typesetting (Fig. **9**). Unlike the Linotype and Monotype, the Ludlow did not have a keyboard but combined both hand and machine production. An operator took matrices from a matrix case similar to a handset type case and placed them into a special composing stick, one by one. The stick would automatically justify or center lines by inserting blank matrices where necessary. Once a line of matrices was assembled, it was placed into a casting device where it was automatically cast into slugs. If a correction was necessary, matrices were inserted into the stick, cast, locked up, and printed. Although partially automated, this process was time consuming. Distributing the matrices back into the type case by hand added to the production time.

Type produced by the Ludlow machine ranged from 6 to 144 points. Its major use was to produce display type for headlines and other purposes requiring larger typefaces. As was true in the case of handset composition, the Ludlow was neither practical nor efficient for setting large volumes of type.

9.
Ludlow linecaster.

Phototypesetting

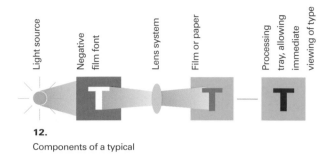

12.
Components of a typical
display phototypesetter.

Phototypesetting is a cold-type process, for type is set not from molten cast metal, but by exposing film negatives of characters onto photographic paper. Although photographic typesetting was explored as early as the 1880s, its potential was not fully recognized until after World War II. As printing advanced from letterpress to offset lithography, typography underwent a similar evolution. Hand composition of metal display type, and cast metal machine-set text type, yielded to photographic typesetting. Two kinds of phototypesetting systems were developed: display phototypesetters, for larger headlines and titles; and keyboard phototypesetters, used to set text type through keyboard input. Phototypesetting gradually replaced metal type during the 1960s, as the technology improved rapidly.

Display phototypesetting

In display phototypesetting machines (Fig. **10**), light is projected through film negatives and a lens to expose letters, numbers, and other symbols onto a strip of photographic paper. While a font of type in hand composition consisted of a drawer full of raised metal letters, a font for display photo composition consists of clear images on a long strip of film (Fig. **11**) wound on two reels. This film font slides between an amber safe light and a lens. Characters are projected onto a strip of photo paper resting in a shallow tray of developer. An operator uses hand cranks to roll the strip from one drum to another, putting the next letter in position to be exposed. By pressing a button, the operator causes a bright white light to flash thorough the lens, exposing the character to the photo paper (Fig. **12**). The character immediately begins to develop, so the operator sees it while using a lever to advance the photo paper. The projected image for the next character is positioned by winding the film strip on the reels with hand cranks. Character by character, a line of display type is exposed on the photo paper, then developed and fixed. Because the operator can view recently set characters as they develop, letterspacing is precisely controlled (Fig. **13**). This spacing flexibility was a major innovation. Many design advantages of display phototypesetting made it the dominant method for setting headlines by the late 1960s. No longer constrained by the fixed sizes of metal type, the designer could now specify display type

set from the film font (whose capitals were about an inch tall) in a wide range of sizes. Type could be enlarged up to two times the master font size, for two-inch capitals, or reduced to a one-fourth size, with capitals as small as a quarter inch high. Enlarged and reduced type retained perfect sharpness, unlike metal type, which became very ragged when enlarged. Metal fonts had a limited number of characters, while photo type had an unlimited number of characters, because the same negative could be exposed over and over again.

The constraints of metal blocks yielded to the elasticity of photographic processes, and innovative designers rapidly explored new possibilities. The lens system permitted photographic distortion. Characters could be expanded, condensed, italicized, and even backslanted (Fig. **14**). The tremendous expense of introducing new metal typefaces, requiring punches, cast letters, and matrices, was replaced by the cost of one economical film font. As a result, many new display typefaces – as well as revivals of earlier styles that were no longer available – were introduced at a rapid pace.

11.
Film font for a display
phototypesetter.

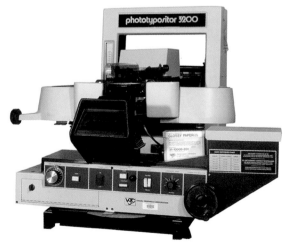

10.
A display phototypesetter.

Typography
Typography
Typography
Typography

13.
Unlike hand composition, where every letter is cast on a block of metal and cannot be easily kerned, display phototype interletter spacing is visually controlled by the operator and can be set wide, normal, tight, or even touching.

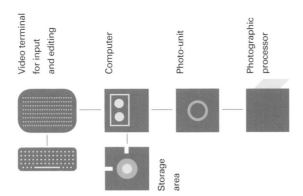

Video terminal for input and editing

Computer

Photo-unit

Photographic processor

Storage area

16.

Components of a typical keyboard phototypesetter.

14.

Normal, expanded, condensed, backslant, and italic (top to bottom).

aaaaaaaa

aaaaaaa
aaaaaaa
a a a a a a

aaaaaaaaa
aaaaaaaaaa
aaaaaaaaaa

aaaaaaaa
aaaaaaaa
aaaaaaa

aaaaaaaa
aaaaaaaa
aaaaaaaa

Keyboard phototypesetters

Keyboard phototypesetters were introduced in 1950. Two major types of phototypesetting systems (Fig. **15**) were developed: photo-optical and photo-scanning systems. They have the same basic components (Fig. **16**); the primary difference is how the photo paper or film is exposed.

Photo-optical systems store characters as a master font on film discs, drums, grids, or strips. The letters, numbers, and other symbols in the text are input on a keyboard. A typical film disc or drum spins at several thousand revolutions a minute, and a computer controls the exposure of light through the negative characters and a lens, onto light-sensitive paper or film. At the same time, the computer advances the paper or film in a transport device, moving it forward by the set width of the previously exposed character and into position for the next character to be exposed. Different lenses are used for different magnifications, so the typesetter can set different sizes of type. The computer makes very precise adjustments in spacing for the specific type size, and increases interletter and interword spacing when setting justified text columns. These systems are capable of setting hundreds of characters per minute. Early phototypesetting systems used a special keyboard to code punched paper tape that was fed into the phototypesetter to control the typesetting process. Paper-tape systems were replaced by magnetic tape systems, then by magnetic disks and diskettes.

A newer generation of photo-scanning typesetters replaced the photo-optical systems with an electronic system. Fonts are stored as electronic data. These digitized characters are projected as typeset text on a cathode ray tube (CRT) screen. A lens focuses the type on the CRT screen onto light-sensitive film or paper. A full page of type, including many different sizes and typefaces, can be divided into a grid of several blocks, each the size of the CRT screen, and stored in the computer's memory. Photo-scanning typesetters are much faster than photo-optical systems. They reproduce sections of the page rapidly, one block at a time, setting up to ten thousand characters per second.

Phototypesetters are flexible and fast, compared to hot-metal typesetting machines, which could set only about five characters per second. Hot-metal machines had many mechanical parts, while phototypesetters were operated electronically. Photo type needs little storage space because it is stored on flat photographic paper or film, while metal slugs are very heavy and require enormous amounts of storage space. Phototypesetting permits electronic editing, with corrections and changes made at the keyboard.

Phototypesetting freed designers from the physical restrictions of metal type. Increased flexibility in spacing typographic elements included greater control over kerning, interletter and interline spacing, overlapping, and special effects such as runarounds (type running around elements such as images). Designers who understood the potential of this technology used it to great advantage.

15.

A keyboard phototypesetter.

Digital typesetting

Digital storage Digitized image CRT scan Lens Film or paper

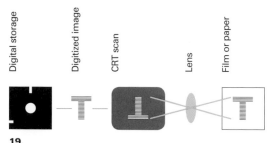

19.
Digital-scanning typesetter.

The digital computer in combination with the high-resolution cathode ray tube (CRT) and laser revolutionized the communications industry. Because digital computers have no mechanical parts and are entirely composed of electronic components, they set and process type at speeds never thought possible. In addition, the text type from digital typesetters has now been developed to rival the quality of phototype.

Knowledge of digital-computer functions is critical to an understanding of digital typesetting. A digital computer is an electronic device that uses electricity to process information. It can perform repetitive logical and arithmetic operations and store the results in memory. A computer system is composed of hardware and software. Hardware consists of the physical components of a computer; software is the program data that controls the operation of the hardware.

The computer component that controls all other parts, performs logical operations, and stores information is the central processing unit (CPU). All components that do not belong to the CPU are called peripherals. A typical digital-typesetting system is composed of a CPU and various peripherals that perform the functions necessary to the setting of type – for example, editing and storing text, displaying text on a screen, and printing typeset copy. In the main memory of a computer, called random access memory (RAM), data is stored and retrieved.

In digital typesetting, when an operator punches a key to enter a letter or issue a command (such as line length or paragraph indent), the computer receives it as binary code. Once information has been entered, it can be stored, edited, and sent to a peripheral device for typesetting.

Digital typesetting systems encode typographic characters digitally on a grid, defining the shape of each letter as a certain number of distinct points. Every detail of a letter is defined, including horizontal strokes, vertical strokes, and curves. The coded characters are stored electronically as digital instructions designating the x and y coordinates of the character on the grid. In the earliest digital typesetters, these instructions were sent to a CRT, where the character is generated onto the computer screen.

A CRT has a vacuum tube with a cathode at one end and a plate of phosphorous and aluminum at the other. When the CRT receives the digital instructions from the computer, defining the shape of the characters, the cathode emits a beam, which scans the tube in a series of parallel back-and-forth sweeps. The light emitted by the plate defines each character being typeset. The type is then digitally exposed to photographic paper.

The degree of resolution in digital letterforms is an important consideration. Basically, the more dots or lines used to describe a letterform, the higher the resolution. Because letters are constructed on a grid, the curved lines consist of a series of stair-stepped contours (Fig. **17**). When more dots are used to represent a curve, the curve appears smoother to the eye. The quality of letterforms is determined not only by their design but also by their digital resolution (Fig. **18**).

Resolution is improved through a process called *hinting* (see Chapter Four), which mathematically encodes letterforms in a manner true to their original design. Each size of a well-designed typeface possesses characters with unique proportional characteristics, and hinting preserves these characteristics, a concern particularly relevant for typefaces of smaller size. Details of curves, strokes, and serifs maintain optical integrity.

Scanning and laser systems

There are two classes of digital typesetters: digital-scanning systems, first introduced in 1972, and digital-laser systems. In digital-scanning systems (Fig. **19**), photographic characters were digitally scanned and recorded electronically on a magnetic disk or tape. The characters were translated into

18.
Examples of digital letterforms, demonstrating decreasing resolution, from top to bottom, as the number of elements is reduced.

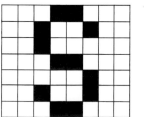

17.

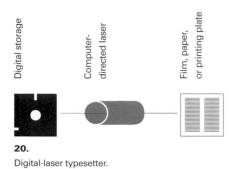

Digital storage

Computer-directed laser

Film, paper, or printing plate

20.
Digital-laser typesetter.

21.
A morphology of multiple-master fonts, originating with four master fonts interpolated along the axes of weight, width, and optical size. Weight and optical size occur along the vertical axis; width occurs along the horizontal axis. Though the variations seem very subtle, each represents an individual font.

22.
Walker, a typeface designed by Matthew Carter, enables designers to "snap-on" five variations of serifs at will.

a grid of extremely high resolution and then transmitted as a set of instructions to a CRT. Next, the characters were generated onto the CRT by a series of scan lines. The letterform images were then projected from the CRT onto paper, film, or an electrostatic drum. Because the output type is digital, it could be modified automatically to reflect a number of typographic variations. For example, it could be made heavier, lighter, slanted, condensed, or expanded at the command of the operator.

Rather than employing a CRT to generate characters, digital-laser systems (Fig. **20**) used a laser beam that scanned photographic paper as it read digital information stored in the typesetter. As the paper was scanned, a series of dots forming the characters were exposed to the paper. The information controlling the laser included the font, as well as spacing, paragraph configuration, hyphenation, and kerning.

Digital typesetting technology continues to improve and evolve, and with the introduction of electronic page design, and the responsibility for typesetting having shifted from a compositor to the designer, the nature of typographic communication has changed drastically. The ability of a designer to dynamically edit and alter individual letterforms and entire fonts with the aid of new software has in many ways redefined the way type is used. For example, multiple-master typefaces, developed by the Adobe Corporation in 1991, readily enable designers to interpolate and therefore change fonts along several design axes (Fig. **21**). These axes include weight, width, optical size, stroke shape, and serif configuration.

Other developments depart entirely from traditional typesetting methods. The typeface Walker, for example, designed in 1995 by Matthew Carter for the Walker Art Center, provides "snap-ons," that is, variant serifs treated as separate characters that can be added to or removed from letters as desired (Fig. **22**). Future innovations in digital typesetting will continue to shape and define typographic culture.

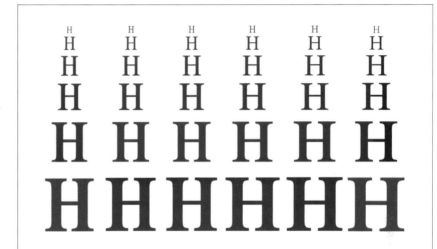

21.

22.

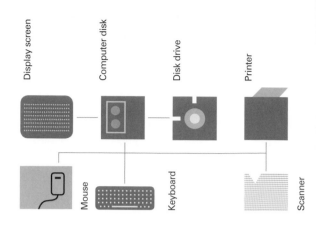

24.
Electronic page design
workstation.

23.
This laptop computer
screen displays type in true
WYSIWYG, for it accurately
shows the image as it
will print.

Digital typesetting moved onto the designer's desktop with the development of more powerful personal computers and software applications during the last two decades. This major leap forward in typographic technology makes it possible to design entire pages on a computer screen, then electronically output them onto paper, film, or even printing plates. Electronic page design, also called desktop publishing, eliminates the need for pasteup, which is the hand-assembly of elements in position for reproduction as a page. Type size, style, spacing, and position can be changed, then viewed on the screen immediately, bringing unprecedented control and freedom to typographic design. Advances in technology are bringing typography closer to WYSIWYG, an acronym meaning "what you see is what you get"; that is, the image on the computer monitor (Fig. **23**) is identical to the image that will be printed as final output.

Hardware components
Hardware, the physical components of the system, consists of the computer and the peripheral devices (Figs. **24** and **25**) that connect to it. Available peripherals include input devices, which are used to feed information into the computer, and output devices, which produce the final product.

Central processing unit. This electronic microprocessor chip does the actual work of the computer by receiving, processing, and storing information. It functions in a manner similar to the CPU of a digital typesetter, discussed earlier.

Input devices. These generate information for processing by the CPU and display on a screen, which uses a cathode-ray tube to produce a visual display of data. The keyboard contains alphabetical and numeric keys to input data. In addition, it contains special keys to perform specified functions, such as arrow keys to direct a pointer around the screen, and a command key that is held down while other keys are pressed, enabling them to send commands to the computer. The mouse is a handheld device that is moved about the desktop; it controls the movement of a pointer on the screen. A button on the mouse is clicked on elements to select them.

When the mouse button is held down, elements on the screen can be moved by moving the mouse. Graphics tablets operate in a manner similar to a mouse, but usea stylus or pointer touched to a flat surface to input information. Scanners are devices that convert images or text into digital form so that they can be stored and manipulated by a computer.

Information storage devices. A disk is a round platter with a magnetic coating similar to recording tape, on which information from the computer is stored in the form of magnetic impulses. A disk drive reads information from and writes information onto disks. Floppy disks are portable and housed in a 3.5-inch hard plastic case; they are inserted into a disk drive, which reads the information on the disk. Hard-disk drives have large rigid disks permanently mounted within the computer or in a separate case. Hard disks have large storage capacity and fast operating speed. Removable hard-disk cartridges combine the portability of floppy disks with the large storage capacity of hard-disk drives. The development of new information storage devices using compact disks and optical, rather than magnetic, systems promises even greater speed and the storage of massive amounts of data.

Output devices. After a design is completed, output devices are used to convert the screen image to printed output. A dot-matrix printer composes characters and image into a pattern of dots. The measure of quality for typographic output is the number of dots per inch (dpi); this determines the resolution of the image. A pin-strike printer uses a series of small pins that strike against an inked ribbon, transferring dots of ink onto paper to form the image. Many pin-strike printers have 72 dpi resolution, identical to the dpi of low-resolution screens.

25.
The contemporary designer's workstation includes a computer, flat-screen monitor, keyboard, mouse, removable storage drives, scanner, and printer.

A laser printer creates images by drawing them on a metal drum with a laser. Dry ink particles are attracted to this image, which is then transferred to paper in a process similar to a photocopying machine. The first-generation laser printers' 300 dpi resolution was called "near typeset quality." The ability of laser printers to output pages combining text and images was made possible by the development of interpretive programming languages that provide a software interface between page-design programs, discussed below, and output devices. The first page-description programming language, PostScript™ by Adobe Systems, Inc., was specifically designed to handle text and graphics and their position on the page; QuickDraw™ by Apple Computer is another programming language that enables the rapid display of typographic elements on a screen.

Imagesetters are high-resolution output devices (Fig. **26**) that consist of two components, a raster image processor (RIP) and a recorder or exposure unit. The RIP is a computer that uses a page-description language (see below) to convert the data files from the designer's workstation into an electronic pixel pattern of the page. Every single point on the page, whether part of a letterform or a pictorial image, is positioned in this pattern, which is sent to the exposure unit as a bitmap of raster lines. A bitmap is a computerized image "made up of dots." Exposure units from various manufacturers use different technologies – such as cathode-ray tube (CRT), gas laser, laser diode, or light-emitting diode (LED) – to record the RIP-composed page on photographic paper or film, plain paper, or even a printing plate.

Imagesetters produce very high resolution 1270 or 2540 dpi output. Imagesetters output type and halftone images in their final reproduction position, and some can output color separation negatives as well. The speed of digital typesetters is rated in characters per second, but imagesetters are rated in inches per minute since they output an entire bitmapped page. Early imagesetters were not capable of the typographic refinement of digital typesetters; however, steady improvement in hardware and software has closed the gap in quality. Imagesetter output of electronically designed pages has rapidly replaced traditional composition and pasteup.

26.
The Linotron 300 imagesetter, shown with its raster image processor, outputs complete pages at 1270 or 2540 dpi resolution.

27.

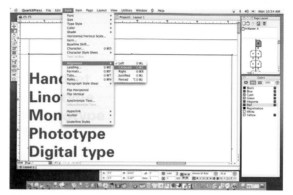

28.

Many typesetting firms have service bureaus to offer imagesetter output for their clients, and large advertising agencies and graphic-design offices have installed imagesetters within their firms. Typefaces are stored electronically in either bitmapped or outline data form. Bitmapped fonts are made up of dots and usually require a separate data set for each size of the typeface. Outline fonts are stored as instructions for drawing the outline of each character, using bezier curves to drawn nonuniform curves (as opposed to uniform curves, which are called arcs). Bezier curves are defined by four points, and their use enables computers to generate smooth images of complex letterforms.

Software

The instructions that tell the computer what to do are called software. An application program is software used to create and modify documents. The principal types of applications used in typographic design are word processors, drawing and painting programs, and page-layout software.

Word-processing programs are used to type in text, then edit, change, move, or remove it. Word-processing software can check grammar and spelling and suggest synonyms. Most text is written with a word-processing program, then transferred to a page-layout program for design.

Drawing and painting programs are used to create images. Early paint programs created images as a series of bitmapped dots, while drawing programs generated objects that are treated as mathematically defined line and arc segments rather than a series of dots. A rectangle created in a paint program can have its corner erased, but in order to move it, all the dots composing it must be selected; by contrast, an object-oriented rectangle can be selected by clicking anywhere on it, then moving it about the space. However, you cannot erase or change details. Most drawing and painting programs can generate and manipulate type, and advanced versions often combine the features of object-oriented draw programs along with bitmapped paint programs.

Page-design programs are used to design pages of typography and combine images with them. The type font, size, and leading can be selected, and text type can be flowed into columns running from page to page. Elements can be moved about the page, and templates of grid lines and standard repeating elements such as page numbers can be established. The screen image provides immediate feedback about the page design because all the elements are visible in their final sizes and spatial positions, and their attributes are capable of infinite change. The paper or film output is in final form, ready for reproduction.

The differences between word-processing programs and page-design programs are decreasing as each incorporates features from the other in updated versions. In general, word-processing programs have greater control over the editing process, whereas page-design programs have greater control over page composition. For example, in page-design programs an element can be selected with the mouse and moved anywhere on the page, but word-processing programs do not have this capability.

Page-design programs were made possible by the development of interpretive programming languages that provide a software interface between page-design programs and output devices.

The new computer-graphics technology has rapidly expanded the range of typeface design as well, for typeface design programs permit more rapid development of a new font than was possible with earlier technologies, while font editors allow the customization of individual letters or entire fonts to meet the needs of a user.

27.

The type menu lists parameters that can be changed on type that has been selected. Here the user has chosen *Size* and clicked the mouse button on *48* to change the selected type from *36-* to *48*-point.

28.

The type menu is being used to change the alignment of the selected type from *Align left* to *Align center.*

29.

When toolbox icons are selected, the mouse-controlled pointer becomes the selected tool. The designer may then select tool variations in secondary tool palettes.

The history of writing is, in a way, the history of the human race, since in it are bound up, severally and together, the development of thought, of expression, of art, of intercommunication, and of mechanical invention.

The history of writing is, in a way, the history of the human race, since in it are bound up, severally and together, the development of thought, of expression, of art, of intercommunication, and of mechanical invention.

30.
The top specimen has an undesirable widow. By changing the tracking of the second line in the bottom example by -1.5 (-1.5/200 em), the spatial interval between characters is deleted slightly, setting the type tighter and pulling the widow up to the last full line.

31.
Using a drawing program, the designer has joined the baseline of the type with an oval and a curved line.

The user interface

A typographic designer's computer workstation has an intuitive user interface; this means the tools are easy to use, permitting the user to focus upon the task at hand. A desktop pasteup metaphor is employed. The user sees the page surrounded by a desktop where elements can be created, held to one side, and then placed into position on the page. This metaphor to traditional pasteup has made it easier for the designers accustomed to traditional methods to design and assemble pages.

In page-design programs, a menu bar across the top of the screen lists major titles. The user moves the mouse to place the pointer on an item on the screen to be changed, then selects it by clicking the mouse button. Then, the pointer is placed on a menu title, and the mouse button is clicked, causing a list of commands to pop down. Under the type menu in one page-design program, for example, a list of commands for making changes to type that has been selected pops down. The user can change the type style, size (Fig. **27**), color, or alignment (Fig. **28**). Page-layout programs also have a palette of tools that are represented by icons (Fig. **29**). After a tool icon is selected, the mouse is

used to perform that operation. Advanced page-design programs permit unprecedented flexibility in typographic design. Minute adjustments of typographic spacing are possible.

Type can be set in sizes from 2 points to 720 points and leaded from –1080 to +1080 points Letter-spacing can be controlled by manually kerning in increments of 1120 or 1/200 em. The user can create kerning tables that automatically kern letter pairs. Tracking can be edited by selecting a range of characters (Fig. **30**), then changing the tracking in increments of 1120 or 1/200 em as well.

Many programs provide the designer with unique capabilities for the manipulation and distortion of typographic forms. Lines of type can be joined to circular, oval, or irregular baselines (Fig. **31**); letterforms can be stretched and distorted in numerous ways (Fig. **32**). Page-design programs compose elements on a page in layers, so elements can be overlapped and layered in space (Fig. **33**). These electronic page-design capabilities are a mixed blessing, for though they can expand the creative range of typography, they can also produce awkward spatial arrangements and typographic forms that are hard to read.

DISTORT TYPE
DISTORT TYPE
DISTORT TYPE
DISTORT TYPE

32.
The bottom letterforms have been stretched excessively, causing the optical relationships to become distorted. The crossbar of the *T* has become too thick; the *S* and *O* extend too far above and below the baseline.

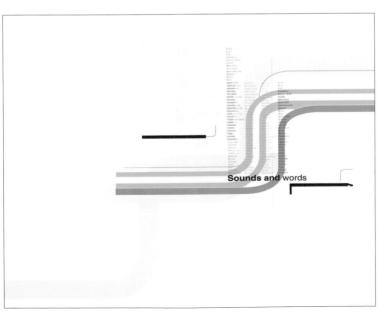

33.

33.
In contrast to the two-dimensional plane of traditional typographic technology, computer software permits the layering of information in space. (Designer: Oak Suwanphanich)

Each major typographic process has its own place in the evolution of technology. Increased efficiency, control, flexibility, and the design of letterforms have been affected by continuous research and innovation. The nature of the typographic image has been changed as well (Fig. **34**). The microphotographs by Mike Cody demonstrate the differences. Letterpress printing of metal type impressed the letterform into the fibers of the paper. Phototype, usually printed by offset lithography, provides a precise image with a comparatively smooth contour. As the micro-photographic enlargement shows, digital type evidences the stepped contour caused by the digitization of the image into discrete elements.

In the most advanced digital-typesetting systems, the discrete elements are so small that they become indiscernible to the naked eye.

Technology develops rapidly, and designers must work to keep abreast of innovations that influence the design process and the typographic image. Designers should view typographers as partners in the design process, for their specialized knowledge of the typesetting system and its capabilities, along with an understanding of typographic refinements, can help the designer achieve the desired quality of typographic communication.

34.
Microphotographic enlargements of letterforms.

Metal type on newsprint

Metal type on coated paper

Phototype

Digital-photo type

As more professional designers become involved in Web site design, the need to preserve typographic integrity in this environment and other interaction design environments is of paramount concern. Marshall McLuhan's "Global Village" has indeed become a reality with nearly 2,000,000,000 billion worldwide users online compared to 16 million in 1995.

Typographic concerns for printed communications are shared by online environments. However, designing with type on-screen poses special challenges, and attempts by designers to simply mimic the appearance of the printed page is a mistake. This chapter discusses the relationship of typography and screen environments, including legibility factors, visual heirarchy, and structuring type on electronic pages.

Rendering type on screen

1.

1.
Digital letterforms have decreasing resolution as the number of pixels is reduced.

The Internet provides a challenging environment for good typography, especially with text sizes. Its problems are inherent in all on-screen font displays, whether designing typography for a laptop, digital notebook, cell-phone display, interactive kiosk, or Web site. When designing on a computer screen – even when the final production will take another form, such as offset printing – the same legibility issues apply to on-screen type. Screen fonts are bitmaps, which are digitized images made up of tiny dots.

To render an outline letterform stored as a Bézier curve on a computer screen, it must be rasterized, or converted into tiny dots called pixels, which is short for picture elements. The relatively low resolution of many contemporary computer screens, which typically have a bitmap matrix of 72 or 96 pixels per inch, cannot display the subtle nuances of a beautifully designed font. When a type's outline is rendered on a screen, details such as stroke weight, subtle curves, and serif detail are reduced to a coarse approximation of the refined forms found in the original design. This occurs because curved and diagonal edges rendered as pixels on a raster-scan display have a jagged stair-step quality, called "the jaggies." The more pixels used to generate the letterform, the higher the resolution (Fig. **1**). When small type appears on-screen with too few pixels to accurately display the subtle forms of the letter, a catastrophic decrease in legibility can occur (Fig. **2**).

2.

3.

4.

5.

2.
This enlargement of an *a*, displayed on a computer screen at a five-pixel height, shows the resulting distortion.
3.
Enlargement of a screen display of an *a* shows "the jaggies" caused by pixels.
4.
Anti-aliasing smooths out the hard, stair-stepped diagonal and curved edges. (Designer: Matt Woolman)

5.
An enlarged antialiased letter *a* demonstrates how colors blend to achieve a smoother look at smaller sizes.

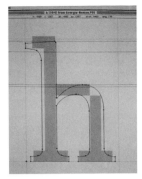

7.

8.

Satisfactory on-screen typographic display blends many factors. These include font enhancement methods such as anti-aliasing, hinting, the use of pixel fonts, and capturing type as image. Computer operating systems and a user's choice of Web browser also play vital roles. These aspects must be considered to achieve optimum typographic outcomes on screen. Operating systems and a user's choice of Web browser also play vital roles. These aspects must be considered to achieve optimum typographic outcomes on screen.

Anti-aliasing

This technique is used to replace the jagged stair-step edges (Fig. **3**) created by pixels with an illusion of the smooth curves found in well-designed typefaces. Pixels around the edges of curved or angled letterforms are rendered in an intermediate tone or color. These pixels are displayed in a blend of the type color and the background color, resulting in an appearance of smoother, more refined letterforms (Fig. **4**). The drawbacks of antialiased type are that the smaller type gets, the fuzzier it appears, which can significantly degrade the original design of the typeface (Fig. **5**).

Hinting

A major factor influencing the legibility of on-screen type is resolution. Where fewer pixels are available to describe letters, resolution decreases. To compensate for this problem, type designers reshape the outlines of characters – a process called "hinting" – to create the best possible image at various point sizes. Hints alter the actual outlines of letters by selectively activating pixels, thus improving the legibility of letters on the screen and from low-resolution output devices. An *unhinted* typeface will typically instruct the computer to turn on a pixel if more than half of its area is covered by the letterform. A *hinted* typeface has the pixels activated to display each letter adjusted to more accurately display it at various sizes (Fig. **6**). Hinting information is built into the software that generates the typeface on the screen and automatically occurs when the type is displayed on the screen.

Two widely used on-screen typefaces were specifically created for use as Web-page text. These are Verdana and Georgia (Fig. **7**), designed by Matthew Carter and hinted by Thomas Rickner. Most digital typefaces are designed as outline fonts that are used to generate bitmapped screen fonts. Verdana and Georgia were first designed as bitmaps of pixels (Fig. **8**), *then* they were translated into outline fonts. As a result, they have better on-screen fidelity than most typefaces originally designed for high-resolution output.

7.
Verdana (left) and Georgia (right) are shown at 9-, 14-, 24-, and 36-point on-screen sizes. Hinting improves legibility by adjusting the design for each size. Note that the 9-point type is bitmapped, while the computer applied antialiasing to the larger sizes. (Font designer: Matthew Carter, hinted by Thomas Rickner)

8.
This screen photograph shows a text-size Georgia *h* as a bitmapped letterform and as an outline letterform. (Designer and photographer: Matthew Carter)

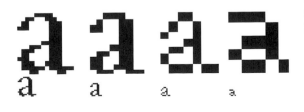

36 point   24 point   18 point   12 point

6.
Four sizes of a hinted letter *a* are shown enlarged and at on-screen reproduction sizes. (Designer: Matt Woolman)

Pixel fonts

These are typefaces specifically designed as bitmapped type. These are designed to the pixel; for example, the characters in Emperor 15 (Fig. **9**) are exactly 15 pixels high. On a 72-dpi screen, these will be the same height as a 15-point typeface, since there are also 72 points in an inch. On a 96-dpi screen, however, a 15-pixel tall bitmap font will appear smaller, about the size of 11-point type. Pixel fonts can degrade when used at larger or smaller sizes than the size for which they are intended. Each of the specimens shown will appear more or less legible at different sizes (Fig. **10**). On screen, care must be taken to scale type for optimum legibility. Pixel fonts are especially useful for very small on-screen text, as they can be designed to maximize legibility when pixellated. The distinctive appearance of these fonts has led to their occasional use as display fonts because their character is expressive of computer technology (Fig. **11**).

Type as image

Type, especially display type, is often converted to a picture file (for example, a GIF), and downloaded as an image on a Web site. The benefits are fidelity to the designer's intent and compatibility with almost all Web-browser software. Since images require more file size than plain text, this slows the downloading of the Web page. If a large number of typographic elements are downloaded as images, this further increases the time required for a browser to display the Web page. Type downloaded as an image is fixed in size and cannot be selected or copied as text. It cannot be scaled or changed in size. Revisions are difficult, because an image, rather than the words in running text, must be revised. When the design of a Web site is changed or updated, each text treated as an image has to be revised individually. Generating type as image in Photoshop provides preset anti-alias settings that enable designers to fine tune typographic images for improved legibility.

9.

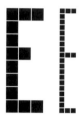

Emperor 8
Emperor 10
Emperor 15
Emperor 19

10.

11.

9.
Emperor is a pixel font with a different design for display at different point sizes, with each pixel equaling one point. Emperor 19, for example, is nineteen pixels tall. (Designer: Zuzana Licko)

10.
Despite their inherent simplicity, abundant variations of pixel fonts exist, each with its own expressive potential.

11.
At a display size, the pixel font used on the welcome page of this portfolio Web site serves as an index for technology and the designer's emphasis on Web design. It also provides a distinct graphic texture on the page. (Designer: Austin Laverty)

history history history
history history history
history history history
history history history
history history history

Content

Because type is viewed as well as read on screen, it is always important to consider the scope and nature of the content. By virtue of shape and proportion, letters possess personalities, attitudes, and emotive qualities that may offer a conceptual fit. Typefaces can also allude to specific time periods, environments, and social and political milieus. Visual distinctions between typefaces are often very subtle and not easily identified. A particular typeface may "feel" right or seem to reveal just the right mood because of a very subtle characteristic such as a unique serif, a peculiar character, or a shape that beckons to another time and place (Fig. **12**).

Some serif typefaces appear dignified, serious, and elegant. Sans serif typefaces appear more informal, and may be associated with simplicity and modernity. Typefaces possessing unusual visual attributes such as odd proportions, angularity, roundness, narrowness, or heaviness can be exploited for their specific communication value.

Simplicity:

Typefaces possessing elemental shapes translate more effectively into the domain of pixels than do typefaces with ornamental and adorned shapes, or typefaces with extreme stroke-to-stroke contrasts (Fig. **13**).

For many years, due to differences in computer operating systems and browsers, Web designers were limited to the selection of default typefaces installed in computer operating systems. Also, they have fought with the inability to consistently control the way type specified for their Web sites is viewed by users on their computers. Users could set their own browser preferences, enabling them to select typefaces, type sizes, font smoothing, colors, and how to view images. The inconsistent rendering of type across platforms and browsers remains a problem, but new technologies have emerged that enable designers to link any number of fonts to their Web pages, thus ensuring that users view pages as intended by the designer.

The introduction of the @font-face feature, for example, allows designers to link any number of fonts from a third-party URL to different browsers. Users can be served designer-selected fonts on their local computer without relying on the limited offerings of their font library. These URL services are working with Web font designers to develop new typefaces and revivals at a quickening pace.

As Web designers gain access to a greater percentage of the world's font libraries, the need to understand typography from historical, technological, and communicative perspectives is critical.

Given the limitations of rendering type on screen, the choice of typeface will either help or hinder legibility. The most readable typefaces exhibit formal characteristics that distinguish them as timeless specimens capable of serving any communicative need. The type families shown in Chapter Twelve, "Type Specimens," display these universal qualities. When considering typefaces for use on the Web or for other on-screen applications, the following guidelines will help in their selection.

12.
Typefaces can visually signify the essence of the content or the meaning of the words they represent. Expressions range from subtle to obvious. The word *history,* set in different typefaces reveals subtle visual inflections.

13.
Simple, bold, and direct, this splash page achieves its purpose without relying on visual decorative devices. A clear hierarchy is achieved by establishing information zones. (Design: Georgiy Kuznetsov)

143

Arial	City	Cheltenham
DIN	Boton	Garamond
Franklin Gothic	Memphis	Georgia
Futura	Officina Serif	Lucida
Rotis Sans	Rockwell	Minion
Trade Gothic	Serifa	Palatino

15.

Many excellent typefaces are suitable for legible screen display. The specimens shown to the left exhibit the formal clarity, simplicity, and proportions required of any typeface befitting for use on digital screens. These antialiased specimens are shown in medium or bold weights at 72 dpi.

Intricate forms lose detail when translated. Elaborate typefaces may gain in legibility when presented at larger sizes, but this gain in visual fidelity may not compensate for how they can potentially detract from the content and message. If used, they must be employed as part of a strategic communicative plan. Many typefaces have simple yet distinctive letterform shapes that render well on screens of various resolutions.

Sans serif and serif typefaces

Because sans serif typefaces are generally more simple in form than serif typefaces and scripts, they achieve a clearer visual presence on the Web. On screen, very small serifs are described by an inordinate number of pixels relative to the rest of the letterform. Comparisons between sans serif typefaces must be made by the designer to ensure that selections are suitable to the content. Usually, a well-proportioned sans serif typeface possesses a medium stroke weight and a balanced ratio of form to counterform. Slightly condensed faces afford more characters per line and thus utilize less

space on the page. Designers may safely select traditional workhorses such as Helvetica, Univers, and Futura, or typefaces embracing similar design characteristics.These classic typefaces still appear fresh when well-spaced and provided with sufficient scale contrast. Sans serif fonts with personality can be equally effective for Web publishing. These include DIN, Franklin Gothic, Gill Sans, Lucida Sans, Meta, and Rotis Sans to name but a few.

When serif typefaces are used, they are best selected on the basis of their legibility on screen at small sizes (Fig. **14**). In the serif category, slab serif fonts provide more legibility than Old Style, Transitional, or Modern typefaces. Typefaces such as Memphis, Rockwell, and Serifa possess moderate contrast between strokes, and blocky serifs that translate well into pixels. All considered typefaces should be tested by comparing their relative legibility on screen at various sizes. Typefaces endowed with sturdy serifs and moderate stroke contrasts hold up best to pixelation on screen (Fig. **14**).

14.

Compare these serif type examples for legibility at various sizes. As type gets smaller on screen, it is described by fewer pixels, which decreases legibility. The specimens shown are antialiased at a resolution of 72 dpi.

Old Style
Old Style
Old Style
Old Style

Transitional
Transitional
Transitional
Transitional

Modern
Modern
Modern
Modern

Slab Serif
Slab Serif
Slab Serif
Slab Serif

16.
While a beloved classic, the typeface Bodoni possesses hairline serifs and an extreme contrast between thin and thick strokes. The antialiased letterform *T*, descending in size from large to small, illustrates how letterforms break down at a screen resolution of 72 dpi.

Scale

At medium resolution, type scaled to larger sizes benefits by the description of more pixels (Fig. **16**). More pixels reveal subtle contours of typographic form and detail. Sufficient contrast in the size of typographic elements should exist in an effort to achieve a lively visual hierarchy. Larger type elements, in relationship to smaller elements not only create drama; they also provide units of information that establish emphasis on the page. The screen environment is forgiving of text scaled to larger sizes. Depending on the size of the screen and resolution, 12- to 16-point type serving as text copy can appear proportionally correct, and not visually overpowering. However, neighboring text units should be sufficiently scaled to maintain contrast.

Combining typefaces

With rare exception, effective Web pages utilize no more than two or three different typefaces. Using more than this number compromises hierarchical clarity. The most important consideration for selecting multiple typefaces is contrast, and variations in contrast are abundant: serif/sans serif, Roman/script, bold/light, thick/thin, simple/complex, and functional/decorative. Plenty of contrast between typefaces ensures that each will effectively fulfill its task. Effective contrasts can also be achieved when using different typefaces within the same family, or using all capital letters in relationship to capitals and lowercase. The process of selecting typefaces is one of comparing several combinations on screen until the best possibilities emerge (Fig. **17**).

17.
Working with a type selection matrix can be an effective and time-saving method for selecting typeface combinations. Contrast between paired typefaces is the most important principle to consider.

	Futura	Garamond	Meta	Rotis Sans	Serifa	Univers
Futura	Futura **Futura**	Garamond **Futura**	Meta **Futura**	Rotis Sans **Futura**	Serifa **Futura**	Univers **Futura**
Garamond	Futura **Garamond**	Garamond **Garamond**	Meta **Garamond**	Rotis Sans **Garamond**	Serifa **Garamond**	Univers **Garamond**
Meta	Futura **Meta**	Garamond **Meta**	Meta **Meta**	Rotis Sans **Meta**	Serifa **Meta**	Univers **Meta**
Rotis Sans	Futura **Rotis Sans**	Garamond **Rotis Sans**	Meta **Rotis Sans**	Rotis Sans **Rotis Sans**	Serifa **Rotis Sans**	Univers **Rotis Sans**
Serifa	Futura **Serifa**	Garamond **Serifa**	Meta **Serifa**	Rotis Sans **Serifa**	Serifa **Serifa**	Univers **Serifa**
Univers	Futura **Univers**	Garamond **Univers**	Meta **Univers**	Rotis Sans **Univers**	Serifa **Univers**	Univers **Univers**

17.

Legibility factors
for on-screen typography

Making type legible on screen requires the utmost attention to how type is translated into pixels and how it works spatially on the page. It also requires paying attention to typographic syntax: the connecting of typographic signs to form words and sentences on the electronic page. Cohesive and readable pages establish a visual gestalt through typographic space and visual hierarchy.

Capital and lowercase letters
As in print, using only capital letters for extensive text settings severely slows reading. Using capital and lowercase letters provides rhythmic word sequences and characteristic word images that promote readability. However, use of all capitals in heads or small amounts of text can effectively be used to create emphasis and visual elegance when sensitively spaced. (Fig. **18**). When displaying text with all capital letters on screen, a minimum tracking value of 110–120% is recommended.

Interletter and interword spacing
Especially at smaller sizes, interletter spacing should be increased to compensate for the spread of antialiased type and the illumination of the screen. Otherwise, pixels from one letterform appear to visually "flood" into the next, causing overly tight interletter spacing (Fig. **19**). Interword spacing should be proportionally adjusted to interletter spacing so that, as in print, letters flow rhythmically and gracefully into words, and words into lines. Essentially, typographic elements living on a Web page require slightly more spatial separation than do those abiding on the printed page.

Line length and interline spacing
Line lengths on the display are best viewed and perceived when viewed at a glance. Readers scan text in chunks, establishing fixation points throughout paragraphs. 45–65 characters per line provide an optimum number of characters for ease of visual scanning (Fig. **20**).

18.

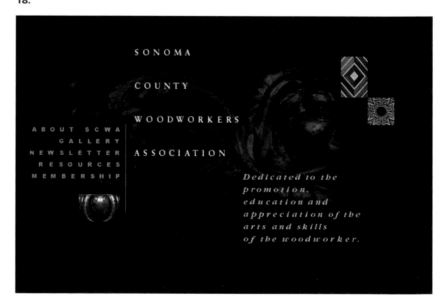

19.

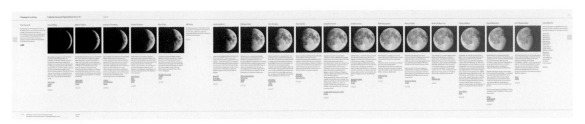

22.
This landscape page from the Web site *Thinking for a Living,* promotes readability by keeping paragraphs short and succinct, and by creating a colorful narrative of the phases of the moon. (Designers: Duane King, Ian Coyle, Shane Bzdok, Frank Chimero.)

Hesign was established in Berlin,Germany in 2002. In 2005, the branch company in Shanghai was established, and the other branch in Hang zhou was set up in 2008. In addition to graphic design, branding, art and design book publishing, they also organize art and cultural activities.

1
2
3
4
5

home
back

20.

The whole duty of typography, as with calligraphy, is to communicate to the imagination, without loss by the way, the thought or image intended to be communicated by the author. And the whole duty of beautiful typography is not to substitute for the beauty or interest of the thing thought and intended

The whole duty of typography, as with calligraphy, is to communicate to the imagination, without loss by the way, the thought or image intended to be communicated by the author. And the whole duty of beautiful typography is not to substitute for the beauty or interest of the thing thought and intended

The whole duty of typography, as with calligraphy, is to communicate to the imagination, without loss by the way, the thought or image intended to be communicated by the author. And the whole duty of beautiful typography is not to substitute for the beauty or interest of the thing thought and intended

The whole duty of typography, as with calligraphy, is to communicate to the imagination, without loss by the way, the thought or image intended to be

21.
Compare these three text settings. Lines of type without sufficient leading inhibit onscreen legibility.

Generous interline spacing is recommended for displaying text on a computer display. A reasonable guideline suggests that the interline spacing equal 140 percent of the type size. Measured in pixels, for example, type with an overall height of 10 pixels will require a measure of 14 pixels from the baseline of one line of type to the baseline of the next. Type on screen is measured in pixels, ems, xx-small, and the relative percentages of surrounding text. Ultimately, interline spacing must rely on optical judgement and an experienced designer's eye. As text settings get smaller on screen, they require more interline spacing for improved legibility (Fig. **21**).

Weight and width
When letterforms appear too heavy or too light on screen, they lose the visual balance between form and counterform, a critical relationship that enables readers to distinguish one letter from another. This principle holds true also for extremely condensed and expanded letterforms.

Alignment
Flush-left, ragged-right text alignments are easiest to read, whether implemented in print or in electronic display applications. Right side line terminations quickly and imperceptibly cue the reader from one line to the next. Other text structures (flush-right, ragged-left; centered; justified; and thought unit typography) may serve a viable purpose, but these alignments do suffer a loss in legibility.

Units of text
On screen, short paragraphs and the introduction of small units of text invite readers into the content. Text can be structured with the goal of bringing clarity and understanding to ideas, and preventing the monotony of vast seas of text, which severely inhibits the reading process (Fig. **22**).

There are many ways in which Web sites can be built, and designers often rely upon specific methods and tools that work best for their needs. However, designing Web sites generally involves three layers of functionality: structure, presentation, and behavior. HTML controls the display structure of content, CSS controls the presentation of the content, and JavaScript, a scripting language that is usually embedded directly into HTML pages, provides Web sites with interactive capabilities, thus controlling a Web site's interactive behavior. These three computer languages provide capabilities for controlling the layout of content, typographical specifications such as font, size, and spacing selection, and interactivity on the Web.

HTML

(Hyper Text Markup Language) is a page description or display language that utilizes formatting tags (coded programming instructions) to control page composition. The basic HTML environment is the browser window itself, where text is formatted to stream into the browser window from left to right and top to bottom. Alignment tags enable designers to control text alignment within the window frame. An HTML designer can only specify elemental text settings and an approximate size measure. Specific typographical specifications such as tracking, linespacing (sometimes called line height by Web designers), and wordspacing are usually arbitrary. HTML is governed by two basic formats:

1. HTML tables provide more specific page structuring by dividing the browser window into a number of fixed blocks (Fig. **23**). In Web design, this is the equivalent of the typographic grid used in print (Fig. **24**). Consisting of rows and columns, tables provide modular environments for organizing and placing page elements, including text, images, and typographic support elements such as ruled lines and shapes. Unlike the traditional grid, however, the size and proportion of modules in HTML tables are determined by the the content itself; each time an element is added or changed, the entire structure changes.

23.

24.

23.
A traditional typographic grid governs the placement of text and other visual elements. Modularity enables the flow of elements over one or several grid lines, bringing proportional consistency throughout a printed, exhibition, or environmental design application.

24.
HTML tables consist of rows and columns divided by borders. Designers assign various content to these spaces for an ordered hierarchy. These spatial units – whose size corresponds to the size of the content elements – remain unaffected by the scale of the browser window, enabling users to experience a layout as intended by the designer.

2. HTML frames enable designers to divide the browser window into independent, autonomous zones. Frames can behave as separate browser windows on the page, and they can be assigned different functions: one may be fixed while another scrolls. Designers often use them to separate navigational control panels from the page content they control.

CSS, JavaScript, and JavaScript Libraries
CSS (Cascading Style Sheets) give designers even more control over the presentation of content. Using them, designers have the ability to flexibly control page composition, to specify exact type sizes, weights, and styles, and to manipulate interletter, interline, and interword spacing. As discussed in Chapter Four, these aspects are major determinates of typographic legibility. CSS come a step closer to giving designers the control provided by other page design software such as QuarkXpress and InDesign. Style sheets can be embedded within a single HTML file, or externally. Unfortunately, style sheets fail for those users who have outdated browsers, or who have set contradictory preferences in their browsers.

JavaScript is a scripting language widely used to create dynamic, interactive Web pages. It is maintained as source code embedded into HTML pages, which are otherwise static rather than dynamic. Web developers use JavaScript to validate form input, create image rollovers, and the ubiquitous pop-up windows, among other things.

Supporting JavaScript are cross-browser JavaScript Libraries, collections of JavaScript code that emphasize interaction between JavaScript and HTML. A popular example is JQuery, a fast and concise Library containing a store of commonly used functions, shortcuts and animation effects that allow designers to create interactive interfaces for web applications. Other Libraries include ProtoType, YUI Library (Yahoo), Moo Tools, Scriptaculous, and Dojo.

The Web site case studies presented on pages 152–160 utilize some or all of these programming tools.

Operating systems (OS) and Web browsers
People often view Web pages set in typefaces that are not installed on their computers. This results in a carefully designed Web page being rendered on many viewers' screens in different fonts than those used in the original design. Different set widths and letterform designs can totally change the appearance of the page layout and type. Fonts can be imbedded into Web pages, but often these are not downloaded and displayed. Some Web-design software permits a designer to list a string of commonly available fonts (for example, Georgia, Times New Roman, Times) that are frequently installed on computers. The computer will set the text in the first available font from the list.

Accurate on-screen type display largely depends upon the operating system in use and a user's choice of Web browser. Every Web browser features a layout engine that decides how it will render type on the screen. These engines determine how Web designs are generated and visualized. Most browsers, however, defer to the text-rendering engines of the operating system to determine the look of the typography. What this means for the Web designer is that browser/OS combinations must be checked to ensure that particular fonts are accurately rendered on the Web.

On a Macintosh computer, each and every Web browser utilizes Core Text, the system default text-rendering engine, along with OS font-smoothing (antialiasing) settings. Browser preferences do not affect the way type is antialiased. Therefore, the appearance of typography on a Macintosh remains the same regardless of the browser in use. This, however, is not true of every OS/browser combination.

Site structure and architecture

The scope of this chapter prevents an in-depth investigation into the complex realm of Web site architecture and navigation. It remains important to emphasize, however, that the ability to successfully travel through a site depends on navigational hierarchies. Users must be assured that they can move efficiently about a site's pages and get where they need to go without getting lost in the process.

Web sites consist of a series of pages connected topologically by hyperlinks. The number and pattern of these links define the site's information architecture. Two fundamental structural schemas exist: 1) networks or webs, which are a collection of pages connected by a fixed number of hyperlinks, and 2) trees, which organize information into a descending hierarchy. The majority of Web sites combine these two models, enabling users to navigate the site's pages from many different directions (Figs. **25–27**). The most effective Web sites limit the number of links, and organize them into a logical site hierarchy.

Page structure and spatial organization

The possibilities for designing Web pages and controlling their appearance continues to improve. Compared to the infancy of Web design, designers enjoy many technological advances that contribute to improved legibility, page organization, visual hierarchy, aesthetics, efficiency, consistency, and adaptability to change. The following considerations enable designers to optimize typographic functions and aesthetics on electronic pages.

Designing grids for any application requires a thoughtful analysis of content, but designing grids for Web applications presents additional challenges. Unlike the fixed media size in print, where type and other elements are scaled and positioned by the designer in relation to established proportions, designing for the Web is challenged by the variable nature of OS platforms, screen size, and the actual devices used for viewing sites. In addition, users have the option of changing font sizes, resizing browser windows, and altering screen resolution. With this in mind, effective grid systems for the Web adapt to the user's potential changes, and retain the original proportions of the page.

Layout grids for Web pages can exist as relative or absolute structures. Relative grid structures, also known as adaptive structures, are based on the use of percentages or relative measurements, while the values of absolute or fixed grids are measured in pixels (Fig. **28**).

25.
Web sites consist of pages connected by hyperlinks. These site configurations determine a site's architecture. The most flexible but unrefined site is a collection of pages connected arbitrarily by hyperlinks.

26.
A tree structure organizes information into a family tree: parents beget children, children beget grandchildren, and grandchildren beget great-grandchildren. Aberrant connections between these branches revert a tree structure to a network structure.

27.
Optimally, a site combines a network with a tree, allowing a limited number of hyperlinks to move through the structure. These hyperlinks aid in the site's hierarchical structure.

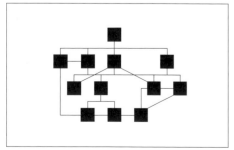

25.

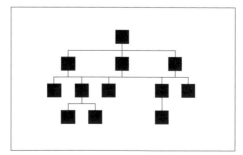

26.

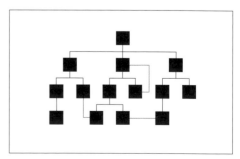

27.

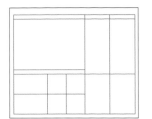
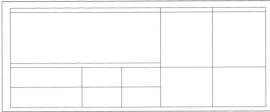

28.

The proportions of a page are altered in the process of changing the dimensions of the browser window.

28.

Adaptive grid systems lend themselves well to Web page design since they are independent of specific units of measurement. These systems are constructed from ratios such as 1:3, 2:1, 3:2, or some percentage of parts to a greater whole (Fig. **29**). This "whole" may be the entire browser window, and when the size of the window is changed, the proportional properties of the grid also changes. More complex ratios, such as the golden section (1:1.618) are referred to as irrational ratios (see Chapter Five, *The Typographic Grid*). Flexible width designs scale to the user's resolution, and therefore to the browser window. The downside is that when stretched, flexible pages can look proportionally distorted.

Fixed grid systems provide the designer with more control over the typographical appearance of the site on different browsers (unless, of course the user tinkers with browser settings). With a growth in CSS-based sites, there has been an increase in the use of column-based fixed grids, ranging from two to many columns, depending on the complexity of the content. These grid systems provide a more stable structure than table-based HTML grids, and more typographic flexibility while retaining structure, consistency, and legibility (Fig. **29**).

Regardless of the kind of grid system used, the designer's task is to organize elements into a clear and easily perceived visual hierarchy, a requirement for successful page and site navigation. Without hierarchy, users are easily frustrated and left to trial and error. Visual hierarchy refers to the relationships of each part to other parts and to the whole. An effective hierarchy is achieved by carefully connecting and/or separating elements in space. As discussed in Chapter Four, when elements are separated by means of size, weight, color, and spatial interval, they achieve independence and emphasis.

Similar to film titles that welcome viewers and set the stage for what they will experience, Web sites begin with an opening page, sometimes referred to as a home or splash page. On this initial page, designers must set the stage for the rest of the site by laying out clear hierarchical zones for navigation and content.

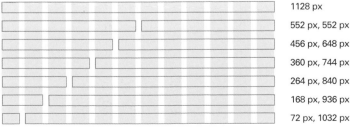

1128 px

552 px, 552 px

456 px, 648 px

360 px, 744 px

264 px, 840 px

168 px, 936 px

72 px, 1032 px

29.

In light of new programming technologies, column-based grid layouts are gaining ubiquitous use; they are easy to create, fairly stable across multiple platforms, and they do not degrade to the same degree as table-based layouts. These grids are measured and designed in screen pixels.

Museum of Design Zurich
http://www.museum-gestaltung.ch

The case studies on the following pages reflect the typographical, navigational, and aesthetic qualities associated with effective Web page design and other digital, on-screen applications. These attributes include simplicity, typographic legibility, clear navigation, and adaptability to change.

Design: Andreas Kohli and Benjamin Schudel

Through its collection and programs, this museum chronicles the aspirations and products of design in Switzerland and around the world. Design categories include product, interior, environmental, and graphic design.

The site's home page features an animated grid of square tiles. The lower left tile presents the name of the museum in white Helvetica on a red background. Current exhibition venues are identified in adjacent squares upon a kinetic photographic montage (Fig. **30**).

As the cursor passes over these venue squares, their backgrounds are replaced by squares of solid color that slide together from the top and bottom of the grid. Clicking on these venues links to pages containing additional information. Filling the entire grid are representative images that continually refresh with new images (Fig. **31**).

A menu at the top of each page provides the primary avenue for searching the site. Links include Exhibitions, Collections, Education, eMuseum, Membership, Shop, and Information (Fig. **32**).

30.

31.

32.

33.

Clicking *Exhibitions* (Fig. **33**) links to a page containing submenus that list current and future exhibitions. These link further to descriptive information about each of the exhibitions.

Clicking on *Collections* takes visitors to a page containing background information and links to the museum's collections, including the design, graphics, posters, and applied arts categories. At the top of each of these pages, a band of representational images can be viewed by scrolling through them. Clicking on an image zooms it forward for a clearer look (Fig. **34**).

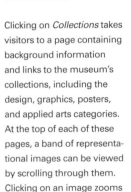

This is an altogether flexible interface, where visitors learn about the museum and retrieve information about events from a varied number of directions. Users can freely navigate between pages to learn about the museum or find the information they are seeking.

This kinetic and resonant site provides users with a lively, memorable experience and a virtual mini-tour of the museum and its collections.

34.

Design of Web site: Students of the course *Schmid Today* under Victor Malsy and Philipp Teufel, Professors at Fachhochschule, Duesseldorf

The *Helmut Schmid: Design is Attitude* site (Fig. **35**) reflects the results of the "Schmid Today" project, a three-year research project about the designer and typographer Helmut Schmid. The results of the project are an international exhibition; a book, *Design is Attitude;* a project documentary; and this Web site. Schmid's prodigious work and career spans forty years.

After training as a typesetter, Schmid (b. 1942 in Ferlach, Austria) studied at the Schule fur Gestaltung in Basel (Basel School of Design) under Emil Ruder, Kurt Hauert, and Robert Buchler.

The Web site reflects the essence of Schmid's typographical work: an integration of clarity, functionality, and visual poetry. The Dutch designer Wim Crouwel has said, "Helmut Schmid... his typography has rhythm... it is created by the eye and resembles a musical score."

After selecting a preferred language on the splash page, visitors enter the home page (Fig. **36**) containing links to five content areas: on Helmut Schmid (Fig. **37**), the archive, the exhibition, the book, and the sponsors.

35.

36.

37.

This Web site is arranged as a simple tree structure, enabling visitors to further select options within subcategories.

After clicking *the archive,* a random thumbnail collection of works from the archive emerges. From a submenu, viewers can select work from more specific categories, including medium, year, client, and collection.

A search engine identifies these selections, enabling visitors to study the works from different perspectives (Fig. **38**). Clicking on specific thumbnails displays a larger image of the subject (Fig. **39**).

Text at the left of the page reveals facts about the object: title, object number, year, medium, format, color, and client. In the case of multi-component designs, such as books, users can scroll through a representative selection of spreads and parts (Figs. **40, 41**).

Clicking *search* enables viewers to scroll through thumbnails of the entire collection (nearly 500 images) presented in chronological order (Fig. **42**).

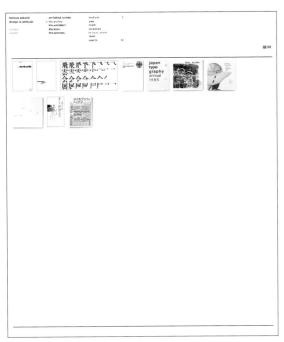

38.

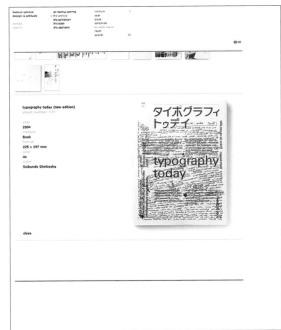

39.

40.

41.

42.

Bauhaus-Archive / Museum of Design Berlin
http://www.bauhaus.de

43.

Design: Veronika Bongartz, Marketing Factory

The aura and spirit of the Bauhaus is captured in the form and structure of the Bauhaus-Archive Website. It is powered by an open source Content Management System (CMS). CMS enables designers to develop Web sites without the technical skill required by HTML programming. These systems are becoming increasingly popular, and when well-matched to content, they yield effective and elegant results.

From this site's home page (Fig. **43**), viewers may select content areas from a visual/verbal menu. As the cursor rolls over the series of square images, they are highlighted by color frames to identify the following catagories: *bauhaus-archive, building, museum, bauhaus 1919–33, focus, news, bauhaus shop, and information.*

Upon clicking any one of these categories, visitors enter selected content pages where thick vertical and thin horizontal rules serve visually as arrows to aid in site navigation. The main menu appears at the top of pages, and as the cursor moves over content headings, the horizontal rule changes in color and lengthens to underscore the heading (Fig. **44**).

Upon clicking a link, visitors enter a new page and the vertical rule shifts to the assigned color to match the horizontal rule.

Near the top of the vertical rules, submenus appear for each content area. As submenu items are selected, small white arrows indicate where visitors are located within the site.

The content management framework selected to structure this site not only complements the site's content, but also provides for legible, flush-left, ragged-right text settings; clean and simple page composition; ease of navigation; and the ability to adapt easily to change. Period photographs and artifacts lend authenticity to the site, and provide viewers with a glimpse of what the Bauhaus-Archive has to offer.

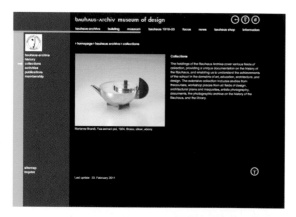

44.

Nicholas Davidson Design
http://www.nicholasdavidson.net

45.

Design: Nicholas Davidson

This bold and direct Web site showcases the work of designer Nicholas Davidson.

The site opens to a page containing a list of design projects set in large, tightly spaced capital letters. Set in Trade Gothic Bold Condensed No. 20, the scale and dense texture of this typographical listing makes it the most dominant element on the page, and its imposing presence invites visitors to explore the site (Fig. **45**).

Clicking on the links opens image panels featuring examples of the projects (Figs. **46, 47**). This causes the remainder of the list to slide down the page, contributing to a resonant, kinetic effect. Clicking on alternate projects opens new panels while closing previous ones. Activating the same link a second time closes a panel.

Clicking anywhere on an open panel slides the current image to the left, revealing the next in the form of a slideshow. Numerical tabs at the top of the panels enable visitors to explore elements of each project in any order whatsoever.

The interactivity of this Web site is appropriately functional, for it gives visitors the freedom to fluidly wander through Davidson's work and to examine its many aspects in detail.

46.

47.

48.

Design: Hesign Design Team

As read on the Web site,
"Hesign was established in
Berlin, Germany in 2002.
In 2005, the branch company
in Shanghai was established,
and the other branch in
Hangzhou was set up in 2008.
In addition to graphic design,
branding, art and design book
publishing, they also organize
art and cultural activities."

The Hesign International Web
site combines whimsical
animated typography with
utter navigational clarity.
Upon entering it, the site's
homepage appears as a
cacophony of indecipherable
abstract forms (Fig. **48**).
Once rolling the cursor over
this configuration, the main
navigational menu emerges,
unraveling as a vertical list
of hyperlinks (Fig. **49**). Each
letter of each word consists of
a different eccentric typeface
that creates a menagerie
of letterforms.

Consisting of a basic tree
structure, users click on any
one of these links to discover
sub-content menus (Fig.
50). Clicking on *Profile,* for
example, takes one to a sub-
menu consisting of numerals
(Fig. **51**). Clicking on different
numerals leads to pages
containing varied aspects of
the firm. Informational text
is set in Courier.

49.

Profile
Blog
Works
Curating
Shop
Contact
Links
Jobs

50.

Hesign was established in Berlin,Germany in 2002. In 2005,
the branch company in Shanghai was established, and the
other branch in Hang zhou was set up in 2008. In addition
to graphic design, branding, art and design book publishing,
they also organize art and cultural activities.

1
2
3
4
5
home
back

Space and Time. Posters by Jianping He

For some years now, Chinese graphic designers have won international acclaim for their
works. The poster is having a new renaissance in China. Emerged has a generation of graphic
designers that sees international poster art with a fresh and unspoiled eye, using these
influences for an own visual language, without plagiarizing or negating the own tradition.

A wide range of individual expressions marks the current Chinese poster. All means of
visual design are being used – from free drawing to digitally altered photography. It seems
that the young Chinese graphic design scene has emphatically reintroduced the emblematic as
an essential aspect of the poster, into public awareness. The Chinese tradition of
scripture, which is especially obligated to the emblematic, might be a root of that.

In his works, Jianping He manages to establish a bridge between Europe and Asia. The
graphic artist studied Visual Communication at the Chinese Academy of Arts in Hangzhou,
continuing his studies at the Academy of Arts in Berlin (from 1997-2001), where he became a
pupil of Prof. Hans-Jürgen Kristhan. Today, he is an artistic assistant at this academy.
Dividing his time between China and Germany, he has rendered outstanding services to making
international graphic design popular in China. With "Life + Design" and "Master +
Students," he has designed and published a series of books which introduce their readers to
the lives, views, and works of artists he admires as role models. The care and the artistic
noblesse of the book's designs do not only give a hint at the level of respect with which
Jianping He sees his subjects. These features also show how much of his talent as a designer of
books, his subtle handling of image and scripture, his feeling for the material.

The posters of Jianping He surprise with their subjects that on the one hand seem
familiar, on the other hand are defamiliarized at the same time. He likes using the human
head as a significant image, employing one of the most popular and also most variable
motives of the 20th century poster. The human head is always the mirror of our identity,
too. This explains the big suggestive force that each of these motives has. Identification
or distance are established at once.
We perceive each and every alteration of the face or the head as an attack on ourselves,
which immediately alerts our attention. In his posters for the Eurasia Language Institute,
Jianping He writes with colorful letters over faces, to evoke connotations of language- and
thought-confusions and the possibilities of their resolution. The faces and heads are
anonymous and individual at the same time. They are eye-catching, but not because of
extravaganza;they appear as ordinary as you and me.

The poster for Amnesty International, made in the year 2000, shows a face resembling Holy
Sebastian, tortured with needles, emerging from darkness. Pain, but also resistance are
expressed and merge into a motive of accusation. Similarly, in his poster for the Human
Rights Day from the same year, the graphic artist uses an arm with a fist, violated by
needles, as a gesture of accusation and protest.

In "Water is Life," the close-up of a face shows huge cracks, dried-up paths, resembling a
torn soil. We ourselves are nature. Jianping He always looks for the immediate connection.
There are no locations outside of our being. We are always affected. The clarity of this
stance is also being expressed by the reflection of current political discourse. The

Like the world around him

1
2
3
4
5
home
back

Like the world around him, Jianping He is a graphic designer
in a state of constant change.
Vivid imagination, strong concepts, high aesthetic standards
and perfect detailing all describe his designs.
Jianping He's art combines East and West, artistry and message
in a unique way.
Kari Piippo Finland, 2007

51.

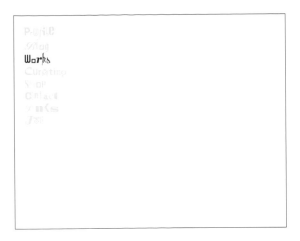

52.

53.

The *Works* link (Fig. **52**) leads to a sub-menu page providing three options (Fig. **53**). Selecting one of these takes users to yet another sub-menu where a wide scope of work is listed and shown by project (Fig. **54**). Except for the featured work, all page elements appear in black and white for a vivid visual environment.

Other links lead to informative content, including the firm's blog, which provides an ongoing narrative about projects, events, and ideas (Fig. **55**).

Clicking *Links* takes visitors to related Web sites where visitors are exposed to animated commentary of the many cultural events and programs sponsored by this multifaceted design and publishing firm.

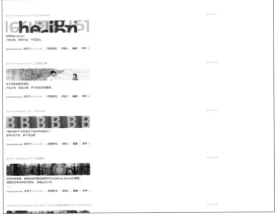

54.

55.

60.   **61.**

Design: Philippe Vendrolini
and Martin Venezky

This Web site introduces
Appetite Engineers, Martin
Venezky's San Francisco–
based graphic design studio,
and also entices visitors
with a tasty and unforgettable
visual treat.

The splash page opens with
a curious array of symbolic
images appearing to orbit
around a central sphere: the
planet saturn (search for
the unknown), a collection of
mischievous cats (curiosity),
a baby (creative innocence),
and a content menu (Fig. **56**).

When clicking on main-menu
links, kaleidoscopic transitions
provide viewer entertainment
and a sense of the studio's
playful creative attitude.
In one transition, a cat leaps
into space to catch a spinning
ball; while in another a
typographic poster spins
into view (Fig. **57**).

The submenu, *This is what
we do,* leads to a selection
of project catagories, and
from there to specific projects
(Fig. **58** and **59**). The screen
remains in constant flux
as visitors navigate the site's
pages (Fig. **60** and **61**).

56.

57.

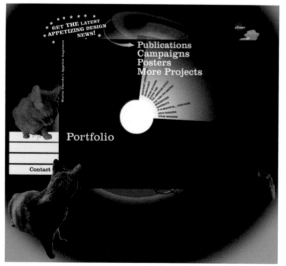

58.

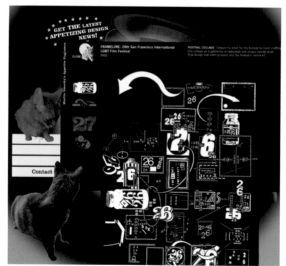

59.

9 Case Studies in Typographic Design

Many of the educational projects in the following chapter represent theoretical and exploratory investigations. They are structured to teach typographic history, theory, spatial concepts, form, and meaning. The goal of typographic education is to prepare young designers for the complexity of applied problem solving. The case studies presented in this chapter describe specific typographic design problems encountered in professional practice. The nature of each problem is analyzed, and the rationale for the solution is discussed.

These eight studies cover a wide range of typographic design problems: integrating type and image on posters, publication designs, environmental typography, branding, Web-site design, and typographic motion-picture titles.

Integrating type and image in poster design

1.

Alignment of the letterspaced type along the angled edges of the stars unifies word and image. (Designer: Jean-Benoît Lévy; photographer: Tom Wedell)

A remarkable integration of type with image is found in posters designed by Jean-Benoît Lévy, who has studios in Basel, Switzerland, and San Francisco, California. Lévy collaborates with photographers; he approaches their images as three-dimensional fields whose space is activated and extended by type. On the last day of class when Lévy was a student, teacher Armin Hofmann told him to place type *in* the photograph rather than *on* the photograph. Lévy says, "From that moment on, I knew what to do." In his inventive designs, words and images become a unified composition.

The large star in a "Happy New Year" poster (Fig. **1**) for the Basel studio AND (Trafic Grafic) conveys a sense of energy and motion through repetition on a diagonal axis. The background transition from orange to blue signifies earth to sky. *Happy* aligns with the two white stars, unifying the type and background. The sky is signified in three ways: symbolic stars; a photograph of clouds; and the lines and dots of a star chart. Subtle symbols of the world's major religions, and small type identifying each religion's deity or founder, date, and number of adherents, add another level of meaning in the bold celebratory message.

Grid structures for graphic designs are often implied, but in a poster (Fig. **2**) for the fashion store Inflagranti, the horizontal and vertical pattern of window blinds superimposed with a double portrait of a fashion model provides a visible structure of the placement of type. The translucency and graded tones of the vertical store name echo the translucent portrait and blended tones of the blinds, further uniting word and image.

The curved forms of watch parts, their shadows, and watch-face numerals were photographed in atmospheric space for a Montres et Bijouterie Bosch watch and jewelry store poster (Fig. **3**). Widely letterspaced type set in arcs reflects the curves in the photograph. Color is used to create harmony, for the yellow, white, and orange letters repeat the photograph's warm tones in contrast to the predominantly gray background. Lévy says the orange dots from the text signify seven planets, with the Sun in the exact center.

1.

2.

Three different sizes and amounts of tracking create variety, while using the same typeface brings unity to the design. (Designer: Jean-Benoît Lévy; photographer: Jean-Pascal Imsand)

3.

The simple geometry and spatial dispersion of the type echos these qualities in the photograph. (Designer: Jean-Benoît Lévy; photographer: Franz Werner)

2.

3.

4.

By making the x-height of the larger words the same height as the smaller words, a strong visual relationship is maintained. (Designer: Jean-Benoît Lévy; photographer: Jean-Pascal Imsand)

5.

Lévy carefully retained enough of the overlapped letters to ensure their legibility. (Designer: Jean-Benoît Lévy; photographer: Alexandre Genoud)

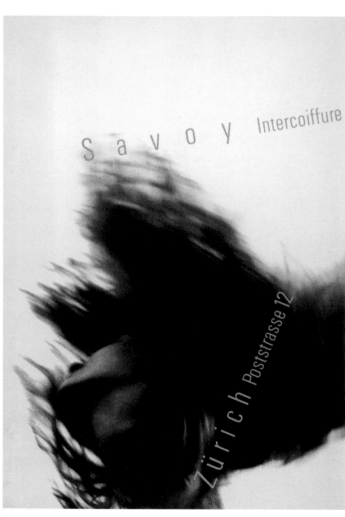

4.

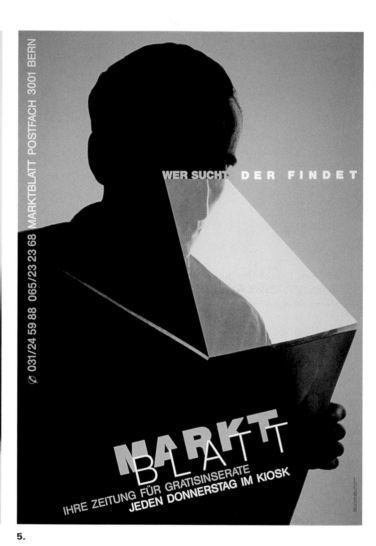

5.

For the Savoy Intercoiffure hair salon poster (Fig. **4**), Lévy used a photograph shot from a low viewpoint of a woman moving her head, causing her hair to fling about in a blurred shape. The photograph was carefully cropped to bleed on the right side and bottom, making a dynamic dark shape against the soft flat background. Two diagonal lines of condensed sans serif type are a sharp contrast to the blurred shape. One line links the top and bottom of the head, while the other links the top of the hair to the edge of the poster. The first word in each line is larger, and the tracking is increased for emphasis.

The *Markt Blatt* is a free newspaper of advertisements in Bern, Switzerland. A sidelit man (Fig. **5**) reads the paper against a warm yellow background. A trapezoid of light becomes a symbol for the process of reading, connecting the reader's eyes with the printed page. Alignment of the typography with the angles of the horizontal and vertical edges of the poster, and the diagonal of the newspaper page creates a structured relationship. By making the type on the photograph yellow and the type on the background white, further integration is achieved. The bold and light type, and overlapping of the two words of the title, produce an arresting visual element.

6.

Across the top, eight rows of modules are filled in with a darker pencil tone to spell the bookstore name in geometric letterforms. The condensed all-capital sans serif type at the bottom of the poster is two modules tall; this unifies with the labyrinth. (Designer and photographer: Jean-Benoît Lévy)

7.

The letters of the bookstore name were executed in outline slab-serif letterforms that are drawn to conform to the horizontal, vertical, and diagonal movements of the labyrinth image. (Designer and photographer: Jean-Benoît Lévy)

6.

7.

In this poster (Fig. **6**) for the Labyrinth bookstore in Basel, the maze or labyrinth appearing on the poster reinforces the store's name. Lévy carefully drew his complex labyrinth in pencil on a modular grid. The soft pencil tones bring warmth to the rigid geometry. This labyrinth can actually be solved by a viewer standing at the poster kiosk.

A photograph of a young man reading a book is superimposed over the labyrinth. "Reading," Lévy says, "is like entering a labyrinth." The organic properties of the human image provide contrast to the stark geometry of the labyrinth, softening and enriching the poster.

In a subsequent poster (Fig. **7**) for the Labyrinth bookstore, Lévy created an image of a three-dimensional labyrinth moving back into space. This compelling image fades back into an out-of-focus, tightly cropped photograph of a reader. These hover in space over the labyrinth; their openness and transparency echo its edges and open channels. A three-dimensional graphics program and Photoshop™ were used to execute this poster. As in Lévy's other posters, a dynamic integration of word and image is achieved through unexpected and original compositional relationships between pictorial and typographic forms.

The U.S. National Park Service Unigrid System

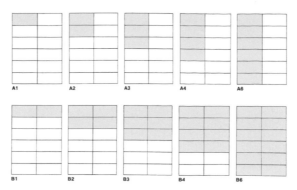

9.
Ten basic publication formats are derived from the Unigrid structure.

The United States National Park Service (NPS) developed the Unigrid System as a design system to unify the design of hundreds of site folders, while bringing harmony and economy to its publications program. Unigrid (Fig. **8**) is based on a sheet 965 by 1270 millimeters (about 16.5 by 23.5 inches), which folds into twelve panels that are 99 by 210 millimeters (about 4 by 8.25 inches). Ten basic formats (Fig. **9**) can be derived from the Unigrid ranging from one-panel leaflets to twelve-panel foldout broadsides. Each side of a folder is treated as a unified graphic surface that is completely unfolded by the user, just as one fully opens a map. The fold lines and the panels they create become background rather than a dominant structure, because the typical folder user quickly unfolds it to its full size; users rarely open a folder panel by panel. These standard formats permit great production economy because paper can be purchased in volume in two flat sizes or in web rolls. Most folders are printed in five of the available formats, further simplifying planning.

Grid modules for the folder formats measure 7 picas wide and 80 points high. Vertical spaces between modules are 1 pica wide; horizontal spaces between modules are 10 points high. Horizontal measurements are always made in picas, while vertical measurements are always made in 10-point units or modules. These spatial intervals provide a structure for organizing type, illustrations, photographs, and maps into an orderly whole.

Helvetica was selected as the type family for the Unigrid System because of "its crisp, clean details and typographic texture that make it aesthetically pleasing and easy to read." It was also determined that Helvetica would strengthen and unify the NPS map series that accompanies the folder program. Other considerations are Helvetica's clearly defined hierarchy of sizes and weights with predictable results, large x-height with good line strength and consistent color, and outstanding printing characteristics. Text type is usually set in 8/10 or 9/10 Helvetica or Helvetica Medium in columns two or three modules wide (15 or 23 picas wide, measuring two or three modules plus spatial intervals between them).

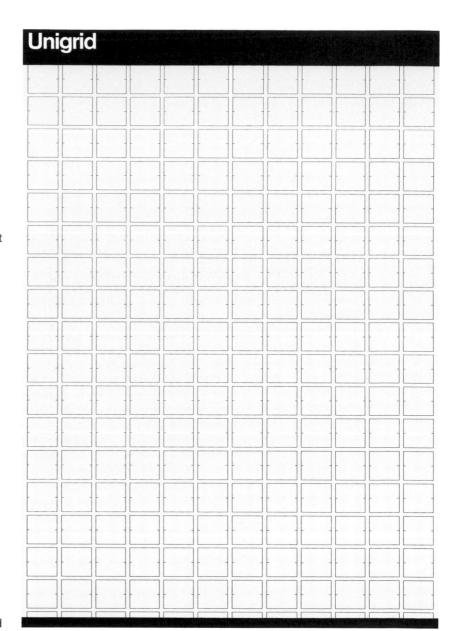

8.
The Unigrid was created by Massimo Vignelli (consulting designer), Vincent Gleason (art director), and Dennis McLaughlin (graphic designer).

10–11.
Copy the Unigrid on the preceding page onto transparent material and place it over these folders to study the underlying structure of the designs.

12.
The black bars and consistent typography on folder covers become a visual identification.

10.

Text type is often justified, and columns are aligned top and bottom to create horizontal movement. Sometimes the last column will run short. One line space, rather than indentations, is used to separate paragraphs.

Captions are set one or two modules wide (7 or 15 picas wide) in 7/7, 7/8, or 8/9 Helvetica Regular or Medium, and may be either roman or italic. This variety of weight, posture, and leading provides flexibility to create a value and texture that complements and contrasts with other typographic and pictorial elements. Captions are set rag-right, and this helps create a strong separation between text and captions, as do contrasts between text and caption textures, weights, and line lengths.

Major display type can be set in 12-, 18-, or 24-point Helvetica Medium and is often positioned 10 points above the related text on a horizontal band of white space, frequently 40 points high, running above the text. The variety of display sizes gives the designer the flexibility needed to create appropriate scale relationships between display type, the size of the folder, image sizes, and density of text type. The margin below the text type is always a spatial interval at least 20 points high.

The cover panels of all folders have a 100-point black band that bleeds at the top and on both sides. Titles reverse from this bar and are set in standard sizes of Helvetica Medium for park names with fewer than twelve letters. When site designation and location appear reversed from the black bar, these are set in 12/14 or 8/9 Helvetica Medium and align on the seventh grid module. Service designations are the same size and align on the tenth grid module. Cover panel type is always positioned 10 points down from the top edge of the band. This horizontal black band with its standardized title type becomes a consistent visual identification device for the National Park Service.

12.

Horizontal movement is accentuated through the placement of the type, the horizontal margins, and internal bars that divide the space into zones of information. These bars are 25 points wide and correspond to the title bar. They may be complementary colors, contrasting colors, or black. One bar is always placed across the bottom of the folder. Display type is sometimes reversed from the bars.

The Unigrid System emphasizes clarity by clearly separating the elements. Type seldom overlaps images, and maps are not obscured by picture inserts or overlaps. Neutral grays and beiges, used to create backgrounds behind text areas or unify groups of images, are part of a standard palette of twenty-four colors, created from four-color process inks and a limited selection of secondary colors. This color palette creates continuity between various park publications.

Planning layouts are created using computer-generated typography, images, map windows, and the master grid sheets. A typesetter with a contract to set National Park Service typography uses electronic page makeup to format and position type, rules, and bars, providing repro-quality output for mechanicals.

Standardized formats and typographic specifications enable National Park Service designers to focus on content and design, rather than developing formats and specifications for each project. The Unigrid System is flexible, permitting unique solutions appropriate to specific messages, while leading to consistent graphic excellence and a unified visual identification.

Massimo Vignelli was the inventor and remains consulting designer for the Unigrid System. The program gained its vitality because the original design team remained intact over the first dozen years, and included Vincent Gleason (chief), Melissa Cronyn, Nicholas Kirilloff, Linda Meyers, Dennis McLaughlin, Phillip Musselwhite, and Mitchell Zetlin.

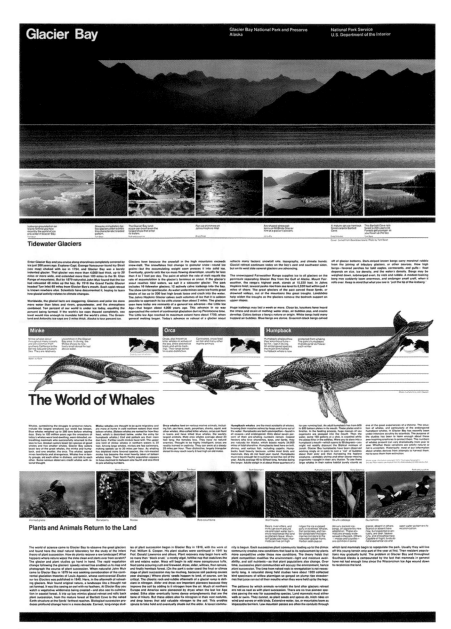

11.

Book Design:
VAS: An Opera in Flatland

13.
On the cover of *VAS,* a system of veins meandering beneath flesh introduces readers to an epic story about the human body. The book's title, bleeding blood red, emerges from a detail of DNA data.

14.
A page showing the typographical (analog) structure of the book, a "double helix" armature consisting of five vertical hairlines.

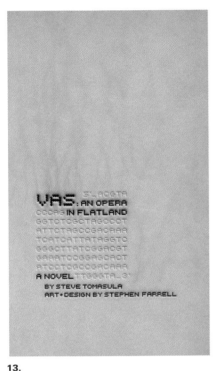

13.

14.

Co-authored by Steve Tomasula and Stephen Farrell, and designed by Stephen Farrell, *VAS: An Opera in Flatland,* provides an uncommon, multi-modal reading experience. A plethora of texts and images combine to reveal dynamic layers of subtexts and expanded narratives. "Authoring" *VAS* evolved more as a process of structuring and organizing masses of ideas and information than of weaving a linear tale.

Combining the processes of writing and design, the authors worked as a team for a period of six years to juggle research and source material, bits of writing, raw manuscripts, design concept sketches and developing spreads. Based on a leap-frog method of writing, designing, and researching, the book was built from the inside out: the subject matter provided the generative mechanism – the material, the guidelines, and the constraints – for the book's organization and structure. The result fuses subject matter with literary and typographic structure into an expansive work of 370 pages.

The authors scoured material sources from popular, literary, and scientific arenas, both classic and contemporary. Raw materials included evolutionary biology and anthropology books, eugenics books, government databases, chromosome charts, genetics supply catalogs, internet plastic surgery and egg donor sites, medical books, doll catalogs, and many other sources accumulated over several years. Some material was used unaltered as "evidence," some was deconstructed and reconstituted, while others were used as structural frameworks. Also, the authors generated many of their own images and illustrations.

The book's subject matter involves the general theme of human biology. But more specifically, the text-image novel explores the myriad ways in which the human body is represented in words and images, and how these representations shift the way we see, perceive, and relate to our bodies.

The book's protagonist, Square, is a writer married to Circle. He considers having a vasectomy, but having doubts about the procedure, traverses realms of science, medicine, bioengineering, and information technology, pondering the ways these domains reveal aspects of the human body through graphic and literary portrayal.

Square focuses on one biological aspect in particular: DNA, the engine of life on earth. But the phenomenon of DNA is too small and too complex to depict in its reality. Square observes science continuously abstracting it, analogizing it, reframing, and repackaging it, each incarnation offering a representation of DNA anew.

Farrell further explains, "DNA's most frequented analog is a string of letters that casts our genetic selves as a piece of writing, a grand text, a magnum opus that science has dubbed 'the book of life.' Through this analog, a human body is suddenly a stream of text, a living novel, a reference guide and technical manual, a printing press running off copies of itself, an agglutination of letters that, when sequenced, form flesh and blood. The genome is a raw manuscript with stories of longevity or disease, chemical balance, sexual development, the acquisition and loss of motor skills and language – a many-layered story which a body acts out and carries to conclusion."

15.

A page revealing the essence of *VAS,* a story about how we represent our biology, and how these representations allow us to see our bodies, think about them, and manipulate them in various ways.

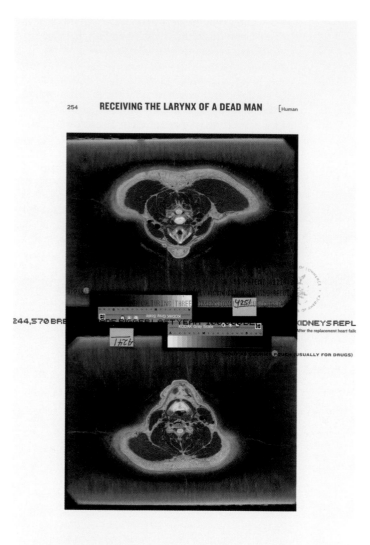

15.

16.

The grid lines as DNA strand provide the structure for interpenetrating text and images. The grid lines transform into a suture, visually piercing the page as if skin.

While reading *VAS,* one comes to realize that the concept of DNA and the popular analogy of DNA as a long text chain provides both the subject matter and structural framework for the book. *VAS* draws together this language model and the double helix model of DNA to build the book's narrative structure and its compositional and typographic structure.

A symmetrical five-column grid of hairlines running vertically through the pages stand for the unwound DNA scaffold of the double helix. Readers feel as if they are travelling a tiny stretch of genome and reading its contents. Three layers of historical, ontological and narrative text threads assigned to the scaffolding cascade down the pages in a coiled sequence mimicking DNA. This grid provides the armature that adheres the texts and constrains them to discrete horizontal positions. This grid slips into other guises throughout the book: the lines are hair, a scalpel's path, suturing thread dipping in and out of flesh, a musical staff.

17.

A sample spread reveals an intricate typographic structure, a "DNA" armature where texts of multilayered content and typographical expression spin downwardly as part of a greater, all-encompassing story.

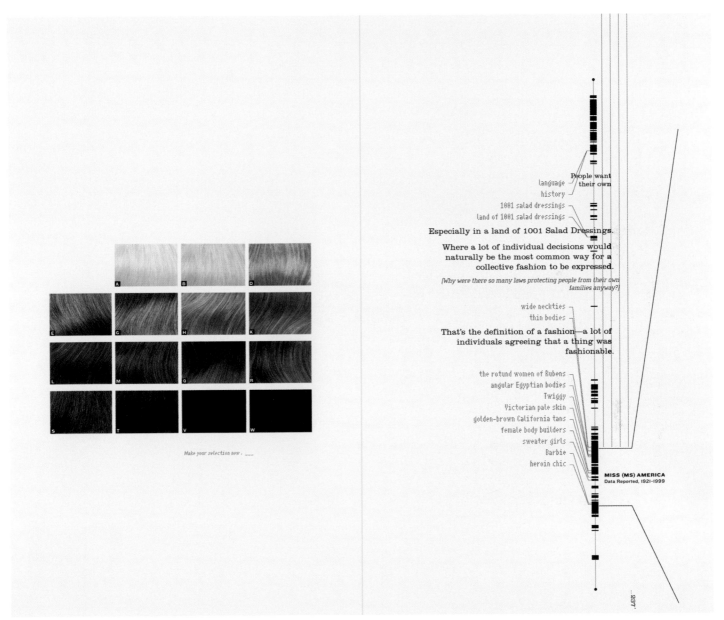

17.

In one spread, the lines swirl into flight patterns of moths to a flame, light rays plotted in curved space, Galileo's telescope, and an abstract plot of normal vs. mentally ill children. Quotes from influential scientists, government officials, famous authors and the like pierce the DNA strand with ideologies, each given the authority of an encyclopedic tab.

In *VAS,* fonts make flesh, and print technologies are analogous to body technologies where materiality of the body and materiality of the body of the text become one. Readers become fully immersed in a book printed in three colors: black, flesh, and blood.

(Farrell actually matched the red to a drop of his own blood, and the "flesh" color to Crayola's discontinued "flesh" crayon which happens to be a very close match to 3M's official designation of "flesh" for their medical supplies.)

Three dominant typefaces were selected for the three dominant voices of the book: Clarendon, Univers, and Cholla. Many accent faces were also used, including Synchro, Fell, Winchester, and Comic Sans. The choreography of the texts, and the palette of typefaces provide a sense of coherence, intelligibility, and narrative pacing to the disparate and interlocking narrative fragments.

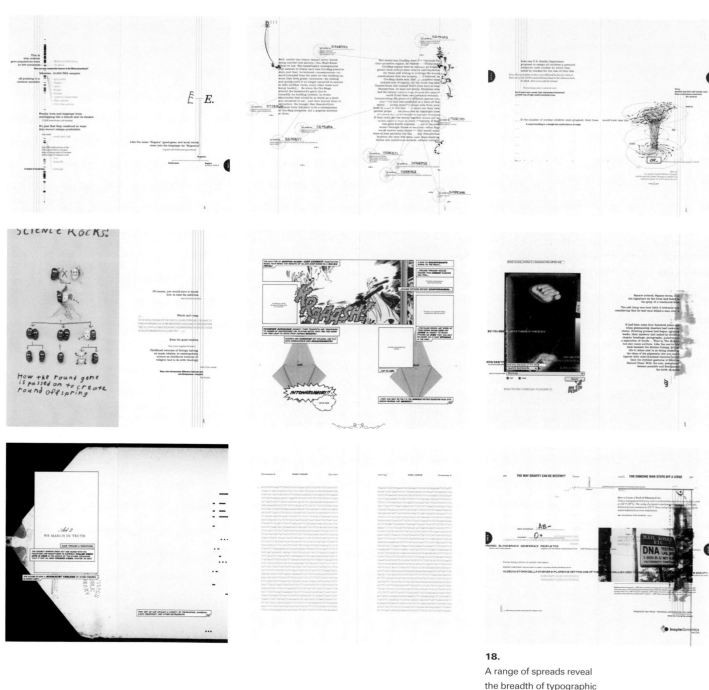

18.
A range of spreads reveal the breadth of typographic expression and the intermingling of texts and images within the governing structure of DNA.

Referring to a movie advertisement that used letterforms "painted by light," typographic historian Beatrice Warde wrote, "After forty centuries of the necessarily static Alphabet, I saw what its members could do in the fourth dimension of Time, 'flux,' movement. You may well say that I was electrified." Through advanced animation and computer graphics techniques, graphic designers are transforming typographic communication into kinetic sequences that might almost be called "visual music."

Richard Greenberg has distinguished himself as a leading innovator in graphic design for film titles, movie previews, special effects, and television commercials. He considers film titles to be a "visual metaphor" for the movie that follows, setting "the *tone* of the movie. You have to take the people who have just arrived at the theater and separate them from their ordinary reality – walking onto the street, waiting in line; you bring them *into* the movie. You want to tell them how to react: that it's all right to laugh, that they are going to be scared, or that something serious is going on."

In the titles for the Warner Brothers film *Superman – The Movie,* bright blue names and the Superman emblem streak through space like comets, stop for a moment, then evaporate into deep space (Fig. **19**). The speed and power of this film's fantasy superhero are evoked. This effect is accomplished by tracking rear-illuminated typography in front of an open camera lens. Each frame captures a streak of light that starts and stops slightly before the light streak recorded on the next frame. When shown at twenty-four frames per second, this series of still images is transformed into a dynamic expression of zooming energy.

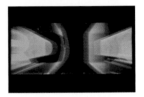

19.

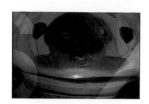

For the Warner Brothers movie *Altered States,* the title sequence opens with a wide-angle image of a researcher in an isolation tank (Fig. **20**). Superimposed over this image, the two words of the title – transparent, as if they are windows cut from a black background – overlap each other as they move slowly across the screen. The film credits are superimposed in white typography in front of this lively pattern of typographic forms and counterforms. Behind the title the background slowly darkens while the camera pulls away from it, causing the letterforms to become smaller and smaller. Finally, the complete title, *Altered States,* appears in its entirety before the totally black screen. In the title, set in Avant Garde Demi, the repetition of this unusual configuration unifies the two words and serves to make the title a unique and memorable signification.

An ominous mood is created in the title sequence for the Twentieth Century-Fox production *Alien* (Fig. **21**). Deep in outer space, the dark side of an immense planet (suggested by a sweeping curved edge) moves slowly onto the screen. Gradually, it passes from right to left, engulfs the screen in blackness, and then continues until it disappears from sight. As the planet passes, small white rectangles appear one by one, then undergo a metamorphosis to form a five-letter title letterspaced across the screen. An elevated sense of mystery is achieved by the harmonious juxtaposition of the passing planet and the typographical transformation. The impending arrival of aliens is evoked.

20.

21.

A striking three-dimensional effect is achieved in the seamless title sequences for *True Lies,* a film about a secret agent who learns about his wife's extramarital affair and pursues her using intelligence resources available in his profession, which is a job he kept secret from her. The title begins with four faint blue streaks that start to rotate in space (Fig. **22**). As the lines rotate, the flat, planar letters of the word *true* are revealed. These letterforms continue to rotate, appearing as independent cubelike structures, with the final sequence revealing the letters of the word *lies,* reversed and appearing in black on the adjacent surfaces of the structures. This simple and elegant visual transformation provides a surprising tension between the two opposing words of the film's title.

Martin Riggs, the lead character in the film *Lethal Weapon 3,* finally meets his match in Lorna Cole, a beautiful but tough policewoman. Together with his partner, Roger Murtaugh, the three attempt to expose the illegal arms racket of a fellow police officer. The heightened suspense of the film is established with the visceral image of fire licking the surface of a calm body of water. As the flames erupt from left to right along the screen, typography presenting the names of the film's stars follows their movement (Fig. **23**). In this film title, the synergistic relationship between type and image is fully developed as they move in time and space. This film title provides an excellent example of the integration of type into image, unlike many designs where type is merely added to, or placed upon, an image.

The time-space orientation of digital media enables the typographic designer to add motion, scale change, sequence, and metamorphosis to alphabet communication. As demonstrated by the work of Richard Greenberg, this opens new vistas of expressive communication.

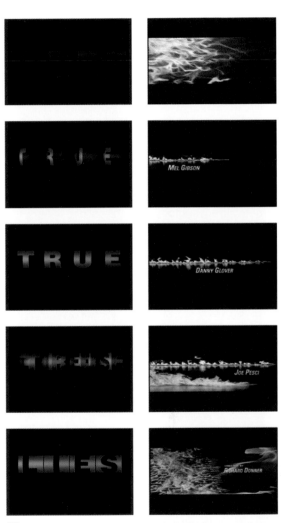

22.

23.

Buenos Aires Underground (Subte)

Buenos Aires, the capital of Argentina, is a culturally diverse city with a population of approximately twelve million people. The firm Diseño Shakespear has made a lasting impression on many facets of the city's visual culture and information infrastructure. Ronald Shakespear, founder and principal of this multi-disciplinary firm describes his design mission as "making the city legible."

A dramatic example of this quest is the Buenos Aires subway system, a mega-wayfinding project designed by Ronald Shakespear and his sons, Lorenzo and Juan. The system inherited the name "Subte" (from subterráneo), the colloquial term for subway used by residents of the city. This memorable term functions as a brand alongside the Tube in London, the Metro in Paris and Washington D.C., and the Subway in New York.

The Buenos Aires subway system originated in 1913 with the introduction of a first station and grew rapidly in later years to keep pace with a burgeoning population. Before the design transformation by Diseño Shakespear, the "system" constituted nothing more than a chaotic collection of vernacular elements. (Fig. **24**).

In separater stages between 1995 and 2007, Diseño Shakespear pursued separate stages of the subway's branding and wayfinding transformation for the existing five lines. The team relied on their established design methodology: "research, analysis, synthesis, drafts, final project, implementation." Sketches and graphic notations served to visualize and synthesize ideas and concepts (Fig. **25**).

24.

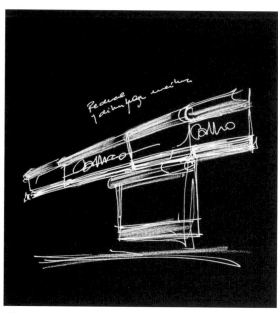

25.

26.

An early subway map lacks the typographic organization, hierarchy, and diagrammatic clarity required for adequate interpretation.

27.

The redesigned map diagrams the cityscape into a translatable model based upon simple geometry. City streets form a secondary lattice beneath the subway lines, orienting riders to their position in the city.

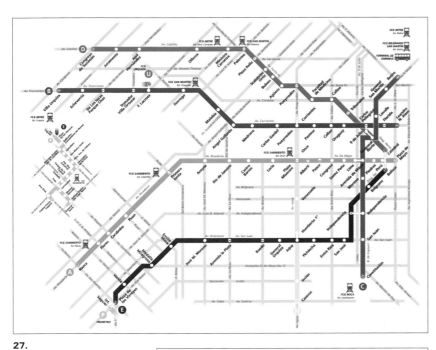

27.

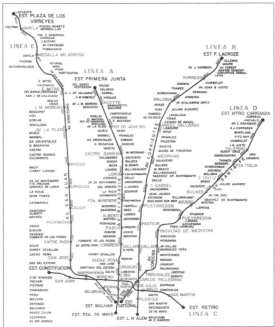

26.

A successful wayfinding system relies on a combination of on-site research and what Ronald refers to as "verified intuition." Two fundamental criteria regarding its signs must govern any system: 1) they must be easy to find and their locations predictable, and 2) they must be easy to understand. Ronald believes that designers have an obligation "to listen to people, to decipher their codes, to discover their yearnings, and to give them an answer."

Research and evaluation of the existing system stimulated the development of a rational and functional graphic language that clearly communicates, providing travellers with the sense and assurance that they will reach their destinations without a problem. In addition, the design solution would require adaptation to 86 subway stations, each with unique physical conditions.

An adaptable but consistent program governs Subte, and a well-considered hierarchy of information is delivered using a bold, clear, and concise visual syntax.

An early task was to design a new map. Prior renditions, relying on actual interpretations of topology, were visually dense and difficult to interpret (Fig. **26**). Influenced by the map of the London Underground designed in 1933 by Henry C. Beck, and the New York Subway system map designed by Massimo Vignelli, the Subte map was reduced to a comprehensible network of linear elements and typographic labels positioned horizontally, vertically, and at 45-degree angles. The simplified, diagrammatic structure provides a legible gestalt for riders en route (Fig. **27**).

28.

29.

A grid system accommodates a variety of sign types, from interior station signage to exterior directional signage (Fig. **28**). As shown in figure **29,** each of the six subway lines (A–F) is assigned a color from a vivid palette of primary and secondary hues. The contrast between colors brands each of the lines, making it easy for riders to pinpoint where they are and how to plan their route. The color scheme corresponds to the Subte map.

Station signage consists of 41 signs in a typical station configuration. Station identification bands run parallel to the tracks at a consistent height of 2.2 meters from the platform floor. This creates a 220-meter "perpetual belt," through the interiors of the stations. The station name repeats every 2.5 meters, helping riders to readily identify their stops from within the trains (Fig. **30**).

Ronald Shakespear attests that signs are "active expressions of identity that go beyond just giving directions and solving basic circulation and communication problems." They must integrate into the surrounding environment and contribute to a sense of place.

Observations revealed critical psychological concerns; for example, the express need for riders to leave the underground environment as soon as possible. As Ronald puts it, "The exit sign is the most important symbol to people on the subway: How do you escape? It is unnatural to be underground in the city" (Fig. **31**).

28.
This drawing reveals the dimensions of the prominent Subte station entrance signs. The proportional system shown here relates to the grid structures used in all other system components.

29.
Contrasting colors brand subway lines, making it easy for riders to distinguish and identify each of them.

30.

31.

30.

Running the entire length of each station platform, an information rail typographically repeats the station name, reassuring travellers of their arrival destination. The station name is easily viewed whie riding the train.

31.

Exit signs are easily identified in the information hierarchy. Once stepping out of trains, travellers immediately seek escape from the underground.

32–34.

The prominent circular columns, viewed at a distance and from any angle, mark subway entrances and provide information about links to other lines. The Retiro station sign was one of the first to be implemented. Illuminated at night, the station signs are highly readable, encouraging 24-hour travel.

34.

Frutiger was selected as the system typeface, not only for its superb legibility, but also for its informal, friendly appearance. Set in Frutiger Bold, the name Subte provides a distinctive word picture for a memorable brand. Different weights and sizes of Frutiger are applied to the signage to establish a decipherable information hierarchy. Type was scaled to optimize readability at various viewing distances.

The final phase of the Subte transformation was the design of above-ground signage. Since a specific design program had not been employed in a hundred years, the entrance conditions, including signage, varied widely. The Shakespear team adapted visual aspects of the interior signage, but reconfigured them at an appropriate scale to help travellers identify the seven different transit lines.

The circular support elements identifying various lines on interior signage were integrated into illuminated sign boxes as rotated, three-dimensional spherical columns. Because of their spatial orientation, and bold forms and colors, these signs serve as prominent landmarks for Subte stations (Figs. **32–34**). As a major urban feature, the Subte system contributes enormously to the functionality and ambience of Buenos Aires, and to the pride of its residents.

Credits:
Directors: Lorenzo Shakespear, Juan Shakespear, Ronald Shakespear; Team: Gonzalo Strasser, Cecilia Bonnefon, Martina Mut, Lucia Diaz, Juan Cerdá; Photos: Juan Hitters, Lorenzo Shakespear, Alejandro Calderone; Legal Advisor: Victor Levy, Construction Advisor, Atlas SAIC.

32.

33.

Ingenious, brave, impressive and absolutely unique – these are terms often used to describe the work of graphic designer Joost Grootens. His books on subjects of art, architecture, and urban spaces all share an analytical and intelligent approach to the subject matter.

Prior to Grootens' design of *Metropolitan World Atlas,* there had been no way of directly comparing worldwide metropolises. Written by Arjen van Susteren and published by 010 Publishers, this remarkable atlas offers a unique survey of global trade networks and their impact on metropolitan spaces.

This book documents a total of 101 metropolises, analyzing them in easy-to-read ground plans. The atlas redefines cities as more than densely built-up areas. It chooses to define metropolitan areas as "regions where global relationships dominate over local ones and which are characterized spatially by a high concentration of global connections and a high concentration of people." These areas having a global range of influence are compared via information graphics in terms of population, density, pollution, travel time, data traffic, air and water travel, and the size of Central Business Districts, among other pertinent factors.

The unexpected combination of ground plans and statistics makes this atlas a unique work of reference where for the first time metropolitan areas like Beijing, Lagos, London, Los Angeles, Rio de Janeiro, and Tokyo can be compared with one another and in terms of their position in the global urban network. The atlas conveys this information with transparent clarity, making readers sense instinctively that they are immersed in the language of cities.

35.

Metropolitan World Atlas: Anchorage, Antwerp-Brussels, Athens, Atlanta, Auckland, Baghdad, Bangalore, Bangkok, Barcelona, Beijing, Berlin, Bogotá, Boston, Buenos Aires, Busan, Cairo, Calcutta, Charlotte, Chennai, Chicago, Cincinnati, Copenhagen, Dallas-Ft. Worth, Denver, Detroit, Dhaka, Djakarta, Dubai, Durban, Frankfurt, Geneva, Hamburg, Hong Kong, Houston, Hyderabad, Indianapolis, Istanbul, Jerusalem-Tel Aviv, Johannesburg, Kaohsiung, Karachi, Kinshasa, Kobe-Osaka-Kyoto, Kuala Lumpur, Lagos, Lahore, Las Vegas, Le Havre, Lima, Lisbon, London, Los Angeles, Louisville, Madrid, Manila, Melbourne, Memphis, Mexico City, Miami, Milan, Minneapolis-St.Paul, Monterey, Montreal, Moscow, Mumbai, Nagoya, New Delhi, New Orleans, New York, Orlando, Oslo, Paris, Perth, Philadelphia, Phoenix, Pittsburgh, Randstad Holland, Rhine-Ruhr, Rio de Janeiro, Rome, Sacramento, San Francisco-Oakland, Santiago de Chile, São Paulo, Seattle, Seoul-Incheon, Shanghai, Singapore, St. Louis, St. Petersburg, Stockholm, Sydney, Taichung, Taipei, Tangier, Tehran, Tianjin, Tokyo-Yokohama, Toronto, Vancouver and Washington-Baltimore.

36.

The *Metropolitan World Atlas* utilizes various weights of Akkurat – designed by Laurenz Brunner in 2004 – as the primary type family. This highly legible, sans-serif type family enables easy, unencumbered reading, and its friendly image urges readers into statistical information without trepidation. In contrast to complex content, the design of the atlas design exhibits restraint, taking on the responsible and critical task of clearly presenting the information without the use of unnecessary decorative devices. The cover invites readers to enter the content by means of a generic map printed in orange dayglo ink. This map corresponds to the scale of maps found throughout the atlas, becoming a part of the entire system. The orange color functions throughout the book to signify population distribution and the intensity of other statistical values. The back cover readily identifies the 101 featured metropolitan areas as a continuous list (Figs. **35** and **36**).

Front and back end sheets and paste-downs provide at-a-glance maps of the globe that pinpoint locations of the major metropolitan areas. Serving as a visual index, page numbers attached to these areas indicate where they can be found in the pages of the atlas. Along with organizing the content alphabetically, this device helps readers find their way in the atlas (Fig. **37**).

After the introduction, a new section presents global (and historical) statistics, such as "The world's 10 largest cities through the ages," and "The worlds largest seaports" (Fig. **38**).

Each of the 101 metropolitan areas are shown consistently using the same organizational structure. The designers began with a geographically projected world map and zoomed into each area to establish a 162 x 130 km framework and a 1:750,000 scale.

This means that 1 cm on the map corresponds to 7.5 kilometers on the ground. For comparison purposes, each map has the same scale, grain, frame, and legend. Grain adjusts in density according to elevation. The legend indicates bodies of water, land area, land elevation, railways, motorways, built-up areas, airports, and seaports. A concentration of contrasting orange on these maps indicates built-up areas.

The statistical data for each metropolitan area are displayed next to each map using two methods: as diagrams, and as figures and text. The diagrammatic display shows proportions in relation to the maximum value that a given characteristic of the region can reach: a small orange dot represents a relatively low value, and a large dot a relatively high value. Maps appear on the right-hand page of the spread, while statistical information appears on the left, enabling readers to seamlessly flip through the book to compare one area to another (Fig. **39**).

37.

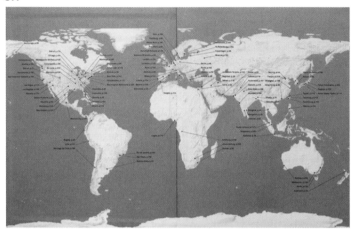

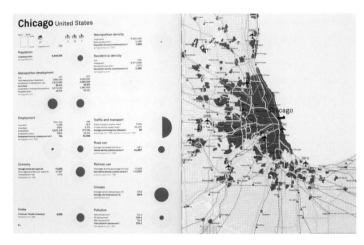

38.

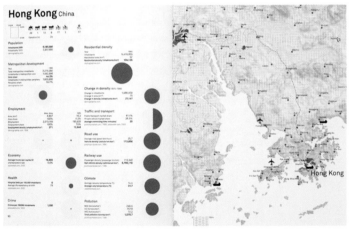

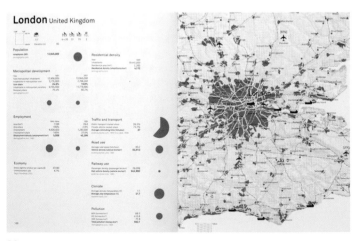

37.
The book's interior is sandwiched between inside front and back covers and end sheets showing maps of the globe. The geographical locations of the 101 metropolitan areas are shown together with the page numbers of where they are located in the atlas. The color orange indicates the most populous regions.

38.
Introductory pages present lists of metropolitan areas having the most significant global impact in terms of the size of population, seaports, airports, and telecom ports. These criteria determined the final selection of 101 metropolitan areas. Grootens finds these lists to "have a poetry of their own."

39.

The second section of the atlas (Fig. **40**) compares data for the metropolitan areas on a global perspective by topic. Dots representing the areas are positioned on simplified world maps. The size of dot refers to regional values in relationship to specific data. Readers can compare areas in terms of passenger airports, flight movements, telecom ports, population, built-up areas, average temperatures, and income per capita, among others.

The design of the Metropolitan Atlas provides an extraordinary typographical reference work for comparing the differences and similarities of metropolitan regions from varying perspectives.

39, 40.

These sample spreads reveal the three basic ingredients used in the design of the atlas: a map, consistently framed and scaled; a system of dots to show intensity and regional variance; and a systematic use of statistical data that can be compared.

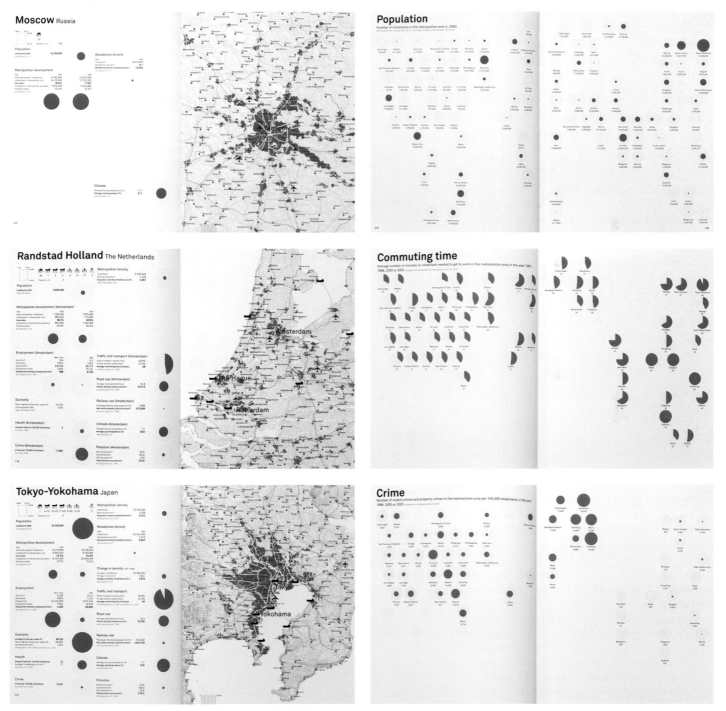

40.

A typographic program
for the 17th Street Farmers' Market

41.
The bold, vector-based tractor silhouette, straightforward spatial composition, and vivid color are characteristics that would define the essence of the Market's graphic program.
42.
The sun sets on a horizon of aligned text type in this implied farm landscape.

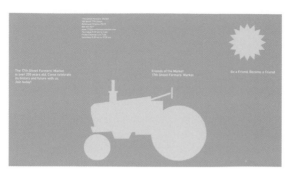

42.

The 17th Street Farmers' Market in the Shockoe Bottom district of Richmond, Virginia, is one of America's first public markets. It originated as an outdoor market around 1737 and was officially established in 1779. The first structure on the site was an open wooden shed, replaced two years later with a brick building and colonnade. The Market expanded in the years to follow, and by 1854 a larger brick building – The First Market House – was built on the corner of 17th Street and Main. During the Civil War, this building served as a strategic gathering place for Confederate soldiers. Later in the war, Union troops occupied it as barracks. After the war and into the 1900s, the market prospered; but by mid-century the Shockoe Bottom district declined and the Market could no longer be sustained; the First Market House was demolished in the 1960s. The Market was again revived in the 1980s, and the current open-air pavillion was built during this time.

In recent years, the Market has thrived as a vital center for various community events, and as a venue for farmers, artists, flea and antique dealers, and bakers to sell their products.

The current success of the 17th Street Farmers' Market is largely attributable to a visionary period of time when the Market's manager departed from the conservative thinking of the city officials and the advisory board to embrace the power of forward-thinking graphic design and typography.

Initially, John Malinoski was asked to design a poster for one of the Market's events. The poster proved so successful that it soon became the pilot project for the Market's identity and the inspiration for developing the graphic program (Fig. **41**). The visual language of the program is based on compelling ideas and bold, iconographic forms rather than what might be considered the obvious market vernacular – nostalgic photographs and engravings laden with obvious period typography. The silhouetted icon of the farm tractor serves as the Market's identity mark and as a central unifying element in posters, postcards, bumper stickers, and various other printed materials (Fig. **42**).

17TH STREET
FARMER'S MARKET

SHOCKOE TOMATO	JULY 24	11 AM — 3 PM
THE VIRGINIA HARVEST CELEBRATION	SEPTEMBER 19	12 — 5 PM
SHIMMERING SHOCKOE LIGHTS	DECEMBER 3	7 PM — 9 PM
SHOCKOE OPEN HEIRLOOM MARKET	SUNDAYS	9 AM — 4 pm
MARKET & RUMBA EN LA CALLE	SATURDAYS	4:30 PM — 7 PM

ph: 780—8597

41.

45.

46.

43.

44.

Malinoski can be considered a second generation modernist who pays allegiance to the universal principles of rationality, simplicity, and visual economy. He nurtures these ideals like a dedicated parent, but does so with wit, humor, and intelligence. It is possible that several visits to Holland contributed to shaping his design vision, for Dutch design has street presence and is a reflection of the processes and pragmatics of everyday living. Malinoski adheres to the idea that understatement is the most potent statement.

Malinoski's work for the Market is also street savvy. The striking simplicity and boldness of the posters and other materials command the attention of people both walking and driving. Often the tractor combines with other images or typography to excite the curiosity of viewers.

In one poster, a tractor hauls a giant tomato to create a highly exaggerated and memorable image (Fig. **43**). In another example, the wheel of a farm tractor is substituted for the letter *o* in the word *tomato*. The large scale and oblique angle of the type, and the hot color set the stage for a hot summer event (Fig. **44**).

Other farm implements are sometimes used in combination with type to create thought-provoking messages. Examples include a postcard for the *International Brunswick Stew Festival,* where the tractor, a passenger jet, and a bowl are objectively displayed as a series of international symbols (Fig. **45**); and a brochure featuring a wheelbarrow loaded with type (Fig. **46**).

Sometimes type and image combine in surprising ways to tell a story or to convey an abbreviated narrative. For a Market event focused on pets, a tractor is placed in a doghouse (Fig. **47**), and in an announcement for *Saturday Arts on the Market,* a living room setting with a framed image of the tractor suggests that art was purchased at the Market (Fig. **48**).

When departing from farm-related images, as in a poster announcing the Market's opening season, the consistent use of robust icons preserves visual unity (Fig. **50**).

The universal feel of the graphic system is supported by the use of DIN as the text typeface. Designed by H. Berthold AG in 1936, *DIN* stands for *German Industrial Standard,* and is the face used for road signage throughout many parts of Europe. When larger amounts of text occur in materials, it is set into basic flush-left, ragged-right blocks, as seen in a flyer for a film festival. (Fig. **49**). But the inherent simplicity of the graphic program belies the careful attention paid to every conceivable typographic detail.

47.

48.

49.

50.

47, 48.
Incongruent combinations of type and image challenge the expectations of viewers.

49.
Multiple readings of typographic images can add mystery, intrigue, and humor to messages. The highlighted *esp* reveals "extra sensory perception."

50.
Here, the word *opening* refers to the Market's new season and the emergence of a spring flower. The typeface selected for the word is both organic and geometric, effectively corresponding to the flower.

The rapid advance of technology and the expanding role of visual and audio-visual communication
in contemporary society have created new
challenges for typographic education. Faced
with a complex communications environment,
and the changes that are occurring and are
anticipated, how can a designer nurture sensitivity
to typographic form and communication? An
appreciation of our typographic heritage, an
ability to meet the standards of contemporary
design practice, and an innovative spirit in facing
tomorrow's challenges are required.

The following assignments, ranging from basic
theoretical exercises to complex applied projects,
were selected to provide an overview of contemporary typographic design education. An effective
curriculum is composed of perceptual and
conceptual development, technical training, and
processes for solving multifaceted design problems. These projects were selected with emphasis
upon building the perceptual and conceptual
abilities that provide a foundation for effective and
innovative typographic design practice.

Generation of a typographic sign from a gestural mark

P. Lyn Middleton

North Carolina
State University

Students were asked to make gestural question marks (Figs. **1–3**), giving consideration to the visual-design qualities of their sketches. Proportion, stroke weight, negative space, and details such as the relationship of the dot to the curved gesture were evaluated. One of the student's question marks was selected and became the basis for designing a freehand typographic sign.

Students generated a variety of graphic signs, exploring a range of forms that can function as a question mark. Executing the typographic version develops visual and manual acuity and an understanding of the differences between written and typographic signs.

1.
 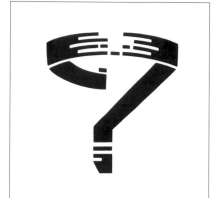

2.

3.

1.
Designer: Alexandre Lock
2.
Designer: Maxine Mills
3.
Designer: Angela Stewart

Letter/digit configurations

Urban letterform studies

Rob Carter

Virginia Commonwealth
University

Thomas Detrie

Guest Lecturer
Winter Session in Basel
Rhode Island
School of Design

Visual configurations were invented by combining a letter from the English alphabet with a single-digit number (Figs. **4–7**). Scale, proportion, weight, and shape relationships between two different signs were explored.

Objectives of this exercise include introducing letterform drawing and drafting skills, using typographic joinery to unify the two distinct forms into a visual gestalt, and understanding the variety of spatial relationships that can exist among characters.

4.
Designer: Penny Knudsen
5.
Designer: Penny Knudsen
6.
Designer: Colene Kirwin
7.
Designer: Linda Evans

8.

Letterforms in an old section of a European town were studied and documented through drawing, rubbings, and found material. A black-and-white letter composition was developed, depicting graphic qualities found in the assigned area.

On a formal level, compositional issues such as dynamic asymmetrical composition and form-counterform relations are explored. On an interpretive level, the ambience of a historical area is translated into a typographic configuration.

4.

5.

6.

7.

8.
Designer: J. P. Williams

Inventing sign systems

Letterform analysis

Greg Prygrocki

North Carolina
State University

Ben Day

Boston University

A modular grid of horizontal, vertical, and diagonal units was established and used to draw variations of a letterform (Fig. **11**). The sans serif *E* has been transformed into expanded and condensed variations. A grid sequence from four to twelve vertical units and from five to ten horizontal units was used.

In Figure **12,** the form has been elaborated upon by opening the space between the vertical stroke and the three horizontal strokes.

The purpose of this project is to understand the allowable tolerance for the alteration of letterform proportions without losing sign legibility.

In addition, the internal structure of a letter is analyzed and manipulated. This project introduces students to the formal variety that is possible and to the process of logo design.

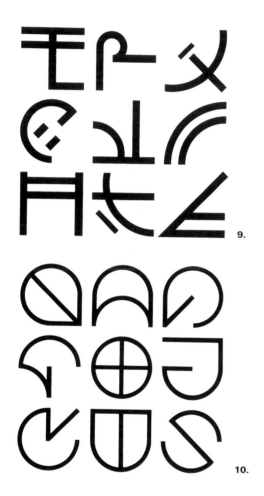

9.

10.

A set of nine signs were invented (Figs. **9,10**). Each was required to be a distinctive mark, with unique optical characteristics, yet harmonious with all the other signs and clearly recognizable as part of the set.

The focus of this project is to make students aware of the properties that bring unity to any typographic system. These include stroke weight and direction, stress, form repetition, and intersection.

9.
Designer: Joe Easter
10.
Designer: Paul Dean

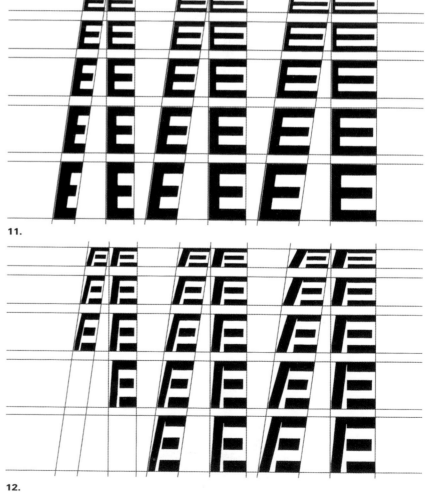

11.

12.

Designer: Tim Barker

Flowering typography

13.

Dennis Y. Ichiyama

Purdue University

Selected letters of the alphabet were combined with images of flowers that have been reduced into visually simplified forms. Each letter is coupled with a flower whose generic name begins with the chosen letter. In the examples shown, *A* is for Alyssum (Fig. **13**), *K* is for Kirengeshoma (Fig. **14**), *J* is for Jalap Root (Fig. **15**), and *H* is for Hollyhock (Fig. **16**).

A primary objective of this project is to achieve a harmonious synthesis between type and image, and in the process create a new visual configuration. It is essential in the process of creating this hybrid form that the recognizability of both the letterform and flower be preserved. Another fundamental concern is to explore the dynamic relationship between positive and negative space.

13–17.
Designer: Li Zhang

14.

15.

16.

Sequential typographic forms in space

Akira Ouchi

Virginia Commonwealth University

By cropping, shifting, rotating, and scaling a large sampling of single letterforms within square modules, students discover the dynamic relationships between form and counterform and the resulting effect upon visual space. Students then proceed with a study of typographic kinetics by organizing selected modules into a linear sequence of ten modules (Figs. **18–21**). Similar to musical scores, diagram sketches enable students to articulate and test sequences with respect to rhythmic patterns, shape and value transitions, and the flow of typographic elements (Fig. **22**).

18–22.
Designers: Virginia Commonwealth University sophomores

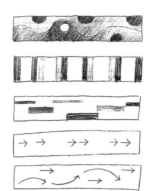

22.

18–21.

17.

191

Greg Prygrocki

North Carolina State
University

Students developed linear
grid structures, then created
a series of plates, organizing
found typographic materials
into spatial compositions
based upon this underlying
structure (Figs. **23, 24**).

This project introduces
the grid structure as a formal
design element. The grid
module is the basic compositional unit, bringing order
to the arrangement. Students
consider contrast, structure,
positive and negative space,
balance, texture and tone, and
rhythm as design properties.

23.

23.
Designer: Craig McLawhorn
24.
Designer: Matt Monk

24.

Lisa Fontaine

Iowa State University

Using letterforms as the primary visual elements, students learned how individual designs can function as a cohesive system. Six square compositions were designed (Figs. **25–30**) using a limited range of colors and letterforms. The success of each individual design relied not only on its composition but also on its systematic potential: each square had to bring both unity and variety to the series to result in a cohesive visual system.

To prove the systematic integrity of their six designs, students create a series of nine-unit grid patterns (Figs. **31** and **32**), where any combination of the smaller designs are placed in the larger grid. If the system is successful, a wide range of patterns is possible through repetition and rotation of the six designs. If the patterns generated are too similar, the system needs more variation of font, color, size, or placement. When the patterns lack continuity, the student needs to more clearly define or limit the visual elements of their system.

25–32.
Designer: Jasmine Friedl

25–30.

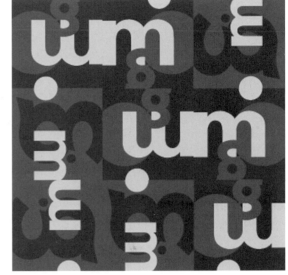

31, 32.

Designing with
a single letter

Typography and
image transformations

Cece Cutsforth

Portland Community
College

Gordon Salchow

University of Cincinnati

A series of designs each used
one or more copies of a single
letter to demonstrate a series
of design concepts:
scale, communicating large
and small by comparison;
positive and negative space,
with the spaces surrounding
the letter becoming equal
to the letter itself; *pattern,*
using repetition to create a
distinctly articulated pattern;
congestion, where letters
encroach upon one another's
space; *tension,* with placement and angle conveying
instability; and *playfulness,*
with letters conveying a
carefree sensation.

The examples shown here
are from the pattern segment
of the project. The choice of
letterform, size, angle, and
figure/ground relationships
determines the tonal density
and degree of consonance
or dissonance.

33–35.
Designers: Portland
Community College students

33.

34.

35.

36.

37.

A letter has been altered in
a series of steps until it is
transformed into a simple
object, an abstract shape,
or another letterform (Figs.
36–38). An understanding
of typographic sequencing,
permutation, and kinetic
properties is developed.
Students can gain an awareness of form and counterform
relationships, and the
unity that can be created in
complex configurations.

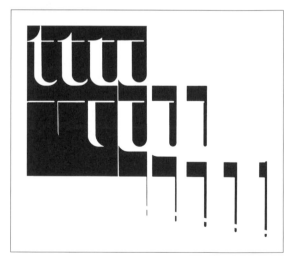

38.

36–38.
Designers: University of
Cincinnati sophomores

**Experimental compositions
with found typography**

Katherine McCoy

Cranbrook Academy of Art

Using all of the typography
found on a product label,
a grid-based composition
was produced exploring
size relationships, spatial
interval, and weight (Fig. **39**).
A second composition was
generated with more dynamic
movement and scale change
(Fig. **40**). Visual notations
were made of each, analyzing
eye movement, massing,
and structure (Figs. **41, 42**).
Tone, texture, and shape are
substituted for the typographic
elements.

This project is designed to
encourage an understanding
of the abstract properties
inherent in existing typographic forms. An exploratory
attitude toward space
and visual organization
is developed.

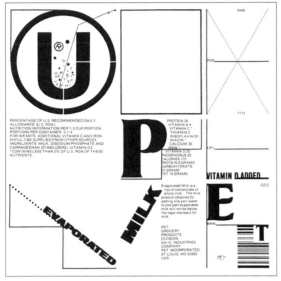

39.

40.

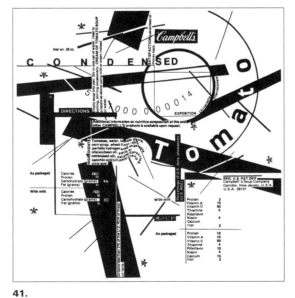

41.

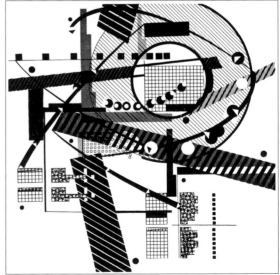

42.

39–42.
Designer: Ryoji Ohashi

Frank D'Astolfo

Rutgers University-Newark

An onomatopoeic term
(a word that sounds like the
thing or action denoted) was
selected and used in syntactic
explorations. The first level
involved drawings exploring
syntactic variations using a
grid to create visual relationships. These studies evolved
into complex type compositions expressing the term.

Level two saw an additional
word added as a simple linear
element. Unexpected yet
meaningful relationships were
sought. Visual relationships
were created through
alignment, balance, juxtaposition, and direction.

In level three, a photograph
was added, completing the
composition and forming
a meaningful message.
Unexpected, ironic, or
complex associations were
encouraged. A spectator or
fan at a sporting event (Fig.
43) adds a new dimension
to the *ver* sound of a fan.
Rabbit ears cause *schhh* (Fig.
44) to denote the static of
poor television reception.
The meaning of the word
croak (Fig. **45**) is changed by
the gun. The *ding-dong* (Fig.
46) comes from the bell in
a boxing match after a prize
fighter is added to the design.

This project addresses a
complex set of issues. Type
style, size, and placement
can express the meaning of
words. Effective visual
organization is achieved with
the help of a grid. Words and
pictures strengthen and even
alter each other's meaning.

FAN

43.

static

44.

croak

45.

ready *di*

46.

43.
Designer: Elisa Robels;
Ver, fan, and spectator.

44.
Designer: Kelly Olsen;
Schhh, static, and rabbit ears.

45.
Designer: Cheri Olsen;
Ribbitt, croak, and gun.

46.
Designer: Paris Jones;
Ding Dong, ready, and boxer.

Type chronology booklet

R. Roger Remington

Rochester Institute
of Technology

A comparative study of ten
typefaces was made by each
student. The information was
organized chronologically in
a booklet with four pages
devoted to each typeface.
In Figure **47**, the opening
spread juxtaposes descriptive
text and a complete font
opposite a large letterform.
The following spread contains
a historical application of the
type opposite a contemporary
application created by the
student.

This problem involves
developing research skills, an
understanding of typographic
history, and an ability to work
with different typefaces. Large
amounts of complex data are
organized; a consistent format
is developed; diversity is
created within this format.

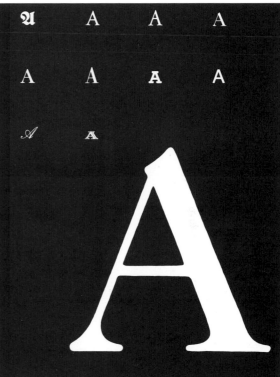

47.

47.
Designer: Heinz Klinkon

Expressive typography: form amplifies message

Douglas Higgins

University of Cincinnati

Design students were introduced to computer typography in a project that explored the potential of computer techniques to intensify typographic messages. Content derived from scientific newsletters was used to create typographic identifiers that clearly summarize factual information contained in the article. By employing a source of subject matter that is usually designed routinely, the temptation to appropriate a solution was minimized.

Special attention was given to the role of visual hierarchy and typographic contrast while developing computer drafting skills useful in professional practice. The ease with which the computer generated variations facilitated visual refinements.

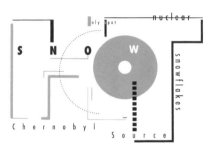

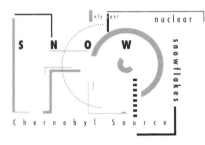

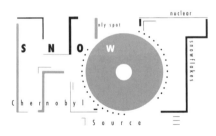

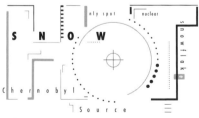

48.

49.

50.

48–50.
Designers: University of Cincinnati juniors

Computer improvisation and manipulation

Douglas Higgins

Ringling School of Art and Design

Two letterforms in structural opposition were combined to create a "seed" configuration (Figs. **51, 52**). Successive improvisations depart from the original while preserving the basic structural form, as basic computer operations are learned (Fig. **52**). Parallels are established between typographic concepts and computer techniques needed to explore them. Electronic page layout software was used to document the entire design process in book form.

Using a computer to deconstruct and manipulate digital type images allows students to hasten their understanding of letterform analysis and elemental structures governing each letter's legibility. Assignment goals include an understanding of letterform complexities and using forms inherent in a letter's design as points of departure for applied problem-solving.

51.
Designer: Michelle Carrier
52.
Designer: Teresa Leard

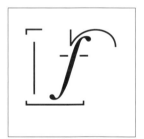

51.

52.

Observing systems
in our surroundings

Levi Hammett
Titus Nemeth

Virginia Commonwealth University,
Doha, Qatar

Students were first challenged to identify distinctive man-made, modular grid structures found within the environment, or to create them using physical materials. Once a grid structure was selected, the system was playfully explored in an effort to generate a "dot-matrix," Latin, or Arabic alphabet. In other words, typographical characters were constructed from modules distilled from the larger grid structure. The constructed letterforms were analyzed for visual attributes that could be shared among characters to provide a unique font.

The design of the alphabet was informed by studying a well-designed, existing typeface and the underlying visual qualities that coalesce a set of diverse characters into a unified font.

These emerging fonts were recorded as sets of photographs, which enabled the students to compare characters, evaluate legibility, and make changes as appropriate to improve the unity among characters.

Each alphabet design evolved from the unique structures and limitations inherent in the initial grids.

This project was realized as a collection of individual letterforms recorded on photographic cards and integrated into a poster presenting the results (Fig. **53**).

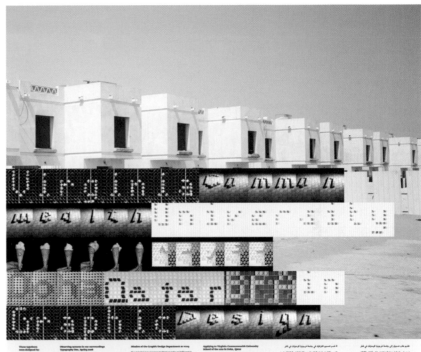

53.

53.
Designers:
Aisha Bushawareb
Aldana Al-Malki
Fatema Al-Doh
Fatma Al-Remaihi
Fatma Al-Jassim
Kholoud Al Sada
Mariam Gasan
Maryam Al-Homaid
Reem AlHajri
Rihab Mohamed
Rouda Al Thani

Sarah Husni
Abeer Al-Kubaisi
Angela Guy
Asma Al-Thani
Esra Abduljawad
Fatima Zainal
Hadeer Omar
Najla Al-Kuwari
Riam Ghani
Sahwa Elnakhli
Sara Qubrosi

Jan Conradi

Ball State University

David Colley

University of Illinois
at Champaign-Urbana

Students design multiple solutions with the same content as a way to explore the relationship between legibility. Innovation is pursued while working within strict parameters and investigating the impact of typeface selection, size, leading, position, line length, tonal contrast, and tactile qualities. In the first of an eight-composition series, each student tries to maximize legibility while using a uniform type font, size, and weight, with no tonal variations. Subsequent compositions introduce geometric grids, then organic forms and multiple type weights and sizes (Figs. **54**, **55**). Images are added but remain subordinate to type. The final compositions emphasize texture and emotional impact rather than legibility (Figs. **56**, **57**).

Students are encouraged to reflect on the visual hierarchy of information and logical reading flow. The consequences of illegibility and people's emotional response to design are considered. Students learn that type can be as potent as images in achieving unique and identifiable communicative designs, and black and white can equal the visual impact of full color.

54.

55.

56.

57.

58.

A series of posters was designed to encourage local high school students to attend symphony concerts (Fig. **58**). Emphasis was placed on writing interpretive copy and selecting typefaces appropriate to that message. Diversity of expression to parallel the concert season was an important consideration. (These posters were printed by offset and donated to the symphony.)

This project introduces the student to the importance of the message in typographic communication. Language devices including metaphor, sound repetition, and rhyme were used to make the content memorable. The relationship of form and meaning was addressed; the nature of each composer's music was considered in the selection of typeface, size, placement, and color. In the examples shown, typographic dissonance in the Stockhausen poster parallels the composer's musical dissonance; word substitution occurs in the Brahms poster; and an auditory double meaning is found in the Bach poster.

58.
Designers: University of Illinois undergraduate students

54.
Designer: Dennis Good
55.
Designer: Dennis Good

56.
Designer: Autumn Musick
57.
Designer: Pam Lemming

Information design:
changing typographic parameters

Marcia Lausen

University of Illinois
at Chicago

Selecting their own subject matter, students explore changing typographic parameters and the resulting effect of these changes upon communication in four exercises. Typographic variables change for each exercise: one size and one weight; two sizes or two weights; any number of sizes and weights; and incorporation of an image with any number of type sizes and weights.

Projects presented here are based upon a Chicago Transit Authority timetable (Figs. **59–62**), and statistical data for a student's vintage muscle car (Figs. **63–66**).

Related goals of the project include instructing students in the use of numeric figures in typography, the relationship of subject and data to visual presentation, the different forms of emphasis and hierarchy in typography, the interaction of type and image, and the basic systems of structure and alignment in typography.

Information design is a growing specialty of graphic design. The ability of designers to interpret, envision, and communicate information in typographical and graphical terms has become increasingly important. The Internet and other information media requiring nonlinear forms of communication are becoming increasingly important in the study and practice of visual communication.

59–62.
Designer: Eric Roth
63–66.
Designer: Tim Russow

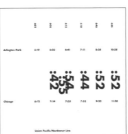

59–62.

63–66.

R. Roger Remington

Rochester Institute
of Technology

Josef Godlewski

Indiana University

A visual presentation combining typography, images, and symbols was created as an extension of a self-assessment study by advanced design students (Figs. **67–69**). The students made a formal analysis of their past experiences and future goals. This part of the project stressed research and information gathering. The collected materials were evaluated for their communicative effectiveness in a complex design.

Transforming diverse information into a three-dimensional cube poses a complex design problem. Each side of the cube functions as part of a totality; the four contiguous sides are graphically and communicatively integrated.

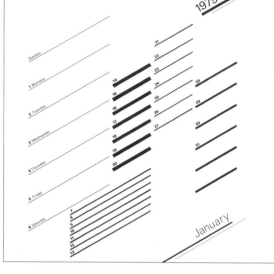

67.

Calendar pages were designed using typographic elements to organize the space and direct eye movement on the page (Fig. **73**). Emphasis was placed upon experimentation, creating unity and movement on each page, and developing a visual elaboration over twelve pages. A grid structure was established and used to achieve diversity and order within a sequence of twelve designs. Graphic elements were limited to typography and rules.

This assignment enables students to explore interrelationships between graphic elements and the surrounding space.

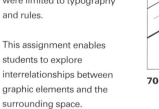

68.   **69.**

70.

67.
Designer: Beth April Smolev
68.
Designer: Katherine St. James
69.
Designer: Bruce Morgan

70.
Designer: Jean
Brueggenjohann

Unity of form and communication

Christopher Ozubko

University of
Washington at Seattle

After selecting a historical
event as subject, students
were asked to develop a
typographic message using
the visual properties of type
and space to amplify content
(Figs. **71–74**). This project
develops an understanding
of the inventive potential
of typographic form. As a
message carrier, typography
can intensify and expand
content and meaning.

71.
Designer: Steve Cox
72.
Designer: Kyle Wiley
73.
Designer: Bill Jolley
74.
Designer: Susan Dewey

71.

72.

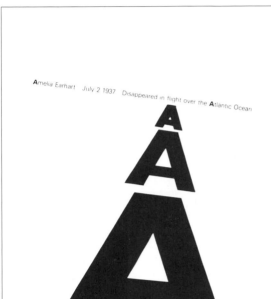

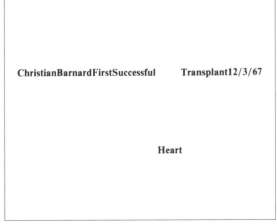

73.

74.

Typeface history posters

Jan Baker

Rhode Island
School of Design

Each student in the class was assigned a typeface to study and use in a poster design, communicating its essential characteristics (Figs. **75**, **76**). Letterforms that reveal the unique properties of the typeface were emphasized. The typeface name and entire alphabet were required components of the design.

This project enables students to establish a visual hierarchy in a poster format, while introducing them to the visual characteristics of typefaces.

75.
Designer: Holly Hurwitz
76.
Designer: Luci Goodman

75.

76.

Self-initiated typographic identity program: Holland Air

Rob Carter
William Culpepper
Sandra Wheeler

Virginia Commonwealth University

In a senior studio class, students propose a project that complements their portfolio of work, and which challenges their visual communication abilities and experience. Corey Hall conceived Holland Air, a fictitious airline company in need of a visual identity program. His research and process culminated in a manual addressing a broad scope of applications, from printed matter and environmental signage to livery graphics (Figs. **77–79**).

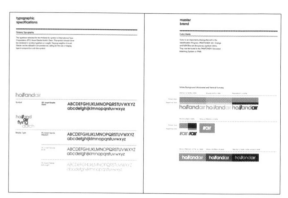

77.

77–79.
Designer: Matthew Corey Hall

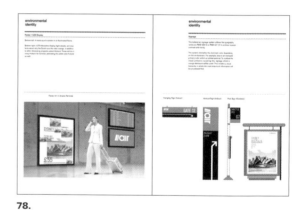

78.

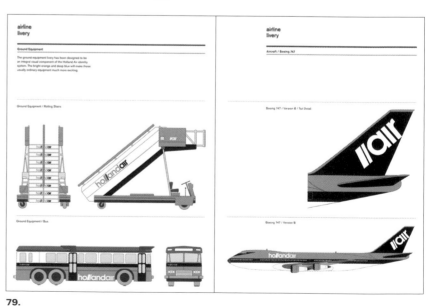

79.

Type in motion

Blending Latin and non-Latin typographic forms

80.

Claudia Dallendörfer
Jean-Benoît Lévy

Academy of Art University
Department of Computer Arts
and New Media, San Francisco

Levi Hammett
Leland Hill

Virginia Commonwealth University,
Doha, Qatar

This project, taught by two designers from different areas of expertise – one new media and the other print – focuses on the development and production of two-dimensional, black-and-white animations. Students first select a small toy that is accompanied by a set of non-verbal instructions revealing how the toy is assembled. (Fig. **80**). Using words and sentences, these instructions are interpreted verbally and translated into typographic compositions (Fig. **81**). These compositions serve as "scores" for typographic animations that communicate the process of assembling each toy. A primary objective of the project is to explore the communicative potential of moving typography and sound (Fig. **82**).

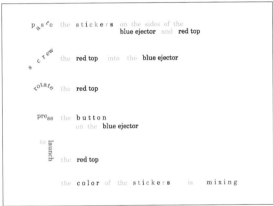

81.

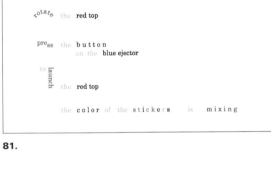

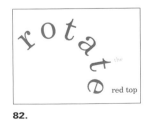

82.

83.

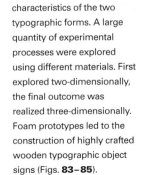

84.   **85.**

Objectives of this project included a rigorous process of form generation. After selecting an existing Latin letterform from a provided list, the students were asked to identify a non-Latin letterform having similar but also contrasting formal characteristics. The students were then instructed to create a unique symbol, a blend of the visual characteristics of the two typographic forms. A large quantity of experimental processes were explored using different materials. First explored two-dimensionally, the final outcome was realized three-dimensionally. Foam prototypes led to the construction of highly crafted wooden typographic object signs (Figs. **83–85**).

Type and image
in the third dimension

Marcia Lausen

University of Illinois
at Chicago

In 1952, Charles and Ray
Eames created the House of
Cards, a set of interlocking
playing cards for children
and adults. This project is an
adaptation of this now-famous
design system.

The two-sided cards enable
students to study on opposite
sides of the twenty individual
cards the structural and
conceptual dualities (as
related to semiotics, color
theory, symbolism, etc.) of
their chosen subject matter.
The interlocking feature of the
cards allows for an exploration of type and image in
dimensional form and space.

Three excellent examples of
this project include *Fourteen
Generations,* the Holing
family lineage traced to the
voyage of the Mayflower
(Fig. **86**); *Catalog of Building
Materials* (Fig. **87**); and *Cards
of Mystery,* where type and
image are manipulated to
express different emotions
and sensations (Fig. **88**).

86.
Designer: Allison Holing
87.
Designer: Chul Kam
88.
Designer: Kyra Jacobs

86.

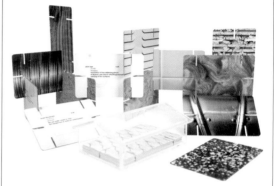

87.

88.

Comparative relationships: type and image

Jan Conradi

Ball State University

In this two-part project, students considered visual relationships between type and image. After selecting photographs, students chose typefaces and letterforms that related to the image through visual characteristics such as shape, weight, decorative embellishments, and other design attributes. Part one involved hand drawing the letterform in a side-by-side comparison of form (Figs. **89**, **90**).

In part two, the relationship was explored further by integrating the letterform into the image (Figs. **91**, **92**). Attention to typeface selection, scale, repetition, color, and balance allowed the merger of type and image into a single entity.

This project helps students who are innately image-oriented to understand how design characteristics of typefaces are individualized and distinctive. Selection of an appropriate font can enhance the communicative message, and type and image can be composed into a unified composition.

89.
Designer: Brandon Luhring
90.
Designer: Brandon Luhring
91.
Designer: Trina Denison
92.
Designer: Kara Holtzman

89.

90.

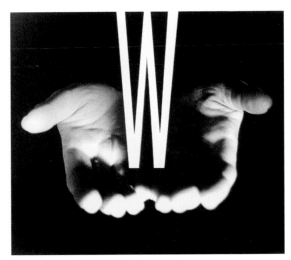

91.

92.

**Directional poster:
from your house to the university**

95.   **96.**

Malka E. Michelson

Philadelphia University

Typographic posters reveal
the directional path between
students' homes and the
university. Message content,
hierarchy, sequencing of
letters, words, and lines
of type were explored to
enhance the development of
a typographic landscape.
Bumpy, smooth, straight,
jagged, curvy, up, down, slow,
traffic jams, smooth sailing,
bumper to bumper, confusing,
farmland, city, over water, and
through tunnels are examples
of concepts explored through
typographic space to amplify
and expand content, context,
and meaning (Figs. **93–96**).

93.
Designer: Todd Duchynski
94.
Designer: Monique Maiorana
95.
Designer: Erin Roach
96.
Designer: Susan Ulsh

93.

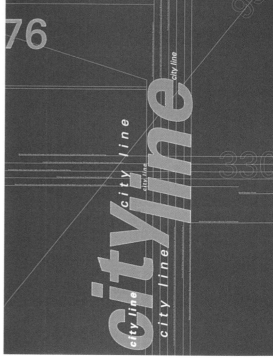

94.

Graphic-design history posters and booklet

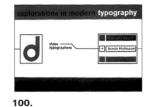

100.

Paul Nini

Ohio State University

Students create a series of three typographic history posters, each based upon one of the following structural themes: 1) orthogonal/grid, 2) diagonal/integral, and 3) combination of orthogonal and diagonal. An orthogonal/grid structure enables a composition consisting of flush-left typographic elements arranged within a grid structure (Fig. **97**). Compositions based on a diagonal/integral structure consist of flush-left typographic elements arranged upon a diagonal axis (Fig. **98**), and a combination structure provides students with an opportunity to explore in a fluid manner the interpretation of information (Fig. **99**).

Phase two of the project is the design of an accordion-fold booklet profiling any three of the modern typographers appearing on the posters. Students conduct research about the typographers, gathering information and images for inclusion in the booklet. Shown here is a sample cover (Fig. **100**).

97–100.
Designer: Matthew Franco

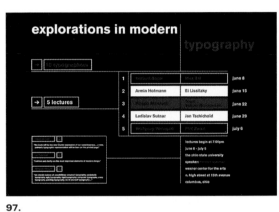

97.

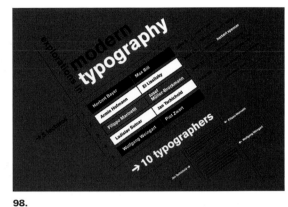

98.

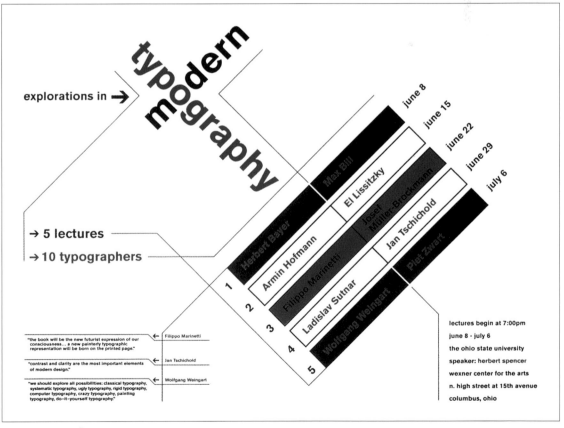

99.

Animated Web site pages

Sandra Wheeler

Virginia Commonwealth
University

Using only the letters of the alphabet and punctuation, students created a ten-second (120 frame) typographic narrative with an expressive aspect. After concepts were developed through preliminary sketches, storyboards were produced to explore the conversion of still images to sequential frames representing motion over time. The storyboards reveal and emphasize that type as a formal element is rooted not only in space but also in time. As such it offers endless possibilities for exploring rhythmic and sequential structures.

The storyboards provided the plan for the animated sequence using a 550 pixel x 400 pixel stage size and frame rate of twelve frames per second. Designing ten-second typographic animations develops an ability to create kinetic typographic splash pages for Web sites.

The animation of two "Gs and a Dot" brings energy to the screen (Fig. **101**). A large Ultra Bodoni capital *G* appears on the screen, then a Futura sans serif capital *G* enters from the left and moves in front of the bolder letter. A turquoise dot resting on the Ultra Bodoni *G* begins to roll through the circle of the Futura letter, while the two letters rotate in space, creating a series of dynamic shape configurations. At the end of the animated sequence, the turquoise dot falls from the screen and the *G*s return to their normal position.

In "Little ä in Traffic" (Fig. **102**), an *ä* with an umlaut (German accent consisting of two dots over a vowel) looks to the left and right, then its "eyes" widen as a stampede of letters rushes past it. Finally, after the letters go by, the little *a*s mother, a capital *A*, arrives to comfort and protect its child. Letters, motion, and color are used to tell a complex metaphorical story in a few seconds.

"Truth/Fiction" (Fig. **103**) explores the metamorphosis of the word *Truth* into the word *Fiction*. Starting as a horizontal word, the letters swing into a vertical position as they transform, ending with a stacked configuration of letters. Going from a five- to a seven-letter word is nicely resolved by treating the two *l*s as offshoots from the capital *T*.

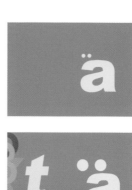

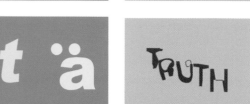

101.
Designer: Bryan Keplesky
102.
Designer: Nancy Digman
103.
Designer: April Meyer

101.   102.   103.

Typezine: my favorite typeface

Rob Carter
Henk Groenendijk

Virginia Commonwealth University

After considering many possibilities, students were asked to select their favorite typeface – one with which they would choose to have a "love affair." On the basis of the selected typefaces, six pages were designed by each student to be combined into a single collection (Figs. **104**, **105**). The content for each page consists of the following: title, type specimens, image having a metaphorical relationship to the typeface, love letter to the typeface, experimental interpretation of the typeface, and a page revealing the research process.

This project exposes students to the enormous range of available typefaces, creating an awareness of the history, form, and function of different typefaces.

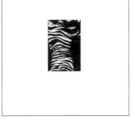

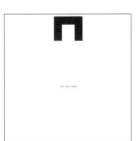

104.
Designer: C.J. Hawn
105.
Designer: Jung Kwon

104.

105.

Type history posters

Larry Clarkson

Weber State University

After thorough investigation into all aspects of a particular period in graphic design history, student teams designed a large poster. Preliminary research included an examination of issues having an impact on the period, including economic conditions of the time, prevailing and developing technologies, popular culture, key design figures, design theory and style, and examples of significant work. This research culminated into a poster composed of the most pertinent content gleaned: a period identity mark, text and captions, examples of work, design theory score, and historic timeline. Each poster was designed in the vernacular of the period communicated (Figs. **106–108**).

106.

107.

108.

106.
Designers: Miki Eto,
Shinsuke Ito

107.
Designers: Anthony Alestra,
Romelle Domingo
108.
Designers: Hana Sullivan,
Lisa Olson, Christine Burton

Typeface design: mind/machine

Max Kisman
Rob Carter
Henk Groenendijk

Virginia Commonwealth
University

This project was launched by Max Kisman as part of a visiting lecture series. Due to the short length of his visit, the project was completed under the tutelage of Rob Carter and Henk Groenendijk. Students were asked to design a typeface based on the concept mind/machine. Kisman's premise that "an alphabet can be anything and anything can be an alphabet," encouraged students to pursue open-ended and unique designs. Typefaces derived from a variety of methods and tools were realized using font design software (Figs. **109, 112**). Other components of the project include a short movie about each typeface (Figs. **110, 113**), a folder containing specimens and a poster (Figs. **111, 114**). The two examples shown are the typefaces *Alphemotibots* and *Franklin Zombie*.

109.

112.

110, 111.

113, 114.

109–111.
Designer: Erin Hall
112–114.
Designer: Ginny Winston

Experimental typographic system

Sandie Maxa
Mark Sanders

Pratt Institute

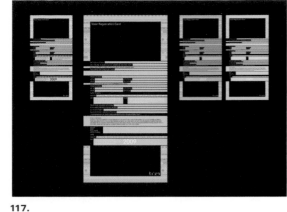

117.

Italo Calvino's 1972 novel, *Invisible Cities* can be used as a basis for typographic experimentation and expression. In conversations between Marco Polo and Kublai Khan, 55 cities are described as physical spaces but also as impressions of residents and memories of visitors. With poetic prose, Calvino presents an alternative to how we usually think about cities, using metaphors based on human nature, linguistics and semiotics. These metaphors provide a springboard for typographic play and manipulation, thereby teaching students how to achieve more expressive communication.

Students select one of the cities from the book. Experimentation begins with identifying descriptive words and aphorisms for the chosen city. Students explore how type can clarify a message, function symbolically, or emphasize meaning in a conceptual way. Work continues with physical alteration of letterforms, integration of texture or other images and composition studies in an effort to create an authentic, impressionable representation of the city's geography, activities, and citizens. These investigations culminate in a book about the city (Fig. **115**). Other system elements include a two-sided poster with a calendar of events (Fig. **116**), voter registration cards (Fig. **117**), and various digital materials.

115.

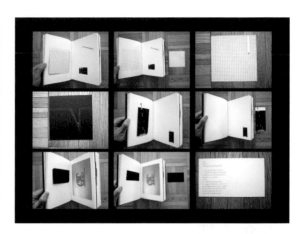

116.

115–117.
Designer: Chiu-Ping Chiu

Ned Drew

Rutgers University-Newark

Cultural diversity serves as the underlying context for this project. Students are asked to design a series of banknotes in three sequential denominations, both front and back sides (Figs. **118, 119**). They begin by researching the country of their origin, engaging in word lists, mindmaps, visual notations, and image gathering. The goal of the project is to design a currency system revealing pertinent historical, social, and environmental aspects of the home country, providing the system with functionality and aesthetic beauty.

Ultimately, the new banknote designs should attempt to surpass the quality and communicative effectiveness of those currently in use.

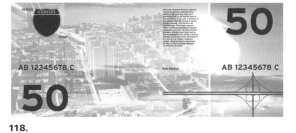

118.
Designer: Alan Bayot
119.
Designer: Christian Pearson

118.

119.

Type as metaphor

Warren Lehrer

SUNY Purchase

About this project, Lehrer states, "Students investigate a subject. Working with one to three primary texts, they develop four panels that approach typography as metaphor. The first panel is composed of paragraphs, sentences, phrases. The second panel, individual words. The third panel, syllables. The last panel, individual letters. Through research, critical thinking, mind-mapping, and experimentation, students give form to metaphoric implications through compositional arrangement, juxtaposition, and typographic manipulation. This project can really help design students go beyond utilitarian, over-literal, or pre-ordained approaches to typography. The examples shown here are from my Advanced Typography class at the School of Art+Design, SUNY Purchase, and from an Experimental Typography class I taught at The Cooper Union. I was first introduced to a variation of the Type as Metaphor project by Mike Schmidt (University of Memphis) who picked it up from Andrew Blauvelt."

122.

120.
Designer: Kerry De Bruce
121.
Designer: Nakyoung Sung
122.
Designer: Rob Dieso

121.

120.

Form and counterform, scale and proportion: "Ne var, ne yok?"

Erik Brandt

Minneapolis College
of Art and Design

"Ne var, ne yok?" An old-fashioned Turkish greeting which translates roughly to "What is, what isn't?" These conglomerate posters represent the culmination of a series of five typographic experiments, each investigating critical aspects of form and counterform. Literally, what is, and what isn't? The formal challenge is to incorporate each and every one of the hundreds of hand-drawn sketches they have created, organize and perhaps resolve a few of them, and project this essential question. Inspired by the introduction to Ara Güler's seminal book, *Memories of Istanbul.*

123.

124.

125.

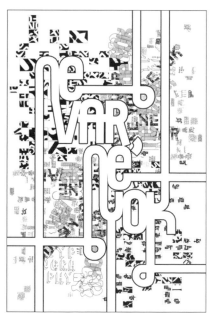

126.

123.
Designer: Brian Mueller
124.
Designer: Clarissa Hamilton
125.
Designer: Peter Steineck
126.
Designer: Sara Zahedi

The creative process is a struggle with the unknown. Whether composing music, making a painting, or designing a chair, one is faced with the challenge of how to begin and how to end. Every project offers unique challenges, and no fail-safe formula exists for solving problems.

The design process can range from the use of highly structured methods to the serendipity of chance operations. Often, designers work in a realm somewhere between these two extremes – somewhere between intuition and logic. The solution to a problem emerges on rare occasion as a brilliant scrawl on a dinner napkin; but most often the problem-solving process is a journey that requires courage and patience, and confidence in finding one's way through uncertain terrain.

The design process is a sequence of events that begin as soon as the designer takes on a problem. It continues until either a deadline is reached or problem criteria have been met. Rarely is the process predictible, a progression in a straight line from point A to point B. The design process is more like reading a road map; there are many ways of reaching the final destination. If side roads are taken, it will probably take longer to get to the destination. But side roads are almost always more interesting than well-travelled highways.

A traditional model

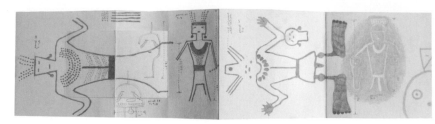

2.

This chapter explores the design process and its role in typographic problem solving. Many models exist that schematically represent the design process. But in fact, there is no single process or method for working through problems. Most designers approach their work in a highly individual manner, some using a combination of traditional and digital tools and methods. Digital technology has played an enormous role in the evolution and individualization of design processes.

A well-known model of the design process consists of five steps, which are explained below. Traditionally, these steps have been thought to occur in a linear manner, beginning with *defining* the problem and progressing toward *realizing* the solution. But rarely, if ever, is the process so smooth and predictable. Design formulas certainly can be devised and followed letter by letter, ending in solutions lacking imagination and mental rigor. But perhaps it is more helpful to think of the process as five fields of activity that overlap each other in a multidimensional environment of intellectual discourse. The process is not linear; rather, it is one of interaction and ambiguity where paths appear to meander aimlessly toward durable and innovative solutions (Fig. **1**).

Defining. Immersion into the design process begins by defining the problem and its parameters. What are the client's needs, and what is the sphere of the client's activity? What are the goals and objectives of a potential solution? Who is the audience? What are the budget and production limitations? To answer these and other pertinent questions is to set the problem's parameters. These parameters may change at any time during the process and should not be too tightly defined.

Gathering. This phase provides the essential information needed by the designer regarding all aspects of the problem. This includes gathering information about the client, problem content, and production requirements. While gathering information, designers should make use of all available resources. Experts, libraries, museums, antique shops, and movie theatres are all excellent information-gathering venues. The Internet is also an invaluable information-gathering resource.

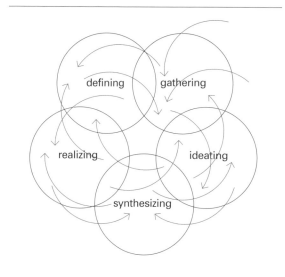

1.
This typographic diagram reveals the design process as a flexible, dynamic, and unpredictable mental journey. Diverse lines of thought and activity lead eventually to closure.
2.
A process book unfolding in time, documents the petroglyphs and pictographs of the Anasazi and Fremont cultures of the American southwest desert region. (Designer: Rob Carter)

As new developments arise later in the process, designers may find it necessary to gather additional information. A designer's curiosity is the key to informed practice, and the ability to openly and clearly communicate with colleagues and clients.

Ideating. The worst enemy of the design process is thinking inside the proverbial "box." The mind should be open to lateral, sideways, and unconventional thinking. Often, experienced designers rely upon formula or knowledge-based intuition to solve problems. But these approaches often limit the vast potential for new possibilities.

Synthesizing. Whereas the ideation phase is concerned with expanding possibilities, the synthesis phase concentrates on narrowing options and coming to closure. Often, the most effective solutions are readily apparent; they meet initial problem criteria and are formally and aesthetically superior to weaker solutions. Short of using sophisticated marketing techniques, the best way to evaluate the effectiveness of a solution is to weigh it point by point against the criteria established at the outset of the problem. However, if necessary and appropriate, the original criteria can change at this stage and the solution can be adjusted.

Realizing. Implementation cannot go forward without client approval. Usually, designers and clients communicate on a regular basis throughout the process, which prevents confusion and misunderstanding at the end. More often than not, clients are not visually oriented people, thus making it the designer's responsibility to educate them and communicate with them clearly and without the use of jargon or highly technical language. Such communication breeds mutual trust and respect. Upon final approval, the design moves into final production. Successful implementation requires the designer to manage production processes such as printing and manufacturing with an eye on intermediate and final deadlines.

Processing typographic form and ideas

The typographic design process involves a search for typographic form and its meaning. Any change in form (syntactics) results in a shift in meaning (semantics). The goal of typographic problem solving is to formulate ideas based on form and its meaning. The following methods and techniques aid the designer in this search.

Sketchbooks and process books

Highly curious individuals, designers crave visual stimuli and make a habit of recording daily visual experiences. Through camera lens and sketchbook, they record thoughts and images by drawing, writing, photographing, and collecting.

Effective sketchbooks do not resemble typical scrapbooks. They reflect ordinary as well as extraordinary experiences during the course of everyday working and living. Sketchbooks function as a collection, a repository of things found and observed, of the visible and invisible, of the concrete and abstract. They are both public and private.

Sketchbooks contain a variety of content – from nonsensical doodles to visual schemas of scientific phenomena. Growing and expanding regularly, they reflect the individual designer's mental flights, observances, and voice (Fig. **3**).

While a sketchbook is an continuing exercise in recording visual and verbal ideas, a process book records specific processes as they unfold (Fig. **2**). Keeping a process book aids the designer in staying consciously aware of the activities and thinking leading to problem solutions.

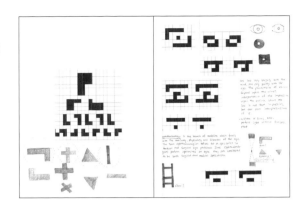

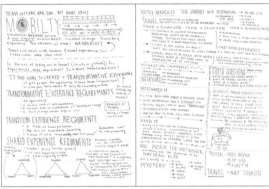

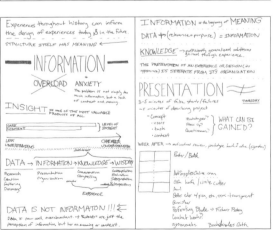

3.
Selected spreads from sketchbooks reveal process drawings, thoughts, and visual notations. (Designers: Yoon-Young Chai, Brent McCormick, Matthew Stay)

219

Any subject can serve as the nucleus for a mind map. Mindmapping is an invaluable exercise where the designer's thought processes are revealed as an ever-expanding universe of possibility and potential. (Designer: Matt Klimas)

Polar opposition occurs in both the syntactic and semantic realms. In this example, the letters *S* and *T* stand syntactically in opposition in terms of shape and weight. The lightness and solitude of peace stand in opposition to the heaviness and aggressiveness of war.

5.

Brainstorming. Brainstorming is perhaps the most familiar ideation strategy for design teams. Though it has its detractors, it remains an effective approach if conducted according to basic ground rules. These include deferring judgement of all ideas during a session, generating as many ideas as possible, and being open to both good and bad ideas. The basic theory is that the group is a deep reservoir of experience, and that one idea leads to new and unique possibilities.

Mindmapping. Related to free association, mindmapping is a nonlinear brainstorming process with a word or concept at its nucleus. By making lighting-quick associations of the concept, a web of related themes reflecting mental patterns emerges (Fig. **4**). The satellite concepts generated from mindmapping help designers identify areas of possible content, both visual and verbal.

Word lists and interaction matrix structures
Making lists of analogous words and descriptive phrases related to specific umbrella topics, or spontaneously generating random words derived from brainstorming or mindmapping can stimulate thinking and open the mind to broader visual possibilities. When lists of words are integrated into the structure of a matrix, new and improbable relationships can be forged between unlikely and contrasting word pairs. Often the most intriguing concepts emerge from the interaction of polar or nearly polar opposites. A sign is understood more clearly and achieves greater impact when juxtaposed with an opposite sign (Fig. **5**). Interaction matrix structures can also accommodate the interaction of words with images, or images with other images. Collecting an abundance of material related to given content and applying it to an interaction matrix can aid the designer in identifying and defining a problem, or in developing fresh ideas outside of conventional thinking. When engaging in these processes, it is helpful to unleash the "play instinct," release the child within, and hush any tendency toward self-criticism. In the sample matrix structure, the red dots are placed at points of potential interaction (Fig. **6**).

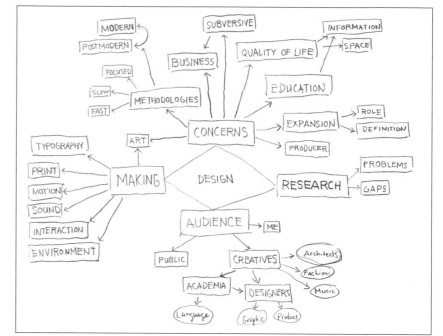

4.

	fear	courage	hate	lust	resentment	anger	trust	seduction	happiness	frustration
elephant										
giraffe						●				
possum		●								
chipmunk										
whale					●					
eagle						●			●	
ant										
rattlesnake	●									
iguana				●						
porcupine										

6.

7.
Gathering images and organizing them thematically aids in generating ideas. (Designer: Jessica Salas)

8.
Preliminary visual notations exploring a wide range of concepts and typographic concerns. (Designer: Alan Bayot)

9, 10.
Sketches with accompanying notes explore thematic possibilities. (Designer: Chinedue Chukwu)

11.
Small but highly articulated thumbnail notations search for a typographic system that will unify the series of banknotes. (Designer: Roland Ilog)

12, 13.
A distinct progression in visual refinement can be seen in this comparison of a preliminary and a final comprehensive. (Designer: Roland Ilog)

Visual notations and comprehensives

Ideas that remain only in the mind and not articulated visually do little to move the process ahead. Design students often convey their ideas to teachers and classmates verbally. This is where ideas begin, but until they are expressed visually in the form of sketches or notations, their effectiveness cannot be evaluated. Thumbnail notations can be created with a variey of tools and materials – from pencil and paper to computer.

The design process can be thought of as beginning at the broad base of an inverted pyramid. Options are expansive at first, but as one moves through the pyramid toward its apex, the vision of a viable outcome – the solution to a problem – becomes more specific. The process may begin as a mindmapping session, progress into a series of general notations, then advance to comprehensive sketches. A project conducted at Rutgers University by Professor Ned Drew is used to illustrate this progression. Visual notations and sketches leading to the design of banknotes are shown (Figs. **7–13**); and see Chapter Ten, Figures **118** and **119**.

7.

8.
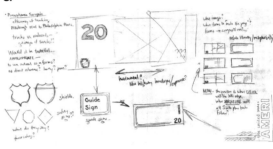

9.
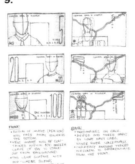

10.
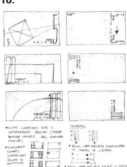

11.
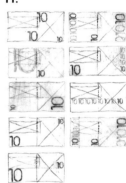

12.

13.

14.

'DOES THE IMAGE *DUPLICATE* CERTAIN ITEMS OF *INFORMATION* IN THE TEXT, BY A *PHENOMENON* OF

ROLAND BARTHES

REDUN DANCY

1

OR DOES THE TEXT ADD A BRAND NEW ITEM OF INFORMATION TO THE IMAGE?'

Metaphorical thinking

In language, a metaphor is a subset of analogy, a figure of speech suggesting that something appears, sounds, or behaves like something else. Letterforms can suggest objects and ideas beyond their function as symbols for spoken language. They possess visual qualities and can be manipulated to suggest other objects, sounds, and images. Typographic metaphors are derived through any number of syntactic manipulations, including those of spacing, position, rhythmic sequencing, and color. Metaphorical thinking is a conceptual process focused on finding relationships between dissimilar ideas and objects; some are highly abstract, others more concrete. Metaphors are successful when the mind makes a conceptual leap and perceives shifts in context. New contexts are established when visual signs are combined to make new signs or when the mind makes an association based on past experience. Fragmented and exploding letterforms suggest fireworks; forms organized into a syncopated rhythm imply a jazz orchestra. Every typeface is also a potential metaphor capable of suggesting meaning beyond the mere content of the words and text. Some typefaces march, others dance (Figs. **14, 15**).

14.
Reorganizing letters in the word *redundancy* translates into a typographic metaphor of the word. (Designer: Todd Timney)

15.
Selected letters from the alphabet, *Dutch Doubles,* with designs by thirty-seven Dutch type designers. Designers of the letters shown:

A: Jacques Le Bailly
I: Assi Kootstra
K: Sander Kessels
M: Marc Lubbers
O: Harmen Liemburg
P: Peter Bil'ak
S: Swip Stolk
T: Richard Niessen
Y: Mark van Wageningen
?: Rutger Middendorp
*: Martin Majoor
.,_: Max Kisman

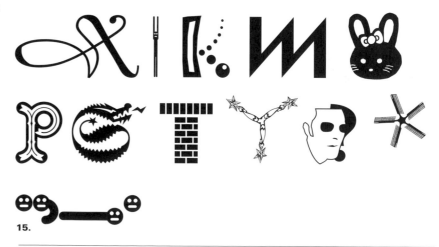

15.

16.
A pasteboard in a computer application measuring approximately 36 x 16 inches serves as a large digital sketch pad for the development and processing of form and ideas. (Designer: Guilherme Villar)

Typographic processes and the computer

The introduction of the computer as a major design tool has dramatically changed the typographic design process, and many designers have adopted hybrid problem-solving methods. Some begin with hand-drawn sketches and proceed to the computer to refine and produce the final designs. Others scan rough sketches and import them as templates into chosen applications, which are then rendered digitally. In a reciprocal process, Swiss designer Jean-Benoît Lévy often begins with hand sketches, redraws them on a computer, prints them out, applies changes and color by hand, and returns to the computer once again. Designer Guilherme Villar creates digital pasteboards often containing hundreds of elements that are combined and manipulated in search of problem solutions (Fig. **16**). It is not unusual for designers to begin the problem-solving process by going directly to the computer and developing ideas by means of digital sketches and permutations. All approaches are valid as long as the process delivers an effective and creative solution. Each designer is faced with embracing a unique relationship with the computer and all other methods, tools, and techniques that may be on the horizon.

Whenever working at the computer, it is advisable to save documents using the "save as" command rather than simply using the "save" command. Each new design permutation can be given a new name, which preserves the last permutation for possible future reference. Otherwise the process is lost in cyberspace. File management is now an essential part of the design process, and is a design problem in and of itself. A major challenge facing designers is how to adequately archive digital files for future reference and, as appropriate, for posterity.

Morphologies

A morphology is a menu of visual possibilities. It consists of a list of syntactic and/or semantic variables that can be systematically or randomly explored in a search for typographic solutions (Fig. **17**). Morphologies can be tailored in size and scope to accommodate a wide range of problems and applications. Just as the twenty-six letters of the alphabet are combined to form an infinite number of words, so too, can morphological factors be employed to achieve a vast number of typographic effects. When used freely and creatively, morphologies liberate rather than constrain the creative mind. Several precedents exist for the development and use of morphologies in typographic design practice, including the pioneering work of Karl Gerstner who developed logical morphologies based on the formal language of type. Gerstner believes that working with "morphological boxes" enables randomness, serendipity, and a kind of invention. He writes, "Working by the morphological method is value-free and unprejudiced – and at least makes it easier to find pioneer solutions where they are possible."

17.

The morphology to the left features a collection of typographic factors that can be freely appropriated in the course of solving typographic problems. The challenge and joy of using a morphology is to combine the components of the various categories in a search for visual alternatives.

The boxes in this morphology filled with black represent other possibilities that may be added as needed.

Typographic factors

	1	2	3	4	5	6	7	8	9
1.1 case	1.1.1 upper	1.1.2 lower	1.1.3 combination						
1.2 face	1.2.1 serif	1.2.2 sans serif	1.2.3 script	1.2.4 decorative	1.2.5 combination				
1.3 size	1.3.1 small	1.3.2 medium	1.3.3 large	1.3.4 combination					
1.4 slant	1.4.1 slight	1.4.2 medium	1.4.3 extreme	1.4.4 combination					
1.5 weight	1.5.1 light	1.5.2 medium	1.5.3 heavy	1.5.4 combination					
1.6 width	1.6.1 narrow	1.6.2 medium	1.6.3 wide	1.6.4 combination					

Form factors

	1	2	3	4	5	6	7	8
2.1 blending	2.1.1 linear	2.1.2 radial	2.1.3 combination					
2.2 distortion	2.2.1 fragmenting	2.2.2 skewing	2.2.3 bending	2.2.4 stretching	2.2.5 blurring	2.2.6 inverting	2.2.7 mutilating	2.2.8 combination
2.3 elaboration	2.3.1 addition	2.3.2 subtraction	2.3.3 extension	2.3.4 combination				
2.4 outline	2.4.1 thin	2.4.2 medium	2.4.3 thick	2.4.4 broken	2.4.5 combination			
2.5 texture	2.5.1 fine	2.5.2 coarse	2.5.3 regular	2.5.4 irregular	2.5.5 combination			
2.6 dimensionality	2.6.1 volumetric	2.6.2 shadowing	2.6.3 combination					
2.7 tonality	2.7.1 light	2.7.2 medium	2.7.3 dark	2.7.4 combination				

Space factors

	1	2	3	4	5
3.1 balance	3.1.1 symmetrical	3.1.2 asymmetrical	3.1.3 combination		
3.2 direction	3.2.1 horizontal	3.2.2 vertical	3.2.3 diagonal	3.2.4 circular	3.2.5 combination
3.3 ground	3.3.1 advancing	3.3.2 receding	3.3.3 combination		
3.4 grouping	3.4.1 consonant	3.4.2 dissonant	3.4.3 combination		
3.5 proximity	3.5.1 overlapping	3.5.2 touching	3.5.3 separating	3.5.4 combination	
3.6 repetition	3.6.1 few	3.6.2 many	3.6.3 random	3.6.4 pattern	3.6.5 combination
3.7 rhythm	3.7.1 regular	3.7.2 irregular	3.7.3 alternating	3.7.4 progressive	3.7.5 combination
3.8 rotation	3.8.1 slight	3.8.2 moderate	3.8.3 extreme	3.8.4 combination	

Support factors

	1	2	3	4	5	6	7	8	9
4.1 ruled lines	4.1.1 horizontal	4.1.2 vertical	4.1.3 diagonal	4.1.4 curved	4.1.5 stair-stepped	4.1.6 thin	4.1.7 medium	4.1.8 thick	4.1.9 combination
4.2 shapes	4.2.1 geometric	4.2.2 organic	4.2.3 background	4.2.4 adjacent	4.2.5 combination				
4.3 symbols	4.3.1 normal	4.3.2 manipulated	4.3.3 combination						
4.4 images	4.4.1 background	4.4.2 adjacent	4.4.3 contained	4.4.4 manipulated	4.4.5 combination				

20.

The range of potential solutions to a typographic problem is seemingly infinite. Variations, permutations, and transformations can be developed, exploring changes in both fundamental aspects and subtle details. Processing typographic form in search of solutions involves a process of insertion, substitution, and omission. After freely exploring ideas and selecting those for further development, the designer explores many permutations by inserting elements into the typographic space. The space may be organized by a predetermined grid structure, or the visual dynamics of the elements may define their own structures. This initial process enables the designer to consider the placement of parts, and most importantly, the relationship of the parts to the whole. Limiting initial elements to the same size and weight provides a solid base for the expansion of syntactic possiblities.

The substitution process replaces initial elements with alternative elements in an effort to test and improve the hierarchy and legibility of the text, as well as to heighten visual resonance. This is achieved by assigning different sizes, weights, spacings, positions, as well as other syntactic variations.

The omission phase eliminates superfluous or meaningless elements, reduces elements to their essential form, and simplifies the typographic field as a whole. The process then repeats itself until all possibilities are exhausted and a viable solution to the problem is revealed.

For the design of a title-page, designer Thomas Detrie developed a sequence of possible solutions. Detrie's approach to the design process is based on his beliefs that "solutions come from within the problem" and "ideas come from working with the material and are not supplied or preconceived."

18.

This project commenced in the postgraduate program in graphic design at the Basel School of Design, Switzerland. The encouragement and criticism of Wolfgang Weingart are gratefully acknowledged.

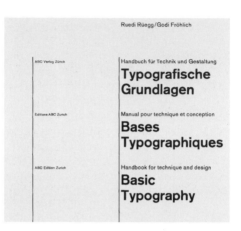

19.

20.

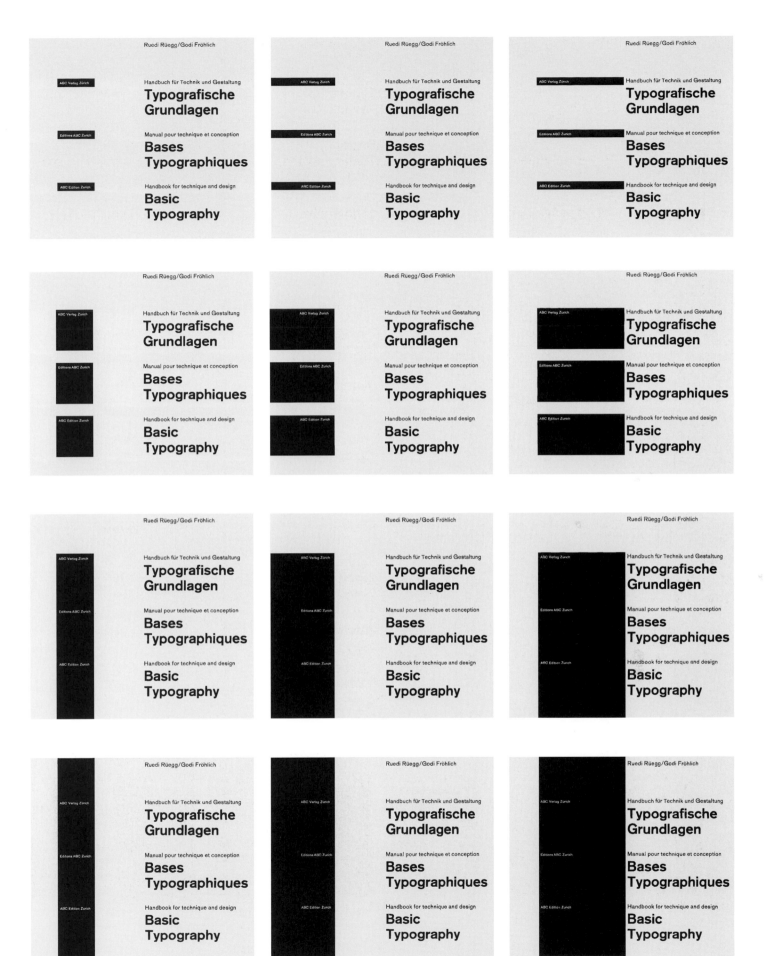

21a.

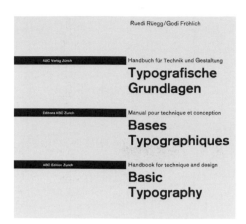

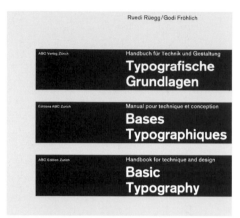

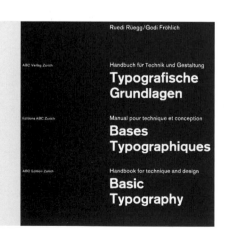

21b.

Detrie's personal problem-solving method is a three-stage design process: preliminary exploration, message investigation, and visualization of solutions. In his preliminary exploration, Detrie considered the nature and content of the problem and made sketches to explore possible directions. Typographic information (title, subtitle, authors, and publisher) was assigned priority.

Detrie raised the question, "For the book *Basic Typography,* what is basic to typography that can be signified in a visual solution?" His answer established parameters appropriate to the given problem: a right-angled system, black on white, printed and unprinted areas, and a clear message. These considerations became the criteria for the investigation.

To investigate the range of typographic possibilities for the clear presentation of the manuscript, actual type was set and used in the initial visualizations for accuracy. A sans-serif face was chosen, and the message was printed in three sizes and two weights for use as raw material in these typographic studies. While maintaining the message priorities determined in the first stage, a variety of visual solutions were executed.

Decisions were made through subtle comparisons of type sizes and weights to select those that provided the best visual balance and message conveyance. Detrie did not place the type upon a predetermined grid; rather, he allowed the organizational structure to evolve from the process of working with the type proofs. Selecting the basic typographic arrangement was an intermediate step in the design process (Fig. **18**).

Next, Detrie developed a series of variations of this arrangement by investigating the application of horizontal and vertical lines, positive and negative shapes with positive type, and positive and negative shapes with positive and reversed type. Figure **19** demonstrates nine permutations with the application of vertical lines to the basic typographic schema. Permutations range from type alone to the addition of linear and rectilinear elements to a solid black page with reversed type (Fig. **20**). A graded arrangement of twenty-four of the many solutions is shown in Figure **21**. Observe the horizontal and vertical sequencing.

Unlimited solutions are possible in typographic design, and selection becomes an integral part of the design process. Not every possible solution is appropriate; the designer must continually evaluate each one against the problem criteria.

24.

25.

Ernest Bernhardi engaged in a series of free typographic experiments with the intent of broadening his understanding of typographic syntax and exploring new forms of typographic expression. For this project, he thought of typography not as an end or a result but rather as part of a continuous, transformative process shared by other forms of expression: automatic writing/drawing, collage, and photography.

To carve out a focused span of time for intense investigation, Bernhardi isolated himself in his work space for a period of several months. He states, "I purposely shut myself off from the outside in an effort to enter fractions of bliss, and to lead my thoughts effortlessly into a state of peace and humility. The process, the activity of graphic design, became my sanctuary."

Seldom sitting, Bernhardi worked on his feet. He explains, "standing forces me out of the comfortable chair – the chair where slouching and chin-resting-on-the-hand occurs. These seemingly irrelevant and harmless behaviors mark the beginning of disengagement in the design process." Over time, his dance-like movements formed patterns of behavior resembling a performance.

Bernhardi's minimal studio, located in a small attic space, was primarily analog in scope. It was equipped with paper, a copy machine, traditional tools and supplies, and two studio lights. He used digital tools: a computer, digital camera, printer, and scanner. He utilized these conventional tools and materials as a brazen nonconformist.

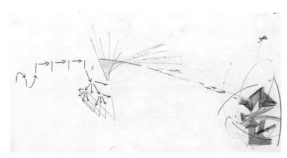

22.
A kinetic notation reveals
the process of thought
transformed into visible
language.

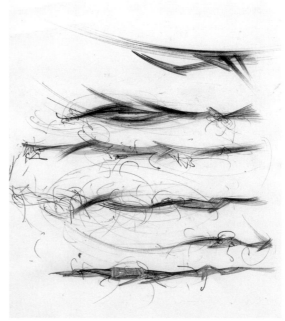

23.

23–26.
Having roots in Surrealist Automatism, "visual sentences" emerge through automatic writing.

27.
Automatic writing and sketching combined with spontaneous typographic fragments unveils an intricate and expressive typographic environment.

He began – without predetermined expectations or intentions – a process of automatic writing and sketching. Responding to visual and verbal stimuli, he sought to master the art of response rather than the art of planning, for response suggests process, and planning suggests product. This exercise encouraged mental and physical agility, and response through action and improvisation (Figs. **22–26**). These highly focused yet unconscious notations then served as typographic material for new explorations in typographic form and structure (Fig. **27**).

Bernhardi responded to various content using a wide variety of materials and processes. Hand-drawn and computer-generated elements were liberally combined in search of uncommon visual effects.

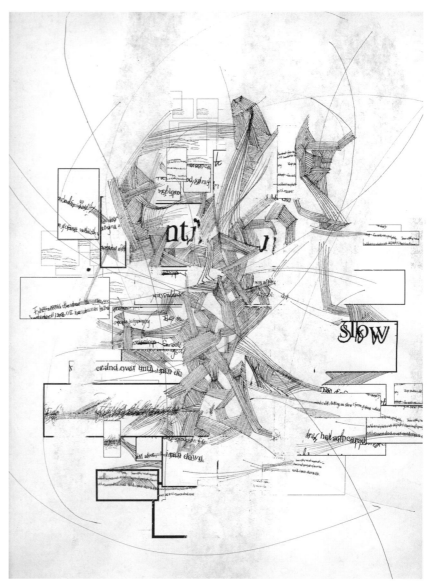

26.

28–31.
Armed with an attitude described by the late designer Paul Rand as the "play instinct," Bernhardi, rather unconsciously and spontaneously, transformed typographic elements in search of possible new forms and meaning.

Operations were quickly executed and included cutting, slicing, tearing, crumpling, scratching, scribbling, and taping (Figs. **28–31**). He repeated particular actions until evocative and enigmatic forms emerged, and he remained open to abruptly break away in search of new typographic effects (Fig. **32**). Working with physical material drove the process.

Compositions developed by adding and subtracting elements. Discarded parts, such as excess paper trimmed from previous exercises, were often used in subsequent studies. Adding type provoked subtraction and an urge to further tear at the surface. Conversely, tearing suggested the adding of new layers. Eventually, an abstract, formal language emerged.

Previous experiments were combined and manipulated into new forms using a combination of tools and techniques. For example, using the copy machine unconventionally (Figs. **33–36**), manipulating paper to suggest topographic space (Fig. **37**), and photographing through "windows" to expose hidden layers (Fig. **38**) lent unusual visual effects.

28.

29.

30.

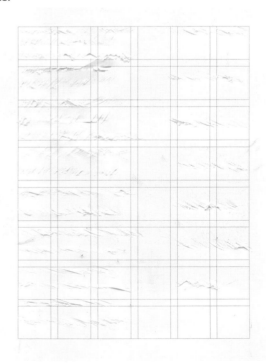

31.

32.
An extension of automatic writing, Bernhardi scratched sentences onto a typographic grid.

33–36.
Typographic elements are further processed into compelling images through the serendipitous effects of a copy machine.

33.

34.

37.
Hand-molded strands of typographic text suggest three-dimensional topographical maps.

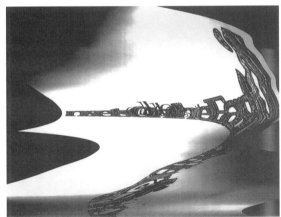

35.

36.

38.
A digital camera is used to capture a typographic layer discovered through a "window."

Visual transformations occurred instinctively and seamlessly. Various kinds of tape, including clear packaging tape, contributed to amorphous layers characterized by light, reflection, and fragmentation (Figs. **39–41**). These mystifying surfaces force the viewer's eye into and out of focus, providing mystery and intrigue.

Bernhardi's typographic approach is one of adaptability and expansion. The attitude is similar to that of the composer John Cage who viewed the random sounds of the surrounding environment – car horns, voices, falling objects, and footsteps – as a sonic system of signs comprising an abstract language. From within a seeming clutter, Bernhardi identified unusual spatial relationships, the emergence of unusual forms and textures, and the potential for new meaning and applications.

39, 40.
Layer upon layer of typographic forms and textures were embedded in clear tape. Details of this evolving tapestry provided new vignettes that were photographed and integrated as material into further explorations.

39.

40.

41.
Reflected light, shadow, and impromptu photography were explored to provide typographic form with sensory qualities.

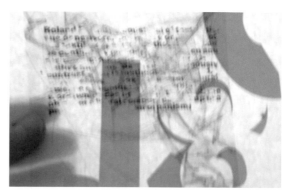

These posters represent a
final stage in Bernhardi's
investigations, but they also
beg further transformation in
a perpetual design process.

The investigation culminated as a series of large-scale, tiled posters constructed from Bernhardi's amassed collection of typographic experiments (Figs. **42–45**). These conclusive permutations visually and verbally recorded and expressed his growth and transformation as a typographic designer.

42.

43.

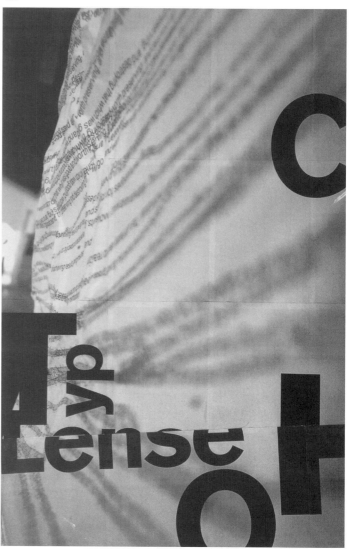

46.

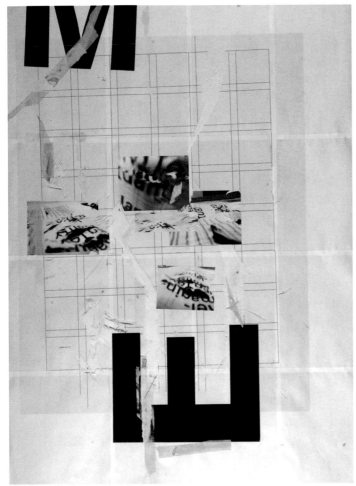

47.

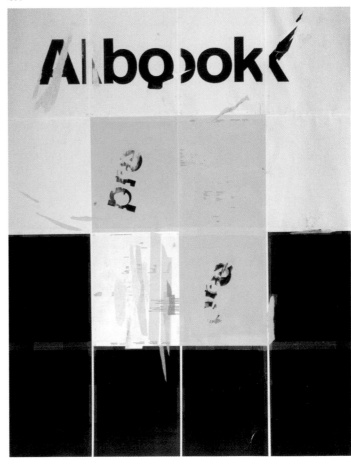

Now Projector: Design as Projection

49.
Impressions of inked and printed styrofoam blocks reveal mysterious forms called "Styroglyphs."

Now Projector is the culmination of a research project in which inquiry influenced both the creative process and the project's outcome. An interactive gallery installation, *Now Projector* looks at how meaning is made in the minds of both designers and their audiences. *Now Projector* is a gallery installation comprising a grid of 48 layered, laser-printed units.

Bret Hansen metaphorically linked his creative process to a pseudoscientific investigation guided by a textbook outlining a process of scientific inquiry. This process followed four fundamental steps: 1) search for a problem, 2) collect data through experimentation, observation, and field research, 3) arrange data, and finally 4) form and test the hypotheses. When the creative process is viewed as inquiry, focus on a final product shifts from the struggle for a singular, brilliant idea to insights gained by curious making and imaginative observation.

It often requires several attempts before a meaningful research question is identified, and *Now Projector* was no exception. The spark providing a hypothesis for this inquiry was the discovery that the Italian name for a designer is "progettista," or "projector." This term led Hansen to think of the design process as generally relating to many aspects of human endeavor. As he put it, "If you throw things, work on projects, daydream, watch movies, read novels, admire others, develop crushes, or cast shadows, then you are a projector."

The Italian title prompted a desire to understand what it means to be called a projector working in a discipline called projection. Concepts of projection were culled from psychology, philosophy, literature, physics, and cartography. Studio time was devoted to conducting visual experiments that played with these notions. A back-and-forth process ensued where textual research and visual experiments served equal roles. This etymological approach became a conceptual springboard after Hansen was well into the project.

48.
Ordinary styrofoam packing blocks contain fascinating protrusions and intrusions that seem to convey cryptic codes.

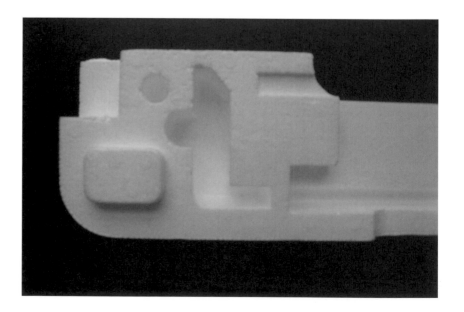

53.
Close-up photographs captured at extreme angles refer to distortions as by-products of projection.

  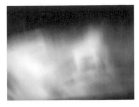

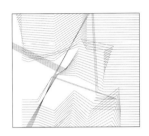

50, 51
Resembling the language of topographic maps, vector drawings were superimposed upon photographic images of styrofoam blocks.

52.
Rorschach inkblots provide projective tests in which a subject's perceptions and associations are recorded and analyzed. Hansen's investigation into projection begged for a brief foray into the world of inkblots.

The first round of experiments involved a study of styrofoam packing blocks (Fig. **48**). Imagining these ubiquitous objects as artifacts from the future, Hansen projected sci-fi meanings onto these perplexing forms. Each three-dimensional protrusion appeared to contain a secret code, and in an effort to isolate and extend this idea, a series of prints were made by inking the styrofoam surfaces and stamping their shapes onto paper (Fig. **49**). These inked impressions were then vectorized and transformed into a system of typographic marks named "styroglyphs."

Further experiments were conducted – each building on previous investigations – to explore notions about projection. Cartographic projections, for example, which map the globe as two-dimensional surfaces, unavoidably distort topographic reality. Vector drawings resembling topographic projections became a major sub-problem (Fig. **50**). These drawings were combined with styrofoam forms to enhance their strange geometry. The synthesis seemed to suggest futuristic landscapes (Fig. **51**).

Abstract images are often embued with visual traits that imply content; they provoke the mind into projecting meaning upon them. The Rorschach inkblot test used for psychological testing provides an applicable example of these phenomena. Hansen made numerous "inkblot" images as an exercise in stimulating mental projections of meaning (Fig. **52**).

Continuing with distortion as subject matter, Hansen viewed classic films and snapped images with a camera held at extreme angles. The contorted faces and skewed architectural settings suggested how perception is warped through projection (Fig. **53**).

Another step in the research involved the arrangement of data. Studio experiments resulted in visual forms comprising "data sets." By combining and arranging visual data, new insights emerged. Combinations of distorted film stills, styroglyphs and typographic forms resulted in digital collages providing opportunities for new readings. These compositions prompted the viewer – either the designer in the act of composing or the audience in the act of viewing – to seek and attach meaning (Fig. **54**).

The final step in the inquiry process was to form and test the projection hypothesis. Related to the design process, this parallels the formation of a creative concept. Looking at design as projection revealed a complex enterprise, for the process of projection is present in all aspects of design and communication.

Now Projector evolved into an installation combining a mural, a book, and a performance. Three prototypes preceded the final realization.

Content for the first prototype consisted of Hansen's large compilation of experiments and collages. These elements were structured into a double-sided, 48-module mural (Fig. **55**). Each of these modules were perforated into spreads, and an audience of 6 participants were invited to randomly remove the spreads and compile them into several 16-page booklets. The activity enabled participants to project their own interpretations as the mural was deconstructed and the books were constructed (Fig. **56**).

54.
Remniscient of Moholy Nagy's "Photoplastics," Hansen renders the familiar strange by combining found imagery, photography, and drawing into unusual perspectives.

55.

A prototype of the mural consisted of 48 perforated spreads and a total dimension of approximately 4 x 12 feet.

56.

Six participants gradually shifted their activities from randomly extracting spreads to reassembling them into one-of-a-kind books.

55.

The second prototype was an effort to elaborate and to solve problems encountered in the first iteration. In this version, rather than experiencing a blank surface after pages were removed, Hansen layered several murals where removal of a page would reveal yet another layer. The perforations, which proved awkward in the first prototype, were replaced with printed pads of paper. As viewers removed layers, fragments of underlying murals were revealed. Each top mural featured a large, distorted face, while subsequent layers provided text from *Plato's Allegory of the Cave.*

A digital projector beamed a wash of light on the mural, and as participants removed pages, their shadows were cast onto the surface, just as the shadows of chained people in the allegory were cast onto the wall of the cave.

Prototype three was similar to the previous version, but now typography played a more dominant role, and the number of mural layers increased to twelve for a total of 576 pages. This change added significantly to the transformational possibilities of the system. Adding to the cinematic effect, isolated images of styrofoam appeared to move along a trajectory the entire length of the mural.

57.

58.

57.
At a distance, participants perceived the mystifying image of a woman's eyes. Up close, the image faded into abstraction, yielding typographic detail.

58.
As participants peeled away pages and deconstructed the initial mural, new layers revealed uncanny, cubist juxtapositions.

Three pages were left blank whereupon a video of the entire process was projected (Fig. **57, 58**).

Finally, *Now Projector* was realized as a series of murals deconstructed by viewers who transform the modular parts into books. The system consisted of four double-sided murals, each comprising 48 modules or pages printed on two sides. Using simple binding supplies, visitors compiled books with pages they removed. These pages, called "projectiles" were mapped from top to bottom with a numeric system: A1–A12, B1–B12, C1–C12, and D1–D12. The back side of each projectile featured one of 192 unique back pages (Fig. **59**).

As pages were peeled off, parts of underlying murals were exposed. Except for the very first visitors, no one saw the entire first mural. The final mural system achieved Hansen's goal of creating a highly immersive, resonant, and participatory typographic environment wherein each participant projects his own meaning (Fig. **60**).

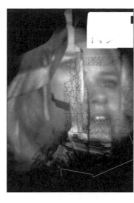

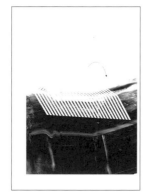

59.
Shown here are 15 of 192 unique back pages. These were generated spontaneously and unconsciously in a process designed to trigger unconscious projections.

60.
Two manifestations of the final mural reveal the kinetic, multi-faceted system. Radiating concentric circles suggest the projection process.

Typographic Book Covers

Designer Anne Jordan focuses passionately on the design of book covers, fortified by a belief that these artifacts contribute significantly to shaping culture. She applies a rigorous, hands-on design process, beginning by reading a text thoroughly, marking key words and phrases, trimming notes to a few salient themes, and sketching ideas for layouts with pen and paper.

The best of these ideas, which emerge from the text itself, launch her into highly experimental procedures, where through a wide variety of tools and materials she discovers compelling and communicative typographic images. The ample number of possible solutions springing from this process requires a thoughtful, curatorial eye for the final selection.

A City of Churches by Donald Barthelme

Imagine a city where streets are solidly lined with churches. The scene at first glance appears normal and wholesome; but in reality, quite the opposite is true. People live and work in the churches. The buildings are identified by different names and architectural styles, but as a group, they are all churches void of diversity and vitality. This is an unsettling story about reality and illusion, filled with absurd, dreamlike imagery.

Using vellum and a variety of other papers, Jordan cut letterforms and silhouettes resembling churches. These were layered together in multiple combinations, and then photographed to create shadowy and foreboding images.

61.
A spread from Jordan's sketchbook showing notes from reading and initial ideation sketches.

62.
A selection of photographic experiments employing church cutouts to search for engaging and memorable images.

63.
The final cover combines an image of ghost-like, blurred churches integrated with splintered type to suggest a dysfunctional town.

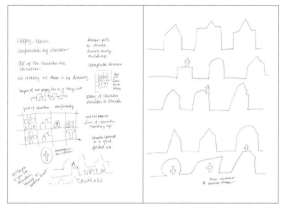

61.

62.

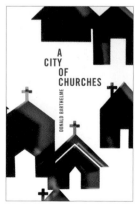

63.

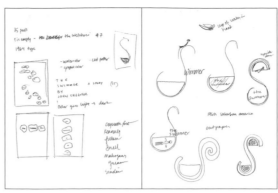

64.
Early investigations attempt to distill the essence of the story into a simple but comprehensive typographic configuration.

65.
These studies reveal an evolution in design thinking and an eagerness to explore many possible variations on a singular theme.

The Swimmer by John Cheever

Neddy Merrill swims home from a party at the Westerhazys' via an imaginary chain of swimming pools. He becomes more despondent and disillusioned the farther he swims, and as he gets closer to home, it becomes clear that things have gone terribly awry. Toward the end of the journey, Neddy's world is nothing as he remembers it, and when he finally arrives home, he ponders why his family is no longer there.

Beginning with the letter *S* to signify a path or journey, Jordan painted the letterform with watercolor to capture the shimmering quality of swimming pool water. This form was then surrounded by a chaotic nest of swimming pool outlines. Finally, a ladder was introduced as an entry point to the montage, inviting readers to climb in and lose their way with Neddy.

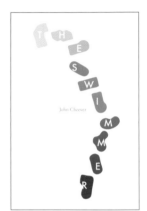

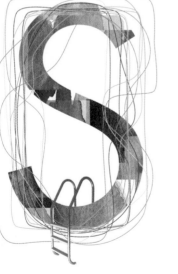

the Swimmer
JOHN CHEEVER

66.
Despite a great variety of typographic forms and images, unity and hierarchy are achieved in the final cover by a thoughtful juxtaposition of disparate elements.

67.
A page of notes taken while reading, and a sketchbook spread showing initial sketches and a comprehensive list of items carried by soldiers during war.

The Things They Carried by Tim O'Brien

Tim O'Brien exposes the realities of war by cataloging the ordinary objects soldiers carry on their bodies. These items, including weapons, photographs, floss, and socks result in feelings of fear, guilt, danger, love, grief, courage, and cowardliness.

Jordan identified the most iconic items from the list: helmets, weapons, canteens, dog tags, and the pervasive images of the female form. She then created outline patterns from these elements, and using Japanese stencil papers, layered them into repetitive patterns to suggest camouflage. These patterns were then scanned to produce negative images. Again, using a scanner, type was sandwiched into the images, capturing light in a way that suggests a jungle environment.

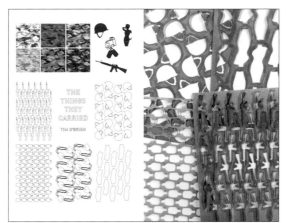

68.
A process book spread includes research into camouflage, pattern generation, and a collection of the original stencil sheets.

69.
Stencil sheets were layered to test various patterns.

70.
Jordan's thorough process typically lends numerous possible solutions. The small sampling shown here did not make the final cut.

71.
For the final cover, type and image integrate to form a unified gestalt, and a pattern reminiscent of camouflage.

68.

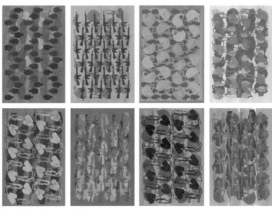

69.

70.

71.

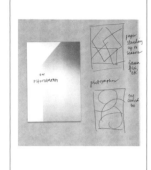

On Photography by Susan Sontag

Sontag analyzes how photographs alter the way we look at ourselves and the world. She argues that photography resembles an act of violence, not unlike firing a weapon and committing a murder. Photographs slice out moments and reinforce "a nominalist view of social reality as consisting of small units of an apparently infinite number... through photographs, the world becomes a series of unrelated, freestanding particles; and history, past and present, a set of anecdotes and *faits divers.* The camera makes reality atomic, manageable, and opaque."

Jordan responded to this violent shattering of our world by slicing paper into many pieces, folding it, piling it, and scanning it. The title typography was deconstructed into syllables and arranged in space to complement the paper structures.

73.

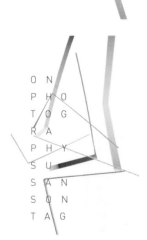

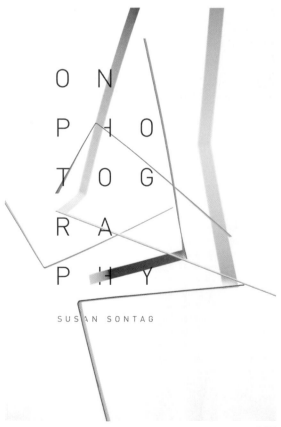

74.
For the final cover, a kinetic constellation of sliced forms suggest the uncertainty and mutability of photographic interpretation.

73.
A scanning bed provides a stage whereupon fragmented shards move about freely to suggest the fragmented, ambiguous, and particulate nature of photographs in human experience. Organizing the title typography into discrete syllables reinforces this concept.

75.

The Rotifer by Mary Gavell

A woman pieces together experiences that take place over many years, amounting to a greater story about how our lives carry us "in our own dimensions, like people passing on different escalators." We exist in different realities, separated by space and time, and conditions of which we are not aware. When different realities converge, as when the gentle nudge of a human finger creates a cataclysm inside a drop of pond water, these moments of intersection make the separateness of our individual dimensions evident. The story's title comes from the rotifer, a microscopic animal existing in its own world inside such a drop of pond water. Jordan explored ideas of separation and intersection by combining orbiting lines and type. This configuration, lasercut and pinned to a wall to cast a miniscule shadow, was combined with a blurred image of a city. The final composite image was then captured photographically.

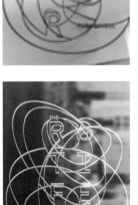

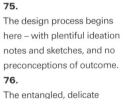

75.
The design process begins here – with plentiful ideation notes and sketches, and no preconceptions of outcome.

76.
The entangled, delicate lasercut of the spiraling typographic configuration further transforms via combinations of light, shadow, and photography.

77.
By blurring the city image in the final cover, it refers generically to any urban environment, reinforcing the idea that realities exist in both macro and micro spheres.

76.

77.

78.

The Peach Stone by Paul Horgan

A young couple's two-year-old daughter has burned to death and the family is on their way to the funeral. During the drive, the passengers reflect inside their heads on the tragic situation, and on their own lives. The resonating spirit of the story is about love in a family, love that "itself is ever-living," a testament to the fact that love cannot be measured or proven by words. The child's death marks a changing of seasons in all of their lives, bringing about a new season that is terribly sad yet that brings hope and strength for the future.

Co-designed by Anne Jordan and Meaghan Dee, the leaf was chosen as the visual metaphor for life and death, the changing of seasons, and the preciousness of human life. A laser cutter was used to etch typography into actual leaves, using the element of fire itself to generate the title.

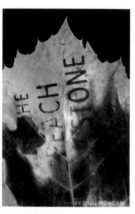

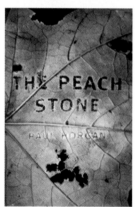

79.

80.

78.
The designers experimented with laser cutter settings to achieve a range of effects with the type, from very light engraving to a full burn through the leaf that left only the skeletal veins intact.

79.
A selection of viable cover designs. By observing their shapes, colors, and textures, the leaves were framed into poetic compositions.

80.
The final cover's title typography provides not a separate, disconnected element; rather, it emerges from the leaf as if a natural part of its evolution.

The uses of typographic specimens by graphic designers have changed dramatically in the age of digital technology. Earlier generations of designers used specimens to determine which fonts and sizes to specify and order from typesetting companies, and for reference or tracing purposes when drawing layouts. A limited range of sizes were manufactured, and specimen sheets or books showed all available sizes.

Digital computers make an infinite range of sizes and style variations available, and designers can study and purchase fonts from digital type foundry Web sites. Today printed specimens are used for study and comparison purposes. The typeface specimens in this chapter were selected from outstanding type families to provide examples of the major historical classifications: Old Style, Transitional, Modern, Egyptian, and Sans Serif. More extensive specimens of Old Style and Sans Serif fonts are included, for these are the most widely used categories.

A bewildering number of typeface variations are available today, including versions originally designed for hand-, machine-, or phototype composition. Excellent newer varieties have been designed specifically for digital media. Designers need to study the subtlety of form and spacing in fonts, because their quality can vary widely.

ORONTII FINEI

DELPHINATIS, REGII MATHEMA=
TICARVM PROFESSORIS, DE
ARITHMETICA PRACTICA
LIBRI QVATVOR.

LIBER PRIMVS, DE INTEGRIS: HOC EST,
eiusdem speciei, siue denominationis tractat numeris.

¶ *De fructu, atq́ dignitate ipsius Arithmeticæ: Procemium.*

NTER LIBERALES MA=
thematicas, quæ solæ disciplinæ vocátur,
Arithmeticam primum locum sibi vendi=
casse: nemo sanæ mentis ignorat. Est enim
Arithmetica omnium aliarum disciplina=
rum mater, & nutrix antiquissima: nume=
rorũ qualitates, vim, & naturam, ac id ge=
nus alia demonstrans, quæ absolutum vi=
dentur respicere numerum. Cuius prin=
cipia tanta excellunt simplicitate, vt nul=
lius artis videatur indigere suffragio: sed cunctis opituletur artibus. Ad
cuius puritatem illud etiam plurimum facit: quoniam nulla diuinitati
adeò cõnexa est disciplina, quantùm Arithmetica. Nam vnitas omniũ
numerorũ radix & origo, in se, à se, ac circum seipsam vnica vel impar=
tibilis permanet: ex cuius tamen coaceruatione, omnis cõsurgit & ge=
neratur, omnísque tandem in eam resoluitur numerus. Quemadmo=
dum cuncta quæ seu discreta, siue composita inspectentur Vniuerso, à
summo rerum conditore in definitum digesta, redactáve sunt, & demũ
resoluenda numerum. ¶Quot autem vtilitates cognita, quótve laby=
rinthos ignota præbeat Arithmetica: conspicere facile est. Numerorũ
etenim ratione sublata, tollitur & musicarum modulationũ intelligen=
tia: geometricorum, cælestiúmve arcanorum subtilis aufertur ingres=
sio: tollitur & vniuersa Philosophia, siue quæ diuina, seu quæ contem=
platur humana: imperfecta relinquitur legũ administratio, vtpote, quæ

Dignitas
arithmeticę.

Fructus
arithmeticę.

A.iij.

Old Style

Garamond
Minion

Additional
Old Style fonts

1.

Page 3 of the French
Renaissance book *Arithmetica*
by Oronce Fine, printed by
Simon de Colines in Paris,
1535.

Although Old Style typefaces trace their heritage
to the printers of the Italian Renaissance, their
heritage extends to an earlier time, for Roman
inscriptional letterforms (see Chapter One, Fig. **18**)
inspired their capital-letter design. The Caroline
Minuscules (see Chapter One, Fig. **27**) from
medieval manuscripts inspired writing styles
during the fifteenth century, and these became
the model for Old Style lowercase letters.

Many Old Style typefaces bear the name of
Claude Garamond, a leading typeface designer
and punchcutter working in Paris when the book
Arithmetica (Fig. **1**) was published. In the heading
material, the designer has used bold capitals

for the author's name, two sizes of capitals for the
title, and italics for the subhead. The spatial intervals between these units have been established
with great care. Fleurons (printer's flowers), paragraph marks, a woodcut headpiece, and a large
initial letter *I* intricately carved on a woodblock
bring vibrancy to this elegant example of French
Renaissance book design and letterpress printing.

For more than five hundred years, designers have
created lively typeface variations inspired by Italian
and French Old Style fonts of the fifteenth and
sixteenth centuries. The specimens in this section
display digitized versions of traditional typefaces
with distinctive design attributes.

Adobe Garamond

A digital version designed by Robert Slimbach for Adobe Systems and released in 1992.

abcdefghij

klmnopq

rstuvwxyz

$1234567

890(,'"-;:)!?

140 point

ABCDEF
GHIJKL
MNOPQ
RSTUV
WXYZ&

140 point

abcdefghijklmnopqrstuvwxyz
ABCDEFGHIJKLMNOPQR
STUVWXYZ$1234567890
(.,'''-;:)!?&

abcdefghijklmn

opqrstuvwxyz

ABCDEFGHIJK

LMNOPQRSTU

VWXYZ$12345

67890(.,'''-;:)!?&

abcdefghijklmnopqrstuvwxyz
ABCDEFGHIJKLMNOPQRS
TUVWXYZ1234567890
(., ''"-;:)!?&

25 point

abcdefghijklmno

pqrstuvwxyz

ABCDEFGHIJK

LMNOPQRSTU

VWXYZ$12345

67890(,'"".;.:)!?&

81 point

abcdefghijklmnopqrstuvwxyz
ABCDEFGHIJKLMNOPQR
STUVWXYZ$1234567890
(.,'''-;:)!?&

26 point

abcdefghijklmno
pqrstuvwxyz
ABCDEFGHIJK
LMNOPQRST
UVWXYZ$1234
567890(,'''-;:)!?&

81 point

Adobe Garamond

abcdefghijklmnopqrstuvwxyz
ABCDEFGHIJKLMNOPQRSTUVWXYZ
$1234567890(.,'"-;:!)!?&
abcdefghijklmnopqrstuvwxyz
ABCDEFGHIJKLMNOPQRSTUVWXYZ
8 point $1234567890(.,'"-;:)!?&

abcdefghijklmnopqrstuvwxyz
ABCDEFGHIJKLMNOPQRSTUVWXYZ
$1234567890(.,'"-;:)!?&
abcdefghijklmnopqrstuvwxyz
ABCDEFGHIJKLMNOPQRSTUVWXYZ
9 point $1234567890(.,'"-;:)!?&

abcdefghijklmnopqrstuvwxyz
ABCDEFGHIJKLMNOPQRSTUVWXYZ
$1234567890(.,'"-;:)!?&
abcdefghijklmnopqrstuvwxyz
ABCDEFGHIJKLMNOPQRSTUVWXYZ
10 point $1234567890(.,'"-;:)!?&

abcdefghijklmnopqrstuvwxyz
ABCDEFGHIJKLMNOPQRSTUVWXYZ
$1234567890(.,'"-;:)!?&
abcdefghijklmnopqrstuvwxyz
ABCDEFGHIJKLMNOPQRSTUVWXYZ
12 point $1234567890(.,'"-;:)!?&

The whole duty of typography, *as with calligraphy,* is to communicate to the imagination, without loss by the way, the thought or image intended to be communicated by the author. And the whole duty of beautiful typography is not to substitute for the beauty or interest of the thing thought and intended to be conveyed by the symbol, a beauty or interest of its own, but, on the one hand, to win access for that communication by the clearness and beauty of the vehicle, and on the other hand, to take advantage of every pause or stage in that communication to interpose some characteristic & restful beauty in its own art. We thus have a reason for the clearness and beauty of the first and introductory page and of the title, and for the especial beauty of the headings of chapters, capital or initial letters, and so on, and an opening for the illustrator as we shall see by and by. Further, in the case of poetry, verse, in my opinion, appeals by its form to the eye, as well as to the ear, and should be placed on the page so that its structure may be taken in at a glance and

8/10

The whole duty of typography, *as with calligraphy,* is to communicate to the imagination, without loss by the way, the thought or image intended to be communicated by the author. And the whole duty of beautiful typography is not to substitute for the beauty or interest of the thing thought and intended to be conveyed by the symbol, a beauty or interest of its own, but, on the one hand, to win access for that communication by the clearness and beauty of the vehicle, and on the other hand, to take advantage of every pause or stage in that communication to interpose some characteristic & restful beauty in its own art. We thus have a reason for the clearness and beauty of the first and introductory page and of the title, and for the especial beauty of the headings of chapters, capital or initial letters, and so on, and an opening for the illustrator as we shall see by and by. Further, in the case of poetry, verse, in

8/12

The whole duty of typography, *as with calligraphy,* is to communicate to the imagination, without loss by the way, the thought or image intended to be communicated by the author. And the whole duty of beautiful typography is not to substitute for the beauty or interest of the thing thought and intended to be conveyed by the symbol, a beauty or interest of its own, but, on the one hand, to win access for that communication by the clearness and beauty of the vehicle, and on the other hand, to take advantage of every pause or stage in that communication to interpose some characteristic & restful beauty in its own art. We thus have a reason for the clearness and beauty of the first and introductory page and of the title, and for the especial beauty of the headings of chapters, capital or initial letters, and so on, and an opening for the illustrator as we shall see by and

9/11

The whole duty of typography, *as with calligraphy,* is to communicate to the imagination, without loss by the way, the thought or image intended to be communicated by the author. And the whole duty of beautiful typography is not to substitute for the beauty or interest of the thing thought and intended to be conveyed by the symbol, a beauty or interest of its own, but, on the one hand, to win access for that communication by the clearness and beauty of the vehicle, and on the other hand, to take advantage of every pause or stage in that communication to interpose some characteristic & restful beauty in its own art. We thus have a reason for the clearness and beauty of the first and introductory or

9/13

The whole duty of typography, *as with calligraphy,* is to communicate to the imagination, without loss by the way, the thought or image intended to be communicated by the author. And the whole duty of beautiful typography is not to substitute for the beauty or interest of the thing thought and intended to be conveyed by the symbol, a beauty or interest of its own, but, on the one hand, to win access for that communication by the clearness and beauty of the vehicle, and on the other hand, to take advantage of every pause or stage in that communication to interpose some characteristic & restful beauty in its own art. We thus have a reason for the clearness and beauty of the first and introductory page and of the

10/12

The whole duty of typography, *as with calligraphy,* is to communicate to the imagination, without loss by the way, the thought or image intended to be communicated by the author. And the whole duty of beautiful typography is not to substitute for the beauty or interest of the thing thought and intended to be conveyed by the symbol, a beauty or interest of its own, but, on the one hand, to win access for that communication by the clearness and beauty of the vehicle, and on the other hand, to take advantage of every pause or stage in that communication to interpose some characteristic & restful beauty in its own art. We thus have a reason

10/14

The whole duty of typography, *as with calligraphy,* is to communicate to the imagination, without loss by the way, the thought or image intended to be communicated by the author. And the whole duty of beautiful typography is not to substitute for the beauty or interest of the thing thought and intended to be conveyed by the symbol, a beauty or interest of its own, but, on the one hand, to win access for that communication by the clearness and beauty of the vehicle,

12/14

The whole duty of typography, *as with calligraphy,* is to communicate to the imagination, without loss by the way, the thought or image intended to be communicated by the author. And the whole duty of beautiful typography is not to substitute for the beauty or interest of the thing thought and intended to be conveyed by the symbol, a beauty or interest of its own, but, on the one hand, to win access for that communication

12/16

The Minion type family was
designed by Robert Slimbach
for Adobe Systems in 1990.

abcdefghij

klmnopqr

stuvwxyz

$123456 78

90(.,’’”-;:)!?

ABCDEF
GHIJKL
MNOPQ
RSTUV
WXYZ&

abcdefghijklmnopqrstuvwxyz
ABCDFGHIJKLMNOPQRSTU
VWXYZ$1234567890
(.,'''-;:)!?&

25 point

abcdefghijklmn
opqrstuvwxyz
ABCDEFGHIJKL
MNOPQRSTU
VWXYZ$12345
67890(,'''-;:)!?&

75 point

abcdefghijklmnopqrstuvwxyz
ABCDFGHIJKLMNOPQRSTU
VWXYZ$1234567890
(.,'"''-;:)!?&

25 point

abcdefghijklmno
pqrstuvwxyz
ABCDEFGHIJKL
MNOPQRSTU
VWXYZ$1234567
890(.,'"''-;::)!?&

75 point

abcdefghijklmnopqrstuvwxyz
ABCDFGHIJKLMNOPQ
RSTUVWXYZ$1234567890
(.,'''-;:)!?&

25 point

abcdefghijklmn
opqrstuvwxyz
ABCDEFGHIJKL
MNOPQRSTU
VWXYZ$12345
67890(,'''-;·)!?&

74 point

Adobe Minion
Regular

abcdefghijklmnopqrstuvwxyz
ABCDEFGHIJKLMNOPQRSTUVWXYZ
$1234567890(.,'"-;:!)!?&
abcdefghijklmnopqrstuvwxyz
ABCDEFGHIJKLMNOPQRSTUVWXYZ
8 point *$1234567890(.,'"-;:)!?&*

abcdefghijklmnopqrstuvwxyz
ABCDEFGHIJKLMNOPQRSTUVWXYZ
$1234567890(.,'"-;:!)!?&
abcdefghijklmnopqrstuvwxyz
ABCDEFGHIJKLMNOPQRSTUVWXYZ
9 point *$1234567890(.,'"-;:)!?&*

abcdefghijklmnopqrstuvwxyz
ABCDEFGHIJKLMNOPQRSTUVWXYZ
$1234567890(.,'"-;:)!?&
abcdefghijklmnopqrstuvwxyz
ABCDEFGHIJKLMNOPQRSTUVWXYZ
10 point *$1234567890(.,'"-;:)!?&*

abcdefghijklmnopqrstuvwxyz
ABCDEFGHIJKLMNOPQRSTUVWXYZ
$1234567890(.,'"-;:)!?&
abcdefghijklmnopqrstuvwxyz
ABCDEFGHIJKLMNOPQRSTUVWXYZ
12 point *$1234567890(.,'"-;:)!?&ß*

The whole duty of typography, *as with calligraphy,* is to communicate to the imagination, without loss by the way, the thought or image intended to be communicated by the author. And the whole duty of beautiful typography is not to substitute for the beauty or interest of the thing thought and intended to be conveyed by the symbol, a beauty or interest of its own, but, on the one hand, to win access for that communication by the clearness and beauty of the vehicle, and on the other hand, to take advantage of every pause or stage in that communication to interpose some characteristic & restful beauty in its own art. We thus have a reason for the clearness and beauty of the first and introductory page and of the title, and for the especial beauty of the headings of chapters, capital or initial letters, and so on, and an opening for the illustrator as we shall see by and by. Further, in the case of poetry, verse, in my opinion, appeals by its form to the eye, as well as to the ear, and should be placed on the page so that its structure may be taken in at
8/10

The whole duty of typography, *as with calligraphy,* is to communicate to the imagination, without loss by the way, the thought or image intended to be communicated by the author. And the whole duty of beautiful typography is not to substitute for the beauty or interest of the thing thought and intended to be conveyed by the symbol, a beauty or interest of its own, but, on the one hand, to win access for that communication by the clearness and beauty of the vehicle, and on the other hand, to take advantage of every pause or stage in that communication to interpose some characteristic & restful beauty in its own art. We thus have a reason for the clearness and beauty of the first and introductory page and of the title, and for the especial beauty of the headings of chapters, capital or initial letters, and so on, and an opening for the illustrator as we shall see by and
8/12

The whole duty of typography, *as with calligraphy,* is to communicate to the imagination, without loss by the way, the thought or image intended to be communicated by the author. And the whole duty of beautiful typography is not to substitute for the beauty or interest of the thing thought and intended to be conveyed by the symbol, a beauty or interest of its own, but, on the one hand, to win access for that communication by the clearness and beauty of the vehicle, and on the other hand, to take advantage of every pause or stage in that communication to interpose some characteristic & restful beauty in its own art. We thus have a reason for the clearness and beauty of the first and introductory page and of the title, and for the especial beauty of the headings of chapters, capital or initial letters, and so on, and an opening for the illustrator as we shall
9/11

The whole duty of typography, *as with calligraphy,* is to communicate to the imagination, without loss by the way, the thought or image intended to be communicated by the author. And the whole duty of beautiful typography is not to substitute for the beauty or interest of the thing thought and intended to be conveyed by the symbol, a beauty or interest of its own, but, on the one hand, to win access for that communication by the clearness and beauty of the vehicle, and on the other hand, to take advantage of every pause or stage in that communication to interpose some characteristic & restful beauty in its own art. We thus have a reason for the clearness and beauty of the first and introductory
9/13

The whole duty of typography, *as with calligraphy,* is to communicate to the imagination, without loss by the way, the thought or image intended to be communicated by the author. And the whole duty of beautiful typography is not to substitute for the beauty or interest of the thing thought and intended to be conveyed by the symbol, a beauty or interest of its own, but, on the one hand, to win access for that communication by the clearness and beauty of the vehicle, and on the other hand, to take advantage of every pause or stage in that communication to interpose some characteristic & restful beauty in its own art. We thus have a reason for the clearness and beauty of the first
10/12

The whole duty of typography, *as with calligraphy,* is to communicate to the imagination, without loss by the way, the thought or image intended to be communicated by the author. And the whole duty of beautiful typography is not to substitute for the beauty or interest of the thing thought and intended to be conveyed by the symbol, a beauty or interest of its own, but, on the one hand, to win access for that communication by the clearness and beauty of the vehicle, and on the other hand, to take advantage of every pause or stage in that
10/14

The whole duty of typography, *as with calligraphy,* is to communicate to the imagination, without loss by the way, the thought or image intended to be communicated by the author. And the whole duty of beautiful typography is not to substitute for the beauty or interest of the thing thought and intended to be conveyed by the symbol, a beauty or interest of its own, but, on the one hand, to win access for that communication by the clearness
12/14

The whole duty of typography, *as with calligraphy,* is to communicate to the imagination, without loss by the way, the thought or image intended to be commu nicated by the author. And the whole duty of beautiful typography is not to substitute for the beauty or inter est of the thing thought and intended to be conveyed by the symbol, a beauty or interest of its own, but, on the one
12/16

Caslon Regular

abcdefghijklmnopqrstuvwxyz
ABCDEFGHIJKLMNOPQRSTUV
WXYZ$1234567890(.,'"-;:)!?&

Caslon Bold

**abcdefghijklmnopqrstuvwxyz
ABCDEFGHIJKLMNOPQRSTUV
WXYZ$1234567890(.,'"-;:)!?&**

Centaur

abcdefghijklmnopqrstuvwxyz
ABCDEFGHIJKLMNOPQRSTUVWX
YZ$1234567890(.,'"-;:)!?&

Centaur Bold

**abcdefghijklmnopqrstuvwxyz
ABCDEFGHIJKLMNOPQRSTUVW
XYZ$1234567890(.,'"-;:)!?&**

Goudy Old Style

abcdefghijklmnopqrstuvwxyz
ABCDEFGHIJKLMNOPQRSTUVW
XYZ$1234567890(.,'"-;:)!?&

abcdefghijklmnopqrstuvwxyz
ABCDEFGHIJKLMNOPQRSTUV
WXYZ$1234567890(.,'"-;:)!?&

abcdefghijklmnopqrstuvwxyz
ABCDEFGHIJKLMNOPQRSTUV
WXYZ$1234567890(.,'"-;:)!?&

abcdefghijklmnopqrstuvwxyz
ABCDEFGHIJKLMNOPQRSTUV
WXYZ$1234567890(.,'"-;:)!?&

abcdefghijklmnopqrstuvwxyz
ABCDEFGHIJKLMNOPQRSTUV
WXYZ$1234567890(.,'"-;:)!?&

abcdefghijklmnopqrstuvwxyz
ABCDEFGHIJKLMNOPQRSTVW
XYZ$1234567890(.,'"-;:)!?&

Im VERLAG DES BILDUNGSVERBANDES der Deutschen Buchdrucker,
Berlin SW 61, Dreibundstr. 5, erscheint demnächst:

JAN TSCHICHOLD
Lehrer an der Meisterschule für Deutschlands Buchdrucker in München

DIE NEUE TYPOGRAPHIE

**Handbuch für die gesamte Fachwelt
und die drucksachenverbrauchenden Kreise**

Das Problem der neuen gestaltenden Typographie hat eine lebhafte
Diskussion bei allen Beteiligten hervorgerufen. Wir glauben dem Bedürf-
nis, die aufgeworfenen Fragen ausführlich behandelt zu sehen, zu ent-
sprechen, wenn wir jetzt ein Handbuch der **NEUEN TYPOGRAPHIE**
herausbringen.

Es kam dem Verfasser, einem ihrer bekanntesten Vertreter, in diesem
Buche zunächst darauf an, den engen Zusammenhang der neuen
Typographie mit dem **Gesamtkomplex heutigen Lebens** aufzuzei-
gen und zu beweisen, daß die neue Typographie ein ebenso notwendi-
ger Ausdruck einer neuen Gesinnung ist wie die neue Baukunst und
alles Neue, das mit unserer Zeit anbricht. Diese geschichtliche Notwen-
digkeit der neuen Typographie belegt weiterhin eine kritische Dar-
stellung der **alten Typographie**. Die Entwicklung der **neuen Male-
rei**, die für alles Neue unserer Zeit geistig bahnbrechend gewesen ist,
wird in einem reich illustrierten Aufsatz des Buches leicht faßlich dar-
gestellt. Ein kurzer Abschnitt „**Zur Geschichte der neuen Typographie**" leitet zu dem wichtigsten Teile des Buches, den **Grundbegriffen
der neuen Typographie** über. Diese werden klar herausgeschält,
richtige und falsche Beispiele einander gegenübergestellt. Zwei wei-
tere Artikel behandeln „**Photographie und Typographie**" und
„**Neue Typographie und Normung**".

Der Hauptwert des Buches für den Praktiker besteht in dem zweiten
Teil „**Typographische Hauptformen**" (siehe das nebenstehende
Inhaltsverzeichnis). Es fehlte bisher an einem Werke, das wie dieses Buch
die schon bei einfachen Satzaufgaben auftauchenden gestalterischen
Fragen in gebührender Ausführlichkeit behandelte. Jeder Teilabschnitt
enthält neben **allgemeinen typographischen Regeln** vor allem die
Abbildungen aller in Betracht kommenden **Normblätter** des Deutschen
Normenausschusses, alle andern (z. B. postalischen) **Vorschriften** und
zahlreiche Beispiele, Gegenbeispiele und Schemen.

Für jeden Buchdrucker, insbesondere jeden Akzidenzsetzer, wird „Die
neue Typographie" ein **unentbehrliches Handbuch** sein. Von nicht
geringerer Bedeutung ist es für Reklamefachleute, Gebrauchsgraphiker,
Kaufleute, Photographen, Architekten, Ingenieure und Schriftsteller,
also für alle, die mit dem Buchdruck in Berührung kommen.

INHALT DES BUCHES

Werden und Wesen der neuen Typographie
Das neue Weltbild
Die alte Typographie (Rückblick und Kritik)
Die neue Kunst
Zur Geschichte der neuen Typographie
Die Grundbegriffe der neuen Typographie
Photographie und Typographie
Neue Typographie und Normung

Typographische Hauptformen
Das Typosignet
Der Geschäftsbrief
Der Halbbrief
Briefhüllen ohne Fenster
Fensterbriefhüllen
Die Postkarte
Die Postkarte mit Klappe
Die Geschäftskarte
Die Besuchskarte
Werbsachen (Karten, Blätter, Prospekte, Kataloge)
Das Typoplakat
Das Bildplakat
Schildformate, Tafeln und Rahmen
Inserate
Die Zeitschrift
Die Tageszeitung
Die illustrierte Zeitung
Tabellensatz
Das neue Buch

**Bibliographie
Verzeichnis der Abbildungen
Register**

typ. tschichold

**Das Buch enthält über 125 Abbildungen, von
denen etwa ein Viertel zweifarbig gedruckt ist,
und umfaßt gegen 200 Seiten auf gutem Kunst-
druckpapier. Es erscheint im Format DIN A5 (148×
210 mm) und ist biegsam in Ganzleinen gebunden.**

Preis bei Vorbestellung bis 1. Juni 1928: **5.00** RM
durch den Buchhandel nur zum Preise von **6.50** RM

Bestellschein umstehend ➤

Sans Serif

**Univers
Meta
Futura**

**Additional
sans serif fonts**

2.

Prospectus designed by Jan Tschichold for his book *Die neue Typographie,* 1928.

Sans serif typefaces have elemental letterforms stripped of serifs and decorations. Although sans serifs first appeared early in the nineteenth century, their use accelerated during the 1920s. "Form follows function" became the design dictum, and the functional simplicity of sans serif typefaces led many designers to look upon them as the ideal typographic expression of a scientific and technological century.

In Jan Tschichold's influential book *Die neue Typographie,* he advocated a new functional style for a rational era. In the prospectus for the book, he used sans serif type as an expression of the age (Fig. **2**). The page also demonstrates asymmetrical balancing of elements on a grid system, visual contrasts of type size and weight, and the

importance of spatial intervals and white space as design elements.

During the 1950s, Univers and Helvetica were both designed as more contemporary versions of Akzidenz Grotesque, a German turn-of-the-century sans serif. Compare the text setting and the display specimens of Helvetica with their Univers counterparts. There are subtle differences in the drawing of many letterforms. The Univers family is renowned for its remarkable graphic unity, which enables the typographic designer to use all twenty-one fonts together as a flexible, integrated typographic system.

Univers was designed by
Adrian Frutiger and released
in 1957.

abcdefgh
ijklmnop
qrstuvwx
yz$12345
67890!?

124 point

ABCDEF
GHIJKLM
NOPQRS
TUVWX
YZ&(.,'""::)

abcdefghijklmnopqrstuv
wxyzABCDEFGHIJKLMN
OPQRSTUVWXYZ$12345
67890(.,'"-;:)!?&

26 point

abcdefghijklmn
opqrstuvwxyz
ABCDEFGHIJKL
MNOPQRSTUV
WXYZ$1234567
890(.,'"-;:)!?&

72 point

abcdefghijklmnopqrstuv
wxyzABCDEFGHIJKLMN
OPQRSTUVWXYZ12345
67890(.,'"-;:)!?&

26 point

abcdefghijklmn
opqrstuvwxyz
ABCDEFGHIJKL
MNOPQRSTUV
WXYZ$1234567
890(.,'"-;:)!?&

72 point

abcdefghijklmnopqrstuv
wxyzABCDEFGHIJKLMN
OPQRSTUVWXYZ$12345
67890(.,'"-;:)!?&

26 point

abcdefghijklmn
opqrstuvwxyz
ABCDEFGHIJKL
MNOPQRSTUV
WXYZ$1234567
890(.,'"-;:)!?&

72 point

Univers 55

abcdefghijklmnopqrstuvwxyz
ABCDEFGHIJKLMNOPQRSTUVWXYZ
$1234567890(.,'"-;:)!?&
abcdefghijklmnopqrstuvwxyz
ABCDEFGHIJKLMNOPQRSTUVWXYZ
8 point *$1234567890(.,'"-;:)!?&*

abcdefghijklmnopqrstuvwxyz
ABCDEFGHIJKLMNOPQRSTUVWXYZ
$1234567890(.,'"-;:)!?&
abcdefghijklmnopqrstuvwxyz
ABCDEFGHIJKLMNOPQRSTUVWXYZ
9 point *$1234567890(.,'"-;:)!?&*

abcdefghijklmnopqrstuvwxyz
ABCDEFGHIJKLMNOPQRSTUVWXYZ
$1234567890(.,'"-;:)!?&
abcdefghijklmnopqrstuvwxyz
ABCDEFGHIJKLMNOPQRSTUVWXYZ
10 point *$1234567890(.,'"-;:)!?&*

abcdefghijklmnopqrstuvwxyz
ABCDEFGHIJKLMNOPQRSTUVWXYZ
$1234567890(.,'"-;:)!?&
abcdefghijklmnopqrstuvwxyz
ABCDEFGHIJKLMNOPQRSTUVWXYZ
12 point *$1234567890(.,'"-;:)!?&*

The whole duty of typography, *as with calligraphy,* is to communicate to the imagination, without loss by the way, the thought or image intended to be communicated by the author. And the whole duty of beautiful typography is not to substitute for the beauty or interest of the thing thought and intended to be conveyed by the symbol, a beauty or interest of its own, but, on the one hand, to win access for that communication by the clearness and beauty of the vehicle, and on the other hand, to take advantage of every pause or stage in that communication to interpose some characteristic & restful beauty in its own art. We thus have a reason for the clearness and beauty of the first and introductory page and of the title, and for the especial beauty of the headings of chapters, capital or initial letters, and so on, and an opening for the illustrator as we shall see

8/10

The whole duty of typography, *as with calligraphy,* is to communicate to the imagination, without loss by the way, the thought or image intended to be communicated by the author. And the whole duty of beautiful typography is not to substitute for the beauty or interest of the thing thought and intended to be conveyed by the symbol, a beauty or interest of its own, but, on the one hand, to win access for that communication by the clearness and beauty of the vehicle, and on the other hand, to take advantage of every pause or stage in that communication to interpose some characteristic & restful beauty in its own art. We thus have a reason for the clearness and beauty of the first and introductory

9/11

The whole duty of typography, *as with calligraphy,* is to communicate to the imagination, without loss by the way, the thought or image intended to be communicated by the author. And the whole duty of beautiful typography is not to substitute for the beauty or interest of the thing thought and intended to be conveyed by the symbol, a beauty or interest of its own, but, on the one hand, to win access for that communication by the clearness and beauty of the vehicle, and on the other hand, to take advantage of every pause or stage in that communication to interpose

10/12

The whole duty of typography, *as with calligraphy,* is to communicate to the imagination, without loss by the way, the thought or image intended to be communicated by the author. And the whole duty of beautiful typography is not to substitute for the beauty or interest of the thing thought and intended to be conveyed by the symbol, a beauty or interest of its own, but, on the one hand, to win

12/14

The whole duty of typography, *as with calligraphy,* is to communicate to the imagination, without loss by the way, the thought or image intended to be communicated by the author. And the whole duty of beautiful typography is not to substitute for the beauty or interest of the thing thought and intended to be conveyed by the symbol, a beauty or interest of its own, but, on the one hand, to win access for that communication by the clearness and beauty of the vehicle, and on the other hand, to take advantage of every pause or stage in that communication to interpose some

9/13

The whole duty of typography, *as with calligraphy,* is to communicate to the imagination, without loss by the way, the thought or image intended to be communicated by the author. And the whole duty of beautiful typography is not to substitute for the beauty or interest of the thing thought and intended to be conveyed by the symbol, a beauty or interest of its own, but, on the one hand, to win access for that communication by the clearness and beauty of

10/14

The whole duty of typography, *as with calligraphy,* is to communicate to the imagination, without loss by the way, the thought or image intended to be communicated by the author. And the whole duty of beautiful typography is not to substitute for the beauty or interest of the thing thought and intended to be conveyed by the symbol, a beauty

12/16

Meta was designed by Erik
Spiekermann and released by
Fontshop in 1991.

abcdefghij
klmnopq
rstuvwxyz
$1234567
890!?

ABCDEF
GHIJKLMN
OPQRSTU
VWXYZ&
(',"''_-:;)

abcdefghijklmnopqrstuvw
xyzABCDFGHIJKLMNOPQRS
TUVWXYZ$1234567890
(.,'"-;:)!?&

26 point

abcdefghijklmnop
qrstuvwxyzABCDE
FGHIJKLMNOPQRS
TUVWXYZ$123456
7890(.,'"-;:)!?&

72 point

abcdefghijklmnopqrstuvw
xyzABCDFGHIJKLMNOPQRS
TUVWXYZ1234567890
(.,'"-;:)!?&

26 point

abcdefghijklmnop
qrstuvwxyzABCDE
FGHIJKLMNOPQRS
TUVWXYZ$123456
7890(.,'"-;:)!?&

72 point

279

abcdefghijklmnopqrstuvw
xyzABCDEFGHIJKLMNOPQRS
TUVWXYZ$1234567890
(.,'"'-;:)!?&

26 point

abcdefghijklmnop
qrstuvwxyzABCDE
FGHIJKLMNOPQRS
TUVWXYZ$123456
7890(.,'";:)!?&

72 point

Meta Normal

abcdefghijklmnopqrstuvwxyz
ABCDEFGHIJKLMNOPQRSTUVWXYZ
$1234567890(.,'"-;:)!?&
abcdefghijklmnopqrstuvwxyz
ABCDEFGHIJKLMNOPQRSTUVWXYZ
8 point *$1234567890(.,'"-;:)!?&*

abcdefghijklmnopqrstuvwxyz
ABCDEFGHIJKLMNOPQRSTUVWXYZ
$1234567890(.,'"-;:)!?&
abcdefghijklmnopqrstuvwxyz
ABCDEFGHIJKLMNOPQRSTUVWXYZ
9 point *$1234567890(.,'"-;:)!?&*

abcdefghijklmnopqrstuvwxyz
ABCDEFGHIJKLMNOPQRSTUVWXYZ
$1234567890(.,'"-;:)!?&
abcdefghijklmnopqrstuvwxyz
ABCDEFGHIJKLMNOPQRSTUVWXYZ
10 point *$1234567890(.,'"-;:)!?&*

abcdefghijklmnopqrstuvwxyz
ABCDEFGHIJKLMNOPQRSTUVWXYZ
$1234567890(.,'"-;:)!?&
abcdefghijklmnopqrstuvwxyz
ABCDEFGHIJKLMNOPQRSTUVWXYZ
12 point *$1234567890(.,'"-;:)!?&*

The whole duty of typography, *as with calligraphy,* is to communicate to the imagination, without loss by the way, the thought or image intended to be communicated by the author. And the whole duty of beautiful typography is not to substitute for the beauty or interest of the thing thought and intended to be conveyed by the symbol, a beauty or interest of its own, but, on the one hand, to win access for that communication by the clearness and beauty of the vehicle, and on the other hand, to take advantage of every pause or stage in that communication to interpose some characteristic & restful beauty in its own art. We thus have a reason for the clearness and beauty of the first and introductory page and of the title, and for the especial beauty of the headings of chapters, capital or initial letters, and so on, and an opening for the illustrator as we shall see by and by. Further, in the case of poetry, verse, in my opinion, appeals by its

8/10

The whole duty of typography, *as with calligraphy,* is to communicate to the imagination, without loss by the way, the thought or image intended to be communicated by the author. And the whole duty of beautiful typography is not to substitute for the beauty or interest of the thing thought and intended to be conveyed by the symbol, a beauty or interest of its own, but, on the one hand, to win access for that communication by the clearness and beauty of the vehicle, and on the other hand, to take advantage of every pause or stage in that communication to interpose some characteristic & restful beauty in its own art. We thus have a reason for the clearness and beauty of the first and introductory page and of the title, and for the especial beauty of the headings of chapters,

8/12

The whole duty of typography, *as with calligraphy,* is to communicate to the imagination, without loss by the way, the thought or image intended to be communicated by the author. And the whole duty of beautiful typography is not to substitute for the beauty or interest of the thing thought and intended to be conveyed by the symbol, a beauty or interest of its own, but, on the one hand, to win access for that communication by the clearness and beauty of the vehicle, and on the other hand, to take advantage of every pause or stage in that communication to interpose some characteristic & restful beauty in its own art. We thus have a reason for the clearness and beauty of the first and introductory page and of the title, and for the especial beauty of the headings of chapters, capital or

9/11

The whole duty of typography, *as with calligraphy,* is to communicate to the imagination, without loss by the way, the thought or image intended to be communicated by the author. And the whole duty of beautiful typography is not to substitute for the beauty or interest of the thing thought and intended to be conveyed by the symbol, a beauty or interest of its own, but, on the one hand, to win access for that communication by the clearness and beauty of the vehicle, and on the other hand, to take advantage of every pause or stage in that communication to interpose some characteristic & restful beauty in its own art. We thus have a reason

9/13

The whole duty of typography, as with calligraphy, is to communicate to the imagination, without loss by the way, the thought or image intended to be communicated by the author. And the whole duty of beautiful typography is not to substitute for the beauty or interest of the thing thought and intended to be conveyed by the symbol, a beauty or interest of its own, but, on the one hand, to win access for that communication by the clearness and beauty of the vehicle, and on the other hand, to take advantage of every pause or stage in that communication to interpose some characteristic & restful beauty in its own art. We

10/12

The whole duty of typography, as with calligraphy, is to communicate to the imagination, without loss by the way, the thought or image intended to be communicated by the author. And the whole duty of beautiful typography is not to substitute for the beauty or interest of the thing thought and intended to be conveyed by the symbol, a beauty or interest of its own, but, on the one hand, to win access for that communication by the clearness and beauty of the vehicle, and on the other hand, to

10/14

The whole duty of typography, *as with calligraphy,* is to communicate to the imagination, without loss by the way, the thought or image intended to be communicated by the author. And the whole duty of beautiful typography is not to substitute for the beauty or interest of the thing thought and intended to be conveyed by the symbol, a beauty or interest of its own, but, on the one hand, to win access for that

12/14

The whole duty of typography, *as with calligraphy,* is to communicate to the imagination, without loss by the way, the thought or image intended to be communicated by the author. And the whole duty of beautiful typography is not to substitute for the beauty or interest of the thing thought and intended to be conveyed by the symbol, a beauty or interest of

12/16

Futura Book

Futura was designed Paul
Renner; the first fonts were
released in 1927.

abcdefgh
ijklmnopq
rstuvwxyz
$12345
67890!?

125 point

ABCDEF
GHIJKLM
NOPQRS
TUVWXY
Z&(.,'"-;:)

125 point

283

abcdefghijklmnopqrstuvwx
yzABCDFGHIJKLMNOPQ
RSTUVWXYZ$123456789
0(.,'"-;:)!?&

26 point

abcdefghijklmn
opqrstuvwxyz
ABCDEFGHIJKL
MNOPQRSTUV
WXYZ$123456
7890(.,'"-;:)!?&

72 point

284

abcdefghijklmnopqrstuvw
xyzABCDFGHIJKLMNOPQR
STUVWXYZ1234567890
(.,'"-;:)!?&

26 point

abcdefghijklmnc

pqrstuvwxyzABC

DEFGHIJKLMNO

PQRSTUVWXYZ

$1234567890

(,'"-;:)!?&

72 point

abcdefghijklmnopqrst
uvwxyzABCDEFGHIJKL
MNOPQRSTUVWXYZ$
1234567890(.,'"-;:)!?&

26 point

abcdefghijklmn
opqrstuvwxyz
ABCDEFGHIJKL
MNOPQRSTUV
WXYZ$123456
7890(.,'"-;:)!?&

68 point

Futura Book

abcdefghijklmnopqrstuvwxyz
ABCDEFGHIJKLMNOPQRSTUVWXYZ
$1234567890(.,'"-;:)!?&
abcdefghijklmnopqrstuvwxyz
ABCDEFGHIJKLMNOPQRSTUVWXYZ
8 point   *$1234567890(.,'"-;:)!?&*

abcdefghijklmnopqrstuvwxyz
ABCDEFGHIJKLMNOPQRSTUVWXYZ
$1234567890(.,'"-;:)!?&
abcdefghijklmnopqrstuvwxyz
ABCDEFGHIJKLMNOPQRSTUVWXYZ
9 point   *$1234567890(.,'"-;:)!?&*

abcdefghijklmnopqrstuvwxyz
ABCDEFGHIJKLMNOPQRSTUVWXYZ
$1234567890(.,'"-;:)!?&
abcdefghijklmnopqrstuvwxyz
ABCDEFGHIJKLMNOPQRSTUVWXYZ
10 point   *$1234567890(.,'"-;:)!?&*

abcdefghijklmnopqrstuvwxyz
ABCDEFGHIJKLMNOPQRSTUVWXYZ
$1234567890(.,'"-;:)!?&
abcdefghijklmnopqrstuvwxyz
ABCDEFGHIJKLMNOPQRSTUVWXYZ
12 point   *$1234567890(.,'"-;:)!?&*

The whole duty of typography, *as with calligraphy,* is to communicate to the imagination, without loss by the way, the thought or image intended to be communicated by the author. And the whole duty of beautiful typography is not to substitute for the beauty or interest of the thing thought and intended to be conveyed by the symbol, a beauty or interest of its own, but, on the one hand, to win access for that communication by the clearness and beauty of the vehicle, and on the other hand, to take advantage of every pause or stage in that communication to interpose some characteristic & restful beauty in its own art. We thus have a reason for the clearness and beauty of the first and introductory page and of the title, and for the especial beauty of the headings of chapters, capital or initial letters, and so on, and an opening for the illustrator as we shall see by and by. Further, in the case of poetry, verse,

8/10

The whole duty of typography, *as with calligraphy,* is to communicate to the imagination, without loss by the way, the thought or image intended to be communicated by the author. And the whole duty of beautiful typography is not to substitute for the beauty or interest of the thing thought and intended to be conveyed by the symbol, a beauty or interest of its own, but, on the one hand, to win access for that communication by the clearness and beauty of the vehicle, and on the other hand, to take advantage of every pause or stage in that communication to interpose some characteristic & restful beauty in its own art. We thus have a reason for the clearness and beauty of the first and introductory page and of the title, and for the especial beauty of the

8/12

The whole duty of typography, *as with calligraphy,* is to communicate to the imagination, without loss by the way, the thought or image intended to be communicated by the author. And the whole duty of beautiful typography is not to substitute for the beauty or interest of the thing thought and intended to be conveyed by the symbol, a beauty or interest of its own, but, on the one hand, to win access for that communication by the clearness and beauty of the vehicle, and on the other hand, to take advantage of every pause or stage in that communication to interpose some characteristic & restful beauty in its own art. We thus have a reason for the clearness and beauty of the first and introductory page and of the title, and for the

9/11

The whole duty of typography, *as with calligraphy,* is to communicate to the imagination, without loss by the way, the thought or image intended to be communicated by the author. And the whole duty of beautiful typography is not to substitute for the beauty or interest of the thing thought and intended to be conveyed by the symbol, a beauty or interest of its own, but, on the one hand, to win access for that communication by the clearness and beauty of the vehicle, and on the other hand, to take advantage of every pause or stage in that communication to interpose some characteristic & restful

9/13

The whole duty of typography, *as with calligraphy,* is to communicate to the imagination, without loss by the way, the thought or image intended to be communicated by the author. And the whole duty of beautiful typography is not to substitute for the beauty or interest of the thing thought and intended to be conveyed by the symbol, a beauty or interest of its own, but, on the one hand, to win access for that communication by the clearness and beauty of the vehicle, and on the other hand, to take advantage of every pause or stage in that communication to interpose some characteristic & restful beauty in its own art.

10/12

The whole duty of typography, *as with calligraphy,* is to communicate to the imagination, without loss by the way, the thought or image intended to be communicated by the author. And the whole duty of beautiful typography is not to substitute for the beauty or interest of the thing thought and intended to be conveyed by the symbol, a beauty or interest of its own, but, on the one hand, to win access for that communication by the clearness and beauty of the vehicle, and on the other hand, to

10/14

The whole duty of typography, *as with calligraphy,* is to communicate to the imagination, without loss by the way, the thought or image intended to be communicated by the author. And the whole duty of beautiful typography is not to substitute for the beauty or interest of the thing thought and intended to be conveyed by the symbol, a beauty or interest of its own, but, on the

12/14

The whole duty of typography, *as with calligraphy,* is to communicate to the imagination, without loss by the way, the thought or image intended to be communicated by the author. And the whole duty of beautiful typography is not to substitute for the beauty or interest of the thing thought and intended to be conveyed by the

12/16

Akzidenz Grotesk

abcdefghijklmnopqrstuvwxyz
ABCDEFGHIJKLMNOPQRSTUVW
XYZ$1234567890(.,'"-;:)!?&

Akzidenz Grotesk Bold

abcdefghijklmnopqrstuvwxyz
ABCDEFGHIJKLMNOPQRSTUV
WXYZ$1234567890(.,'"-;:)!?&

Din Regular

abcdefghijklmnopqrstuvwxyz
ABCDEFGHIJKLMNOPQRSTUVWX
YZ$1234567890(.,'"-;:)!?&

Din Bold

abcdefghijklmnopqrstuvwxyz
ABCDEFGHIJKLMNOPQRSTUVWX
YZ$1234567890(.,'"-;:)!?&

Franklin Gothic Book

abcdefghijklmnopqrstuvwxyz
ABCDEFGHIJKLMNOPQRSTUVW
XYZ$1234567890(.,'"-;:)!?&

abcdefghijklmnopqrstuvwxyz
ABCDEFGHIJKLMNOPQRSTU
VWXYZ$1234567890(.,'"-;:)!?&

Frutiger Roman

abcdefghijklmnopqrstuvwxyz
ABCDEFGHIJKLMNOPQRSTUVWX
YZ$1234567890(.,' "-;:)!?&

Frutiger Bold

abcdefghijklmnopqrstuvwxyz
ABCDEFGHIJKLMNOPQRSTUVW
XYZ$1234567890(.,'"-;:)!?&

Scala Sans

abcdefghijklmnopqrstuvwxyz
ABCDEFGHIJKLMNOPQRSTUVWXY
Z$1234567890(.,'"-;:)!?&

Scala Sans Bold

abcdefghijklmnopqrstuvwxyz
ABCDEFGHIJKLMNOPQRSTUVWX
YZ$1234567890(.,'"-;:)!?&

P. VIRGILII MARONIS

GEORGICON.

LIBER SECUNDUS.

Hactenus arvorum cultus, et fidera cœli:
Nunc te, Bacche, canam, nec non filveftria tecum
Virgulta, et prolem tarde crefcentis olivæ.
Huc, pater o Lenæe; (tuis hic omnia plena
5 Muneribus: tibi pampineo gravidus autumno
Floret ager; fpumat plenis vindemia labris)
Huc, pater o Lenæe, veni; nudataque mufto
Tinge novo mecum direptis crura cothurnis.
    Principio arboribus varia eft natura creandis:
10 Namque aliæ, nullis hominum cogentibus, ipfæ
Sponte fua veniunt, campofque et flumina late
Curva tenent: ut molle filer, lentæque geniftæ,
Populus, et glauca canentia fronde falicta.
Pars autem pofito furgunt de femine: ut altæ
15 Caftaneæ, nemorumque Jovi quæ maxima frondet
Aefculus, atque habitæ Graiis oracula quercus.
Pullulat ab radice aliis denfiffima filva:
Ut cerafis, ulmifque: etiam Parnaffia laurus
Parva fub ingenti matris fe fubjicit umbra.
20 Hos natura modos primum dedit: his genus omne
Silvarum, fruticumque viret, nemorumque facrorum.
Sunt alii, quos ipfe via fibi repperit ufus.
Hic plantas tenero abfcindens de corpore matrum

Depofuit

Transitional

Baskerville

**Additional
Transitional fonts**

3.
Type page for the second book of Virgil's *Georgics,* designed and printed by John Baskerville, 1757.

Transitional type appeared during the eighteenth century, a period of typographic evolution. Steady technical advances allowed more refined punches, matrices, and typecasting. Designers were able to gradually increase the contrast between thick and thin strokes, apply sharper and more horizontal serifs to their characters, and make the stress of rounded letterforms more vertical. By the century's end, Old Style typefaces had evolved into the Modern styles with hairline serifs and geometric proportions: typefaces designed during the middle of this period of evolving designs were *transitional.*

Simplicity and understated elegance were achieved through the use of John Baskerville's masterful Transitional typefaces, seen in the title page of Virgil's *Georgics* (Fig. **3**). Generous margins, careful letterspacing of display type, and thoughtfully considered interline and wordspacing are present. The great Roman poet is presented to the reader with clarity and dignity in a book that "went forth to astonish all the librarians of Europe."

If the words *Transitional* and *Baskerville* have become interwoven in the lexicon of typography, it is because the Transitional typefaces produced by John Baskerville of Birmingham, England, have an unsurpassed beauty and harmony. Many Transitional typefaces in use today, including most of the specimens in this section, are inspired by the exquisite beauty of Baskerville's work.

291

Baskerville Regular

Early twentieth-century
adaptations were released
by American Type Founders,
Linotype, and Monotype.

abcdefghi

jklmnopq

rstuvwxyz

$1234567

890(,''"-;:)!?

130 point

ABCDEF
GHIJKL
MNOPQ
RSTUV
WXYZ&

abcdefghijklmnopqrstuvw
xyzABCDEFGHIJKLMNO
PQRSTUVWXYZ
$1234567890(.,'''-;:)!?&

27 point

abcdefghijklmn

opqrstuvwxyz

ABCDEFGHIJK

LMNOPQRSTU

VWXYZ$12345

67890(.,'''-;:)!?&

78 point

abcdefghijklmnopqrstuvwxyz
ABCDEFGHIJKLMNOPQ
RSTUVWXYZ$123456
7890(.,""'-;:)!?&

27 point

abcdefghijklmnop
qrstuvwxyz
ABCDEFGHIJKL
MNOPQRSTU
VWXYZ$123456
7890(.,""'-;:)!?&

78 point

abcdefghijklmnopqrst
uvwxyzABCDFGHIJKL
MNOPQRSTUVWXYZ
$1234567890(.,'''-;:)!?&

25 point

abcdefghijklmn
opqrstuvwxyz
ABCDEFGHIJK
LMNOPQRSTU
VWXYZ$123456
7890(,''-;:'')?&

72 point

296

Baskerville Regular

abcdefghijklmnopqrstuvwxyz
ABCDEFGHIJKLMNOPQRSTUVWXYZ
$1234567890(.,'''-;:)!?&
abcdefghijklmnopqrstuvwxyz
ABCDEFGHIJKLMNOPQRSTUVWXYZ
8 Point *$1234567890(.,'''-;:)!?&*

abcdefghijklmnopqrstuvwxyz
ABCDEFGHIJKLMNOPQRSTUVWXYZ
$1234567890(.,'''-;:)!?&
abcdefghijklmnopqrstuvwxyz
ABCDEFGHIJKLMNOPQRSTUVWXYZ
9 Point *$1234567890(.,'''-;:)!?&*

abcdefghijklmnopqrstuvwxyz
ABCDEFGHIJKLMNOPQRSTUVWXYZ
$1234567890(.,'''-;:)!?&
abcdefghijklmnopqrstuvwxyz
ABCDEFGHIJKLMNOPQRSTUVWXYZ
10 Point *$1234567890(.,'''-;:)!?&*

abcdefghijklmnopqrstuvwxyz
ABCDEFGHIJKLMNOPQRSTUVW
XYZ$1234567890(.,'''-;:)!?&
abcdefghijklmnopqrstuvwxyz
ABCDEFGHIJKLMNOPQRSTUVW
12 Point *XYZ$1234567890(.,'''-;:)!?&*

The whole duty of typography, *as with calligraphy,* is to communicate to the imagination, without loss by the way, the thought or image intended to be communicated by the author. And the whole duty of beautiful typography is not to substitute for the beauty or interest of the thing thought and intended to be conveyed by the symbol, a beauty or interest of its own, but, on the one hand, to win access for that communication by the clearness and beauty of the vehicle, and on the other hand, to take advantage of every pause or stage in that communication to interpose some characteristic & restful beauty in its own art. We thus have a reason for the clearness and beauty of the first and introductory page and of the title, and for the especial beauty of the headings of chapters, capital or initial letters, and so on, and an opening for the illustrator as we shall see by and by. Further, in the case of poetry, verse, in my opinion, appeals by its form to the eye, as well as to the ear, and should be placed on the page so that its structure may be
8/10

The whole duty of typography, *as with calligraphy,* is to communicate to the imagination, without loss by the way, the thought or image intended to be communicated by the author. And the whole duty of beautiful typography is not to substitute for the beauty or interest of the thing thought and intended to be conveyed by the symbol, a beauty or interest of its own, but, on the one hand, to win access for that communication by the clearness and beauty of the vehicle, and on the other hand, to take advantage of every pause or stage in that communication to interpose some characteristic & restful beauty in its own art. We thus have a reason for the clearness and beauty of the first and introductory page and of the title, and for the especial beauty of the headings of chapters, capital or initial letters, and so on, and an opening for the illustrator as we shall
8/12

The whole duty of typography, *as with calligraphy,* is to communicate to the imagination, without loss by the way, the thought or image intended to be communicated by the author. And the whole duty of beautiful typography is not to substitute for the beauty or interest of the thing thought and intended to be conveyed by the symbol, a beauty or interest of its own, but, on the one hand, to win access for that communication by the clearness and beauty of the vehicle, and on the other hand, to take advantage of every pause or stage in that communication to interpose some characteristic & restful beauty in its own art. We thus have a reason for the clearness and beauty of the first and introductory page and of the title, and for the especial beauty of the headings of chapters, capital or initial letters, and so on, and an opening for the illustrator as we shall
9/11

The whole duty of typography, *as with calligraphy,* is to communicate to the imagination, without loss by the way, the thought or image intended to be communicated by the author. And the whole duty of beautiful typography is not to substitute for the beauty or interest of the thing thought and intended to be conveyed by the symbol, a beauty or interest of its own, but, on the one hand, to win access for that communication by the clearness and beauty of the vehicle, and on the other hand, to take advantage of every pause or stage in that communication to interpose some characteristic & restful beauty in its own art. We thus have a reason for the clearness and beauty of the first and introductory
9/13

The whole duty of typography, *as with calligraphy,* is to communicate to the imagination, without loss by the way, the thought or image intended to be communicated by the author. And the whole duty of beautiful typography is not to substitute for the beauty or interest of the thing thought and intended to be conveyed by the symbol, a beauty or interest of its own, but, on the one hand, to win access for that communication by the clearness and beauty of the vehicle, and on the other hand, to take advantage of every pause or stage in that communication to interpose some characteristic & restful beauty in its own art. We thus have a reason for the clearness and beauty of the first
10/12

The whole duty of typography, *as with calligraphy,* is to communicate to the imagination, without loss by the way, the thought or image intended to be communicated by the author. And the whole duty of beautiful typography is not to substitute for the beauty or interest of the thing thought and intended to be conveyed by the symbol, a beauty or interest of its own, but, on the one hand, to win access for that communication by the clearness and beauty of the vehicle, and on the other hand, to take advantage of every pause or stage in that
10/14

The whole duty of typography, *as with calligraphy,* is to communicate to the imagination, without loss by the way, the thought or image intended to be communicated by the author. And the whole duty of beautiful typography is not to substitute for the beauty or interest typographyof the thing thought and intended to be conveyed by the symbol, a beauty or interest of its own, but, on the one hand, to win access for that communication by the clearness and beauty
12/14

The whole duty of typography, *as with calligraphy,* is to communicate to the imagination, without loss by the way, the thought or image intended to be communicated by the author. And the whole duty of beautiful typography is not to substitute for the beauty or interest typographyof the thing thought and intended to be conveyed by the symbol, a beauty or interest of its own, but, on the one hand, to win
12/16

Georgia, drawn for clarity
on a computer screen, was
designed by Matthew Carter
in 1993 for the Microsoft
Corporation.

abcdefghij

klmnopq

rstuvwxyz

$1234567

890(,'",-;:)!?

110 point

ABCDEF

GHIJKL

MNOPQ

RSTUV

WXYZ&

110 point

abcdefghijklmnopqrstuv
wxyzABCDFGHIJKLMN
OPQRSTUVWXYZ
$1234567890(.,'"-;:)!?&

27 point

abcdefghijklmn

opqrstuvwxyz

ABCDEFGHIJK

LMNOPQRSTU

VWXYZ$12345

67890(.,'"-;:)!?&

72 point

abcdefghijklmnopqrstu
wxyzABCDEFGHIJKLM
NOPQRSTUVWXYZ
$1234567890(.,"'-;:)!?&

27 point

abcdefghijklmnop
qrstuvwxyzABC
DEFGHIJKL
LMNOPQRSTU
VWXYZ$123456
7890(.,"'-;:.)!?&

78 point

abcdefghijklmnopqrst
uvwxyzABCDEFGHIJKL
MNOPQRSTUVWXYZ
$1234567890(.,'''-;:)!?&

25 point

abcdefghijklmn
opqrstuvwxyz
ABCDEFGHIJK
LMNOPQRSTU
VWXYZ$123456
7890(.,'''-;:!)?&

60 point

Georgia Regular

8 Point
abcdefghijklmnopqrstuvwxyz
ABCDEFGHIJKLMNOPQRSTUVWXYZ
$1234567890(.,'"-;:)!?&
abcdefghijklmnopqrstuvwxyz
ABCDEFGHIJKLMNOPQRSTUVWXYZ
$1234567890(.,'"-;:)!?&

9 Point
abcdefghijklmnopqrstuvwxyz
ABCDEFGHIJKLMNOPQRSTUVWXYZ
$1234567890(.,'"-;:)!?&
abcdefghijklmnopqrstuvwxyz
ABCDEFGHIJKLMNOPQRSTUVWXYZ
$1234567890(.,'"-;:)!?&

10 Point
abcdefghijklmnopqrstuvwxyz
ABCDEFGHIJKLMNOPQRSTUVWXYZ
$1234567890(.,'"-;:)!?&
abcdefghijklmnopqrstuvwxyz
ABCDEFGHIJKLMNOPQRSTUVWXYZ
$1234567890(.,'"-;:)!?&

12 Point
abcdefghijklmnopqrstuvwxyz
ABCDEFGHIJKLMNOPQRSTUVW
XYZ$1234567890(.,'"-;:)!?&
abcdefghijklmnopqrstuvwxyz
ABCDEFGHIJKLMNOPQRSTUVW
XYZ$1234567890(.,'"-;:)!?&

The whole duty of typography, *as with calligraphy,* is to communicate to the imagination, without loss by the way, the thought or image intended to be communicated by the author. And the whole duty of beautiful typography is not to substitute for the beauty or interest of the thing thought and intended to be conveyed by the symbol, a beauty or interest of its own, but, on the one hand, to win access for that communication by the clearness and beauty of the vehicle, and on the other hand, to take advantage of every pause or stage in that communication to interpose some characteristic & restful beauty in its own art. We thus have a reason for the clearness and beauty of the first and introductory page and of the title, and for the especial beauty of the headings of chapters, capital or initial letters, and so on, and an opening for the illustrator as we shall see by and by. Further, in the case of poetry, verse, in my opinion, appeals by its

8/10

The whole duty of typography, *as with calligraphy,* is to communicate to the imagination, without loss by the way, the thought or image intended to be communicated by the author. And the whole duty of beautiful typography is not to substitute for the beauty or interest of the thing thought and intended to be conveyed by the symbol, a beauty or interest of its own, but, on the one hand, to win access for that communication by the clearness and beauty of the vehicle, and on the other hand, to take advantage of every pause or stage in that communication to interpose some characteristic & restful beauty in its own art. We thus have a reason for the clearness and beauty of the first and introductory page and of the title, and for the especial beauty of the headings of chapters,

8/12

The whole duty of typography, *as with calligraphy,* is to communicate to the imagination, without loss by the way, the thought or image intended to be communicated by the author. And the whole duty of beautiful typography is not to substitute for the beauty or interest of the thing thought and intended to be conveyed by the symbol, a beauty or interest of its own, but, on the one hand, to win access for that communication by the clearness and beauty of the vehicle, and on the other hand, to take advantage of every pause or stage in that communication to interpose some characteristic & restful beauty in its own art. We thus have a reason for the clearness and beauty of the first and introductory page and of the title, and for the

9/11

The whole duty of typography, *as with calligraphy,* is to communicate to the imagination, without loss by the way, the thought or image intended to be communicated by the author. And the whole duty of beautiful typography is not to substitute for the beauty or interest of the thing thought and intended to be conveyed by the symbol, a beauty or interest of its own, but, on the one hand, to win access for that communication by the clearness and beauty of the vehicle, and on the other hand, to take advantage of every pause or stage in that communication to interpose some characteristic & rest-

9/13

The whole duty of typography, *as with calligraphy,* is to communicate to the imagination, without loss by the way, the thought or image intended to be communicated by the author. And the whole duty of beautiful typography is not to substitute for the beauty or interest of the thing thought and intended to be conveyed by the symbol, a beauty or interest of its own, but, on the one hand, to win access for that communication by the clearness and beauty of the vehicle, and on the other hand, to take advantage of every pause or stage in that communication to interpose some characteristic & restful beauty in its own art. We

10/12

The whole duty of typography, *as with calligraphy,* is to communicate to the imagination, without loss by the way, the thought or image intended to be communicated by the author. And the whole duty of beautiful typography is not to substitute for the beauty or interest of the thing thought and intended to be conveyed by the symbol, a beauty or interest of its own, but, on the one hand, to win access for that communication by the clearness and beauty of the vehicle, and on the other hand, to

10/14

The whole duty of typography, *as with calligraphy,* is to communicate to the imagination, without loss by the way, the thought or image intended to be communicated by the author. And the whole duty of beautiful typography is not to substitute for the beauty or interest of the thing thought and intended to be conveyed by the symbol, a beauty or interest of its own, but, on the one hand, to win access for that

12/14

The whole duty of typography, *as with calligraphy,* is to communicate to the imagination, without loss by the way, the thought or image intended to be communicated by the author. And the whole duty of beautiful typography is not to substitute for the beauty or interest of the thing thought and intended to be conveyed by the symbol, a beauty or interest of

12/16

Bookman Light

abcdefghijklmnopqrstuvwxyz
ABCDEFGHIJKLMNOPQRSTUVWXYZ
$1234567890(.,'"-;:)!?&

Bookman Demi

abcdefghijklmnopqrstuvwxyz
ABCDEFGHIJKLMNOPQRSTUV
WXYZ$1234567890(.,'"-;:)!?&

Cheltenham

abcdefghijklmnopqrstuvwxyz
ABCDEFGHIJKLMNOPQRSTUV
WXYZ$1234567890(.,'"-;:)!?&

Cheltenham Bold

abcdefghijklmnopqrstuvwxyz
ABCDEFGHIJKLMNOPQRSTU
VWXYZ$1234567890(.,'"-;:)!?&

Mrs Eaves Roman

abcdefghijklmnopqrstuvwxyz
ABCDEFGHIJKLMNOPQRSTUVWX
YZ$1234567890(.,'"-;:)!?&

abcdefghijklmnopqrstuvwxyz
ABCDEFGHIJKLMNOPQRSTUVW
XYZ$1234567890(.,'"-;:)!?&

abcdefghijklmnopqrstuvwxyz
ABCDEFGHIJKLMNOPQRSTUV
WXYZ$1234567890(.,'"-;:)!?&

abcdefghijklmnopqrstuvwxyz
ABCDEFGHIJKLMNOPQRSTUV
WXYZ$1234567890(.,'"-;:)!?&

abcdefghijklmnopqrstuvwxyz
ABCDEFGHIJKLMNOPQRSTU
VWXYZ$1234567890(.,'"-;:)!?&

abcdefghijklmnopqrstuvwxyz
ABCDEFGHIJKLMNOPQRS
TVWXYZ$1234567890(.,'"-;:)!?&

63.

Modern

Bodoni

**Additional
Modern fonts**

4.
Page 250 from the *Manuale Tipographico,* 1818.

The word *modern* is a relative term. Often, we use it interchangeably with the term *contemporary;* sometimes it is used to identify movements in the arts representing a radical break with tradition. In typographic design, *Modern* identifies typefaces of the late 1700s with flat, unbracketed serifs, extreme contrasts between thick-and-thin strokes, and geometric construction. The influence of writing and calligraphy upon type design was replaced by mathematical measurement and the use of mechanical instruments to construct letterforms.

After the death of type designer and printer Giambattista Bodoni, his widow and foreman published the *Manuale Tipographico,* displaying specimens of the approximately three hundred

type fonts designed by Bodoni. The page reproduced here in its actual size shows the dazzling contrasts and vigorous proportions found in Modern-style typefaces (Fig. **4**). Thick-and-thin oxford or scotch rules (see Fig. **17**, Chapter 3) echo and complement the letters' stroke weight.

Modern-style typefaces were widely used for book text type during the nineteenth century and have enjoyed continued acceptance for more than two centuries. Numerous variations – from extreme fineline versions to ultrabolds; and from very narrow, condensed fonts to wide, expanded letterforms – have been designed. Many contemporary fonts bear the names of eighteenth-century designers: Bodoni, Didot, and Walbaum.

**Bauer Bodoni
Regular**

This version was released
by the Bauer type foundry
in Germany in 1926.

abcdefghij

klmnopq

rstuvwxyz

$1234567

890(.,'"")-;:)!?

ABCDEF
GHIJKL
MNOPQ
RSTUV
WXYZ&

abcdefghijklmnopqrstuv
wxyzABCDEFGHIJKLMN
OPQRSTUVWXYZ12345
67890(.,'"-;:)!?&

27 point

abcdefghijklmn
opqrstuvwxyz
ABCDEFGHIJK
LMNOPQRSTU
VWXYZ$1234
567890(.,'"-;:)!?&

81 point

abcdefghijklmnopqrstuvw
xyzABCDEFGHIJKLMNO
PQRSTUVWXYZ1234567
890(.,'''-;:)!?&

27 point

abcdefghijklmno
pqrstuvwxyz
ABCDEFGHIJK
LMNOPQRSTU
VWXYZ$12345
67890(.,'''-;:)!?&

61 point

abcdefghijklmnopqrstuvw
xyzABCDFGHIJKLMNOP
QRSTUVWXYZ$12345678
90(.,'''-;:)!?&

25 point

abcdefghijklmn
opqrstuvwxyzw
xyzABCDEFGHI
JKLMNOPQRST
UVWXYZ$1234
567890(.,'''-;:!)?&

72 point

Bauer Bodoni
Regular

abcdefghijklmnopqrstuvwxyz
ABCDEFGHIJKLMNOPQRSTUVWXYZ
$1234567890(.,'"-;:!)?&
abcdefghijklmnopqrstuvwxyz
ABCDEFGHIJKLMNOPQRSTUVWXYZ
8 point *$1234567890(.,'"-;:)!?&*

abcdefghijklmnopqrstuvwxyz
ABCDEFGHIJKLMNOPQRSTUVWXYZ
$1234567890(.,'"-;:)!?&
abcdefghijklmnopqrstuvwxyz
ABCDEFGHIJKLMNOPQRSTUVWXYZ
9 point *$1234567890(.,'"-;:)!?&*

abcdefghijklmnopqrstuvwxyz
ABCDEFGHIJKLMNOPQRSTUVWXYZ
$1234567890(.,'"-;:)!?&
abcdefghijklmnopqrstuvwxyz
ABCDEFGHIJKLMNOPQRSTUVWXYZ
10 point *$1234567890(.,'"-;:)!?&*

abcdefghijklmnopqrstuvwxyz
ABCDEFGHIJKLMNOPQRSTUVWXYZ
$1234567890(.,'"-;:)!?&
abcdefghijklmnopqrstuvwxyz
ABCDEFGHIJKLMNOPQRSTUVWXYZ
12 point *$1234567890(.,'"-;:)!?&*

The whole duty of typography, *as with calligraphy*; is to communicate to the imagination, without loss by the way, the thought or image intended to be communicated by the author. And the whole duty of beautiful typography is not to substitute for the beauty or interest of the thing thought and intended to be conveyed by the symbol, a beauty or interest of its own, but, on the one hand, to win access for that communication by the clearness and beauty of the vehicle, and on the other hand, to take advantage of every pause or stage in that communication to interpose some characteristic & restful beauty in its own art. We thus have a reason for the clearness and beauty of the first and introductory page and of the title, and for the especial beauty of the headings of chapters, capital or initial letters, and so on, and an opening for the illustrator as we shall see by and by. Further, in the case of poetry, verse, in my opinion, appeals by its form to the eye, as well as to the ear.
8/10

The whole duty of typography, *as with calligraphy*; is to communicate to the imagination, without loss by the way, the thought or image intended to be communicated by the author. And the whole duty of beautiful typography is not to substitute for the beauty or interest of the thing thought and intended to be conveyed by the symbol, a beauty or interest of its own, but, on the one hand, to win access for that communication by the clearness and beauty of the vehicle, and on the other hand, to take advantage of every pause or stage in that communication to interpose some characteristic & restful beauty in its own art. We thus have a reason for the clearness and beauty of the first and introductory page and of the title, and for the especial beauty of the headings of chapters, capital or initial letters, and so
8/12

The whole duty of typography, *as with calligraphy*; is to communicate to the imagination, without loss by the way, the thought or image intended to be communicated by the author. And the whole duty of beautiful typography is not to substitute for the beauty or interest of the thing thought and intended to be conveyed by the symbol, a beauty or interest of its own, but, on the one hand, to win access for that communication by the clearness and beauty of the vehicle, and on the other hand, to take advantage of every pause or stage in that communication to interpose some characteristic & restful beauty in its own art. We thus have a reason for the clearness and beauty of the first and introductory page and of the title, and for the especial beauty of the headings of chapters, capital or
9/11

The whole duty of typography, *as with calligraphy*; is to communicate to the imagination, without loss by the way, the thought or image intended to be communicated by the author. And the whole duty of beautiful typography is not to substitute for the beauty or interest of the thing thought and intended to be conveyed by the symbol, a beauty or interest of its own, but, on the one hand, to win access for that communication by the clearness and beauty of the vehicle, and on the other hand, to take advantage of every pause or stage in that communication to interpose some characteristic & restful beauty in its own art. We thus have a reason
9/13

The whole duty of typography, *as with calligraphy*; is to communicate to the imagination, without loss by the way, the thought or image intended to be communicated by the author. And the whole duty of beautiful typography is not to substitute for the beauty or interest of the thing thought and intended to be conveyed by the symbol, a beauty or interest of its own, but, on the one hand, to win access for that communication by the clearness and beauty of the vehicle, and on the other hand, to take advantage of every pause or stage in that communication to interpose some characteristic & restful beauty in its own art.
10/12

The whole duty of typography, *as with calligraphy*; is to communicate to the imagination, without loss by the way, the thought or image intended to be communicated by the author. And the whole duty of beautiful typography is not to substitute for the beauty or interest of the thing thought and intended to be conveyed by the symbol, a beauty or interest of its own, but, on the one hand, to win access for that communication by the clearness and beauty of the vehicle, and on the other hand,
10/14

The whole duty of typography, *as with calligraphy*; is to communicate to the imagination, without loss by the way, the thought or image intended to be communicated by the author. And the whole duty of beautiful typography is not to substitute for the beauty or interest of the thing thought and intended to be conveyed by the symbol, a beauty or interest of its own, but, on the one hand, to win access for that
12/14

The whole duty of typography, *as with calligraphy*; is to communicate to the imagination, without loss by the way, the thought or image intended to be communicated by the author. And the whole duty of beautiful typography is not to substitute for the beauty or interest of the thing thought and intended to be conveyed by the symbol, a beauty or interest of
12/16

Bodoni Book

abcdefghijklmnopqrstuvwxyz
ABCDEFGHIJKLMNOPQRSTUVWXYZ
$1234567890(.,'"-;:)!?&

Bodoni Bold

abcdefghijklmnopqrstuvwxyz
ABCDEFGHIJKLMNOPQRSTUVW
XYZ$1234567890(.,'"-;:)!?&

Bodoni Poster

abcdefghijklmnopqrstuvwxyz
ABCDEFGHIJKLMNOPQRSTUV
WXYZ$1234567890(.,'"-;:)!?&

Century Schoolbook Regular

abcdefghijklmnopqrstuvwxyz
ABCDEFGHIJKLMNOPQRSTUVW
XYZ$1234567890(.,'"-;:)!?&

Century Schoolbook Bold

abcdefghijklmnopqrstuvwxyz
ABCDEFGHIJKLMNOPQRSTUV
WXYZ$1234567890(.,'"-;:)!?&

abcdefghijklmnopqrstuvwxyz
ABCDEFGHIJKLMNOPQRSTUV
WXYZ$1234567890(.,'"-;:)!?&

abcdefghijklmnopqrstuvwxyz
ABCDEFGHIJKLMNOPQRSTUV
WXYZ$1234567890(.,'"-;:)!?&

abcdefghijklmnopqrstuvwxyz
ABCDEFGHIJKLMNOPQRSTUVWXYZ
$1234567890(.,'"-;:)!?&

abcdefghijklmnopqrstuvwxyz
ABCDEFGHIJKLMNOPQRSTUVWXYZ
$1234567890(.,'"-;:)!?&

abcdefghijklmnopqrstuvwxyz
ABCDEFGHIJKLMNOPQRSTUVWXYZ
$1234567890(.,'"-;:)!?&

NEW LINE BETWEEN
ALBANY & NEWBURG

LANDING AT

Hamburgh, Marlborough, Milton, Poughkeepsie, Hyde Park, Kingston, Rhinebeck, Barrytown, Redhook, Bristol, Westcamp Catskill, Hudson, Coxsackie, Stuyvesant, Baltimore & Coeymans.

On and after MONDAY, October 15th,

The Superior Low Pressure Steamer

ST. NICHOLAS

CAPTAIN WILSON,

Will run as a Passage and Freight Boat between Newburgh and Albany, leaving Newburgh

MONDAYS, WEDNESDAYS & FRIDAYS

AT SEVEN O'CLOCK A.M.,

And ALBANY on Tuesdays, Thursdays & Saturdays, at half-past 9 o'clock A.M.

Albany, Oct. 9th, 1849.

Egyptian

Serifa

**Additional
Egyptian fonts**

5.
Broadsheet, 1849. This slab-serif display type has been lightly inked, and the textured grain of the wooden type is clearly visible, as in the words *St. Nicholas.*

Egyptian or slab-serif typefaces first appeared in the early nineteenth century and enjoyed great popularity. Their bold, machinelike qualities offered a dynamic expression of the industrial age. During the Industrial Revolution, letterpress printers delighted in using bold slab-serif display fonts to give their messages graphic impact (Fig. **5**). Rectangular serifs, uniform or almost uniform stroke weight, and geometric letterform construction give Egyptian typefaces a bold, abstract quality. Egyptian styles whose abrupt right-angle joinery is tempered by curved bracketing include the Clarendon, Century, and Cheltenham type families.

Serifa was designed Adrian
Frutiger in 1966.

abcdefghi

jklmnopqr

stuvwxyz

$12345678

90(,'"-;:)!?

ABCDEF
GHIJKL
MNOPQR
STUVWX
YZ&

120 point

abcdefghijklmnopqrstuvw
xyzABCDEFGHIJKLMNO
PQRSTUVWXYZ$1234567
890(.,'"-;:)!?&

26 point

abcdefghijklmn
opqrstuvwxyz
ABCDEFGHIJK
LMNOPQRSTU
VWXYZ$123456
7890(.,'"-;:)!?&

72 point

abcdefghijklmnopqrstuvw
xyzABCDEFGHIJKLMNO
PQRSTUVWXYZ12345678
90(.,'""-;:)!?&

26 point

abcdefghijklmn
opqrstuvwxyz
ABCDEFGHIJK
LMNOPQRSTU
VWXYZ$12345
67890(.,'"-;:)!?&

72 point

abcdefghijklmnopqrstu
vwxyzABCDEFGHIJKL
MNOPQRSTUVWXYZ
$1234567890(.,'"-;:)!?&

abcdefghijklmn
opqrstuvwxyz
ABCDEFGHIJK
LMNOPQRSTU
VWXYZ$12345
67890(.,'"-;:)!?&

Serifa Roman

8 point

abcdefghijklmnopqrstuvwxyz
ABCDEFGHIJKLMNOPQRSTUVWXYZ
$1234567890(.,'"-;:)!?&
abcdefghijklmnopqrstuvwxyz
ABCDEFGHIJKLMNOPQRSTUVWXYZ
$1234567890(.,'"-;:)!?&

9 point

abcdefghijklmnopqrstuvwxyz
ABCDEFGHIJKLMNOPQRSTUVWXYZ
$1234567890(.,'"-;:)!?&
abcdefghijklmnopqrstuvwxyz
ABCDEFGHIJKLMNOPQRSTUVWXYZ
$1234567890(.,'"-;:)!?&

10 point

abcdefghijklmnopqrstuvwxyz
ABCDEFGHIJKLMNOPQRSTUVWXYZ
$1234567890(.,'"-;:)!?&
abcdefghijklmnopqrstuvwxyz
ABCDEFGHIJKLMNOPQRSTUVWXYZ
$1234567890(.,'"-;:)!?&

12 point

abcdefghijklmnopqrstuvwxyz
ABCDEFGHIJKLMNOPQRSTUVWXYZ
$1234567890(.,'"-;:)!?&
abcdefghijklmnopqrstuvwxyz
ABCDEFGHIJKLMNOPQRSTUVWXYZ
$1234567890(.,'"-;:)!?&

The whole duty of typography, *as with calligraphy,* is to communicate to the imagination, without loss by the way, the thought or image intended to be communicated by the author. And the whole duty of beautiful typography is not to substitute for the beauty or interest of the thing thought and intended to be conveyed by the symbol, a beauty or interest of its own, but, on the one hand, to win access for that communication by the clearness and beauty of the vehicle, and on the other hand, to take advantage of every pause or stage in that communication to interpose some characteristic & restful beauty in its own art. We thus have a reason for the clearness and beauty of the first and introductory page and of the title, and for the especial beauty of the headings of chapters, capital or initial letters, and so on, and an opening for the illustrator as we shall see

8/10

The whole duty of typography, *as with calligraphy,* is to communicate to the imagination, without loss by the way, the thought or image intended to be communicated by the author. And the whole duty of beautiful typography is not to substitute for the beauty or interest of the thing thought and intended to be conveyed by the symbol, a beauty or interest of its own, but, on the one hand, to win access for that communication by the clearness and beauty of the vehicle, and on the other hand, to take advantage of every pause or stage in that communication to interpose some characteristic & restful beauty in its own art. We thus have a reason for the clearness and beauty of the first and introductory page and of the

8/12

The whole duty of typography, *as with calligraphy,* is to communicate to the imagination, without loss by the way, the thought or image intended to be communicated by the author. And the whole duty of beautiful typography is not to substitute for the beauty or interest of the thing thought and intended to be conveyed by the symbol, a beauty or interest of its own, but, on the one hand, to win access for that communication by the clearness and beauty of the vehicle, and on the other hand, to take advantage of every pause or stage in that communication to interpose some characteristic & restful beauty in its own art. We thus have a reason for the clearness and beauty of the first and introductory

9/11

The whole duty of typography, *as with calligraphy,* is to communicate to the imagination, without loss by the way, the thought or image intended to be communicated by the author. And the whole duty of beautiful typography is not to substitute for the beauty or interest of the thing thought and intended to be conveyed by the symbol, a beauty or interest of its own, but, on the one hand, to win access for that communication by the clearness and beauty of the vehicle, and on the other hand, to take advantage of every pause or stage in that communication to interpose

9/**13**

The whole duty of typography, *as with calligraphy,* is to communicate to the imagination, without loss by the way, the thought or image intended to be communicated by the author. And the whole duty of beautiful typography is not to substitute for the beauty or interest of the thing thought and intended to be conveyed by the symbol, a beauty or interest of its own, but, on the one hand, to win access for that communication by the clearness and beauty of the vehicle, and on the other hand, to take advantage of every pause or stage in that communication to interpose

10/12

The whole duty of typography, *as with calligraphy,* is to communicate to the imagination, without loss by the way, the thought or image intended to be communicated by the author. And the whole duty of beautiful typography is not to substitute for the beauty or interest of the thing thought and intended to be conveyed by the symbol, a beauty or interest of its own, but, on the one hand, to win access for that communication by the clearness and beauty of

10/14

The whole duty of typography, *as with calligraphy,* is to communicate to the imagination, without loss by the way, the thought or image intended to be communi-cated by the author. And the whole duty of beautiful typography is not to substitute for the beauty or interest of the thing thought and intended to be conveyed by the symbol, a beauty or interest of its own,

12/14

The whole duty of typography, *as with calligraphy,* is to communicate to the imagination, without loss by the way, the thought or image intended to be communi-cated by the author. And the whole duty of beautiful typography is not to substitute for the beauty or interest of the thing thought and intended to be conveyed

12/16

Archer, designed by Hoefler &
Frere-Jones in 2001 combines
the bold architecture of
twentieth-century Geometrics
with the friendly ball terminals
of earlier Antique styles.

abcdefghi

jklmnopq

rstuvwxyz

$1234567

890(,'"-,;)!?

132 point

ABCDEF
GHIJKL
MNOPQ
RSTUV
WXYZ&

abcdefghijklmnopqrstuvw
xyzABCDEFGHIJKLMNO
PQRSTUVWXYZ$1234567
890(.,"'-;:)!?&

26 point

abcdefghijklmn
opqrstuvwxyz
ABCDEFGHIJK
LMNOPQRST
UVWXYZ$12345
67890(.,"'-;:)!?&

72 point

abcdefghijklmnopqrstuvw
xyzABCDEFGHIJKLMNO
PQRSTUVWXYZ12345678
90(.,"'''-;:)!?&

26 point

abcdefghijklmn
opqrstuvwxyz
ABCDEFGHIJK
LMNOPQRST
UVWXYZ$12345
67890(.,"'''-;:)!?&

72 point

abcdefghijklmnopqrstuvw
xyzABCDEFGHIJKLMNOP
QRSTUVWXYZ
$1234567890(.,'''-;:)!?&

26 point

abcdefghijklmno

pqrstuvwxyz

ABCDEFGHIJKL

MNOPQRSTU

VWXYZ$123456

7890(.,'''";:)!?&

72 point

Archer Book

abcdefghijklmnopqrstuvwxyz
ABCDEFGHIJKLMNOPQRSTUVWXYZ
$1234567890(.,'":;)!?&
abcdefghijklmnopqrstuvwxyz
ABCDEFGHIJKLMNOPQRSTUVWXYZ
$1234567890(.,'":;)!?&

8 point

abcdefghijklmnopqrstuvwxyz
ABCDEFGHIJKLMNOPQRSTUVWXYZ
$1234567890(.,'":;)!?&
abcdefghijklmnopqrstuvwxyz
ABCDEFGHIJKLMNOPQRSTUVWXYZ
$1234567890(.,'":;)!?&

9 point

abcdefghijklmnopqrstuvwxyz
ABCDEFGHIJKLMNOPQRSTUVWXYZ
$1234567890(.,'":;)!?&
abcdefghijklmnopqrstuvwxyz
ABCDEFGHIJKLMNOPQRSTUVWXYZ
$1234567890(.,'":;)!?&

10 point

abcdefghijklmnopqrstuvwxyz
ABCDEFGHIJKLMNOPQRSTUVWXYZ
$1234567890(.,'":;)!?&
abcdefghijklmnopqrstuvwxyz
ABCDEFGHIJKLMNOPQRSTUVWXYZ
$1234567890(.,'":;)!?&

12 point

The whole duty of typography, *as with calligraphy,* is to communicate to the imagination, without loss by the way, the thought or image intended to be communicated by the author. And the whole duty of beautiful typography is not to substitute for the beauty or interest of the thing thought and intended to be conveyed by the symbol, a beauty or interest of its own, but, on the one hand, to win access for that communication by the clearness and beauty of the vehicle, and on the other hand, to take advantage of every pause or stage in that communication to interpose some characteristic & restful beauty in its own art. We thus have a reason for the clearness and beauty of the first and introductory page and of the title, and for the especial beauty of the headings of chapters, capital or initial letters, and so on, and an opening for the illustrator as we shall see by and by. Further, in the case of poetry, verse, in my opinion, appeals by its form to the eye, as well as to the ear, and

8/10

The whole duty of typography, *as with calligraphy,* is to communicate to the imagination, without loss by the way, the thought or image intended to be communicated by the author. And the whole duty of beautiful typography is not to substitute for the beauty or interest of the thing thought and intended to be conveyed by the symbol, a beauty or interest of its own, but, on the one hand, to win access for that communication by the clearness and beauty of the vehicle, and on the other hand, to take advantage of every pause or stage in that communication to interpose some characteristic & restful beauty in its own art. We thus have a reason for the clearness and beauty of the first and introductory page and of the title, and for the especial beauty of the headings of chapters, capital or initial letters, and so on, and

8/12

The whole duty of typography, *as with calligraphy,* is to communicate to the imagination, without loss by the way, the thought or image intended to be communicated by the author. And the whole duty of beautiful typography is not to substitute for the beauty or interest of the thing thought and intended to be conveyed by the symbol, a beauty or interest of its own, but, on the one hand, to win access for that communication by the clearness and beauty of the vehicle, and on the other hand, to take advantage of every pause or stage in that communication to interpose some characteristic & restful beauty in its own art. We thus have a reason for the clearness and beauty of the first and introductory page and of the title, and for the especial beauty of the headings of chapters, capital or

9/11

The whole duty of typography, *as with calligraphy,* is to communicate to the imagination, without loss by the way, the thought or image intended to be communicated by the author. And the whole duty of beautiful typography is not to substitute for the beauty or interest of the thing thought and intended to be conveyed by the symbol, a beauty or interest of its own, but, on the one hand, to win access for that communication by the clearness and beauty of the vehicle, and on the other hand, to take advantage of every pause or stage in that communication to interpose some characteristic & restful beauty in its own art. We thus have a reason

9/13

The whole duty of typography, *as with calligraphy,* is to communicate to the imagination, without loss by the way, the thought or image intended to be communicated by the author. And the whole duty of beautiful typography is not to substitute for the beauty or interest of the thing thought and intended to be conveyed by the symbol, a beauty or interest of its own, but, on the one hand, to win access for that communication by the clearness and beauty of the vehicle, and on the other hand, to take advantage of every pause or stage in that communication to interpose some characteristic & restful beauty in its own art. We thus have a reason for the clearness

10/12

The whole duty of typography, *as with calligraphy,* is to communicate to the imagination, without loss by the way, the thought or image intended to be communicated by the author. And the whole duty of beautiful typography is not to substitute for the beauty or interest of the thing thought and intended to be conveyed by the symbol, a beauty or interest of its own, but, on the one hand, to win access for that communication by the clearness and beauty of the vehicle, and on the other hand, to take advantage of every pause

10/14

The whole duty of typography, *as with calligraphy,* is to communicate to the imagination, without loss by the way, the thought or image intended to be communicated by the author. And the whole duty of beautiful typography is not to substitute for the beauty or interest of the thing thought and intended to be conveyed by the symbol, a beauty or interest of its own, but, on the one hand, to win access for that communication by the clearness

12/14

The whole duty of typography, *as with calligraphy,* is to communicate to the imagination, without loss by the way, the thought or image intended to be communicated by the author. And the whole duty of beautiful typography is not to substitute for the beauty or interest of the thing thought and intended to be conveyed by the symbol, a beauty or interest of its own, but, on the one hand, to

12/16

City Light

abcdefghijklmnopqrstuvwxyz
ABCDEFGHIJKLMNOPQRSTUVWXYZ$123
4567890(.,'"-;:)!?&

City Bold

abcdefghijklmnopqrstuvwxyz
ABCDEFGHIJKLMNOPQRSTUVWXYZ
$1234567890(.,'"-;:)!?&

Clarendon

abcdefghijklmnopqrstuvwxyz
ABCDEFGHIJKLMNOPQRSTU
VWXYZ$1234567890(.,'"-;:)!?&

Clarendon Bold

abcdefghijklmnopqrstuvwxyz
ABCDEFGHIJKLMNOPQRSTU
VWXYZ$1234567890(.,'"-;:)!?&

Memphis Light

abcdefghijklmnopqrstuvwxyz
ABCDEFGHIJKLMNOPQRSTUVW
XYZ$1234567890(.,'"-;:)!?&

abcdefghijklmnopqrstuvwxyz
ABCDEFGHIJKLMNOPQRSTUVW
XYZ$1234567890(.,'"-;:)!?&

abcdefghijklmnopqrstuvwxyz
ABCDEFGHIJKLMNOPQRSTUV
WXYZ$1234567890(.,'"-;:)!?&

abcdefghijklmnopqrstuvwxyz
ABCDEFGHIJKLMNOPQRSTUVW
XYZ$1234567890(.,'"-;:)!?&

abcdefghijklmnopqrstuvwxyz
ABCDEFGHIJKLMNOPQRSTUV
WXYZ$1234567890(.,'"-;:)!?&

abcdefghijklmnopqrstuvwxyz
ABCDEFGHIJKLMNOPQRSTU
VWXYZ$1234567890(.,'"-;:)!?&

Typefaces that often defy historical classification are sometimes called decorative or novelty typefaces. Most often these are used as display types or as text when appropriate. These typefaces provide context for typographic messages, adding visual accent and charisma.

Anonymous (Designer: Mark Simonson)

abcdefghijklmnopqrstuvwxyz
ABCDEFGHIJKLMNOPQRSTUVWXY
Z$1234567890(.,'''-;::)!?&

Glas (Designer: AtelierMAChauer)

abcdefghijklmnopqrstuvwxyz
ABCDEFGHIJKLMNOPQRSTUV
WXYZ$1234567890(.,-;::)!?&

Maus (Designer: James Arboghast)

ABCDEFGHIJKLMNOPQRSTUVW
XYZABCDEFGHIJKLMNOPQRSTU
VWXYZ$1234567890(.,)!?&

Montessori Script (Designer: Stefan Hattenbach)

abcdefghijklmnopqrstuvwxyz
ABCDEFGHIJKLMNOPQRSTUV
WXYZ$1234567890(.,'''-;::)!?&

Morpheus (Designer: Eric Oehler)

ABCDEFGHIJKLMNOPQRSTUVWXYZ
ABCDEFGHIJKLMNOPQRSTUV
WXYZ$1234567890(.,"'-;:)!?&

Mosaico (Designer: Alexjandro Paul)

abcdefghijklmnopqrstuvxyz
ABCDEFGHIJKLMNOPQRSTUVXYZ
$1234567890(.,;:)!?&

Overwork (Designer: Bagel & Co.)

abcdefghijklmnopqrstuvwxyz
ABCDEFGHIJKLMNOPQRSTUV
WXYZ$1234567890(.,=;:)!?&

Plexifont BV (Designer: Jess Latham)

ABCDEFGHIJKLMNOPQRS
TUVWXYZ
$1234567890!?

Torn Univers (Designer: Matt Gardner)

abcdefghijklmnopqrstuvwxyz
ABCDEFGHIJKLMNOPQRS
TUVWXYZ$1234567890

A chronology of typeface designs

The dates of design, production, and release of a typeface often differ, and additional fonts in a type family frequently follow later; therefore, many dates listed here are approximate.

Revivals of many typefaces are often named after early designers or authors. These faces were not so named during their epoch; however, their contemporary names are used here for identification purposes.

c. 1450: First Textura-style type, Johann Gutenberg
1467: First Roman-style type, Sweynheym and Pannartz
1470: Jenson,1 Nicolas Jenson
1495: Bembo, Francesco Griffo
1499: Poliphilus, Francesco Griffo
1501: First italic type, Francesco Griffo
1514: Fraktur, Hans Schoensperger
1532: Garamond, Claude Garamond
1557: Civilité, Robert Granjon
c. 1570: Plantin, Anonymous
c. 1570: Canon d'Espagne, the Plantin Office
c. 1582: Flemish bold Roman, the Plantin Office
1616: Typi Academiae, Jean Jannon
c. 1670: Fell Roman, Peter Walpergen
1690: Janson, Nicholas Kis
1702: Romain du Roi, Philippe Grandjean
1722: Caslon Old Style, William Caslon
c. 1743: Early transitional types, Pierre Simon Fournier le Jeune
c. 1746: Fournier decorated letters, Pierre Simon Fournier le Jeune
1757: Baskerville, John Baskerville
c. 1764: Italique Moderne and Ancienne, Pierre Simon Fournier le Jeune
1768: Fry's Baskerville, Isaac Moore
c. 1780: Bodoni, Giambattista Bodoni
1784: Didot, Firmin Didot
c. 1795: Bulmer, William Martin
1796: Fry's Ornamented, RichardAustin
c. 1800: Walbaum, J. E. Walbaum
c. 1810: Scotch Roman, Richard Austin
1815: Two Lines Pica, Antique (first Egyptian style), Vincent Figgins
1815: Five Lines Pica, In Shade (first perspective font), Vincent Figgins
1816: Two-line English Egyptian (first sans serif), William Caslon IV
1820: Lettres Ornées, Fonds de Gille
1828: Roman, Darius Wells
1830: Two-line great primer sans serif, Vincent Figgins
1832: Grotesque, William Thorowgood
1838: Sans serryphs ornamented, Blake and Stephenson
1844: Ionic, Henry Caslon
1845: Clarendon, Robert Besley and Company
1845: Rustic, V. and J. Figgins
1845: Zig-Zag, V. and J. Figgins
1850: Scroll, Henry Caslon
1859: Antique Tuscan Outlined, William Page
1856: National, Philadelphia Type Foundry
c. 1860: P. T. Barnum, Barnhart Brothers and Spindler

c. 1865: French Antique (later called Playbill), Miller and Richard
c. 1865: Old Style Antique (called Bookman in the U.S.), Miller and Richard
c. 1869: Runic, Reed and Fox
c. 1870: Figgins Condensed No. 2, Stevens Shanks
c. 1870: Bank Gothic, Bardhart Brothers and Spindler
1878: Circlet, Barnhart Brothers and Spindler
1878: Glyphic, MacKellar, Smiths and Jordan
c. 1885: Geometric, Central Type Foundry
c. 1890: Ringlet, Marr Typefounding
c. 1890: Gothic Outline No. 61, American Typefounders
c. 1890: Rubens, Marr Typefounding
c. 1890: Karnac, Marr Typefounding
1890: Century, L. B. Benton
1890: Golden, William Morris
1892: Troy, William Morris
1893: Chaucer, William Morris
1894: Bradley, Will Bradley
1895: Merrymount Type, Bertram Goodhue
1895: Century Roman, Theodore Low DeVinne and L. B. Benton
1896: Cheltenham, Bertram Goodhue
1896: Vale Type, Charles Ricketts
1898: Grasset, Eugène Grasset
c. 1898: Paris Metro Lettering, Hector Guimard
1898–1906: Akzidenz Grotesque (Standard), Berthold Foundry
1900: Eckmann-Schrift, Otto Eckmann
1900: Century Expanded, Morris F. Benton
1900: Doves Roman, T. J. Cobden-Sanderson and Emery Walker
1901: Endeavor, Charles R. Ashbee
1901: Copperplate Gothic, Frederic W. Goudy
1901–4: Auriol, Georges Auriol
1902: Behrens-Schrift, Peter Behrens
1902: Subiaco, C. H. St. John Hornby
1903: Brook Type, Lucien Pissarro
1904: Korinna, H. Berthold
1904: Franklin Gothic, Morris F. Benton
1904: Arnold Böcklin, O. Weisert
1904: Linoscript, Morris F. Benton
1907: Behrens-Kursiv, Peter Behrens
1907: Clearface Bold, Morris F. Benton
1907–13: Venus, Bauer Foundry
1908: Behrens-Antiqua, Peter Behrens
1908: News Gothic, Morris F. Benton
1909: Aurora, Wagner and Schmidt Foundry
1910: Kochschrift, Rudolf Koch
1910–15: Hobo, Morris F. Benton
1911: Kennerly Old Style, Frederic W. Goudy
1912: Nicolas Cochin, G. Peignot
1913: Belwe, Georg Belwe

1914: Souvenir, Morris F. Benton
1914: Cloister Old Style, Morris F. Benton
1915: Century Schoolbook, Morris F. Benton
1915–16: Goudy Old Style, Frederic W. Goudy
1916: Centaur, Bruce Rogers
1916: Johnston's Railway Type, Edward Johnston
1919–24: Cooper Old Style, Oswald Cooper
1921: Cooper Black, Oswald Cooper
1922: Locarno (Eve), Rudolf Koch
1923: Windsor, Stephenson Blake Foundry
1923: Tiemann, Walter Tiemann
1923: Neuland, Rudolf Koch
1925: Perpetua, Eric Gill
1926: Weiss Roman, E. R. Weiss
1926: Bauer Bodoni, Bauer Typefoundry
1927–29: Futura, Paul Renner
1927–29: Kabel, Rudolf Koch
1928: Ultra Bodoni, Morris F. Benton
1928–30: Gill Sans, Eric Gill
1928: Modernique, Morris F. Benton
1929: Zeppelin, Rudolf Koch
1929: Golden Cockerel, Eric Gill
1929–30: Metro, William A. Dwiggins
1929: Bernhard Fashion, Lucien Bernhard
1929: Bifur, A. M. Cassandre
1929: Broadway, Morris F. Benton
1929: Novel Gothic, H. Becker
1929: Bembo, Monotype Corporation
1929: Lux, Josef Erbar
1929: Memphis, Rudolf Weiss
1929–30: Perpetua, Eric Gill
1929–34: Corvinus, Imre Reiner
1930: City, Georg Trump
1930: Joanna, Eric Gill
1930: Dynamo, Ludwig and Mayer Foundry
1930: Metro, William A. Dwiggins
1931: Prisma, Rudolf Koch
1931: Times New Roman, Stanley Morison and Victor Lardent
1931: Stymie, Morris F. Benton
1931–36: Beton, Heinrich Jost
1932–40: Albertus, Berthold Wolpe
1933: Agency Gothic, Morris F. Benton
1933: Atlas, K. H. Schaefer
1934: Rockwell, H. F. Pierpont
1935: Electra, William A. Dwiggins
1935: Huxley Vertical, Walter Huxley
1936: Acier Noir, A. M. Cassandre
1937: Peignot, A. M. Cassandre
1937: Stencil, Robert H. Middleton
1937: Onyx, Gerry Powell
1938: Caledonia, William A. Dwiggins
1938: Libra, S. H. De Roos
1938: Lydian, Warren Chappell
1938: Empire, American Typefounders

1939: Chisel, Stephenson Blake Foundry
1940: Trajanus, Warren Chappell
1940: Tempo, Robert H. Middleton
1945: Stradivarius, Imre Reiner
1945: Courier, Bud Kettler
1946: Profil, Eugen and Max Lenz
1948: Trade Gothic, Mergenthaler Linotype
c. 1950: Brush, Harold Brodersen
1950: Michelangelo, Hermann Zapf
1950: Palatino, Hermann Zapf
1951: Sistina, Hermann Zapf
1952: Horizon, K. F. Bauer and Walter Baum
1952: Melior, Hermann Zapf
1952: Microgramma, A. Butti
1953: Mistral, Roger Excoffon
1954: Trump Mediaeval, Georg Trump
1955: Columna, Max Caflisch
1955: Egizio, Aldo Novarese
1955–56: Egyptienne, Adrian Frutiger
1956: Craw Clarendon, Freeman Craw
1956: Murry Hill, E. J. Klumpp
1957: Meridien, Adrian Frutiger
1957: Univers, Adrian Frutiger
c. 1957: Helvetica, Max Miedinger
1960: Aurora, Jackson Burke
1961: Octavian, Will Carter and David Kindersley
1962: Eurostile, Aldo Novarese
1962–66: Antique Olive, Roger Excoffon
1964: Sabon, Jan Tschichold
1965: Americana, Richard Isbell
1965: Snell Roundhand, Matthew Carter
1965: Friz Quadrata, Ernest Friz
1966: Egyptian 505, André Gürtler
1966: Vladimir, Vladimir Andrich
1966: Sabon, Jan Tschichold
1967: Serifa, Adrian Frutiger
1967: Americana, Richard Isbell
1967: Cartier, Carl Dair
1967: Avant Garde Gothic, Herb Lubalin and Tom Carnase
1967: Poppl-Antiqua, Friedrich Poppl
1968: Syntax, Hans E. Meier
1969: Aachen, Colin Brignall
1970: Olympian, Matthew Carter
1970: Machine, Tom Carnase and Ron Bonder
1970: ITC Souvenir, Edward Benguiat
1972: Iridium, Adrian Frutiger
1972: Times Europa, Walter Tracy
1972: University, Mike Daines
1974: American Typewriter, Joel Kadan
1974: ITC Tiffany, Edward Benguiat
1974: Newtext, Ray Baker

1974: Korinna, Ed Benguiat and Vic Caruso
1974: American Typewriter, Joel Kaden and Tony Stan
1974: Serif Gothic, Herb Lubalin and Tony DiSpigna
1974: Lubalin Graph, Herb Lubalin, Tony DiSpigna, Joe Sundwall
1975: ITC Bauhaus, based on Bayer's universal alphabet
1975: ITC Bookman, Ed Benguiat
1975: ITC Century, Tony Stan
1975: ITC Cheltenham, Tony Stan
1975: Concorde Nova, Gunter Gerhard Lange
1975: ITC Garamond, Tony Stan
1975: Marconi, Hermann Zapf
1976: Eras, Albert Hollenstein and Albert Boton
1976: Poppl-Pontiflex, Friedrich Poppl
1976: Zapf Book, Hermann Zapf
1976: Frutiger, Adrian Frutiger
1977: Quorum, Ray Baker
1977: Korinna Kursiv, Edward Benguiat
1977: Italia, Colin Brignall
1977: Benguiat, Edward Benguiat
1977: Zapf International, Hermann Zapf
1977: Fenice, Also Novarese
1978: Basilia, André Gürtler
1978: Bell Centennial, Matthew Carter
1978: Galliard, Matthew Carter
1979: Benguiat Gothic, Edward Benguiat
1979: Glypha, Adrian Frutiger
1979: Zapf Chancery, Hermann Zapf
1980: Fenice, Aldo Novarese
1980: Novarese, Aldo Novarese
1980: Icone, Adrian Frutiger
1980: Marconi, Hermann Zapf
1980: Edison, Hermann Zapf
1981: Adroit, Phil Martin
1981: Barcelonia, Edward Benguiat
1981: Isbell, Dick Isbell and Jerry Campbell
1982: Cushing, Vincent Pacella
1983: ITC Berkeley Old Style, Tony Stan
1983: Weidemann, Kurt Weidemann and Kurt Strecker
1983: Neue Helvetica, Linotype (Stempel) staff designers
1984: Macintosh screen fonts, Susan Kare
1984: Osiris, Gustav Jaeger
1984: Usherwood, Les Usherwood
1984: Veljovic, Jovica Veljovic
1985: Aurelia, Hermann Zapf
1985: Elan, Albert Boton
1985: Emigre, Zuzana Licko
1985: Kis-Janson, Autologic staff designers
1985: Lucida, Charles Bigelow and Kris Holmes
1985: Mixage, Aldo Novarese

1985: Oakland, Zuzana Licko
1986: Linotype Centennial, Matthew Carter
1986: Matrix, Zuzana Licko
1986: Centennial, Adrian Frutiger
1987: Amerigo, Gerard Unger
1987: Charter, Matthew Carter
1987: Gerstner Original, Karl Gerstner
1987: Glypha, Adrian Frutiger
1987: Neufont, David Weinz
1987: Stone Informal, Sans and Serif, Sumner Stone
1987: Charlemagne, Carol Twombly
1987: Belizio, David Berlow
1987: Zapf Renaissance, Hermann Zapf
1988: Visigoth, Arthur Baker
1988: Avenir, Adrian Frutiger
c. 1989: FF Meta, Erik Spiekermann
1989: Adobe Garamond, Robert Slimbach
1989: Giovanni, Robert Slimbach
1989: Helicon, David Quay
1989: Lithos, Carol Twombly
1989: Rotis, Otl Aicher
1989: Trajan, Carol Twombly
1989: Keedy Sans, Jeffery Keedy
1989: Phaistos, David Berlow
1989: Commerce, Greg Thompson and Rick Valicenti
1989–90: Bronzo, Rick Valicenti
1990: Bodega Sans, Greg Thompson
1990: Journal, Zuzana Licko
1990: Adobe Caslon, Carol Twombly
1990: Quay, David Quay
1990: Tekton, David Siegel
1990: Template Gothic, Barry Deck
1990: Dead History, Scott Makela
1990: Myriad, Robert Slimbach and Carol Twombly
1990: Minion, Robert Slimbach
1990: Arcadia, Industria, and Insignia, Neville Brody
1991: Print, Sumner Stone
1991: Exocet, Jonathan Barnbrook
1991: Adobe Caslon, Carol Twombly
1991: Remedy, Frank Heine
1992: Syndor, Hans Edward Meier
1992: Mason: Jonathan Barnbrook
1992: Poetica, Robert Slimbach
1993: Mantinia and Sofia, Matthew Carter
1993: Agenda, Greg Thompson
1994: Barcode, Brian Lucid
1994: Dogma, Zuzana Licko
1994: Big Caslon CC, Matthew Carter
1995: DIN, Albert-Jan Pool
1995: Walker, Matthew Carter
1995: Shogun, Richard Lipton
1996: Filosofia, Zuzana Licko
1996: Mrs Eaves, Zuzano Licko
1997: Vendetta, John Downer
1997–2000: Poynter Old Style, Tobias Frere-Jones
1999: Council, John Downer

1999: Spira, Andy Stockley
1999: Acropolis, Jonathan Hoefler
1999: Leviathan, Jonathan Hoefler
1999: Dispatch, Cyrus Highsmith
1999: Scala, Martin Majoor
2000: Verdana, Matthew Carter
2000: Georgia, Matthew Carter
2000: Seria, Martin Majoor
2000: Gotham, Tobias Frere-Jones
2001: Atma Serif Book, Alan Greene
2001: Dalliance, Frank Heine
2001: Vesta, Gerard Unger
2002: Bau, Christian Schwartz
2002: Gotham, Tobias Frere-Jones
2003: Benton Sans, Tobias Frere-Jones and Cyrus Highsmith
2003: Max, Morten Rostgaart Olson
2003: Page Sans and Serif, Albert Boton
2004: Amira, Cyrus Highsmith
2004: Nexus, Martin Majoor
2005: Dederon Sans, Tomas Brousil
2005: Minah, Jacqueline Sakwa
2005: Titling Gothic, David Berlow
2005: Truth, David Berlow
2006: Omnes, Joshua Darden
2007: Arno, Robert Slimbach
2007: Meta Serif, Christian Schwartz and Erik Spiekermann
2008: Fabiol, Robert Strauch
2009: Allumi PTF, Jean François Porchez
2010: Brandon Grotesque, Hannes von Döhren

A.A. Abbreviation for "author's alteration," used to flag a mistake or correction by the author.

ABA form. Design principle of form interrelationships, involving repetition and contrast.

Accents. Small marks over, under, or through a letterform, indicating specific punctuation or changes in stress.

Agate. Vertical unit used to measure space in newspaper columns, originally five-and-one-half point type. Fourteen agate lines equal approximately one inch.

Alert Box. A message box that appears on a computer screen with information for the user, for example, a "bomb message" when a computer crashes.

Alignment. Precise arrangement of letterforms upon an imaginary horizontal or vertical line.

Alphabet length. Horizontal measure of the lowercase alphabet in a type font, used to approximate the horizontal measure of type set in that font.

Ampersand. Typographic character (&) representing the word *and.*

Antialiasing. The blurring of a jagged line or edge on a screen or output device to give the appearance of a smooth line.

Application program. Computer software used to create and modify documents.

Area Composition. The organization of typographic and other graphic elements into their final positions by electronic means (keyboard, graphics tablets, and electronic pens, etc.), eliminating the need for hand assembly or pasteup.

Ascender. Stroke on a lowercase letter that rises above the mean-line.

ASCII code. Abbreviation for American Standard Code of Information Interchange. The numbers 0 through 127 represent the alphanumeric characters and functions on the keyboard.

Aspect ratio. The ratio of an image, screen, or other medium's height to its width. Images will become distorted if forced into a different aspect ratio during enlargement, reduction, or transfers.

Autoflow. A page-layout program setting for placing blocks of text from page to page without operator intervention.

Autopaging, Automatic pagination. A capability in computer typesetting for dividing text into pages. Advanced autopaging can add page numbers and running heads, and avoid awkward widows and orphans.

Auto-runaround, Automatic runaround. A page-layout program feature that flows text smoothly around graphics or headlines placed within the normal text area.

Base alignment. A typesetter or printer specification that the baseline for all letters should be horizontal, even in a line of mixed sizes or styles; also called baseline alignment.

Baseline. An imaginary horizontal line upon which the base of each capital letter rests.

Baud rate. The number of bits per second, often used as a measure of data transmission; for example, by a modem.

Bezier curves. A type of curve with nonuniform arcs, as opposed to curves with uniform curvature, which are called arcs. A Bezier curve is defined by specifying control points that set the shape of the curve, and are used to create letter shapes and other computer graphics.

Binary Code. Number system using two digits: zero and one.

Bit. Contraction of binary digit, which is the smallest unit of information that a computer can hold. The value of a bit (1 or 0) represents a two-way choice, such as yes or no, on or off, positive or negative.

Bitmap. A computerized image made up of dots. These are "mapped" onto the screen directly from corresponding bits in memory (hence the name). Also referred to as paint format.

Bitmapped Font. A font whose letters are composed of dots, such as fonts designed for dot-matrix printers. Compare *Outline font* and *Screen font.*

Body size. Depth of a piece of metal type, usually measured in points.

Body type. Text material, usually set in sizes from 6 to 12 points. Also called text type.

Boldface. Type with thicker, heavier strokes than the regular font. Indicated as "BF" in type specifications.

Boot. A computer's start-up procedures; coined from "pulling yourself up by your bootstraps."

Bounding box. In drawing or page-description languages, a bounding box is an imaginary box within which an image is located. It represents the rectangular area needed to create the image.

Browser. A graphical user interface to display HTML files for navigating the World Wide Web.

Byte. Unit of computer information. The number of bits used to represent a character. For personal computers, a byte is usually eight bits.

Backslant. Letterforms having a diagonal slant to the left.

C. and l.c. Used in marking copy, to instruct the typesetter to use capitals and lowercase.

C. and s.c. Used in marking copy, to instruct the typesetter to use capitals and small capitals.

Camera ready (or camera-ready copy). Copy and/or artwork that is ready to be photographed to make negatives, which are exposed to printing plates.

Cap height. Height of the capital letters, measured from the baseline to the capline.

Capline. Imaginary horizontal line defined by the height of the capital letters.

Capitals. Letters larger than – and often differing from – the corresponding lowercase letters. Also called uppercase.

Caps. See *Capitals.*

Captions. Title, explanation, or description accompanying an illustration or photograph.

Cascading style sheets. Web-site design software permitting the specification of type characteristics such as type size, letter-, and line-spacing.

Cast off. Determining the length of manuscript copy, enabling a calculation of the area that type will occupy when set in a given size and style of type.

Cathode ray tube (CRT). An electronic tube with a phosphorescent surface that produces a glowing image when activated by an electronic beam.

CD-ROM. An optical data storage device; initials for compact disk read-only memory.

Central processing unit (CPU). Computer component that controls all other parts, performs logical operations, and stores information.

Character. Symbol, sign, or mark in a language system.

Character count. The number of characters in a block of text. In typography, spaces are counted but other nonprinting characters usually are not. In data processing, both printing and nonprinting characters are usually counted.

Chase. Heavy metal frame into which metal type is locked for proofing or printing.

Chip. A small piece of silicon impregnated with impurities that form miniaturized computer circuits.

Chooser. Software that tells a computer which output device and connection port to use.

Ciecero. European typographic unit of measure, approximately equal to the American pica.

Clipboard. A computer's "holding place," a buffer area in memory for the last material to be cut or copied from a document. Information on the clipboard can be inserted (pasted) into documents.

Cold type. Type that is set by means other than casting molten metal. A term most frequently used to indicate strike-on composition rather than photo or digital typesetting.

Colophon. Inscription, frequently placed at the end of a book, that contains facts about its production.

Column guide. Nonprinting lines that define the location of columns of type.

Command. The generic name for an order or instruction to a computer.

Command character. The combination of a command key plus character(s) used to instruct a computer to take an action.

Comp. See *Comprehensive layout.*

Compensation. In visual organization, the counter-balancing of elements.

Composing stick. Adjustable handheld metal tray, used to hold handset type as it is being composed.

Composition. Alternate term for typesetting.

Compositor. Person who sets type.

Comprehensive layout. An accurate representation of a printed piece showing all type and pictures in their size and position. Comps are used to evaluate a design before producing final type and artwork.

Computer. Electronic device that performs predefined (programmed) high-speed mathematical or logical calculations.

Condensed. Letterforms whose horizontal width has been compressed.

Consonance. In design, harmonious interaction between elements.

Copyfitting. Calculating the area that will be occupied by a given manuscript when set in a specified size and style of type.

Counter. Space enclosed by the strokes of a letterform.

Counterform. "Negative" spatial areas defined and shaped by letterforms, including both interior counters and spaces between characters.

CPS. Characters per inch.

CPU. See *Central processing unit.*

CRT. See *Cathode ray tube.*

CSS. See *Cascading style sheets.*

Cursive. Type styles that imitate handwriting, often with letters that do not connect.

Cursor. Term for the pointer or insertion point on a computer screen.

Cut and paste. To move material from one location to another within a document, or from one document to another. This is a computer's electronic equivalent to clipping something with scissors, then using glue to paste the clipping in another location.

Cut off rules. Rules used to separate pages into various units, such as advertisements or news stories.

Daisy wheel. Strike-on printing wheel containing relief characters on spokes, radiating from a central disk. As the wheel spins, a hammer impacts the characters against an inked ribbon.

Data. Information, particularly information upon which a computer program is based.

Data bank. Mass storage of large quantities of information, indexed for rapid retrieval.

Data processing. The storing and handling of information by a computer.

Data transmission. Rapid electronic transfer of coded data via telephone or other communication links.

Dazzle. Visual effect caused by extreme contrast in the strokes of letterforms.

Default. A value, action, or setting that a computer system assumes, unless the user gives an explicit instruction to the contrary; for example, a certain point size and typeface style will be used by a page-layout program unless the user selects another size and font.

Descender. Stroke on a lowercase letterform that falls below the baseline.

Desktop. Refers to the desktop metaphor depicted on the computer screen, with a menu bar across the top, icons for applications and disk drives, and other icons, such as a trash can used to throw away unwanted material.

Desktop publishing. The popular use of this term is incorrect, because publishing encompasses writing, editing, designing, printing, and distribution activities, not just makeup and production. See *Electronic page design.*

Dialogue box. A box displayed on a computer screen requesting information or a decision by the user.

Digital type. Type stored electronically as digital dot or stroke patterns rather than as photographic images.

Digitizer. A computer peripheral device that converts images or sound into a digital signal.

Directory. The contents of a computer disk or folder. Directory contents can be arranged and displayed on a screen by name, icon, date created, size, or kind, etc.

Digital computer. A device that translates data into a discrete number system to facilitate electronic processing.

Disk. Thin, flat, circular plate with a magnetic surface upon which data may be stored. See *Floppy disk* and *Hard disk.* Also, a circular grid containing the master font in some typesetting systems.

Display Postscript. A technology by Adobe Systems that allows PostScript commands (for special graphic effects) to be displayed on the screen.

Display type. Type sizes 14 points and above, used primarily for headlines and titles.

Dissonance. In design, visual tension and contrast between typographic elements.

Dithering. A technique for alternating the value of adjacent dots or pixels to create the effect of an intermediate value. When printing color images or displaying color on a computer screen, dithering refers to the technique of making different colors for adjacent dots or pixels to give the illusion of a third color; for example, a printed field of alternating cyan and yellow dots appears to be green. Dithering gives the effect of shades of gray on a black-and-white display or the effect of more colors on a color display.

Dot-matrix printer. A printer that forms characters out of a pattern of dots; many have pins that strike against an inked ribbon to transfer the pattern of dots making up each character onto paper.

Dots per inch (dpi). A measure of the resolution of a screen image or printed page. Dots are also known as pixels. Some computer screens display 72 dpi; many laser printers print 300 dpi; and imagesetters often print 1270 or 2540 dpi.

Downloadable font. A font can be downloaded into a printer or computerized typesetter, which means that tables telling how to construct the type characters are sent from the computer to the output device. By accepting additional character sets – downloadable fonts – an output device can print many typefaces. To be able to accept downloadable fonts, a printer or typesetter must have sufficient computer memory and processing power to receive and store the images.

Downloading. Transferring information from one computer and storing it on another one.

DRAM. Abbreviation for dynamic random access memory chip; *dynamic* refers to loss of data in memory when a computer is shut off.

Draw program. Computer applications for drawing graphics that are object-oriented; that is, it produces graphics from arc and line segments that are mathematically defined by points located on the horizontal and vertical axes on the screen. Compare *Paint program.*

Drop initial. Display letterform set into the text.

E.A. Abbreviation for "editor's alteration," used to flag errors or corrections made by the editor.

Editing terminal. Workstation consisting of a keyboard and visual display device, used to input and edit copy prior to typesetting.

Egyptian. Typefaces characterized by slablike serifs similar in weight to the main strokes.

Electronic page design. The layout and typesetting of complete pages using a computer with input and output devices.

Elite. Size of typewriter type approximately equal to 10-point typography.

Ellipses. Three dots used to indicate an omission in quoted material.

Em. The square of the body size of any type, used as a unit of measure. In some expanded or condensed faces, the em is also expanded or condensed from the square proportion.

Em dash. A dash one em long. Also called a long dash.

Em leader. Horizontal dots or dashes with one em between their centers.

Em space. A space equal to the width of an em quad.

En. One-half of an em. See *Em.*

En dash. A dash one en long. Also called a short dash.

En leader. Horizontal dots or dashes with one en between their centers.

En space. Space equal to the width of an en quad.

Encapsulated PostScript (ESP). A computer format for encoding pictures. These can be stored, edited, transferred, and output in the form of structured PostScript code.

EPS. See *Encapsulated PostScript.*

Exception dictionary. See *Hyphenation.*

Expanded. Letterforms whose horizontal width has been extended.

Export. To send text, graphics, or layouts created in one program from the computer memory in a form suitable for use with other programs.

Face. The part of metal type that is inked for printing. Also another word for *typeface.*

Family. See *Type family.*

FAX Machine. An electronic device that scans documents and transmits them over telephone lines. Documents are received and output by another FAX machine.

Film font. A photographic film master used in some typesetting machines. Characters from a film font are exposed through lenses of different sizes onto paper or film. Unlike digital typesetting, typesetting systems using film fonts cannot set an entire page complete with graphics.

Finder. A computer program that generates the desktop and is used to access and manage files and disks. See *Multifinder.*

Firmware. Software that has been written into nonchangeable memory that does not need to be loaded into the system for each use. Most printers and output devices store their software in this form.

Fit. Refers to the spatial relationships between letters after they are set into words and lines.

Floppy disks. Portable, flexible disks housed in a 3.5-inch hard plastic case and inserted into a disk drive, which reads the information on the disk.

Flush left (or right). The even vertical alignment of lines of type at the left (or right) edge of a column.

Folio. Page number.

Font. A complete set of characters in one design, size, and style. In traditional metal type, a font meant a particular size and style; in digital typography a font can output multiple sizes and even altered styles of a typeface design.

Font/DA Mover. An application that allows a user to add and/or remove fonts and desk accessories from a file on a disk.

Font substitution. During output of a page, font substitution is the replacement of a requested but unavailable font by another (usually similar) available font.

Footer. An identifying line, such as a page number and/or a chapter title, appearing in the bottom margin of a document. Footers repeated throughout a document are called running footers or running feet.

Footprint. The amount of space a machine such as a computer takes up on a surface such as a desktop.

Format. The overall typographic and spatial schema established for a publication or any other application.

Formatting. In digital typesetting and phototypesetting, the process of issuing specific commands that establish the typographic format.

Foundry type. Metal type used in hand composition.

Furniture. Rectangular pieces of wood, metal, or plastic used to fill in excess space when locking up a form for letterpress printing.

Galley. A three-sided, shallow metal tray used to hold metal type forms before printing.

Galley proof. Originally, a type proof pulled from metal type assembled in a galley. Frequently used today to indicate any first proof, regardless of the type system.

GIF. See *Graphic Interface Format.*

Gigabyte (GB). A unit of data storage equal to 1,000 megabytes.

"Golf" ball. An interchangeable metal ball approximately one inch in diameter with raised characters on its surface, used as the printing element in some typewriters.

Graphic Interface Format (GIF). A graphic image format widely used in Web sites.

Greeking. Type set using random or Greek characters to simulate typeset text in a layout or comp.

Grayscale. An arbitrary scale of monochrome (black to white) intensity ranging from black and white, with a fixed number of intermediate shades of gray.

Grid. Underlying structure composed of a linear framework used by designers to organize typographic and pictorial elements. Also, a film or glass master font, containing characters in a predetermined configuration and used in phototypesetting.

Grotesque. Name for sans-serif typefaces.

Gutter. The interval separating two facing pages in a publication.

Gutter margin. Inner margin of a page in a publication.

Hairline. Thinnest strokes on a typeface having strokes of varying weight.

Hand composition. Method of setting type by placing individual pieces of metal type from a type case into a composing stick.

Hanging indent. In composition, a column format in which the first line of type is set to a full measure while all additional lines are indented.

Hanging punctuation. Punctuation set outside the column measure to achieve an optical alignment.

Hard copy. Computer output printed on paper.

Hard disks. Large rigid disks having large storage capacity, fast operating speed, and permanent installation within the computer or a separate case.

Hardware. The physical equipment of a computer system, such as the CPU, input/output devices, and peripherals.

Header. An identifying line at the top margin of a document. A header can appear on every page and can include text, pictures, page numbers, the date, and the time. Headers repeated throughout a document are called running headers or running heads.

Heading. Copy that is given emphasis over the body of text, through changes in size, weight, or spatial interval.

Headline. The most significant type in the visual hierarchy of a printed communication.

Hertz. One cycle per second. See *Megahertz.*

Hinting. A technique used to add greater realism to a digital image by smoothing jagged edges on curved lines and diagonals.

Hot type. Type produced by casting molten metal.

HTML. See *Hypertext markup language.*

HTML tables. Similar to a typographic grid, HTML tables allow designers to arrange data, text, images, links, and forms into rows and columns of cells on a web page.

Hypertext. Text on a computer screen that contains pointers enabling the user to jump to other text or pages by clicking a computer mouse on highlighted material.

Hypertext markup language. The basic computer-programming language used to design Web sites.

Hyphenation. The syllabic division of words used when they must be broken at the end of a line. In electronic typesetting, hyphenation can be determined by the operator or automatically by the computer.

I-beam pointer. The shape the pointer or cursor on a computer screen usually takes when working with text.

Icon. A pictorial representation. The elemental pictures on a computer screen used to represent disk drives, files, applications, and tools, etc., are called icons.

Import. To transfer text, graphics, or layouts into a program in a form suitable for its use.

Imposition. The arrangement of pages in a printed signature to achieve the proper sequencing after the sheets are folded and trimmed.

Incunabula. European books printed during the first half-century of typography, from Gutenberg's invention of movable type until the year 1500.

Indent. An interval of space at the beginning of a line to indicate a new paragraph.

Inferior characters. Small characters, usually slightly smaller than the x-height, positioned on or below the baseline and used for footnotes or fractions.

Initial. A large letter used at the beginning of a column; for example, at the beginning of a chapter.

Initialize. Electronically formatting a disk to prepare it to record data from a computer.

Input. Raw data, text, or commands entered into a computer memory from a peripheral device, such as a keyboard.

Insertion point. The location in a document where the next text or graphics will be placed, represented by a blinking vertical cursor. A user selects the insertion point by clicking where he or she wishes to work.

Interletter spacing. The spatial interval between letters, also called *letterspacing*.

Interline spacing. The spatial interval between lines, also called *leading*.

Interword spacing. The spatial interval between words, also called *wordspacing*.

Italic. Letterforms having a pronounced diagonal slant to the right.

Jaggies. The jagged "staircase" edges formed on raster-scan displays when displaying diagonal and curved lines. See *Antialiasing*.

Javascript. An embedded scripting language used to create dynamic and interactive Web pages.

JPEG. An acronym for Joint Photographic Experts Group. JPEG is a bitmap format used to transmit graphic images.

Justified setting. A column of type with even vertical edges on both the left and the right, achieved by adjusting interword spacing. Also called *flush-left, flush-right*.

Justified text. Copy in which all lines of a text – regardless of the words they contain – have been made exactly the same length, so that they align vertically at both the left and right margins.

K. Computer term for one thousand twenty-four bytes of memory.

Kerning. In typesetting, *kerning* refers to the process of subtracting space between specific pairs of characters so that the overall letterspacing appears to be even. Compare *Tracking*.

Keyboard. A device having keys or buttons used to enter data into typesetting and computer systems.

Laser. A concentrated light source that can be optically manipulated. Coined from "Light Amplification by Stimulated Emission of Radiation."

Laser printer. A computer printer that creates the image by drawing it on a metal drum with a laser. The latent image becomes visible after dry ink particles are electrostatically attracted to it.

Latin. Type style characterized by triangular, pointed serifs.

Leader. Typographic dots or periods that are repeated to connect other elements.

Lead-in. Introductory copy set in a contrasting typeface.

Leading. (Pronounced "LED-ing") In early typesetting, strips of lead were placed between lines of type to increase the interline spacing, hence the term. See *Linespacing, Interline spacing*.

Letterpress. The process of printing from a raised inked surface.

Letterspacing. See *Interletter spacing*.

Ligature. A typographic character produced by combining two or more letters.

Line breaks. The relationships of line endings in a *ragged-right* or *ragged-left* setting. Rhythmic line breaks are achieved by adjusting the length of individual lines of type.

Line length. The measure of the length of a line of type, usually expressed in picas.

Linespacing. The vertical distance between two lines of type measured from baseline to baseline. For example, "10/12" indicates 10-point type with 12 points base-to-base (that is, with 2 points of leading). See *Leading, Interline spacing*.

Lining figures. Numerals identical in size to the capitals and aligned on the baseline: 1 2 3 4 5 6 7 8 9 10.

Linotype. A machine that casts an entire line of raised type on a single metal slug.

Local area network (LAN). A network of computers and peripherals, usually in the same office or building, connected by dedicated electrical cables rather than telephone lines.

Logotype. Two or more type characters that are combined as a sign or trademark.

Lowercase. The alphabet set of small letters, as opposed to capitals.

LPM. Lines per minute, a unit of measure expressing the speed of a typesetting system.

Ludlow. A typecasting machine that produces individual letters from hand-assembled matrices.

Machine composition. General term for the mechanical casting of metal type.

Majuscules. A term in calligraphy for letterforms analogous to uppercase letterforms, usually drawn between two parallel lines, the capline and the baseline. See *Minuscules*.

Makeup. The assembly of typographic matter into a page, or a sequence of pages, ready for printing.

Margin. The unprinted space surrounding type matter on a page.

Markup. The marking of typesetting specifications upon manuscript copy.

Marquee. A rectangular area, often surrounded by blinking dashed or dotted lines, used to select objects or regions in a application program.

Master page. In a page-layout program, a master page is a template providing standard columns, margins, and typographic elements that appear on a publication's individual pages.

Masthead. The visual identification of a magazine or newspaper, usually a logotype. Also a section placed near the front of a newspaper or periodical containing information such as names and titles of publishers and staff, along with addresses.

Matrix. In typesetting, the master image from which type is produced. The matrix is a brass mold in linecasting and a glass plate bearing the font negative in phototypesetting.

Meanline. An imaginary line marking the tops of lowercase letters, not including the ascenders.

Measure. See *Line length*.

Mechanical. A camera-ready pasteup of artwork including type, images showing position of color and halftone matter, line art, etc., all on one piece of artboard.

Megabyte (MB). A unit of measurement equal to 1024 kilobytes or 1,048,576 bytes.

Megahertz (MHz). A million cycles per second. Describes the speed of computer chips; used to measure of how rapidly a computer processes information.

Menu. A list of choices in a computer application, from which the user selects a desired action. In a computer's desktop interface, menus appear when you point to and click on menu titles in the menu bar. Dragging through a menu and releasing the mouse button while a command is highlighted chooses that command.

Menu bar. A horizontal band across the top of a computer screen that contains menu titles.

Message Box. A box that appears on a computer screen to give the user information.

Microprocessor. A single silicon chip containing thousands of electronic components for processing information; the "brains" of a personal computer.

Minuscules. A term in calligraphy for letterforms analogous to lowercase letters and usually drawn between four parallel lines determining ascender height, x-height, baseline, and descender depth. See *Majuscules*.

Minus Spacing. A reduction of interline spacing, resulting in a baseline-to-baseline measurement that is smaller than the point size of the type.

Mixing. The alignment of more than one type style or typeface on a single baseline.

Modem. Contraction of modulator/demodulator; a peripheral device to send data over telephone lines from a computer to other computers, service bureaus, and information services, etc.

Modern. Term used to describe typefaces designed at the end of the eighteenth century. Characteristics include vertical stress, hairline serifs, and pronounced contrasts between thick and thin strokes.

Monocase alphabet. A language alphabet, such as Hebrew and Indic scripts, having only capital-height letters and no lowercase letterforms.

Monochrome. Refers to material or a display consisting of a single color, typically black or white.

Monogram. Two or more letterforms interwoven, combined, or connected into a single glyph, typically used as abbreviations or initials.

Monoline. Used to describe a typeface or letterform with a uniform stroke thickness.

Monospacing. Spacing in a font with characters that all have the same set width or horizontal measure; often found in typewriter and screen fonts. See *Proportional spacing*.

Monotype. A trade name for a keyboard-operated typesetting machine that casts individual letters from matrices.

Mouse. A small computer device that controls an on-screen pointer or tool when the mouse is moved around on a flat surface by hand. The mouse-controlled pointer can select operations, move data, and draw images.

Multifinder. A computer program permitting several applications to be open at the same time, so that a designer can work back and forth between page-layout and drawing programs, for example, without having to repeatedly open and close programs.

Navigation. The act of manually moving a cursor through an on-screen page or series of pages.

Negative. The reversal of a positive photographic image.

Network. A system connecting multiple computers so they can share printers and information, etc.

Object-oriented. A method in drawing and other computer programs that produces graphics from arc and line segments that are mathematically defined by points located on the horizontal and vertical axes on the screen.

Oblique. A slanted roman character. Unlike many italics, oblique characters do not have cursive design properties.

Offset lithography. A printing method using flat photo-mechanical plates, in which the inked image is transferred or offset from the printing plate onto a rubber blanket, then onto the paper.

Old Style. Typeface styles derived from fifteenth- to eighteenth-century designs, and characterized by moderate thick-and-thin contrasts, bracketed serifs, and a handwriting influence.

Old Style figures. Numerals that exhibit a variation in size, including characters aligning with the lowercase x-height, and others with ascenders or descenders: 1 2 3 4 5 6 7 8 9 10.

Operating System. A computer program that controls a computer's operation, directing information to and from different components.

Optical adjustment. The precise visual alignment and spacing of typographic elements. In interletter spacing, the adjustment of individual characters to achieve consistent spacing.

Orphan. A single word on a line, left over at the end of a paragraph, sometimes appearing at the top of a column of text. See *Widow*.

O.S. See *Operating System*.

Outline font. A font designed, not as a bitmap, but as outlines of the letter shapes that can be scaled to any size. Laser printers and imagesetters use outline fonts. See *Bitmapped font* and *Screen font*.

Outline type. Letterforms described by a contour line that encloses the entire character on all sides. The interior usually remains open.

Output. The product of a computer operation. In computerized typesetting, output is reproduction proofs of composition.

Page Preview. A mode on many word-processing and page-layout programs that shows a full-page view of what the page will look like when printed, including added elements such as headers, footers, and margins.

Pagination. The sequential numbering of pages.

Paint program. A computer application that creates images as a series of bitmapped dots, which can be erased and manipulated by turning the pixels on and off. Compare *Draw program*.

Pantone Matching System (PMS). The trademarked name of a system for specifying colors and inks that is a standard in the printing industry.

Paragraph mark. Typographic elements that signal the beginning of a paragraph. For example, ¶.

Parallel construction. In typography, the use of similar typographic elements or arrangements to create a visual unity or to convey a relationship in content.

Paste. To place a copy of saved material into a computer-generated document or layout.

P. E. Abbreviation for "Printer's Error," used to flag a mistake made by the compositor rather than by the author.

Pen plotter. A printer that draws using ink-filled pens that are moved along a bar, which also moves back and forth. Many plotters have very high resolutions but have slow operation, poor text quality, and poor handling of raster images.

Peripheral. An electronic device that connects to a computer, such as a disk drive, scanner, or printer.

Photocomposition. The process of setting type by projecting light onto light-sensitive film or paper.

Photodisplay typesetting. The process of setting headline type on film or paper by photographic means.

Phototype. Type matter set on film or paper by photographic projection of type characters.

Photounit. Output component of a photocomposition system, which sets the type and exposes it to light-sensitive film or paper.

Pica. Typographic unit of measurement: 12 points equal 1 pica. 6 picas equal approximately one inch. Line lengths and column widths are measured in picas.

PICT. A computer format for encoding pictures. PICT data can be created, displayed on the screen, and printed, thus enabling applications without graphics-processing routines to incorporate PICT data generated by other software.

Pixel. Stands for picture element; the smallest dot that can be displayed on a screen.

Point. A measure of size used principally in typesetting. One point is equal to 1/12 of a pica, or approximately 1/72 of an inch. It is most often used to indicate the size of type or amount of leading added between lines.

Pointer. A graphic form that moves on a computer screen and is controlled by a pointing device; usually a symbolic icon such as an arrow, I-beam, or clock.

Pointer device. A computer input device, such as a mouse, tablet, or joystick, used to indicate where an on-screen pointer or tool should be placed or moved.

Port. An electrical socket where cables are inserted to connect computers, peripheral devices, or networks. Ports are named for the type of signal they carry, such as printer port, serial port, or SCSI port.

PostScript.™ A page-description programming language created by Adobe Systems that handles text and graphics, placing them on the page with mathematical precision.

Preview. To view the final output on a computer screen before printing. Because most screens have lower resolution than an imagesetter or laser printer, fine details are often different from the final output.

Processor. In a computer system, the general term for any device capable of carrying out operations upon data. In phototypography, the unit that automatically develops the light-sensitive paper or film.

Program. A sequence of instructions that directs the operations of a computer to execute a given task.

Proof. Traditionally, an impression from metal type for examination and correction; now applies to initial output for examination and correction before final output.

Proportional spacing. Spacing in a font adjusted to give wide letters (M) a larger set width than narrow letters (I).

Quad. In metal type, pieces of type metal shorter than type-high, which are used as spacing matter to separate elements and fill out lines.

Quoins. Wedges use to lock up metal type in the chase. These devices are tightened and loosened by a quoin key.

Ragged. See *Unjustified type.*

RAM. Abbreviation for *random access memory,* the area of a computer's memory that temporarily stores applications and documents while they are being used.

RAM cache. An area of the computer's memory set aside to hold information from a disk until it is needed again. It can be accessed much more quickly from a RAM cache than from a disk.

Raster display. A raster image is divided into scan lines, each consisting of a series of dots from a thin section of the final image. This dot pattern corresponds exactly to a bit pattern in the computer memory.

Raster image file format. A file format for paint-style color graphics, developed by Letraset USA.

Raster image processor (RIP). A device or program that translates an image or page into the actual pattern of dots received by a printing or display system.

Raster scan. The generation of an image upon a cathode ray tube made by refreshing the display area line by line.

Recto. In publication design, the right-hand page. Page one (and all odd-numbered pages) always appears on a recto. The left-hand page is called the verso.

Resolution. The degree of detail and clarity of a display; usually specified in dots per inch (dpi/ppi). The higher the resolution, or the greater the number of dpi, the sharper the image.

Reverse. Type or image that is dropped out of a printed area, revealing the paper surface.

Reverse leading. A reduction in the amount of interline space, making it less than normal for the point size. For example, 12-point type set on an 11- point body size becomes reverse leading of 1 point.

Revival. A little-used historic typeface previously unavailable in current font formats, now released for contemporary technology.

RIFF. See *Raster Image File Format.*

River. In text type, a series of interword spaces that accidentally align vertically or diagonally, creating an objectionable flow of white space within the column.

ROM. Abbreviation for *read only memory,* which is permanently installed on a computer chip and can be read but cannot accept new or changed data; for example, some laser printers have basic fonts permanently installed in a ROM chip.

Roman. Upright letterforms, as distinguished from italics. More specifically, letters in an alphabet style based on the upright serifed letterforms of Roman inscriptions.

Rule. In handset metal type, a strip of metal that prints as a line. Generally, any line used as an element in typographic design, whether handset, photographic, digital, or hand-drawn.

Run-around. Type that is set with a shortened line measure to fit around a photograph, drawing, or other visual element inserted into the running text.

Run in. To set type without a paragraph indentation or other break. Also, to insert additional matter into the running text as part of an existing paragraph.

Running foot or running footer. A line of text that duplicates a line of text from another page but positioned at or near the bottom of a page.

Running head. Type at the head of sequential pages, providing a title or publication name.

Sans serif. Typefaces without serifs.

Saving. Transferring information – such as an electronic page design – from a computer's memory to a storage device.

Scanner. A computer peripheral device that scans pictures and converts them to digital form so they can be stored, manipulated, and output.

Scrapbook. A computer's "holding place" for permanent storage of images, text, etc.

Screen font. A bitmapped version of an outline font that is used to represent the outline font on a computer screen.

Script. Typefaces based on handwriting, usually having connecting strokes between the letters.

Scroll bar. A rectangular bar that may appear along the right or bottom of a window on a computer screen. By clicking or dragging on the scroll bar, the user can move through the document.

Scrolling. In typesetting and computer-assisted design, moving through a document to bring onto the screen portions of the document not currently displayed.

SCSI. Abbreviation for Small Computer System Interface; pronounced "scuzzy." SCSI is a computer-industry standard interface allowing very fast transfer of data.

Semantics. The science of meaning in linguistics; the study of the relationships between signs and symbols, and what they represent.

Serifs. Small elements added to the ends of the main strokes of a letterform in serifed type styles.

Set width. In metal type, the width of the body upon which a letter is cast. In phototype and digital type, the horizontal width of a letterform measured in units, including the normal space before and after the character. This interletter space can be increased or decreased to control the tightness or looseness of the fit.

Shoulder. In metal type, the flat top of the type body that surrounds the raised printing surface of the letterform.

Sidebar. A narrow column of text, separated from the main text by a box or rule and containing a secondary article.

Side head. A title or other heading material placed to the side of a type column.

Slab serifs. Square or rectangular serifs that align horizontally and vertically to the baseline and are usually the same (or heavier) weight as the main strokes of the letterform.

Slug. A line of metal type cast on a linecasting machine, such as the Linotype. Also, strips of metal spacing material in thicknesses of 6 points or more.

Small capitals. A set of capital letters having the same height as the lowercase x-height, frequently used for cross-reference and abbreviations. Also called small caps and abbreviated "s.c."

Smoothing. The electronic process of eliminating jaggies (the uneven staircase effect on diagonal or curved lines).

Software. Components of a computer system consisting of the programs or instructions that control the behavior of the computer hardware.

Solid. Lines of type that are set without additional interline space. Also called *set solid.*

Sorts. In metal type, material that is not part of a regular font, such as symbols, piece fractions, and spaces. Also, individual characters used to replace worn-out type in a font.

Stand-alone typesetting system. A typesetting system that is completely self-contained, including editing terminal, memory, and character generation.

Startup disk. The computer disk drive containing the system software used to operate the computer.

Stet. A proofreader's mark meaning that copy marked for correction should not be changed; rather, any instructions for changes should be ignored and the text should be left as originally set.

Storage. In computer typesetting, a device (such as a disk, drum, or tape) that can receive information and retain it for future use.

Straight matter. Text material set in continuous columns with limited deviation from the basic typographic specifications.

Stress. The gradual variation in the thickness of a curved character part or stroke; often used for any variation in the thickness of a character part or stroke.

Style sheets. In several word-processing and page-layout programs, style sheets are special files containing formatting instructions for creating standardized documents.

Subscript. A small character beneath (or adjacent to and slightly below) another character.

Superscript. A small character above (or adjacent to and slightly above) another character.

Swash letters. Letters ornamented with flourishes or flowing tails.

Syntax. In grammar, the way in which words or phrases are put together to form sentences. In design, the connecting or ordering of typographic elements into a visual unity.

System. A related group of interdependent design elements forming a whole. In computer science, a complete computing operation including software and hardware (Central Processing Unit, memory, input/output devices, and peripherals or devices required for the intended functions).

System software. Computer files containing the operating system program and its supporting programs needed to make the computer work, interface with peripherals, and run applications.

Tag Image File Format (TIFF). A computer format for encoding pictures as high-resolution bitmapped images, such as those created by scanners.

Telecommunications. Sending messages to distant locations; usually refers to communicating by telephone lines.

Terminal. See *Video display terminal.*

Text. The main body of written or printed material, as opposed to display matter, footnotes, appendices, etc.

Text type. See *Body type.*

Thumbnail. A miniature image of a page, either a small planning sketch made by a designer or a reduction in a page-layout program.

TIFF. See *Tag Image File Format.*

Tracking. The overall tightness or looseness of the spacing between all characters in a line or block of text. Sometimes used interchangeably with *kerning,* which more precisely is the reduction in spacing between a specific pair of letters.

Transitional. Classification of type styles combining aspects of both Old Style and Modern typefaces; for example, Baskerville.

Type family. The complete range of variations of a typeface design, including roman, italic, bold, expanded, condensed, and other versions.

Typeface. The design of alphabetical and numerical characters unified by consistent visual properties.

Type-high. The standard foot-to-face height of metal types; 0.9186 inches in English-speaking countries.

Typescript. Typewritten manuscript material used as copy for typesetting.

Typesetting. The composing of type by any method or process, also called *composition*.

Type specimen. A typeset sample produced to show the visual properties of a typeface.

Typo. See *Typographical error.*

Typographer. A firm specializing in typesetting. Sometimes used to denote a compositor or typesetter.

Typographical error. A mistake in typesetting, typing, or writing.

Typography. Originally the composition of printed matter from movable type. Now the art and process of typesetting by any system or method.

U.C. and l.c. Abbreviation for *uppercase and lowercase,* used to specify typesetting that combines capitals with lowercase letters.

Undo. A standard computer command that "undoes," or reverses, the last command or operation executed.

Uniform Resource Locator (URL). A location pointer name used to identify the location of a file on a server connected to the World Wide Web.

Unit. A subdivision of the em, used in measuring and counting characters in photo- and digital typesetting systems.

Unitization. The process of designing a typeface so that the individual character widths conform to a typesetter's unit system.

Unitized font. A font with character widths conforming to a typesetter's unit system.

Unit system. A counting system first developed for Monotype, used by most typesetting machines. The width of characters and spaces are measured in units. This data is used to control line breaks, justification, and interword and interletter spacing.

Unit value. The established width, in units, of a typographic character.

Unjustified type. Lines of type set with equal interword spacing, resulting in irregular line lengths. Also called *ragged.*

Uploading. Sending information from your computer to a distant computer. See *Downloading.*

Uppercase. See *Capitals.*

URL. See *Uniform Resource Locator.*

User interface. The way a computer system communicates with its user; the "look and feel" of the machine as experienced by the user.

Vector-based software. Software using computer instructions that specify shapes by defining linear elements by specifying starting and ending locations.

Verso. In publication design, the left-hand page. Page two (and all even-numbered pages) always appear on a verso. The right-hand page is called the recto.

Virus. A computer program that invades computers and modifies data, usually in a destructive manner.

Visual display terminal. A computer input/output device utilizing a cathode ray tube to display data on a screen. Information from memory, storage, or a keyboard can be displayed.

Web browser. A utility viewer used to display documents on the World Wide Web, which are usually written in HTML.

Web page. A document written in HTML, typically stored on a Web site and accessible through a Web browser.

Web site. A collection of files on a Web server computer system that are accessible to a Web browser or by Web TV.

Weight. The lightness or heaviness of a typeface, which is determined by ratio of the stroke thickness to character height.

White space. The "negative" area surrounding a letterform. See *Counter* and *Counterform.*

White-space reduction. A decrease in the amount of interletter space, achieved in typesetting by reducing the unit value of typeset characters. See *Tracking.*

Widow. A very short line that appears at the end of a paragraph, column, or page, or at the top of a column or page. These awkward typographic configurations should be corrected editorially.

Width tables. Collections of information about how much horizontal room each character in a font should occupy, often accompanied by information about special kerning pairs or other exceptions.

Windows. An area of a computer screen in which a single document is displayed.

Woodtype. Hand-set types cut from wood by a mechanical router. Formerly used for large display sizes that were not practical for metal casting, woodtype has been virtually eliminated by display photographic typesetting.

Word. In computer systems, a logical unit of information, composed of a predetermined number of bits.

Word-processing program. A computer application used to type in text, then edit, correct, move, or remove it.

Wordspacing. The spatial interval between words. In setting justified body type, space is added between words to extend each line to achieve flush left and right edges. See *Interword spacing.*

World Wide Web. A global graphic media system used to exchange data between computer users.

WORM. Acronym for "Write Once Read Many," usually applied to storage media such as CD-ROMs, which can only be written once but read many times.

WYSIWYG. Abbreviation for "what you see is what you get," pronounced Wizzywig. This means the image on the screen is identical to the image that will be produced as final output.

x-height. The height of lowercase letters in a font, excluding characters with ascenders and descenders. This is most easily measured on the lowercase *x.*

Bibliography

Aicher, Otl. *Typographie*. Berlin: Ernst & Sohn, 1988.

Anderson, Donald M. *A Renaissance Alphabet*. Madison, WI: University of Wisconsin Press, 1971.

————. *The Art of Written Forms*. New York: Holt, Reinhart and Winston, 1969.

Arnheim, Rudolf. *The Power of the Center: A Study of Composition in the Visual Arts*. Berkeley, CA: University of California Press, 1982.

Bellantoni, Jeff, and Woolman, Matt. *Type in Motion*. London: Thames& Hudson, 2000.

Bevington, William. *Typography: The Principles. A Basic Guide to Using Type*. New York: The Center for Design and Typography, The Cooper Union, 1991.

Bigelow, Charles, Duensing, Paul Hayden, and Gentry, Linnea. *Fine Print on Type: The Best of Fine Print on Type and Typography*. San Francisco: Fine Print/Bedford Arts, 1988.

Binns, Betty. *Better Type*. New York: Watson-Guptill, 1989.

Blackwell, Lewis. *20th Century Type*. New York: Rizzoli, 1992.

Bojko, Szymon. *New Graphic Design in Revolutionary Russia*. New York: Praeger, 1972.

Bringhurst, Robert. *The Elements of Typographic Style*. Port Roberts, WA: Hartley and Marks, 1992.

Brody, Neville, and Blackwell, Lewis. *G3: New Dimensions in Graphic Design*. New York: Rizzoli, 1996.

Burns, Aaron. *Typography*. New York: Van Nostrand Reinhold, 1961.

Bruckner, D. J. R. *Frederic Goudy*. New York: Harry Abrams, 1990.

Carter, Rob. *American Typography Today*. New York: Van Nostrand Reinhold, 1989.

————. *Digital Color and Type*. Crans-Près-Céligny Switzerland: RotoVision, 2002.

————. *Working with Type*, Volumes 1–5, Crans-Près-Céligny, Switzerland: RotoVision; and New York: Watson Guptill, 1995–99.

Carter, Sebastian. *Twentieth Century Type Designers*. New York: W. W. Norton & Co., 1995.

Chang, Amos I. *The Tao of Architecture*. Princeton, NJ: Princeton University Press, 1981.

Craig, James, Korol Scala, Irene, and Bevington, William. *Designing with Type: The Essential Guide to Typography*. New York: Watson-Guptill Publications, 2006.

Dair, Carl. *Design with Type*. Toronto: University of Toronto Press, 1967.

Damase, Jacque. *Revolution Typographique*. Geneva: Galerie Mott, 1966.

Doczi, Gregory. *The Power of Limits: Proportional Harmonies in Nature, Art and Architecture*. Boulder, CO: Shambhala Publications, 1981.

Dooijes, Dick. *Mijn Leven Met Letters*. Amsterdam: De Buitenkant, 1991.

Dowding, Geoffrey. *Fine Points in the Spacing and Arrangement of Type*. Point Roberts, WA: Hartley and Marks, 1993.

Drogin, Marc. *Medieval Calligraphy: Its History and Technique*. Montclair, NJ: Allanheld and Schram, 1980.

Dwiggins, William Addison. *Layout in Advertising*. New York: Harper and Brothers, 1948.

Elam, Kimberly. *Expressive Typography: The Word as Image*. New York: Van Nostrand Reinhold, 1990.

————. *Grid Systems: Principles of Organizing Type*. New York: Princeton Architectural Press, 2004.

Felici, James. *The Complete Manual of Typography*. Berkeley, CA: Peachpit Press, 2003.

Friedl, Fiedrich, Ott, Nicolaus, and Stein, Bernard. *Typography: An Encyclopedic Survey*. New York: Black Dog, 1998.

Friedman, Mildred, ed. *De Stijl: 1917–1931, Visions of Utopia*. New York: Abbeville Press, 1982.

Frutiger, Adrian. *Type, Sign, Symbol*. Zurich: ABC Verlag, 1980.

————. *Signs & Symbols: Their Design & Meaning*. New York: Van Nostrand Reinhold, 1989.

Gardner, William. *Alphabet at Work*. New York: St. Martins Press, 1982.

Gerstner, Karl. *Compendium for Literates: A System for Writing*. Translated by Dennis Q. Stephenson. Cambridge, MA: MIT Press, 1974.

Gill, Eric. *An Essay on Typography*. Boston: David R. Godine, 1988.

Goines, David Lance. *A Constructed Roman Alphabet*. Boston: David R. Godine, 1981.

Goudy, Frederic W. *The Alphabet and Elements of Lettering*. New York: Dover, 1963.

————. *Typologia: Studies in Type Design and Type Making*. Berkeley, CA: University of California Press, 1940.

Gray, Nicolete. *Nineteenth Century Ornamented Typefaces*. Berkeley, CA: University of California Press, 1977.

————. *A History of Lettering: Creative Experiment and Letter Identity*. Boston: David R. Godine, 1986.

Harlan, Calvin. *Vision and Invention: A Course in Art Fundamentals*. New York: Prentice Hall, 1969.

Heller, Steven, and Meggs, Philip B. eds. *Texts on Type: Critical Writings on Typography*. New York: Allworth, 2001.

Hiebert, Kenneth J. *Graphic Design Processes: Universal to Unique*. New York: Van Nostrand Reinhold, 1992.

Hinrichs, Kit. *Typewise*. Cincinnati: North Light, 1990.

Hochuli, Jost. *Detail in Typography*. London: Hyphen Press, 2008

Hoffman, Armin. *Graphic Design Manual: Principles and Practice*. New York: Van Nostrand Reinhold, 1992.

————. *His Work, Quest, and Philosophy*. Basel: Burkhäuser Verlag, 1989.

Jaspert, W. Pincus, Berry, W. Turner, Jaspert, W. P., and
    Johnson, A. F. *The Encyclopaedia of Typefaces*. New York:
    Blandford Press, 1986.
Kane, John. *A Type Primer*. Upper Saddle River, NJ: Prentice
    Hall, 2003.
Kelly, Rob Roy. *American Wood Type 1828–1900*. New York: Van
    Nostrand Reinhold, 1969.
Kepes, Gyorgy. *Sign, Symbol, Image*. New York: George
    Braziller, 1966.
Kinross, Robin. *Modern Typography: An Essay in Critical History*.
    London: Hyphen Press, 1992.
Kunz, Willi. *Typography: Macro+Micro Aesthetics*. Switzerland:
    Verlag Arthur Niggli, 1998.
Knobler, Nathan. *The Visual Dialogue*. New York: Holt, Reinhart
    and Winston, 1967.
Lawson, Alexander. *Anatomy of a Typeface*. Boston: David R.
Godine, 1990.
Lewis, John. *Anatomy of Printing: The Influence of Art and
    History on Its Design*. New York: Watson-Guptill, 1970.
Lobell, Frank. *Between Silence and Light: Spirit in the
    Architecture of Louis I. Kahn*. Boulder, CO: Shambhala
    Publications, 1979.
Malsy Victor, Philipp Teufel and Fjodor Gejko. *Helmut Schmid:
    Design is Attitude*. Basel: Birkhäuser Publishers, 2002
McGrew, Mac. *American Metal Typefaces of the Twentieth
    Century*. New Castle, DE: Oak Knoll Books, 1993.
McLean, Ruari. *The Thames and Hudson Manual of Typography*.
    London: Thames and Hudson, 1980.
————. *Jan Tschichold: Typographer*. Boston: David R.
    Godine, 1975.
————. *Jan Tschichold: A Life in Typography*. New York:
    Princeton Architectural Press, 1997.
Meggs, Philip, and Carter, Rob. *Typographic Specimens:
    The Great Typefaces*. New York: John Wiley & Sons, 1993.
Meggs, Philip B., and McKelvey, Roy, eds. *Revival of the Fittest:
    Digital Versions of Classic Typefaces*. New York: RC
    Publications, 2000.
Meggs, Philip B. *Type and Image: The Language of Graphic
    Design*. New York: John Wiley & Sons, 1989.
————. *A History of Graphic Design*, 3rd Edition. New York:
    John Wiley & Sons, 1998.
Morison, Stanley. *First Principles of Typography*. Cambridge,
    England: Cambridge University Press, 1936.
————. and Day, Kenneth. *The Typographic Book:
    1450–1935*. Chicago: University of Chicago Press, 1964.
Müller-Brockmann, Josef. *Grid Systems in Graphic Design:
    A Visual Communications Manual*. Niederteufen, Switzerland:
    Arthur Niggli Ltd., 1981.
Nesbitt, Alexander. *The History and Technique of Lettering*. New
    York: Dover, 1950.

Perfect, Christopher, and Austen, Jeremy. *The Complete
    Typographer: A Manual for Designing with Type*.
    Englewood Cliffs, NJ: Prentice Hall, 1992.
Petersen, Ad. *Sandberg: Designer + Director of the Stedelijk*.
    Rotterdam: 010 Publishers, 2004.
Quay, David, and Broos, Kees. *Wim Crouwel Alphabets*.
    Amsterdam: BIS Publishers, 2003.
Rehe, Rolf F. *Typography: How to Make It Most Legible*. Carmel,
    CA: Design Research Publications, 1974.
Richardson, Margaret. *Type Graphics: The Power of Type in
    Graphic Design*. Gloucester, MA: Rockport, 2000.
Roberts, Raymond. *Typographic Design: Handbooks to Printing*.
    London: Ernest Bend Limited, 1966.
Rogers, Bruce. *Paragraphs on Printing*. New York: Dover, 1980.
Ruder, Emil. *Typography: A Manual of Design*. Switzerland:
    Verlag Arthur Niggli, 1967.
Ruegg, Ruedi. *Basic Typography: Design with Letters*.
    New York: Van Nostrand Reinhold, 1989.
Schmid, Helmut. *Typography Today*. Tokyo: Seibundo
    Shinkosha,1980.
Solt, Mary Ellen. *Concrete Poetry*. Bloomington, IN: University
    of Indiana Press, 1971.
Spencer, Herbert. *Pioneers of Modern Typography*. Londonn:
    Lund Humphries, 1969, and Cambridge, MA:
    MIT Press, 1983.
————. *The Visible Word*. New York: Hastings House, 1969.
————. Editor. *The Liberated Page*. San Francisco:
    Bedford, 1987.
Spiekermann, Erik, and Ginger, E. M. *Stop Stealing Sheep and
    Find Out How Type Works*. Mountain View, CA:
    Adobe Press, 1993.
Stone, Summer. *On Stone*. San Francisco: Bedford Arts, 1991.
Sutnar, Ladislav. *Visual Design in Action – Principles, Purposes*.
    New York: Hastings House, 1961.
Swann, Cal. *Techniques of Typography*. New York: Watson-
    Guptill, 1969.
Tschichold, Jan. Translator, Ruari McLean. *The New Typography*.
    Berkeley, CA: University of California Press, 1998.
Updike, Daniel. *Printing Types: Their History, Form, and Use*.
    New York: Dover, 1980.
VanderLans, Rudy, Licko, Zuzana, and Gray, Mary E. *Emigre:
    Graphic Design in the Digital Realm*. New York: Van
    Nostrand Reinhold, 1993.
Van Kooten, Kees, and Spieker, Ewald. *Letter Lust*. Antwerpen:
    Uitgeverij Manteau, 2003.
Wallis, Lawrence W. *Modern Encyclopedia of Typefaces: 1960–90*.
    New York: Van Nostrand Reinhold, 1990.
Weingart, Wolfgang. *Wolfgang Weingart: My Way to Typography*.
    Baden: Switzerland: Lars Müller, 2000.

(Frontispiece) *Saint Barbara,* 15th-Century German or French polychromed walnut sculpture. (50"H x 23"W x 13"D) 127.0 cm x 58.4 cm x 33.0 cm. The Virginia Museum of Fine Arts, Richmond. The Williams Fund, 1968.

Chapter One

1. Impressed tablet from Godin Tepe, Iran. West Asian Department, Royal Ontario Museum, Toronto.

2. Facsimile of the cuneiform impression on a clay tablet, after Hansard.

3. The Pyramids at Giza, from *The Iconographic Encyclopaedia of Science, Literature, and Art* by Johann Georg Heck, 1851.

4. Egyptian Old Kingdom *False Door Stele,* limestone. The Virginia Museum of Fine Arts, Richmond. Museum Purchase: The Williams Fund.

5. Cuneiform tablet. Sumero-Akkadian. The Metropolitan Museum of Art, New York. Acquired by exchange with J. Pierpont Morgan Library, 1911.

6. Photograph of Stonehenge; courtesy of the British Tourist Authority.

7. Egyptian Polychromed Wood Sculpture, XVIII–XIX Dynasty. Ushabti. The Virginia Museum of Fine Arts, Richmond. Museum Purchase: The Williams Fund, 1955.

8. *The Book of the Dead of Tuthmosis III.* Museum of Fine Arts, Boston. Gift of Horace L. Meyer.

10. Phoenician inscription. The Metropolitan Museum of Art, New York. The Cesnola Collection. Purchased by subscription, 1874–76.

12. Photograph of the Parthenon; courtesy of the Greek National Tourist Office.

13. Photograph of Greek record of sale; Agora Excavations, American School of Classical Studies, Athens.

15. Photograph of a wall in Pompeii, by James Mosley.

17. Photographer anonymous; c. 1895. Private collection.

18. *Funerary inscription of Lollia Genialis.* Marble. The Metropolitan Museum of Art, New York.

19. Photographer anonymous; c. 1895. Private collection.

20. Photograph; courtesy of the Italian Government Travel Office.

24. Detail, "Christ attended by angels," from *The Book of Kells,* fol. 32v; photograph; courtesy of the Irish Tourist Board.

25 and 26. Photographs; courtesy of the Irish Tourist Board.

28. Photograph; courtesy of the French Government Tourist Office.

30. Bronze and copper *Crucifix.* The Virginia Museum of Fine Art, Richmond. Museum Purchase: The Williams Fund, 1968.

32. *Madonna and Child on a Curved Throne.* Wood, 0.815 x 0.490m (32 1/8 x 19 3/8 in.) National Gallery of Art, Washington. Andrew W. Mellon Collection, 1937.

34. Lippo Memmi; Sienese, active 1317–47. *Saint John the Baptist.* Wood, 0.95 x 0.46m (37 1/4 x 18 in.). National Gallery of Art, Washington. Samuel H. Kress Collection, 1939.

35. Photograph courtesy of the Italian Government Tourist Office.

37. Fra Filippo Lippi; Florentine c. 1406–69. *Madonna and Child.* Wood, 0.80 x 0.51m (31 3/8 x 20 1/8 in.). National Gallery of Art, Washington. Samuel H. Kress Collection, 1939.

38. The Rosenwald Collection; The Library of Congress, Washington, DC.

39. Woodcut illustration from *Standebuch* by Jost Amman, 1568.

40. Photographer anonymous; c. 1895. Private collection.

42. Typography from *Lactantu . . . .* Printed by Sweynheym and Pannartz; Rome, 1468. The Library of Congress Rare Book and Special Collections Division, Washington, DC.

43. From *De evangelica praeparatione* by Eusebius Pamphilii. Printed by Nicolas Jenson; Venice, 1470

44. From *The Recuyell of the Historyes of Troye* by Raoul Le Fevre. Printed by William Caxton and Colard Mansion; Burges, c. 1475.

45. Filippino Lippi; *Portrait of a Youth.* Wood, 0.510 x 0.355 m (20 x 13 7/8 in.). National Gallery of Art, Washington, DC. Andrew Mellon Collection, 1937.

46. Erhard Ratdolt, earliest extant type specimen sheet. Published April 1, 1486, in Augsburg, Germany. Bayerische Staatsbibliothek, Munich.

47. Woodcut portrait of Aldus Manutius. Published by Antoine Lafrery; Rome, 16th century.

48. From *De aetna* by Pietro Bembo. Published by Aldus Manutius, Venice, 1495.

49. Page from *Virgil.* Published by Aldus Manutius; Venice, 1501.

50. Photograph by Rommler and Jonas; 1892. Private collection.

53. From *Underweisung der Messung* by Albrecht Durer; Nuremburg, 1525.

54. From *Champ Fleury* by Geoffroy Tory; Paris, 1529.

55. Photograph; courtesy of the French Government Tourist Office.

57. Titian; Venetian c. 1477–1565. *Cardinal Pietro Bembo.* Canvas, 0.945 x 0.765m (37 1/8 x 30 1/8 in.). National Gallery of Art, Washington, DC. Samuel H. Kress Collection, 1952.

58. Title page for *Elementary Geometry* by Oronce Fine. Printed by Simone de Colines; Paris, 1544.

59. From *Hypnerotomachia Poliphili* by Fra Francesco Colonna. Printed by Jacque Kerver; Paris, 1546.

60. El Greco; Spanish 1541–1614. *Saint Martin and the Beggar.* Canvas, 1.935 x 1.030m (76 1/8 x 40 1/2 in.). National Gallery of Art, Washington, DC. Widener Collection, 1942.

61. From *Nejw Kunstliches Alphabet* by Johann Theodor de Bry; Germany, 1595.

62. Photographer anonymous; c. 1895. Private collection.

63. Detail, typographic specimens of Jean Jannon; Sedan, 1621.

64. Page from *Stamperia Vaticana Specimen;* Rome, 1628.

65. Photograph; courtesy of the Government of India Tourist Office.

66. Sir Anthony van Dyck; Flemish, 1599–1641. *Henri II de Lorraine, Duc de Guise.* Canvas, 2.046 x 1.238m (80 5/8 x 48 5/8 in.). National Gallery of Art, Washington, DC. Gift of Cornelius Vanderbilt Whitney, 1947.

67. Jan Vermeer; Dutch 1632–75. *Woman Holding a Balance,* c. 1664. Canvas, 0.425 x 0.380m (16 3/4 x 15 in.). National Gallery of Art, Washington, DC. Widener Collection, 1942.

69. Photograph; courtesy of the British Tourist Authority.

71. Photographer anonymous; 1896. Private collection.

72. From the 1764 specimen book of W. Caslon and Son, London.

73. Photograph; courtesy of the Irish Tourist Board.

74. Title page for *Cato Major, or His Discourse on Old Age* by M. T. Cicero. Printed by Benjamin Franklin; Philadelphia, 1744.

75. Francois Boucher; French 1703–70. *The Love Letter,* 1750. Canvas, 0.813 x 0.741m (32 x 29 1/8 in.). National Gallery of Art, Washington, DC. Timken Collection, 1959.

76. Anonymous; engraved portrait of John Baskerville.

77. From the specimen book of Thomas Cottrell, English typefounder; London, c. 1765.

78. Detail, title page of *Historie de Louis de Bourbon . . . ,* using types and ornaments designed by Pierre Simon Fournier le Jeune. Published by Lottin; Paris, 1768.

79. Johann David Steingruber, 1702–1787. Engraved letter *A* from *Architectonishes Alphabet,* Schwabach, 1773. The Metropolitan Museum of Art. The Elisha Whittelsey Collection, 1955. The Elisha Whittelsey Fund.

80. Photograph; courtesy of the Library of Congress, Washington, DC.

82. Detail, title page using type designed by Bodoni. Dante's *Divine Comedy;* Pisa, 1804.

83. From Thorowgood's *New Specimen of Printing Types, late R. Thorne's, No. 2;* London, 1821.

Picture Credits

84. Jacques-Louis David; French 1748–1825. *Napoleon in his Study,* 1812. Canvas, 2.039 x 1.251m (80 1/4 x 49 1/4 in.). National Gallery of Art, Washington, DC. Samuel H. Kress Collection, 1961.

85–6. From *Specimen of Printing Types* by Vincent Figgins; London, 1815.

87. From *Specimen of Printing Types* by William Caslon IV; London, 1816.

88. From *Manuale Typographico.* Published by Signora Bodoni and Luigi Orsi; Parma, Italy, 1818.

89. From Thorowgood's *New Specimen of Printing Types, late R. Thorne's, No. 2;* London, 1821.

90. Photograph; courtesy of the Virginia State Travel Service.

91. From *Bower, Bacon & Bower's Specimen of Printing Types;* Sheffield, c. 1825.

92. Wood engraving of Darius Wells, from *The Inland Printer;* Chicago, July 1888.

93. From *Specimen of Printing Types* by Vincent Figgins; London, 1833.

94. Poster by the Davy & Berry Printing Office; Albion, England, 1836.

95. From *Specimen of Printing Types by V. & J. Figgins, successors to Vincent Figgins, Letter-Founder;* London, 1836.

96. Courtesy of the Library of Congress Rare Book and Special Collections Division, Washington, DC.

97. Photograph; courtesy of the British Tourist Authority.

98. From *The Specimen Book of Types Cast at the Austin Foundry by Wood & Sharwoods;* London, c. 1841.

99. From *A General Specimen of Printing Types.* Published by W. Thorowgood and Company; London, 1848.

100. Photograph; The Library of Congress Rare Book and Special Collections Division, Washington, DC.

101. Photograph; The Library of Congress Rare Book and Special Collections Division, Washington, DC.

102. From the wood type specimen book of William H. Page & Company; Greenville, Connecticut, 1859.

103. Private collection.

104. Honoré Daumier; French 1808–79. *The Third-Class Carriage.* Oil on canvas, 65.4 x 90.2m (25 3/4 x 35 1/2 in.). The Metropolitan Museum of Art, New York. Bequest of Mrs. H.O. Havemeyer, 1929. The H.O. Havemeyer Collection.

105. Private collection.

106. Private collection.

107. Courtesy of The New York Convention and Visitors Bureau.

108. Private collection.

109. Private collection.

110. Wood engraving from *The Inland Printer;* Chicago, December 1889.

112. Courtesy of the French Government Tourist Office.

113. Photograph; courtesy of the Archives: The Coca-Cola Company.

114. Paul Gauguin; French 1848–1903. *Fatata Te Miti (By the Sea),* 1892. Canvas, 0.679 x 0.915m (26 3/4 x 36 in.). National Gallery of Art, Washington, DC. The Chester Dale Collection, 1962.

117. William Morris. *News from Nowhere.* Published by Kelmscott Press; London, 1892.

118. Title page from *Van nu en Straks.* Designed by Henri van de Velde, 1893.

119. Title page from *Limbes de Lumieres* by Gustave Kahn; Brussels, 1897.

120. From *The Inland Printer;* Chicago, June 1900.

121. Title page from *A Lady of Quality* by Francis Hodgson Burnett. Published by Charles Scribner's Sons; New York, 1897.

122. Cover for Vienna Secession Catalog No. 5; Vienna, 1899.

123. Photograph; courtesy of the French Government Tourist Office.

124. © 2007 Artists Rights Society (ARS), New York / Dedication page from *Feste des Lebens und der Kunst: Ein Betrachtung des Theaters als hochsten Kultursymbols (Celebrations of Life and Art: A Consideration of the Theater as the Highest Cultural Symbol)* by Peter Behrens; Darmstadt, 1900.

125. © 2007 Artists Rights Society (ARS), New York / Filippo Marinetti, Futurist poem, S.T.F., 1914.

126. Cover, *Delikatessen Haus Erich Fromm, Haupt-List 2;* Cologne, c. 1910.

127. © 2007 Artists Rights Society (ARS), New York / Wassily Kandinsky. *Improvisation 31 (Sea Battle),* 1913. National Gallery of Art, Washington, DC. Ailsa Mellon Bruce Fund.

128. War Bond Fund Drive poster for the British government by Bert Thomas, c. 1916.

129. © 2007 Artists Rights Society (ARS), New York / Advertisement for the *Kleine Grosz Mappe (Small Grosz Portfolio)* from *Die Neue Jugend.* Designed by John Heartfield. Published by Der Malik-Verlag, Berlin, June 1917.

130. First cover for *De Stijl,* the journal of the de Stijl movement. Designed by Vilmos Huszar. Published/edited by Theo van Doesburg, The Netherlands; October 1917.

131. © 2007 Artists Rights Society (ARS), New York / Raoul Hausmann. *Poème Phonetique,* 1919.

132. Piet Mondrian; Dutch 1872–1944. *Diamond Painting in Red, Yellow, and Blue.* Oil on canvas, 40 x 40 in. National Gallery of Art, Washington, DC. Gift of Herbert and Nannette Rothschild, 1971.

133. Poster announcing availability of books, by Alexander Rodchenko; Moscow, c. 1923. Private collection.

134. Illustration by Michael Fanizza.

135. © 2007 Artists Rights Society (ARS), New York / Title page from *Die Kunstismen* by El Lissitzky and Hans Arp. Published by Eugen Rentsch Verlag; Zurich, 1925.

136. Proposed universal alphabet. Designed by Herbert Bayer as a student at the Bauhaus.

137. © 2007 Artists Rights Society (ARS), New York / Constantin Brancusi; Romanian 1876–1957. *Bird in Space.* Marble, stone, and wood, hgt. 3.446m (136 1/2 in.). National Gallery of Art, Washington, DC. Gift of Eugene and Agnes Meyer, 1967.

138. Title page for special insert, "Elementare Typographie" from *Typographische Mitteilungen;* Leipzig, October 1925.

139–40. © 2007 Artists Rights Society (ARS), New York / Advertisements by Piet Zwart; courtesy of N. V. Nederlandsche Kabelfabriek, Delft.

141. Trial setting using Futura. Designed by Paul Renner. Published by Bauersche Giesserei; Frankfurt am Main, 1930.

142. Photograph; courtesy of New York Convention and Visitors Bureau.

143. © 2007 Artists Rights Society (ARS), New York / Max Bill. Poster for an exhibition of African Art at the Kunstgewerbemuseum, Zurich.

144. Alexey Brodovitch. Poster for an industrial design exhibition at the Philadelphia Museum of Art.

145. Walker Evans. Photograph, "Fields family, sharecroppers," Hale County, Alabama. The Library of Congress, Washington, DC.

146. Jean Carlu. Advertisement for Container Corporation of America, December 21, 1942.

147. © 2007 Artists Rights Society (ARS), New York / Max Bill. Poster for an exhibition of Art Concrete at the Kunsthalle, Basle.

148. Paul Rand. Title page for *On My Way* by Hans Arp. Published by Wittenborn, Schultz Inc.; New York, 1948.

149. © 2007 Artists Rights Society (ARS), New York / Willem de Kooning. *Painting,* 1948. Enamel and oil on canvas, 42 5/8 x 56 1/8 in. Collection; Museum of Modern Art, New York. Purchase.

150. Ladislav Sutnar. Cover for *Catalog Design Progress* by K. Lonberg-Holm and Ladislav Sutnar. Published by Sweet's Catalog Service; New York, 1950.

151. Illustration by Stephen Chovanec.

152. © 2007 Artists Rights Society (ARS), New York / Henri Matisse; French 1869–1954. *Woman with Amphora and Pomegranates.* Paper on canvas (collage), 2.436 x 0.963m (96 x 37 7/8 in.). National Gallery of Art, Washington, DC. Ailsa Mellon Bruce Fund, 1973.

153. © 2007 Artists Rights Society (ARS), New York / Josef Müller-Brockmann. Poster for a musical concert; Zürich, January 1955.

154. Saul Bass. Advertisement from the *Great Ideas of Western Man* series, Container Corporation of America.

155. Willem Sandberg. Back and front covers for *Experimenta Typographica*. Published by Verlag Galerie der Spiegel; Cologne, 1956.

156. Saul Bass, designer. Film title for *Anatomy of a Murder.* Produced and directed by Otto Preminger, 1959.

157. © 2007 Artists Rights Society (ARS), New York / Photograph; courtesy of the New York Convention and Visitors Bureau.

158. © 2007 Artists Rights Society (ARS), New York / Carlo L. Vivarelli. Cover for *Neue Grafik.* Published by Verlag Otto Walter AG; Olten, Switzerland, 1959.

159. Henry Wolf. Cover for *Harper's Bazaar* magazine, December 1959.

160. Gerald Holton. Symbol for the Campaign for Nuclear Disarmament; Great Britain, c. 1959.

161. Otto Storch. Typography from *McCall's* magazine; July 1959.

162. Karl Gerstner. Poster for the newspaper *National Zeitung;* Zürich, 1960.

163. Herb Lubalin. Advertisement for Sudler and Hennessey Advertising Inc.; New York.

164. George Lois. Advertisement for A.H. Robins Company Incorporated.

165. Photograph; courtesy of the Virginia State Travel Service.

166. Seymour Chwast and Milton Glaser, Push Pin Studios Inc. Poster for the Lincoln Center for the Performing Arts, New York.

167. George Lois. Cover for *Esquire* magazine, October 1966.

168. Seymour Chwast and Milton Glaser, Push Pin Studios Inc. Poster for *Filmsense,* New York.

169. Photograph; courtesy of the Public Relations Department, City of Montreal, Canada.

170. Designer not known. Symbol widely used in the environmental movement.

171. Photograph; courtesy of the National Aeronautics and Space Administration.

172. Wolfgang Weingart. Experimental interpretation of a poem by Elsbeth Bornoz; Basel, Switzerland.

173. Herb Lubalin. Volume 1, Number 1, of *U&lc.* Published by the International Typeface Corporation, New York.

174. Cook and Shanosky, commissioned by the American Institute of Graphic Arts under contract to the U.S. Department of Transportation. From *Symbol Signs,* a series of thirty-four passenger-oriented symbols for use in transportation facilities.

175. Bruce Blackburn, then of Chermayeff and Geismar Associates. Symbol for the U.S. Bicentennial Commission and stamp for the U.S. Postal Service, first released in 1971.

176. Photograph; courtesy of the French Government Tourist Office.

177. Trademark reproduced by permission of Frederic Ryder Company; Chicago, Illinois.

178. Willi Kuntz. Poster for an exhibition of photographs by Fredrich Cantor, FOTO Gallery, New York.

179. Title film for *All That Jazz,* Twentieth Century-Fox. Director/designer Richard Greenberg, R/Greenberg Associates Inc., New York.

180. MTV logo courtesy of Pat Gorman, Manhattan Design, New York.

181. Photograph; courtesy of the Office of the Mayor, Portland, Oregon.

182. Warren Lehrer, designer. Published by ear/say, Purchase, NY, and Visual Studies Workshop, Rochester, NY.

183. Emperor 8, 10, 15 & 19 designed by Zuzana Licko in 1985. Courtesy of Emigre Inc., Berkeley, CA.

184. David Carson, designer; Art Brewer, photographer. *Beach Culture* next issue page, 1990.

185. Ted Mader and Tom Draper, designers. Ted Mader + Associates, Seattle, WA. Published by Peachpit Press Inc., Berkeley, CA.

186. Template Gothic designed by Barry Deck in 1990. Courtesy of Emigre Inc., Berkeley, CA.

187. Exocet Heavy designed by Jonathan Barnbrook in 1991. Courtesy of Emigre Inc., Berkeley, CA.

188. Fetish typeface designed by Jonathan Hoefler. Copyright 1994, The Hoefler Type Foundry Inc.

189. Meta typeface designed by Erik Spiekerman and released by FontShop, c. 1991.

190. Robert Slimbach and Carol Twombly, designers. Myriad Multiple Master typeface designed by courtesy of Adobe Systems Inc., San Jose, CA.

191. Ron Kellum, designer. Courtesy of Kellum McClain, Inc., New York.

192. James Victore, designer. *Racism* poster, 1993.

193. Registered logo of Netscape, used by permission of America Online Inc.

194. Matthew Carter, designer. Walker typefaces, 1994.

195. Landor Associates, designers. Courtesy of Xerox/The Document Company.

196. Stefan Sagmeister, designer. Courtesy of Sagmeister Inc.

197. Frank Gehry, architect. Guggenheim Museum in Bilbao, Spain, 1997. Photograph courtesy of the Tourist Office of Spain, New York.

198. Paula Scher and Keith Daigle, designers. Courtesy of Pentagram Design Inc., New York.

199. Robert Slimbach, designer. Adobe Garamond, 1989. Courtesy of Adobe Systems Inc., San Jose, CA.

200. Janice Fishman, Holly Goldsmith, Jim Parkinson, and Sumner Stone, designers. ITC Bodoni, 1994–95.

201. Mrs Eaves Roman designed by Zuzana Licko in 1996. Courtesy of Emigre Inc., Berkeley, CA.

202. Neville Brody, designer. *Fuse 98: Beyond Typography* poster, 1998.

203. Wolfgang Weingart, designer.

204. Jennifer Sterling, designer. Fox River Paper Company calendar, 2001.

205. Jim Sherraden. Courtesy of Hatch Show Print, a division of the Country Music Foundation, Inc.

206. Emil Ruder, designer. Courtesy of Daniel Ruder.

207. Irma Boom, designer.

208. © 2007 Artists Rights Society (ARS), New York / Philippe Apeloig, designer.

209. Max Kisman, designer.

210. Hesign Design Team. Courtesy of Hesign International, GmbH.

211. Rob Carter, Photographer.

212. Lawrence Weiner, designer/artist. Courtesy of Anderson Gallery.

213. Mevis & Van Deursen, designers. Courtesy of Mevis & Van Deursen.

214. Jean Benoît-Lévy, designer. Courtesy of AND Trafic Grafic.

215. Martin Venezky, designer. Courtesy of Appetite Engineers.

216. Joost Grootens, designer; Arjen van Susteren, author. Courtesy of 010 Publishers.

217. Helmut Schmid, designer. With permission of Victor Malsy, Philipp Teufel and Fjodor Gejko. Courtesy of Birkhäuser Publishers.

218. Experimental Jetset, designers.

219. Lanny Sommese, designer.

220. Ed Fella, designer.

221. Harmen Liemburg, designer.

222. Mirko Ilić, designer. Courtesy of the *New York Times*.

223. Stephen Vitiello, sound artist; Paul Green, photographer. Courtesy of Sydney Park Brickworks, 20th Kaldor Public Art Project.

224. Skolos and Wedell, designers. Poster honoring Matthew Carter.

225. Doug and Mike Starns, artists. © 2011 Doug + Mike Starns. Courtesy of the *New York Times Magazine*.

Chapter Three

3, 7, 14, 30, 54. Frank Armstrong, designer. Courtesy of Armstrong Design Consultants, New Canaan, CT.

4. Willi Kunz, designer. Poster; 14 x 16 1/2 in.

5. Paul Rand, designer. Courtesy of the Estate of Paul Rand.

9. Walter Ballmer, designer. Courtesy of Olivetti.

18. John Malinoski, designer. Courtesy of Anderson Gallery.

19. John Malinoski, designer. Courtesy of Anderson Gallery.

29. Ben Day, designer.

30. Designer: Frank Armstrong; photograph by Sally Anderson-Bruce. Courtesy of Armstrong Design Consultants, New Canaan, CT.

32. Philip B. Meggs, designer.

35. Ben Day, designer.

51 and 56. Paul Rand, designer. Courtesy of the Estate of Paul Rand.

57. Designer: Danne and Blackburn. Courtesy of NASA.

Chapter Five

1. Designer: Jan Tschichold. Title page for special insert, "Elementare Typographie" from *Typographische Mitteilungen;* Leipzig, October 1925.

7. Psalterium, 12th century. Spencer Collection, The New York Public Library, Astor, Lenox and Tilden Foundations.

10. Paul Rand, designer. Courtesy of the Estate of Paul Rand.

11. Courtesy of type-ø-tone.

15. Cover and spread from *Die Weise von Liebe und Tod des Cornets Christoph Rilke* (Insel-Bucherei Nr. 1) 1957. Courtesy of Insel Verlag, Frankfurt.

16. Rob Carter, designer; Leo Divendal, photographer.

17. Victor Levie, designer. Courtesy of Anne Frank House, Amsterdam.

25. Creative Director: Christian Beckwith; designer: Sam Serebin. Courtesy of *Alpinist*.

26. Typography, Interiority & Other Serious Matters, designers. Courtesy of Stichting De Best Verzorgde Boeken.

27. Photograph; courtesy of the Burdick Group.

29. © 2007 Artists Rights Society (ARS), New York / Josef Müller-Brockmann, designer. Courtesy of Verlag Niggli AG, Switzerland.

33. Photograph; courtesy of Graphic Thought Facility, London.

34. Photograph; courtesy of Main Street Design, Inc., Cambridge, MA.

35. Juan Benedit, Web site design. Courtesy of Demographik.

36. Virtual Identity AG, Web site design; Uli Weidner, designer. Courtesy of Vitra.

Chapter Six

1. Eugen Gomringer. "ping pong," from *Concrete Poetry: A World View.* Edited by Mary Ellen Solt, Indiana University Press, 1970.

2. © 2007 Artists Rights Society (ARS), New York / Filippo Tommaso Marinetti, *"Les mots en liberté futuristes."*

3. © 2007 Artists Rights Society (ARS), New York / *Der Dada,* #1, cover.

5. © 2007 Artists Rights Society (ARS), New York / El Lissitzky, *Veshch,* cover, 1921–22.

15. Herb Lubalin, designer. Courtesy of *Reader's Digest*.

20. Photograph; courtesy of Olivetti.

25. © 2007 Artists Rights Society (ARS), New York / Gerrit Rietveld, designer. *Red and Blue Chair,* 1918. Collection Stedelijk Museum, Amsterdam.

26. Stephen Coates, designer. Masthead for *eye, the International Review of Graphic Design.* Courtesy of *eye* magazine.

29. J. Abbott Miller, James Hicks, Paul Carlos, and Scott Davendorf, designers. Courtesy of Pentagram Design Inc., New York.

Chapter Seven

4, 5, and 6. Photographs; courtesy of Mergenthaler Linotype Company.

9. George Nan, photographer.

18. Courtesy of Autologic Inc., Newbury Park, CA.

26. Photograph; courtesy of Mergenthaler Linotype Company.

34. Microphotographs courtesy of Mike Cody, Virginia Commonwealth University, Richmond, VA.

Chapter Eight

7. Matthew Carter, designer. Copyright Microsoft.

8. Matthew Carter, photographer.

9. Emperor 8, 10, 15 & 19 designed by Zuzana Licko in 1985. Courtesy of Emigre Inc., Berkeley, CA.

Chapter Nine

1–7. Courtesy of Jean Benoît-Lévy, designer.

8–11. Courtesy of United States National Park Service.

13–18. Courtesy of Stephen Farrell, designer. Coauthors, Stephen Farrell and Steve Tomasula.

19–23. Courtesy of Richard Greenberg, designer.

24–34. Courtesy of Diseño Shakespear, Buenos Aires, Argentina.

35–40. Joost Grootens, designer. Courtesy of 010 Publishers. Arjen van Susteren, author.

41–50. Courtesy of John Malinoski, designer.

Chapter Eleven

15. Courtesy of Holland Fonts.

18–21b. Courtesy of Thomas Detrie.

22–47. Courtesy of Ernest Bernhardi.

48–60. Courtesy of Bret Hansen.

61–80. Courtesy of Anne Jordan.

Chapter Twelve

5. From *American Advertising Posters of the Nineteenth Century* by Mary Black; courtesy of Dover Publications Inc., New York.

Sources for specimen quotations

Pages i, 259, 265, 275, 281, 287, 279, 297, 303, 313, 323, and 329. From *The Book Beautiful* by Thomas James Cobden-Sanderson. Hammersmith: Hammersmith Publishing Society, 1902.

Page 137. from *The Alphabet and Elements of Lettering* by Frederic W. Goudy, courtesy of Dover Publications Inc., New York.

Index

Page numbers in *italic* refer to illustrations

Printing:	R.R. Donnelley and Sons, Roanoke, Virginia
Binding:	R.R. Donnelley and Sons, Roanoke, Virginia
Cover printing:	R.R. Donnelley and Sons, Roanoke, Virginia
Typography:	9/11 Univers 55 text with 7/11 Univers 55 captions and 9/11 Univers 75 headings
Design:	First edition: Rob Carter, Stephen Chovanec, Ben Day, and Philip Meggs; Second edition: Rob Carter and Philip Meggs; Third edition: Rob Carter, Philip Meggs, and Sandra Wheeler; Fourth edition: Rob Carter and Sandra Wheeler; Fifth edition: Rob Carter and Sandra Wheeler
Web site design:	Andrew Ilnicki
Design Assistance:	First edition: Tina Brubaker Chovanec, Justin Deister, John Demao, Akira Ouchi, Tim Priddy, Anne Riker, Joel Sadagursky, and Jennifer Mugford Weiland; Second edition: Linda Johnson, Jeff Price, and Brenda Zaczek
Photography and digital imaging:	First and second edition: George Nan; Third edition: Rob Carter, Philip Meggs, George Nan, North Market Street Graphics, and Sandra Wheeler; Fourth edition: Rob Carter and Sandra Wheeler; Fifth edition: Rob Carter and Sandra Wheeler

The authors wish to thank the following people for their contributions to the fifth edition of this book. At John Wiley & Sons, Senior Editor Margaret Cummins, Production Director Diana Cisek, Senior Production Editor David Sassian, and Manufacturing Manager Tom Hyland guided this book through the editorial and production phases. Libby Phillips Meggs contributed ongoing consultation and advice. R. Roger Remington generously shared information about contributing designers. Brandi Price provided administrative support. Andrew Ilnicki designed the ancillary Web site and lent a critical eye to Chapter Eight content. At Virginia Commonwealth University, John DeMao offered support and encouragement. The authors extend special thanks to the many contributors of this volume for sharing their significant typographic work.